THE PRACTICAL BOOK OF
INTERIOR DECORATION

PLATE 1

A CASEMENT BOW-WINDOW WITH WILLIAM AND MARY AND QUEEN ANNE FURNITURE
By Courtesy of Messrs. Waring & Gillow, Ltd., London

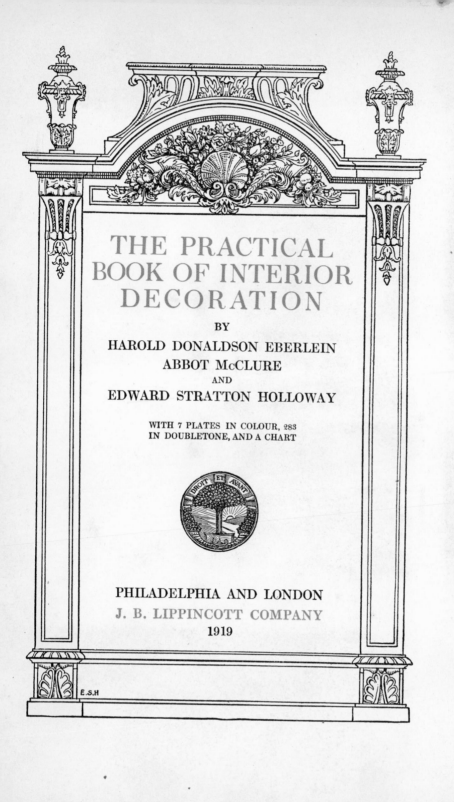

THE PRACTICAL BOOK OF INTERIOR DECORATION

BY

HAROLD DONALDSON EBERLEIN

ABBOT McCLURE

AND

EDWARD STRATTON HOLLOWAY

WITH 7 PLATES IN COLOUR, 283
IN DOUBLETONE, AND A CHART

PHILADELPHIA AND LONDON
J. B. LIPPINCOTT COMPANY
1919

PRINTED BY J. B. LIPPINCOTT COMPANY
AT THE WASHINGTON SQUARE PRESS
PHILADELPHIA, U. S. A.

FOREWORD

It is hard to understand why someone has not written such a book as this before, a book covering the three great needs of anyone approaching in any capacity the matter of household decoration.

History is a treasure house of the crystallised experience that has slowly evolved in past ages, a treasure house ready for us to draw upon as we will. The limit of our taking from its stores is marked only by our capacity to receive. This is especially true in the case of so concrete a subject as interior decoration where many enduring examples of the best achievements of former generations in that field have been preserved for us practically intact.

The truest and sanest originality is the product of a gradual evolution and rational adaptation to present needs of the most obvious and applicable precedents established by our predecessors and tried by the searching test of time. Such originality, too, is largely an unconscious product. The agent is scarcely conscious that he is aiming to be original. Deliberately self-conscious originality that casts aside and contemns all precedent and strives, above all else, to create something the like of which has never been done before, may indeed be original to the extent of being unique, but the chances are ninety-nine out of an hundred that it will also be gauche and crude and without any merit to entitle it to permanence. It wins notice only because it is a curiosity and a freak.

If there were no guiding principles and traditions, if Interior Decoration were to begin to-day, it is probable that furnishing—even of the simplest cottage— would be a chaotic thing. Successful decoration and

v

home-making is a matter not merely of "feeling" or
even of taste, if these necessary qualities be without
knowledge. Decoration is both an art and a science;
it is the result of long centuries of loving thought and
high craftsmanship based upon unalterable principles
of beauty and of use. What wonder is it that the usual
brisk and light-hearted "jumping into" the furnishing
of the home is productive of a result causing the
judicious to grieve! Notwithstanding an improvement
in recent years, the utter waste of money and of effort,
the absence of any praiseworthy result in thousands of
modern homes is still appalling.

Knowledge therefore must come first, and nothing
can be more absorbing than to see the beauty and the
fitness evolved, both from elaborate and from simple
materials, through the various periods of Decoration
and to apply them to our own needs. It would, then,
certainly seem wise to provide the professional decorator, the home-furnisher and the allied professions and
trades with a convenient, thorough-going and well illustrated account and description of the work of the great
decorative periods, since their beginnings, and of the
principles which informed them.

In the first part of this volume the authors have
endeavoured to give a consecutive and synoptic picture
of the art of interior decoration as it has been practised
in England, in France, in Italy, and in Spain since the
beginning of the sixteenth century, adding thereto such
comment as seemed necessary upon American modifications of British usage during the Colonial and early
republican periods. This includes the decorative practice of the Renaissance, Baroque, Rococo and Neo-
Classic systems, and it may be added that in no other
one volume can such a fully described, illustrated and
digested account be found.

In the second part of the volume is made the direct application to modern requirements of the lessons to be drawn from the historical exposition in Part I. As it is manifestly impossible, even were it desirable, to give specific and categorical directions for decorative procedure to suit every case, it has been the policy to set forth *principles* as well as to explain *practice,* and to leave considerable discretionary latitude in which the reader may exercise his or her choice of action. In this way it is believed the utility of the book will prove flexible enough to meet all sorts of needs, both simple and elaborate.

Each age has its own conditions, requirements and developments, and any volume on Modern Decoration that did not take these fully into account would be imperfect. The treatment of the Practical side of Decoration, in Part II, will be found so simple and straightforward as to be readily understood by any intelligent furnisher of his own home, and, while this Part is primarily addressed to him, it is felt that a fresh view of the subject from a point other than the traditions of trade may be of distinct interest to the professional decorator and dealer as well.

The plates constitute a most vital feature of the book and the reader is urged to study carefully the illustrations in connexion with the text in the manner indicated by the text references. Without such comparison and cross reference the purpose of the volume will be in great measure defeated. It will be seen that instant reference may thus be made to any particular feature of the work.

We are living in an age of catholic appreciation which we are optimistic enough to believe is increasing. We believe, also, that with this catholic tendency to appreciate and to lay hold of whatever is intrinsically good in the work of any period, there is rapidly growing an healthy constructive ability on the part of the householder which prompts the individual to beautify his or her home, either through the offices of a decorator or through personal effort.

Our twofold purpose is, in the first place, to stimulate intelligent coöperation with the decorator, to encourage appreciation of what the decorator does, and to afford a sound basis of discriminating criticism and judgment; in the second place, to aid the householder who may elect to achieve either a limited decorative improvement or the execution of an whole constructive scheme. It is also felt that the decorator and the dealer will find in this volume much information compactly arranged for instant reference.

Whether or not the services of a decorator be retained, may we urge the wisdom of not trying to hasten unduly the completion of a scheme. It is infinitely better to proceed deliberately, to accomplish at one time what is unquestionably sound and then to wait for a while, if it be necessary, to secure exactly what is needed, rather than to push for immediate completion at the risk of incorporating features that afterwards prove undesirable and make us rue our impatience.

We have reminded the reader that this is an age of catholic appreciation of whatever was worth while in the practice of the past. In this connexion, it should be pointed out that while it is perfectly permissible, if the householder so chooses, and may at times be thoroughly desirable, to decorate and furnish a room in strict accord with some particular period style, we do not urge such a course. Meticulous reproduction of this sort is apt to savour too much of decorative archæology and to result in a stilted, artificial effect, quite incompatible with a desirable expression of the owner's individuality or with the exercise of rational originality. The outcome is likely to be dead and "correct" instead of being instinct with vital quality as it ought.

It is better to think, to consult principles, which we believe the reader will find lucidly enough set forth, and to employ a rational liberty of selection when attacking a problem of rearrangement or of new composition. The room will then reflect the occupant's personality, a condition that will afford vastly more interest and lively charm than any amount of simian exactitude in reproduction.

No one questions the value of period furnishing, but the question as to how it is to be used in our modern days has been the subject of much discussion indeed. On the one hand we find, in practice, the narrow adherence to one period and one country; on the other, a jumble of everything under the sun from the fifteenth century to the twentieth and from China to Portugal. In Part III of this book is for the first time formulated a logical system of decoration which avoids both the narrow limitations of the one-period method and the pitfalls of eclectic furnishing.

Without wishing to claim undue credit, the writers are under the impression that this volume is the first of the kind to formulate a definite body of decorative *principles* that are applicable under any conditions likely to arise. Scattered precepts and general observations upon the effects attained in individual instances are agreeable and helpful, so far as they go. It is more serviceable, however, to have a digest of principles explaining the "how" and "why", principles simple and flexible enough in their working to be readily applied to meet the varying requirements that may from time to time confront the reader.

It will be seen upon perusal that a great deal of

space and attention have been devoted, both in the historical section and in the sections upon application, to the architectural background and the fixed decorations. The vital importance of this part of interior decoration cannot be overestimated. Without it all efforts in other directions will be robbed of their legitimate result and the expense bestowed will not count for its full value.

The architectural background and the fixed decorations really supply the foundation for which all else is the superstructure. When building an house, no sane person would dream of constructing an elaborate and costly superstructure upon insufficient or poor foundations. It is quite as fatuous to expect a room to look well and to do justice to the pains spent upon it without adequate preparation of the background, or, in other words, the foundation for the subsequent movable decoration. If it be necessary to economise anywhere in the erection of a structure, the economising is not done at the foundation, which cannot be changed later, but above ground in the matter of details that can be subsequently added. In precisely the same way, if there be any limitation in carrying out a decorative scheme, do not stint the background, which has a strongly permanent quality, but postpone completing a part of the movable equipment, which can be added at any time.

The work of interior decoration is not a task that can be undertaken in a haphazard manner and accomplished with creditable results. Nor can it be achieved by the whimsical following of fads. It requires thought, judgment, calm planning and sanity. In the past it has always been a dignified occupation in which the greatest architects and artists have not hesitated to labour assiduously. Its ultimate object, to enrich and beautify the home which is the nucleus of social life and the cornerstone of the state, is a service in which architect and artist, decorator and householder alike may engage with justifiable pride.

In conclusion, the authors wish sincerely to thank all the many who have materially assisted in the preparation of this work, and for numerous courtesies extended to acknowledge their indebtedness, especially to the following: —— the editors of *House and Garden,* of *Good Furniture Magazine* and of *House Beautiful* in arranging for the use of material that has appeared in substance in their pages; to Messrs. Wilson Eyre and McIlvaine, Edmund B. Gilchrist, Willing and Sims, Mellor, Meigs and Howe, Sir Ernest Newton, Barry Parker and Raymond Unwin, George Leland Hunter, William Lawrence Bottomley, the Misses Hewitt, the Misses Owen, Mrs. Abbot Thorndike and Mrs. William Thorndike, the Honourable Jefferson M. Levy, Wolstan Herbert Dixie, Durr Friedley, E. S. Dodge, and Henry Chapman Mercer; to W. H. Ward's "Architecture of the French Renaissance" and George P. Bankart's "Art of the Plasterer"; to the C. M. Traver Co., William Helburn, Inc., B. T. Batsford, Ltd., Messrs. L. Alavoine & Co., Carvalho Brothers, Nicholas Martin, Montillor Brothers, Messrs. Litchfield & Co., Radillo & Pelliti Co., Woodville & Co., the Chapman Decorative Co., Messrs. Robinson and Farr, R. W. Lehne, *Vogue,* the *Architectural Record,* the *International Studio,* Waring & Gillow, Ltd., Edwards & Sons, Bartholomew & Fletcher, Speelman Brothers, Story & Triggs, C. J. Charles, the Aschermann Studio, Newcomb-Macklin Co., A. H. Notman & Co., Edward I. Farmer, Ramsey, Lyon & Humphreys, Inc., Alfred Villoresi, Karl Freund, Mrs. M. Orme Wilson, John Wanamaker; American Art Galleries, Anderson Art Galleries; the Pennsylvania Museum and School of Industrial Arts, the Metropolitan Museum of Art, Brooklyn Museum, and the

Museum of the Cooper Institute for supplying many illustrations and for permission to reproduce others; to the officers and staffs of the Library Company of Philadelphia and of the Philadelphia Free Library; and last, but by no means least, to Mr. Philip B. Wallace for his unfailing help with many of the photographs used.

HAROLD DONALDSON EBERLEIN
ABBOT MCCLURE
EDWARD STRATTON HOLLOWAY

PHILADELPHIA, July, 1919

CONTENTS

PART I

HISTORIC PERIOD DECORATION IN ENGLAND, ITALY, SPAIN AND FRANCE

PART II

PRACTICAL DECORATION AND FURNISHING

xiii

CONTENTS

PART III

INTERNATIONAL-INTER PERIOD DECORATION
AND FURNISHING

ILLUSTRATIONS

ILLUSTRATIONS

PART I

HISTORIC PERIOD DECORATION IN ENGLAND, ITALY, SPAIN AND FRANCE

Finally, there should grow the most austere of all mental qualities; I mean the sense for style. It is an æsthetic sense, based on admiration for the direct attainment of a foreseen end, simply and without waste. Style in art, style in literature, style in science, style in logic, style in practical execution, have fundamentally the same æsthetic qualities, namely, attainment and restraint. The love of a subject in itself and for itself, where it is not the sleepy pleasure of pacing a mental quarter-deck, is the love of style as manifested in that study.

Here we are brought back to the position from which we started, the utility of education. Style, in its finest sense, is the last acquirement of the educated mind; it is also the most useful. It pervades the whole being. The administrator with a sense for style, hates waste; the engineer with a sense for style, economises his material; the artisan with a sense for style, prefers good work. Style is the ultimate morality of the mind.

But, above style and above knowledge, there is something, a vague shape like fate above the Greek gods. The something is Power. Style is the fashioning of power. the restraining of power. But, after all, the power of attainment of the desired end is fundamental. The first thing is to get there. Do not bother about your style, but solve your problem, justify the ways of God to man, administer your province or do whatever else is set before you.

Where, then, does style help? In this, with style the end is attained without side issues, without raising undesirable inflammations. With style, you attain your end and nothing but your end. With style, the effect of your activity is calculable, and foresight is the last gift of gods to men. With style, your power is increased, for your mind is not distracted with irrelevancies, and you are more likely to attain your object. Now style is the exclusive privilege of the expert. Who ever heard of the style of an amateur painter, of the style of an amateur poet? Style is always the product of specialist study, the peculiar contribution of specialism to culture.

"The Organisation of Thought"
By A. N. Whitehead, Sc.D., F.R.S.

London: Williams & Norgate
Philadelphia: J. B. Lippincott Company.

THE PRACTICAL BOOK OF INTERIOR DECORATION

PART I

HISTORIC PERIOD DECORATION IN ENGLAND, ITALY, SPAIN AND FRANCE

CHAPTER I

INTERIOR DECORATION IN ENGLAND PRIOR TO THE EIGHTEENTH CENTURY

*I*NTRODUCTION. — Sixteenth century England will ever be endued with a glamour all its own in the eyes of those over whom history exerts a fascinating hold or in whose mental background a strong sense of love and reverence for our Mother Country and a just pride in our great heritage of English blood and traditions count as potent factors. The vigour, freshness and *naïveté* of the period, added to the full-blooded stability of English characteristics and traditions, combine to cast a subtle spell over the imagination. Even the misdoings of that old reprobate and rapacious spendthrift, Henry VIII, seem to fade into a half-pardoned state of unreality and grow less reprehensible in the enshrouding haze of glowing splendour that radiates from the Field of the Cloth of Gold, and when we think of the marvellous delights of Nonesuch or of the 2600 tapestries that adorned the walls of his palaces we are all too apt to forget whence came the

3

funds to compass the building of the former and that many of the latter he either stole from the monasteries he so ruthlessly pillaged or filched from the possessions of Cardinal Wolsey.

Notwithstanding all this bravery of gorgeous display, there was comparatively little upon which, for our present purpose, we may profitably centre our attention until we come to the days of Queen Elizabeth. During her reign the building of country houses advanced by strides and gave scope for the art of furnishing to develop to a truly national extent. In all this work, which progressed continuously during the rule of Elizabeth and her Stuart successors, the spirit of the Renaissance was the controlling influence, but that influence arrived in England through various channels and manifested itself under varying forms, as we shall presently see, so that it is necessary to divide the epoch embracing the last half of the sixteenth century and the whole of the seventeenth into three phases—the first covering decoration in the time of Queen Elizabeth and during the reigns of King James and King Charles I, a period of consistent, logical and uninterrupted development; the second covering the dour years of the Commonwealth; the third covering the Restoration period, with all its influx of fresh and divers tendencies, and terminating in the medley of Baroque and Oriental fashions that flourished vigorously all through the reign of William and Mary.

In the Elizabethan period the chiefest part of the architectural and mobiliary Renaissance inspiration came into England through Flemish channels. While a powerful Renaissance influence had taken deep root in Flanders and wrought abundant results, nevertheless the Flemings, like the French, had retained a large measure of late Gothic tradition and their interpretation of Renaissance principles was strongly tinged and modified by this residuary leaven of an earlier mode so that the composite result was unmistakably local and individual in character. This body of Flemish forms, upon its transition to England, was grafted upon a stock of British growth and precedent and the pure Italian Renaissance element in it was still further diluted by British conceptions and methods of execution on the part of craftsmen who, then as now, were conservative and retentive of the manner of technique and forms of decorative expression instilled by early training. In spite, however, of the dominating Flemish bias imparted to the Renaissance mode in England, distinct traces of a subsidiary but unadulterated source of Italian inspiration recur again and again in the work of the period, showing that the direct connexion with Italian cultural influence was far stronger and more intimate than is generally supposed. We may the more readily credit the existence and potency of this bond when we look into the literary history of the age and find that between the accession and death of the Virgin Queen there were published in England no fewer than 394 translations from the Italian into English and 72 texts in Italian and Latin. When Italian literature found such a receptive audience as these figures prove, when we remember how closely the arts were interrelated in England, when we study the evidence of trade and imports, and when we consider the presence of not a few able Italian craftsmen, whose continued residence and activity in England are matters of historical record, we may be very sure that Englishmen were not insensible to the enlivening impetus of direct contact with Latin sources in matters of decoration.

We also see in this condition a further link in the powerful chain of evidence showing a wide internationalism in art, an internationalism that we are altogether too prone to ignore in the past and assume as a development of modern times.

Under the Commonwealth we find a period of comparative stagnation and arrested growth in matters of English decoration. Certain Baroque tendencies, it is true, came more into evidence than at an earlier date, but, for the most part, it was an era of drab monotony; the minority who still cherished taste and refinement were in too great trouble or weighed down by disabilities too heavy to permit them to give much encouragement to any form of art, and the greater part of the nation, under the impulse of that strange mania that impelled the rue-faced Roundhead ranters and gloomy Puritan religionists to contemplate in fascinated dread the flaming terrors of hell and to prophesy with savage satisfaction the unalterable damnation of all their kin and neighbours, was much too engrossed in the orgy of morbid introspection to pay much heed to the amenities of architecture or decoration. A few wealthy " worldlings " did indulge in " wicked and unedifying extravagances," but their example did not produce an appreciable effect.

At the Restoration, the pendulum swung to the other extremity of its arc and the arts of architecture and interior decoration gained all the impetus that usually attends long pent up energy suddenly let loose in a congenial and hitherto forbidden field of activity. The impetus was further intensified in London by the necessity of replacing the ruin wrought by the Great Fire. The large numbers of refugees returning from exile on the Continent in the train of the King brought with them not only a fresh set of polite tastes, requirements and broadened conceptions but also a very considerable quantity of household furnishings and luxurious garniture. Court circles and the people of the country at large alike welcomed all the new and newly invigorated influences — French, Italian, Flemish, Dutch, Spanish, Portuguese and Oriental—that successively made their way into England as a result partly of political alliances, partly of expanded trade relations, partly through the immigration of foreign artificers, and partly, though by no means in the least measure, through a new cosmopolitanism that was gradually spreading throughout the country and supplanting the old insularity that had received a mortal wound when King Charles the Martyr was beheaded and got its *coup de grace* when King Charles the Scapegrace, as the Merry Monarch might well have been called, came back from overseas to "enjoy his own again."

The architecture of this complex Restoration period was catholic enough to employ inspiration derived from French, Flemish and Italian interpretations of the Renaissance spirit and also to incorporate Baroque elements when there was occasion. In the field of interior decoration we find an opulent medley of Renaissance, Flemish, Baroque, East Indian and Chinese influences that combined to diversify the mobiliary manifestations of the period to an hitherto unwonted degree.

Architectural Background and Methods of Fixed Decoration.—Allusion has already been made to the domestic architecture of the age of Elizabeth, which was largely a composite of Flemish Renaissance forms grafted upon an English stock of late Gothic provenance. One might characterise the style as a Gothic body with Flemish Renaissance features and clothes.

The rooms and galleries were large, or at the very least commodious, and the ceilings were frequently though not invariably low in comparison to the other dimensions, unless there was an open timbered roof. The window openings were large and might consist of a range of three or more leaded casements separated by upright posts or mullions of wood or stone, or might rise to a great height, filled with tiers of leaded casements (Plate 5) separated both horizontally and vertically by mullions. Again, the whole end of a room might be filled by one great bow window with the mullion divisions, as in the previously noted cases. In any event, the mullions were an invariable as well as a distinctly characteristic and decorative feature. The casements were glazed with small quarries or with little lozenge-shaped panes leaded together. While the leading alone served as an agreeable decoration, heraldic blasonings and other devices in colour, in the centre of a casement, were often employed to lend additional glow and interest.

The walls were panelled with small oaken panels (Plates 3, 4 and 5), separated by broad stiles and rails, for either their whole height or else for the greater part of it, and when any part of the upper wall was left uncoated with wainscot it was plastered. At the top of the panelling was often a carved and moulded frieze. Projections from the panelling, such as door frames and pilasters, were carved in low relief.

The fireplace and its superstructure always formed an highly significant and much decorated feature of the room. The opening of the fireplace was of generous size and the surround was of carved stone (Plate 4), while the massive superstructure or chimney piece might be either of richly carved stone or of wood (Plate 3) carved with an equal degree of elaboration.

PLATE 2

THE HALL, FRANKS, KENT

Note Mullioned Windows, Wainscotted Walls and Plastered Ceiling with Moulded Rib Decoration, Distinctive of the English Renaissance
From "The Mansions of England in the Olden Time," by Joseph Nash

PLATE 3

DINING ROOM IN ENGLISH RENAISSANCE STYLE (EARLY STUART PHASE)
Note Oak Wainscot in Small Panels, Carved Chimney Piece and Moulded Parge Ceiling
Table Jacobean: Chairs Baroque
Courtesy of Mrs. Lyman Kendall, New York City

PLATE 4

LIVING ROOM OF STUART TYPE
Wainscotted Walls in Small Oak Panels, Moulded Parge Ceiling and Stone Fireplace
Trim
Courtesy of Wilson Eyre and McIlvaine, Architects

PLATE 5

LIVING ROOM OF STUART TYPE
Wainscotted Walls in Small Oak Panels and Moulded Parge Ceiling
Courtesy of Wilson Eyre and McIlvaine, Architects

Whether of wood or of stone, the further enrichment of colour and gilding was often added. Equally significant with the fireplace as a conspicuous item in the Elizabethan and Stuart interiors was the staircase, the newel post and the side railing beautifully carved and fretted, which rose by broken flights and landings to the upper floor, sometimes ascending directly from one of the larger rooms, sometimes from a hall or gallery.

Doorways, too, were objects of rich ornamentation (Plate 2), both at the sides, in the shape of either carved pilasters or semi-engaged pillars, and at the top with elaborate carving and moulding, often in the form of armorial bearings with casque, mantlings and supporters. In not a few instances, the actual entrance was surrounded by an elaborately carved and panelled screen extending from the floor part way to the ceiling. The door itself not infrequently bore the adornment of wrought-iron hinges and bands with scrolls. The floors were of stone, of tiles and of wood, the latter being most used. Occasionally simple decorative devices were essayed with stone or tile paving, but as a rule the paving was without any pretense at ornamentation.

The ceilings were of beamed wood or of plaster or else there were open timbered roofs. The beamed ceilings commonly displayed the amenity of chamfering and moulding on the beams and frequently the addition of carving. Colour, too, was apt to play a part in the decorative scheme. Open timbered roofs might or might not be plastered between the timbers and characteristic ornamentation of carving and colour sometimes adorned the woodwork, while decoration was also extended to the plaster surfaces.

The plastered ceilings were either flat or barrel vaulted or coved. In some cases *stucco-duro* or parge (Plates 3 and 4) ornamentation was used for the ceiling

and consistent decoration in the same media extended
to a portion or to the whole of the wall surface above
the oak panelling. The over-mantel decoration, too,
often consisted of a *stucco-duro* or a parge composition
instead of carvings in stone or wood. The art of working in *stucco-duro* was introduced into England in the
time of Henry VIII and was executed by Italian work-
men who continued to ply their craft during a great
part of the reign of Queen Elizabeth, and they taught
some of the more capable English artificers to work
after the same fashion. For various reasons, however,
the art decayed and was eventually supplanted by the
simpler substitute of parge work which, while it required less skill of execution, was also limited in the
scope of delicacy and the range of *motifs* which might
be executed therein. The *stucco-duro* ceilings were
beautifully decorated with moulded ribs and panels,
floriations and other devices, while the plaster portions
of walls above the panelling often bore most intricately
and deftly wrought friezes of hunting scenes, mythological or historical subjects. The same style of device
was likewise used for an over-mantel embellishment
and well-moulded strapwork was employed freely. It
was not at all unusual further to augment the decorative effect of this carefully wrought *stucco-duro* work
by polychrome treatment in tempera colours.

After the hand of the average English plasterer had
somewhat lost its cunning and it became necessary to
descend to the cruder parge work, the modelled decoration continued to be applied in the same places as
previously noted, but the *motifs* were necessarily
simpler and the execution far less delicate. For a full
explication of *stucco-duro* and parge work, for the
methods and *motifs* employed, and for numerous excellent illustrations, the reader is referred to George P.

Bankart's admirable book, "The Art of the Plasterer."

When all the resources of fixed decoration just enumerated were fully utilised, the interior of many an Elizabethan or Stuart room was so replete with decorative variety and interest that it gave the impression of being furnished, even before a stick of movable furniture was put in place. This fact deserves close attention for the emphasis it lends to the reasonable contention that interior decoration is not alone a matter of selecting and arranging an aggregation of movable pieces, but comprehends the creation of an whole and complete composition, a conception of the art that too many are unfortunately disposed to ignore.

The interiors during early Stuart or Jacobean times were substantially the same in their principal features as the Elizabethan rooms already described. Certain *motifs* of carved decoration, such as Romayne work or heads carved on roundels or medallions, fell out of fashion while other *motifs* came into vogue. The differences, however, were not sufficient to require minute elucidation here and may be satisfactorily explained in a subsequent paragraph. During the Commonwealth there was little architectural or decorative activity and it is not until we come to the Restoration that we find another fully distinct interior type of a widely increasing prevalence.

Beginning with the immediate Restoration period and thence onward to the end of the century, two separate and well-defined types of interiors must be taken into consideration. The one was the type with which we are already familiar, substantially the same as the Elizabethan or Stuart interior, which came down as an heritage from the past with only a few minor evolutionary modifications; the other was a type for which we are indebted to the agency of Inigo Jones, followed, after the Restoration, by the work of Sir Christopher Wren and his contemporaries, who designed in a vein of much purer Renaissance inspiration than was apparent in the Elizabethan houses, the creations of Wren, however, being perceptibly tinged by a strong French influence, while the earlier designs by Jones were based directly upon Italian precedents. An infusion of Baroque interpretation entered into the composition of this style as well as the basis of Renaissance precedent.

The most signal points of difference between the old Elizabethan and early Stuart type of interior and that of the newer mode were that in the houses of more recent fashion the ceilings were higher: there was a more general regard for symmetry in the dimensions of rooms which, as a rule, were now broader in proportion to their length than formerly and designed to be approximately square rather than oblong: the window openings were taller and not so wide, double hung sashes instead of leaded casements appeared, and panes of glass considerably larger than the old quarries and lozenges, that had been held in place by strips of lead, were now set in substantial wooden muntins: the panelling of the walls—and this was one of the most momentous changes—was made with far larger divisions (Plate 6) and the mouldings surrounding the panels were of wholly different contour and far bolder: finally, in the treatment of both the plaster ceilings and the wooden floors, the spaces involved were regarded as opportunities for coherent and finished composition in decorative design rather than as bare surfaces to be covered with a relieving pattern.

While oak was still used extensively for panelling, pine, deal or Scottish fir, and even cedar were coming rapidly into fashion for the same purpose. This was the age of Grinling Gibbon, when the art of decorative

PLATE 6

DRAWING ROOM PANELLED IN OAK, WILLIAM AND MARY PERIOD
Note Large Panels Defined by Raised Mouldings, Carved Door Trims (Showing
Baroque Influence), Carved Cornice and Decorated Plaster Ceiling
Courtesy of Mrs. Lyman Kendall, New York City

wood carving reached the acme of perfection. For the new style of carving with all its realism, delicacy and undercutting, oak was too hard and open-grained a medium to be worked with the same ease or with the same dexterity of finish as the other woods just mentioned. Delicate carving in low relief was often employed freely on the mouldings of cornices and the surrounds of panels (Plate 6), while for overdoor ornamentation and still more for the enrichment of the chimney piece swags and drops of flowers, fruit and foliage, with human figures, *amorini*, baskets, urns, birds and other devices in a free and flowing style, with high relief and much undercutting, all together constituted one of the most characteristic aspects of the new mode. These finely wrought carvings were often executed in lime or basswood, which admitted of even more ingenious manipulation than pine, deal or cedar. While the beauty of the woods just mentioned, in their natural state, was fully appreciated, it was also a common practice to paint all the woodwork, carving and all, white or some colour such as grey, greenish grey or blue green and occasionally to apply gilding to mouldings and portions of carving. This practice was especially common towards the end of the century.

Doorways, and very often window casings, were made the objects of decorative wood carving: fluted pilasters with carved capitals, heavy cornices with carved mouldings, overdoor embellishments of an architectural character or panels with carved drops and swags were much used. The overmantel or chimney piece was even to a greater degree the object of careful decorative elaboration. The fireplace surround, with bold bolection mouldings, was sometimes of wood, sometimes of stone or marble. There was no mantel shelf and the chimney piece, reaching all the way to the ceiling, consisted either of a distinctly architectural treatment in classic and Renaissance *motifs,* sometimes with Baroque features also, or else of a large panel surrounded with heavy mouldings and flanked and surmounted with carved flower, fruit and foliage swags and drops in the characteristic Grinling Gibbon manner. In many instances either a portrait or else a decorative still life painting would be framed in the panel. This empanelling of portraits was not confined to the chimney piece, but was likewise practised to some extent for the walls. Toward the end of the century painted panels for overdoor adornment, too, came into favour and now and again decorative niches with coved or shell tops, for urns, vases or sculpture, were introduced into the panelled walls when there was a good opportunity for such symmetrical composition. Another feature of fixed wall decoration also frequently resorted to towards the end of the century was the setting of mirrors into wall and door panels, a device now made readily possible in England, as well as the employment of larger panes for glazing windows, by the establishment of glass works at Lambeth under the patronage of the Duke of Buckingham.

Just as the panelling of the walls had been proportioned and varied in size, according to the space to be filled (Plates 6, 7 and 8), so also was the ceiling space treated with one consistent and sufficient design (Plates 6 and 137) calculated to satisfy the whole area. Cornice, corner and centre ornaments were conceived in one mode and proportioned to the scale of the room. The devices used were ropes and garlands of laurel, flowers and fruit in bold relief cast in plaster as distinguished from the old *stucco-duro* work and the parge work that succeeded it, in which latter the relief or ribbing and flower pats were comparatively low (Plate 3), the designs being worked in the raw *parge* or plaster *in situ*. Colour and gilding were in many instances added to this cast plaster decoration. Decorative paintings also often occurred in the flat surfaces.

While most of the floors were of well-joined boards without ornamental device, the practice was not uncommon, in the more elegant houses, of inlaying or parquetting the floors in patterns wrought in different coloured woods. In her diary, Celia Fiennes alludes to the floor in a cedar room, of the Restoration period, "inlayed with cyphers and the coronet." Geometrical patterns in divers coloured woods were likewise used, " often radiating from a star in the centre of the room." To some such design Evelyn evidently refers in his Diary in an entry anent the Duke of Norfolk's "new palace at Weybridge" when he notes that "the roomes were wainscotted and some of them parquetted with cedar, yew, cypresse, etc." He also notes of another house that "one of the closets is parquetted with plain deal set in diamond exceeding staunch and pretty."

Furniture and Decoration.—During the sixteenth century and the early part of the seventeenth the articles of furniture in common use were somewhat restricted in number. Chests of all sizes and of all degrees of ornamentation were to be found everywhere and may be regarded as the standard mobiliary unit of the period. It was not until the early days of the Stuarts that tables became really common; prior to that time long boards on trestles often served in lieu of the long, narrow refectory tables with heavy legs, underframing and stretchers close to the ground. The wall furniture comprised hanging cupboards, credences or buffets (Plate 136) and hutches in the earlier days and, in the greater houses, there were often cabinets of more or less elaboration in the matter of carving. Bedsteads with heavy carved posts supporting cumbrous panelled and carved tops were the most imposing items of mobiliary equipment. The seating furniture consisted mainly of backless benches or forms and joint stools. Chairs, most commonly with arms, panelled backs and carved cresting, were few in number and usually reserved for the heads of families or for guests of honour. It was not until the fore part of the seventeenth century, during the reigns of James I and Charles I, that there was much variety in the kinds of pieces in general use or that houses were furnished in at all an adequate manner according to our notions. Both in the time of Queen Elizabeth and also through the reigns of the first two Stuarts and the Commonwealth period the furniture, almost without exception, was heavy in structure, robust in its proportions and rectilinear in contour, in all of these respects coinciding very fully with the architectural background (Plate 136). So universally was this the case that the mobiliary creations of the period have been not inappropriately referred to as being, for the most part, a kind of movable architecture. While the paragraphs immediately following are to be understood as applying mainly to the furniture of the first sixty years of the seventeenth century, they may be taken as applying also to the furniture of the sixteenth century so far as the pieces therein discussed existed during the earlier period. It is, however, necessary to remember that certain items of decorative detail and ornamentation that had been characteristic in the time of Queen Elizabeth either almost or entirely disappeared very early in the reign of King James. Such an item of difference, for example, was the "Romayne work." This consisted of human heads carved in relief on roundels or medallions and was popular in the sixteenth century but virtually disappeared at the beginning of the seventeenth. Human figures in ornamentation also dropped almost completely out of fashion.

The pieces of furniture in common use during the reigns of James I and Charles I and the period of the Commonwealth were cupboards of various sorts, cabinets, buffets and dressers, chests, hutches, bedsteads, day-beds, tables of many varieties the most characteristic of which, perhaps, were the long narrow refectory tables, settles and settees, chairs both with and without arms, forms or backless benches, joint stools and footstools. The wood of which these pieces were made was almost invariably oak, although other less durable woods were occasionally used for furniture in humbler houses. The decoration consisted of carving, panelling, inlay or marqueterie, painting and, towards the middle of the century, the application of turned ornaments such as oval bosses, lozenges, split balusters and maces, and the formation of intricate geometrical panels by means of applied mouldings.

Carving of several sorts was used (v. pp. 55 and 56, "Practical Book of Period Furniture": Eberlein & McClure), but the most usual kind was in low but strong relief, often on a sunk ground. The *motifs* included strapwork, diaperwork, *guilloche* patterns, lunettes, tulips, hearts, roses and rosettes, acanthus leaves, foliated and floriated scrolls, grapevines with fruit and leaves, gadrooning, channelling, reeding, fluting, nulling, lozenges, laurelling, palmated chains, pomegranates, notching, "jewelling," geometrical designs and similar devices, all of which were practically echoes of the *motifs* employed in connexion with the panelling or in the embellishment of one or another part of the fixed woodwork.

2

The inlay or marqueterie of divers coloured woods and bone was of simple but effective execution and generally showed an adaptation of some of the *motifs* already mentioned. The aid of colour was more frequently resorted to than many imagine. The carved headboards and panelled canopies of the bedsteads were often enriched with heraldic blasonings and the same form of ornamentation was also applied in other places. There was comparatively little upholstered furniture and such as there was in the early part of the century may usually be traced to a Continental origin; after the principles of the Commonwealth had swept aside tradition regarding the use of chairs and they had become plentiful, we find both seats and backs frequently covered with either leather or "Turkey work." For a full discussion of all the furniture during the first sixty years of the seventeenth century, the reader is referred to Chapter II, "Practical Book of Period Furniture": Eberlein & McClure.

With the access of new and varied influences attending the Restoration and profoundly affecting cultural conditions during the rest of the century, there was not only a vast growth in the taste for luxurious and ample household furnishings but also a perceptible increase in the kinds of articles that came into common use. While the furniture of former days continued in use along with the newer types in a majority of the houses, and while the former styles continued to be copied in country districts, the new modes exercised a far-reaching and modifying effect, completely transformed and enriched the average interior where they had been adopted along with the substantial residuum of earlier equipment, and in houses where only *le dernier cri* of fashion was heeded to the exclusion of all previous vogue—as in the establishments of some of the king's mistresses—produced a revolution in the art of interior decoration.

In addition to the tale of articles previously set forth as usual items of equipment, we must now mention chests of drawers on stands, highboys and low-boys, cabinets with doors on high stands, Chinese lacquered cabinets, with or without doors, on carved stands, chests of drawers without stands, desks or bureaux, bureau bookcases, presses, bookcases, mirrors, tall case clocks and a great assortment of small tables for one special purpose or another. In the matter of contour, we may note that while the old rectilinear principle continued to be strongly felt, the curvilinear influence made its appearance and rapidly gained favour. This curvilinear influence manifested itself plainly in Baroque tendencies and we have such plentiful examples as scrolled legs, hooded tops to cabinet work, curved contours of chair backs in the Portuguese fashion and the beginnings of cabriole leg dominance.

The decorative processes employed included carving, painting and gilding or parcel gilding, veneering, inlay and marqueterie and lacquering. The vogue for lacquered furniture became a positive passion and not only did the importation of numerous Oriental pieces indicate a potent infusion of "the Chinese taste" in interior decoration, but the rage for this species of polychrome embellishment led amateurs to engage extensively in the process and the results of their endeavours often achieved an high degree of excellence. The style of carving that now came into fashion was realistic and wholly different from the methods that had previously prevailed. Much elaborately carved or turned furniture was made of pine, lime, beech, birch and other soft woods and then painted and parcel gilt or wholly gilded. The art of veneering was developed to an extent hitherto unknown and produced admirable results in whose composition were considered not only the pleasing effects to be gained from the contrasting colours of different woods but also the divers agreeable effects of grain and the pattern employed. Akin to veneering, but involving greater scope for the exercise of decorative design and the properties of multi-coloured woods, was the process of marqueterie which, in England, reached the high-water mark of its most skillful expression towards the end of the century. The value of upholstery as a decorative accessory was now fully understood and a great many chairs, settees and stools were covered with needlework of *gros point* and *petit point,* with velvets and brocades, with silks and even with printed linens and chintzes.

Other Decorative Accessories and Movable Decorations.—In no country has skillful needlework ever commanded more sincere admiration or counted a greater number of proficient devotees than in England. It is not surprising, therefore, during the sixteenth and seventeenth centuries to learn of the high esteem in which the decorative products of the loom and of the embroidery frame were held and of the extent to which they were utilised in the adornment of houses. Allusion has already been made to the 2600 tapestries which Henry VIII had in his possession. Nor was he by any means alone as a collector. England was always regarded as a good market for Continental tapestries and an enormous number crossed the Channel to be hung up in English halls and bring brilliant colour into sombre oak-panelled rooms. During the reign of James I the Mortlake looms were set up and the exportation of English-made tapestries from the island was several times forbidden.

Besides numerous tapestries a great many other

hangings were used to liven the walls; velvets with *appliqué* devices, embroideries, and large pieces of the curious multi-coloured zig-zag needlework which we are accutsomed to associate with upholstered seats and chair backs rather than with the adornment of walls. When we remember that needlework was one of the principal occupations of ladies of position and quality, we can more readily understand the abundance of this sort of decoration. Besides the hangings for doors and windows, which were often enriched with embroidery, there were the bed hangings and bedspreads by which so much store was set that they were specifically bequeathed by will as important items of inheritance. These hangings and spreads were not only made of costly material, but were enriched with the most lavish and exquisite needlework as well. In the simpler rooms window hangings and bed hangings were occasionally of printed linen with striking patterns and brilliant colouring.

In addition to the woven and embroidered hangings that decked the walls of oak-panelled rooms, another resource for polychrome decoration was to be found in the stamped, tooled, coloured and sometimes gilded leather that was hung or else fastened tight upon the wall surface. Other wall adornments no less effective were portraits and occasionally other paintings. When neither paintings nor hangings graced the wall, the surface was oftentimes relieved by antlers, heads, fox masques and other trophies of the chase.

Of course, there were numerous small accessories such as candlesticks, sconces, candelabra, and fire dogs, the last named of which were often large and of imposing design. Besides these, such objects as silver and pewter tankards, bowls and platters, pieces of brass and copper, the small brass fireside ornaments and

fittings and brass bracket clocks lent welcome spots
of interest and lustre.

While many of the floors were strewn with rushes,
especially in the fore part of the period under consideration, it was not at all unusual to have rugs made
of rushes woven by hand. In the wealthier houses
Oriental rugs were by no means unknown.

After the Restoration curtains and draperies assumed an importance in the scheme of furnishing
(Plate 1) previously unknown in England. The most
splendid fabrics imported from Venice and Genoa, and
afterwards made in England, were used for this purpose. Curiously enough, although the Mortlake looms
continued in operation during the Restoration period
and tapestries were still imported from the Continent,
the vogue for this particular sort of wall decoration
somewhat languished and abated in use and manufacture, in large measure, no doubt, owing to the new
styles of decoration by means of more pretentious panelling, the use of niches, and the inserting of decorative
paintings as panels and overdoor embellishments—a
change for which Wren and his school were to a great
extent responsible. Bed hangings and bedspreads
maintained their wonted hold on public taste. Linens
and calicoes printed in gay colours and fascinating designs, many of them of Oriental origin, took the place
of the more expensive fabrics for draperies and hangings in rooms of simpler equipment.

Mention has already been made of the use of mirrors set in the panelling as a means of wall decoration.
Mirrors in wonderfully wrought frames were no less
esteemed as an effective factor in furnishing elegantly.
Since the establishment of glass works at Lambeth and
Greenwich it had become possible to obtain the best
glass and of a much larger size than formerly and English decorators were not slow to avail themselves of

this new resource. Some of the mirror frames were made of coloured, bevelled and engraved glass and were exceedingly rich in appearance. This glass of excellent quality was also turned to account in making large, cut lustres or crystals for the admirably designed chandeliers and sconces that now became common. Other chandeliers were made of brass, of iron embellished with colour and gilding and of wood painted and parcel gilt.

Paintings, both portraits and pictures of a decorative character, afforded a constantly used resource. And to all this rich array, we must add the colour and grace of form conveyed by the Oriental porcelains the collection of which had become not only a fashionable hobby but an absolute passion among the people at large. Here, again, the power of Chinoiserie showed itself plainly in the history of decoration. The Dutch were not slow to emulate the Chinese and their Delft soon came to hold nearly as high a place in the esteem of English people. What with porcelains, lacquer and other odds and ends of Eastern luxuries that constantly found their way into England, Oriental influence made a deep impression on the modes of the period.

Materials and Colour.—Up to the end of the Commonwealth period oak had been the staple wood of England for all purposes architectural and mobiliary, although, of course, there were plenty of occasional departures from this precedent and exceptions to the rule. Nevertheless, the period mentioned must be considered *par excellence* the "age of oak." About the time of the Restoration walnut came into popular use, being partly imported and partly derived from native sources which became plentifully available at this time. In addition to walnut, which may be considered the staple wood for fine furniture after the Restoration, other woods were employed for inlay and marqueterie purposes and oak continued to have an accepted position, especially in country districts.

Owing to the revocation of the Edict of Nantes and, to some extent, to a certain tide of immigration into England before that event, great numbers of silk workers came over from France and began to ply their craft in England. They soon made brocades and velvets the equals in gorgeous colour, graceful pattern and excellent texture of the fabrics that had previously been imported in vast quantities from Venice and Genoa.

Throughout the whole of the sixteenth and seventeenth centuries the English colour sense was fresh and vigorous (Plate 1) and, despite the somewhat sombre hue of oak panelled walls, English interiors did not lack for colour and plenty of it. This passion for colour reached its culmination in the latter part of the seventeenth century, so that by 1700 the country was in a very riot of rich, virile, scintillating colour, a condition that was perfectly compatible with good taste because the massive, strong, and rather dark backgrounds of the architectural setting made such treatment not only permissible but absolutely necessary.

Arrangement.—During the earlier part of this period the architectural arrangement was rather fortuitous than formal, and the arrangement of the furniture units was much the same. The units themselves were not overly numerous, so that it was not difficult to place the important pieces in the broad spaces where they would be most effective. The fireplace, of course, was always a centre about which a number of movables would naturally be grouped.

In the latter part of the seventeenth century furniture items were far more numerous and notions of symmetrical arrangement, brought back by the refugees, imparted to the rooms an aspect of orderly and balanced composition.

CHAPTER II

INTERIOR DECORATION IN ENGLAND AND AMERICA DURING THE EIGHTEENTH CENTURY AND THE FIRST THREE DECADES OF THE NINETEENTH

*I*NTRODUCTION.—In England and America, the eighteenth century and the first three decades of the nineteenth, which really belong to the preceding century through stylistic affinities and as a directly logical outcome of influences well under way before the year 1800, constitute a period of the greatest complexity as well as of the greatest interest. It will be understood that what is said in this chapter applies to the American Colonies and the infant republic, after its severance from the Mother Country, as well as to England. But it must also be distinctly understood that all the evolutions of the styles considered reached their full and richest fruition only in England and that they were reflected in America in less elaborate renderings. This statement does not mean to asperse in the slightest degree the culture or taste on our own side of the Atlantic, but the estates that were able to support the expense of the highest decorative achievements of the age were comparatively few in number, and although there were not wanting instances of the greatest elegance and most lavish expenditure in furnishing of various town houses in Philadelphia, in Boston, in Charleston and New York, and of some country houses in Pennsylvania, Maryland, Virginia and South Carolina, the majority of people, from force of circumstances, were obliged to be content with the simpler though not less admirable interpretation of modes that attained an hitherto unparallelled development in the British Isles.

At the very beginning of the eighteenth century we have the heritage of Baroque inspiration remaining over from the seventeenth century. Following close upon it came the severe and somewhat heavy classicism of which Kent was the chiefest and most able exponent. With the middle of the century we find an utterly new influence that was expressed in England by the Brothers Adam and those that followed in their wake, and in France, a little later, by the architects and designers who imparted to the style we know familiarly as "Louis Seize" its peculiar grace and refinement.

The Adam influence was of classic derivation as was also the heavier scheme of interpretation practised by the Kentian school, but it expressed classicism in its more attenuated and refined forms and laid emphasis, as a rule, rather upon the elegancies of decoration than upon the bold masses and the marshalling of vigorous structural or semi-structural members by way of embellishment. Adam delicacy, in turn, was in course of time supplanted by the robust and often severe forms of the Classic Revival, in which the sterner Greek modes and the more heroic Roman phases that at times savoured of bombast were stressed with insistence.

Besides all these well-defined influences, there was "the Chinese taste," which recurred again and again in one form or another throughout the century, adding its charm to the manifold factors that contributed to make the eighteenth century one of the most opulent as well as varied decorative epochs in English history.

Architectural Background and Methods of Fixed Decoration.—One fact of tremendous importance in the art of interior decoration has already been noted in

PLATE 7

EARLY GEORGIAN ROOM WITH PANELLED AND PAINTED WALLS
Removed from Norfolk, England
Composite English Furniture, Queen Anne Mirror
By Courtesy of Messrs. Litchfield & Co., London

the Foreword, but too much stress cannot be laid upon it, and we therefore repeat it here. That fact is that *interior decoration does not consist merely of selection and arrangement of movable furniture and garnishings; the architectural background and the fixed decorations are every whit as vitally essential to a successful and complete composition,* and it is impossible to attach too much emphasis to this truth, a truth that some professional decorators too often minimise while not a few amateurs are even more prone to ignore it. In Part III special attention is paid to the treatment of plain walls where the occupancy of rented quarters, apartments and the like makes it impracticable to effect far-reaching structural changes in the background. In the paragraphs that follow, special attention will be devoted to an analysis of backgrounds and fixed decorations.

The opening years of the eighteenth century witnessed virtually the same features of interior architecture as were in vogue during the last years of the seventeenth century, features of which, however, we shall now give a somewhat more detailed description. There were spacious, high-ceilinged rooms, symmetrically designed with window and door openings so disposed as to contribute to the air of regularity. The window openings were large and high, while their trims were often made the objects of formal ornamentation. Doorways also shared a distinctly decorative and usually architectural treatment, traces of Baroque influence being more or less discernible in such features as continuous segmental pediments or interrupted pediments with urns. (Plate 7.)

The panels of the walls were large (Plates 7 and 8) and were often bounded by boldly profiled (Plate 138) bolection mouldings. In size the panels were graduated according to the parts of the room; shallow and broad panels would be placed between door or window heads and the cornice, tall and narrow panels between windows, a single panel for the chimney piece (Plate 137), whatever its dimensions and shape might be, while the ordinary wall panels were of generous proportions. Elaborate naturalistic carving of foliage, fruits, flowers and figures in swags and drops (Plate 137), wrought in high relief or undercut in the manner of Grinling Gibbon, were still used and were supplemented in many instances by sundry supporting architectural scrolls and by conventional *motifs* in low relief, such as acanthus foliage on a cyma moulding (Plate 6), classic laurelling, and all their well-known affinities.

Very fully developed and elaborate cornices adorned such rooms, and the plaster coves and ceilings, wrought with the utmost dexterity of the plasterer's art, echoed the flowers, fruit, foliage (Plate 137) and figures to be seen in the decorative wood carving. The floors, while usually of plain boards, not infrequently exhibited parquetted patterns, in the manner already mentioned in the preceding chapter, or else a device in chequered tiles of stone or marble.

It is safe to say that there was never a time when interior architectural woodwork was carried to an higher point of development or displayed more admirable characteristics. Even in the simpler houses, where three of the walls of a room would ordinarily be plastered, there was almost invariably some well-proportioned panelling above the fireplace or even covering a greater part of the whole of the wall on that side of the room. For many of the elaborately carved and panelled interiors, the wood used was oak, cedar, deal or pine. The oak and cedar were left unpainted; deal was sometimes merely waxed, or slightly stained and waxed, and sometimes painted; while pine was ordinarily painted, although not invariably, and, when left in its natural state, assumed a mellow golden brown tone from the action of the atmosphere. In at least one instance known to the authors, the panelling of a late seventeenth century house in Pennsylvania, belonging architecturally, however, to the category under discussion, consisted of pine and poplar together. Neither paint nor stain of any kind were ever used upon it and all of the wood took on a rich ginger brown hue of great beauty.

When the panelling was painted, white, which was much favoured in Holland at the time, was sometimes used, but by no means so universally as many people seem to imagine. Grey, grey green, buff, brown, pale yellow, blue, green and green blues of great beauty were in common use and imparted a richness and warmth that strongly commend a wider employment of similar treatments at the present day. These painted interiors were very commonly further embellished with gilding applied to mouldings and carving.*

In the latter part of the seventeenth century, as previously stated, the taste for lacquer became a positive passion. Much lacquer was imported from the East, but the importations could not begin to supply the demand; much furniture was lacquered both by artisans and by amateurs, who regarded skill in this direction

---

* At Graeme Park, Horsham, Pennsylvania, for instance, the home of Sir William Keith, the first coat of paint given the woodwork was a greenish grey, and no other colour has ever since adorned the panelling and the door and window trims. At Stenton, Northern Liberties, in Philadelphia, the home of James Logan, on the other hand, " the taste of the occupants dictated a change of colour from time to time and we find a good deal of variety in the successive coats " of paint. For these instances and other observations anent the practice in America *v.* " The Architecture of Colonial America," p. 149: Harold Donaldson Eberlein; Little, Brown & Co., Boston, 1915. See also "Architectural Record," *passim.*

as an eligible and polite accomplishment.   The vogue
for lacquer endured throughout the reign of Queen
Anne and even lasted for some time afterwards.   What
with the universal admiration for lacquer in an especially colour-loving epoch, and the very considerable
proficiency in lacquer processes attained by British
craftsmen, it is not surprising to find lacquered decoration occasionally extended to the fixed woodwork in
rooms and not reserved solely as a method of mobiliary
embellishment.   It is worth noting that this architectural employment of lacquer has been revived in a few
instances and on a limited scale in our own time, with
admirable results.

In the more sumptuous interiors of this type, the
fireplace surrounds and facings were of carefully
chosen marble or stone, while in the simpler interiors
the surrounds were of wood and the facings frequently
of glazed tiles, sometimes plain, but more usually of
Delft make with monochrome blue or rose devices or
else with polychrome decorations.   The surround commonly consisted of a bold bolection moulding and there
was generally no mantel shelf or else only a very narrow one.

The fixed decorations were rich and adequate.   There
were mirrors empanelled in the walls or set in the doors,
decorative paintings set in panels over doorways, in
chimney pieces and in central positions on the sides of
walls.   There were cupboards (Plate 7) built into the
woodwork, usually in corners, with coved tops carefully scalloped and enriched with carving and sometimes parcel gilt, or with smooth surfaces in the coving
covered with decorative painting.   Coves and the flat
surfaces of ceilings, likewise, in addition to the rich cast
plaster reliefs, were often adorned with paintings.

When the walls were not fully panelled, they were

PLATE 8

BED CHAMBER IN QUEEN ANNE MODE WITH PANELLED PAINTED WALLS
Courtesy of Mrs. Lyman W. Kendall

PLATE 9

DINING ROOM OF GEORGIAN TYPE WITH HEPPLEWHITE
FURNITURE AND ADAM SIDEBOARD
Panelled Walls Painted a Grey Green
Courtesy of Edward Browning, Esq.

PLATE 10

THE BANQUETTING ROOM, CROOME COURT, WORCESTERSHIRE, BY ROBERT ADAM
Characteristic Wall and Ceiling Treatment
From "Robert Adam and His Brothers," by Courtesy of B. T. Batsford, Ltd.

PLATE 11

ADAM DOOR AND OVER DOOR
DECORATION
Courtesy of Mr. Karl Freund

sometimes painted, sometimes covered with wall paper in highly decorative and bright-coloured patterns, and sometimes hung with rich fabrics tacked tightly in place. Occasionally the panels of the doors themselves were embellished with mirrors or with decorative paintings.

Sconces, lanthorns and chandeliers of varied forms in plain brass, in wrought-iron painted and parcel gilt, in wood richly carved and gilt or painted and parcel gilt, and in brass or cut glass profusely hung with crystals added greatly to the rich effect of the permanent background.

Such were the possibilities and characteristics of the fixed architectural interior settings during the reign of Queen Anne and in the years immediately following her demise.

Early in the Georgian period, under the influence of such men as James Gibbs, Sir John Vanbrugh, Sir William Chambers and, above all, Sir William Kent, there was a clearly marked departure from the freedom and flexibility of architectural and decorative interpretation, as practised by Sir Christopher Wren and his immediate school, and a reversion to what was fancied to be a purer and more scholarly presentation of classic principles as set forth by the great architectural exponents of the Italian Renaissance. For this reason the work of Inigo Jones evoked a renewed measure of praise and admiration but, quite apart from any enthusiasm for the achievements of earlier English architects, the men of the day, one and all, placed themselves at the feet of Vitruvius, Vignola and Palladio and followed the precepts of these great men of the past with the most meticulous and sometimes simian precision. To the votaries of the new school Palladio was especially dear and they so generally accepted him as their standard and so glorified his work and precepts that they " raised him in their time almost to the position of a demigod." Actuated as they were by this narrow and almost fanatical admiration for merely one individual's explication of classicism, it is scarcely to be wondered at that they were "unreasonably prejudiced against the work of the Wren period by the discovery that, although classic in principle, the rules laid down by the great architects of the Italian Renaissance had by no means been strictly adhered to." This attitude, quite apart from any other agency, explains in large measure "the prejudice that existed against Sir Christopher at the close of his brilliant career and the exaltation of the earlier work of Inigo Jones." Wren had both displayed a perceptible tinge of French influence and also shown not a little personal independence in his interpretations, and this damned him in the eyes of the early Georgian purists who "accepted so fervently the principles of Italian classicism as the only form of true culture that all buildings which exhibited variations were regarded by them as beneath notice or consideration." In their zeal of archælogical solicitude— to quote Sir Horace Walpole, architecture had "resumed all her rights" and buildings were designed "in the purest style of antique composition"—they often produced work that savoured of pedantry and missed the spontaneous inspiration and elastic quality necessary to give it the vital significance of an understanding contemporary expression.

At the same time, while the spirit of classic purism was dominant, there were numerous successful and acceptable adventures into the realm of Baroque design, as witnessed, for instance, by some of the creations of James Gibbs, but it was restrained and chastened Baroque, conceived and executed in the light of classic severity. Notwithstanding the rigidity of ideals and the conscientious exactitude with which the foremost architects held themselves to precedent, a great proportion of the early Georgian work possessed merit of an high order and exhibited both dignity and charm. It is an enduring memorial to the skill and good taste of the designers and also equally a striking testimony to the intelligence and appreciation of a clientele that made possible the realisation of such designs. It was, indeed, a golden age of appreciative interest and liberal patronage on the part of wealthy laymen in the persons of the great nobles and landed gentry, who found that the "court of the first two Georges offered" them few attractions and that there was little "scope for competion in politics during the long and all-powerful sway of Walpole." Furthermore, in the entire absence of foreign hostilities, there were no openings for gaining distinction in military or naval careers and, consequently, "it would seem that numbers of these great nobles and men of leisure embraced the study of art as the principal occupation of their lives. The particular branch of art which interested them most keenly was the pure classic architecture of Ancient Rome," and their extensive diversions in this field of research rendered them both capable critics and enthusiastic patrons.

The interiors of the great houses then erected displayed a sense of architectural composition that has never been surpassed in English domestic building and even the less pretentious dwellings of the period clearly reflected the prevailing sense of symmetry and architectural amenity that had permeated all ranks of society. So thoroughly had Palladianism and a feeling for elegant proportions taken hold of the popular imagination that they may truly be said to have become endemic among English-speaking people of that day.

3

Both inside and out, houses were planned to convey the impression of symmetrical balance and the same care for symmetrical composition was observed in the treatment of the individual rooms, which were, as a rule, approximately square and high-ceiled. Structural features, that is to say, doorways, windows and fireplaces, were symmetrically placed so as to emphasise the effect of balance (Plate 9) and were given such architectural adornment that they constituted an important item in the decoration of the room and to a great extent dominated the placing of the movable furnishings and determined their character.

The details were vigorous in line and classic in fashion—fluted pilasters with appropriate capitals, correct architectural entablatures, pediments of several types, accurately designed friezes and cornices and bold, well-considered mouldings. Doorways frequently were graced with superimposed pediments (Plate 7), either straight, or interrupted with a central urn or bust, and the same *motif* was apt to be echoed in the chimney piece which extended all the way or almost all the way to the ceiling. When there was no pediment above the doorway, the note of decorous architectural formality was often sustained by a fitly conceived panel with suitable embellishments. The overmantel panel with its imposing architectural setting was made a central feature for the reception of a portrait (Plate 7) or a decorative painting or, when the chimney piece was less structurally elaborate, a mirror in a frame of strongly architectural design, perhaps with the additional decoration of a painting in the head or in side panels, might be placed directly above the mantel shelf. The mantel-piece itself was of wood or of marble (Plates 7 and 137), often elaborately carved with devices inspired by designs of classic provenance pourtrayed in the works of the Renaissance exponents of Greek and Roman antiquity.

About the middle of the century, under the influence of Sir William Chambers, the elaborate chimney piece, reaching nearly to the ceiling, which had received the sanction and best efforts of previous architects, gradually fell into disfavour and gave place to a newer mode of Continental fashion (Plate 9).

"When he [Sir William Chambers] returned to England in 1755 [from the Continent], he was accompanied by Wilton and Cipriani, afterwards so well known as an artist and decorator. He also brought Italian sculptors to carve the marble mantel-pieces he introduced into English houses.

These were made from his own designs, and the ornament of figures, scrolls and foliage was free in character. Strange to say, these mantel-pieces, designed and made by an architect, were yet the means of taking away this important part of interior decoration from the hands of the architect altogether and causing it to become quite a separate production, made and sold along with the grates.

In former times it had been an integrant portion of the room, reaching from floor to ceiling, balanced and made part of the wall by having its main lines carried round in panelling and enriched friezes. It was the keynote of decoration, and the master builder of the times grew fanciful and exerted his utmost skill upon its carving and quaint imagery, centralising the whole ornament of the room around the household shrine.

Mantel-pieces had gradually come down in height, though still retaining much of their finer proportions and classic design. Many causes had contributed to this, the chief being the disuse of wood panelling and the preference given to hangings of damask, foreign leather and wall-paper. In the reigns of Queen Anne and the Little Dutchman the custom of panelling was partially kept up. . . . At this time the upper half of the chimney piece was still retained, but only reached about half way up the wall [in many instances]. Gibbs, Kent, and Ware kept the superstructure as much as they could, but Sir William Chambers dealt it the most crushing blow it had yet received by copying the later French and Italian styles and giving minute detail more consideration than fine proportion. He discarded the upper part altogether and helped to make 'continued chimney pieces' things of the past."—(*Warren Clouston's "Treatise on Chippendale."*)

Window trims, while vigorously designed, were comparatively plain and nearly all of the carved and moulded architectural enrichment was bestowed upon the overdoor decorations, cornices and friezes and, up to the time of Chambers, the chimney piece. The window openings were tall and sufficiently wide and were often somewhat recessed with carefully panelled jambs and soffits. The sashes themselves had heavy muntins and the rectangular panes were the same size or slightly larger than those in use during the Queen Anne period.

During much of the early Georgian era the walls continued to be fully panelled with large panels (Plate 9), frequently of the bevel flush type (Plate 7), separated by broad stiles and rails with thumbnail mouldings. Very often a moulded chair rail separated the base panelling from the upper panels. The panels were generally of a uniform size, but were graduated to the exigencies of space when there was occasion. Cupboards and buffets, and occasionally niches with coved and scalloped tops, continued in many instances to be built into the panelling at appropriate places and were generally given an additional enrichment of intricately wrought mouldings and other carving of a character to correspond with the ornate cornices that not infrequently exhibited a wealth of carved foliation, egg and dart *motifs* or similar devices. It will thus be seen that the carved and panelled woodwork was an highly important item in the decoration of an early Georgian room (Plates 7 and 137).

The ceilings, though sometimes comparatively plain, were also occasionally embellished with lavish foliated and floriated bands and mouldings and other designs, wrought with all the dexterity of which the highly skilled plaster craftsmen were capable. On such ceilings colour and gilding were likewise wont to play an important part. When the walls were not fully panelled—the abandonment of full panelling, as already noted, became more common as the century advanced—they were apt to be covered with rich fabrics, wallpaper or, sometimes, with fine leather appropriately decorated.

It is most important, in our process of visualising the panelled rooms of the early Georgian period, to bear in mind that the use of unpainted woodwork was abandoned comparatively early in the century. We have seen that the earlier architects and decorators, when they did use paint as a variant to the deal, pine, cedar, oak or walnut panelling, did not confine themselves to white or cream white, as people sometimes fancy, but resorted very frequently to colours such as those already mentioned. In the early Georgian epoch, while not eschewing white—white, it is true, was more commonly used in the American Colonies than colours—they quite as often or oftener employed full-bodied tones of cream, cream yellow, green, blue green, drab and brown and these tones contributed materially to give the appearance of richness and "comfort for which the rooms of the period are noted. Frequently additional grandeur was obtained by gilding or partly gilding some of the carving."

In addition to the fixed decoration supplied by the rich woodwork, the stately chimney pieces and the plaster adornment of the ceilings, decorative paintings were often incorporated in the scheme where a suitable over-door or other similar space invited their employment, mirrors were permanently affixed in suitable positions and choice specimens of sculpture were placed in niches especially provided for them or upon pedestals where their presence would contribute to the general aspect of balanced dignity and elegance.

While surveying this particular period of eighteenth century decoration, we must not fail to take due note of two influences that marked a wide and striking departure from the prevailing Palladianism—the "Chinese Taste," fostered by Sir William Chambers, and a fanciful pseudo-Gothic manifestation largely abetted by Sir Horace Walpole. The former movement coincided with and gave especial emphasis to one of the periodic recrudescences of unusual interest in things Oriental whose recurrence in the history of English and Continental decoration afforded an agreeable and inspiring note of variety and gave rise to many features of permanent worth; the latter movement was not happy in its conception, was taken up as a fad by *dilettanti* who were not in sympathy with the Gothic spirit and did not really understand it, and produced no results of lasting importance. The Chinese work of Sir William Chambers, and of those who imitated or emulated his endeavours, was in the main performed in an honest and legitimate manner, created an interesting and not unwelcome relief to the predominant classicism of the period, and extended its application to movable equipment as well as to fixed decoration. The Gothic work of the day was palpably a piece of affectation and even, at times, grotesque in its forms and we may be thankful that its ephemeral course left no momentous traces behind it.

Shortly after the middle of the eighteenth century,

an entirely new architectural influence became paramount and as the introduction of this influence was due
almost wholly to the Brothers Adam, and as they and
their contemporaries and imitators were its accredited
exponents, we shall be justified in calling the second
half of the century, and, indeed, the first decade of the
nineteenth, the Adam Age. Impelled by their extended
studies of classic art and architecture at fountain head,
and realising clearly what their architectural predecessors in England had completely failed to realise—that
classic precedents were susceptible of a far wider and
more elastic interpretation than had hitherto been given
them, that architecture and the decorative arts in the
golden ages of Greek and Roman development had not
been straitly confined by an unalterably rigid set of
rules and interpretative conventions whose authoritative exposition was to be found only in the works of
Vitruvius, Vignola and the other dogmatists to whom
Kent and his school had tightly pinned their faith, and
that classicism, without being adulterated or distorted
and robbed of its fundamental genius, was susceptible
of a previously undreamed of urbanity, refinement and
even playful exuberance of expression—the Adelphi
proceeded to refine, enrich, revivify and even revolu-
tionise the architectural and decorative conceptions of
their day and generation. They not only introduced
the epoch-marking notes of attenuation and slender
grace, along with a more exuberant, lively, diversified
and elegant system of decorative *motifs,* all derived,
however, from classic precedent, but, at the same time,
they also showed how classic architectural interpretation could be thoroughly domestic, intimate and lively
in tone as well as ponderous and monumental. When
they began to practise, domestic architecture in England had fallen somewhat into a groove and was in

danger of becoming narrow, rigid and pedantic. Without sacrificing any principles of classicism, they rendered it human, infinitely more interesting, and elastic
in scope.

The Adelphi were no less formal in their modes of
expression than their predecessors, but their formality
was vastly more varied, richer and intensely genial.
There was a *finesse* and a polish about their conceptions that fully accorded with the spirit of the day, a
period which someone has aptly termed the ''age of the
drawing-room.'' Indeed, they may be regarded as in
no small degree responsible for the creation of that
spirit. One of the eminently pleasing forms in which
their humanised formality found a fresh outlet was in
the varied shapes of the rooms frequently introduced
into their compositions. Hitherto, although rooms were
designed with a due regard for satisfying symmetry in
their proportions, they were habitually rectangular in
shape. Not content with confining themselves to the
monotonous convention of rectangularity, the Brothers
Adam made the very shapes of their rooms fulfill a decorative purpose and frequently designed circular, semi-
circular, octagonal, oval and elliptical apartments or
rooms with semi-circular, arc-shaped, tribune or ar-
caded ends when they deemed that, by so doing, they
could enhance the elegance, vivacity or interest of their
creations. At the same time they made the ceilings
(Plates 10 and 159) and floors enter into a comprehensive and inter-related scheme of decorative unity that
had rarely before been equalled.

To a greater extent, perhaps, than had ever been
done previously, they treated the walls of their more
important rooms as architectural compositions (Plate
10), distinct and complete in themselves, with a due and
ordered disposition of panels (Plate 10), pilasters, cap-

itals, pediments, friezes and cornices. All of these features were usually in low and rather flat projection so as to emphasise the sense of space and prevent them from seeming unduly obtrusive, unless the apartment was so large that it could easily stand a succession of bold projections without their becoming oppressive or destroying the aspect of spacious freedom. The decorative details, both upon these architectural members and upon the panelled or other intervening flat surfaces, were refined and delicate in scale and in low relief. Pilasters, pediments and other dominant projections were sometimes fashioned in carved wood, but more frequently were executed in plaster; the low relief wall panels and other ornamental details were almost invariably done in plaster or compo. Never before had the art of the plasterer or of the worker in compo been given so ample an opportunity to display its manifold possibilities and charms.

The panels, or successions of panels, were often covered with a complete and sufficient decorative design of airy arabesques, urns, pateræ and other *motifs* in low relief and the effect of this rich mural adornment was generally further enhanced by the use of a pale-coloured background in order to throw the raised work into sharp contrast. At other times the wall panels exhibited no plaster or compo relief but were painted, upon a solid body colour, with devices similar to those employed in the reliefs just mentioned.

Even with their plainer and less pretentious walls, on which there was no display of architectural features, decorative panels, either in relief or painted, were used to good effect and constituted a valuable item of fixed embellishment. On walls of a still less elaborate type— walls in the Adam mode varied from the utmost exuberance of detail to the opposite extreme of classic austerity—countersunk panels and niches were introduced, either in conjunction or separately, and were so disposed that the most striking results were obtained from the agreeable alternation of light and shadow, for the Adelphi were masters in the management of this simple but often neglected and misapplied resource, as they also were in their handling of low relief. On the plainest walls, whose surfaces were unbroken by either projections or depressions, the rich and delicate detail of the cornice (Plate 69), along with the decoration of door and window trims, was skillfully manipulated to present an elegant contrast between concentrated ornament and foil. Wooden panelling entered little if at all into the interior decorative schemes of the Brothers Adam for they were too deeply imbued with the ideals they had formed during their travels and researches in classic lands to be much enamoured of this method of wall treatment, notwithstanding the great body of previous English precedent and the materials at their disposal. Instead of wooden panelling, they occasionally employed marble, but their methods of treating plaster were capable of such agreeable variety that there was little need to resort to other means of interior finish. In a great number of cases, especially with the plainer walls, a chair rail or moulding was carried around the room, thus creating the appearance of a base for the treatment above. In some instances, also, fabrics and wall-paper were used, but painted walls seem to have accorded more nearly with the spirit of Adam interior backgrounds. The system of colouring commonly employed will be more fully discussed in a subsequent section, but it seems advisable at this point to call attention to what an extent the *ensemble* of Adam interiors was dependent upon the light, delicate and often pale tones of the flat wall surfaces.

Decorative paintings of landscapes (Plate 159) and architectural subjects, in the Italian manner worthily represented in England by Cipriani and others of his fellow-countrymen who had heeded the invitation of the Adelphi, were plentifully used and were set either in countersunk panels or in flush panels surrounded with plaster or compo mouldings in the fashion of a frame. These panels were introduced with great frequency and in various shapes over (Plate 11) doorways, above fireplaces and wherever else decorative expediency dictated. Wedgwood plaques (Plate 159), with designs by Flaxman or Lady Templetown, were often made the central features of arabesque panels, and large plaster or Wedgwood medallions, with heads or with classic figures in low relief, frequently occurred either with an accompaniment of flowing arabesques to enrich a large wall or overmantel panel, or else in a severely chaste composition as the sole enrichment of one of the smaller countersunk panels already mentioned. Busts or other pieces of sculpture (Plate 10) were sometimes strikingly used for wall decoration and so placed that the shadow of a niche behind them supplied a most impressive background against which they were silhouetted.

Mirrors fulfilled an important function in the fixed decoration of many Adam rooms and were set above mantels, over consoles in symmetrical placings or sometimes in the panelling of doors, the gilded frames being designed to accord with the light and airy interpretations of classicism elsewhere in evidence. Not a few door heads contained semi-elliptical fan lights, filled with clear glass or with mirrors, and traversed with delicately moulded leaden tracery. The effect of these door heads was singularly rich and beautiful.

Mantel pieces, as might be expected, were the objects

of no less solicitous care (Plates 10 and 69) than was lavished upon all the other permanent accessories. They were of the finest white marble carved in the characteristic Adam *motifs,* consisting of urns, swags, drops, flutings and the like, sometimes with a central panel above the fireplace opening exhibiting a Flaxman or a Templetown design in low relief, and frequently yellow (Plate 69), buff, black or green Italian marbles were so combined as to throw the carved devices into conspicuous relief, or else the whole mantel structure was of wood carved in the same refined and delicate fashion or with the more intricate detail modelled in compo and applied to the wooden ground before painting. There were few architectural superstructures or attached and "continued" chimney pieces, as in the days of Kent, and the chimney breast above the mantel shelf was adorned with a mirror or in some one of the other ways previously indicated. For many of the fireplaces, grates of burnished steel or of brass were designed in a fashion to coincide with the rest of the decoration.

The woodwork of doors and of door and window trims (Plate 69) displayed refined mouldings of rather low relief and the same chaste and delicate decorative detail, sometimes elaborate, sometimes simple, as already noted in the wooden mantels and other permanent features. Straight door heads often carried a considerable degree of elaboration and occasionally central panels in the manner shown in Plate 69. The refining effect of flutings and of other close parallel lines was especially well exemplified in Adam woodwork. As the century advanced the size of window panes gradually increased and, although there was no approximation to the horrors of large sheets of glass with which we are now sometimes afflicted and which utterly destroy the character of a window, the lights were perceptibly larger than they were during the first half of the century. The muntins, also, were appreciably pared down in dimensions. Wrought ironwork, while used chiefly in exterior embellishment, also often made its appearance in the composition of stair rails and balustrades and was fashioned in graceful, light and frequently attenuated devices to correspond with the interior *ensemble*.

The ceilings (Plates 10, 69 and 159), designed by the Brothers Adam were among the most beautiful and finished of all their exquisite compositions. The Adelphi not only had a goodly heritage of plaster tradition behind them in the work of English designers and artificers, but they also had constantly in their mind's eye the wonderful ceiling enrichments of the classic precedents upon which they drew so freely for inspiration. In the matter of physical execution they were able to avail themselves of the services of skilled plasterers, adepts in every minute detail of their craft, and also, in addition to this, they made extensive use of a newly perfected process of applying compo ornament in large moulded sections. The low reliefs, which the Adelphi knew how to employ with such marvellous effect upon walls, they used to no less advantage in the decoration of their ceilings. *Motifs* of the same description as those already noted were, of course, employed in ceiling treatment. Sometimes the ceilings were uncoloured, sometimes there was a pale ground colour to throw the low reliefs into sharp contrast, and sometimes whole surfaces were covered with painted panels or frescoes, polychrome enrichment and gilding. A great many of the ceilings were flat, but it was not uncommon to find them coved and still others domed and vaulted. Some of these vaulted and domed ceilings were quite plain except for the ornamentation around the cornice and, we may add, were exceedingly beautiful and effective, one of their great merits being the perfection of their proportions. There was the same relative gradation between the elaboration of ceilings and the elaboration of walls, some of them being exceedingly ornate while others were quite simple, but even where the walls were almost devoid of ornamentation there was usually some attempt at more decorative amenity on the ceiling, especially if it was a flat ceiling and had not the interest of curving lines to fascinate the eye.

Floors were made of both wood and marble and a certain degree of restrained decoration was sometimes employed, but in most cases the floor was either regarded as a plain foundation for the rest of the composition or else intended to be carpeted so that a fixed decoration thereon would have been lost. The increasing vogue of full-sized carpets or rugs, both of which were often especially designed and woven for the rooms in which they were to be used, discouraged the elaborate ornamental parquetting of floors, a fashion that had obtained at an earlier date when large floor coverings were not so numerous.

A survey of the elements entering into the fixed decoration of Adam rooms, as indicated in the foregoing paragraphs, shows that a hitherto unprecedented degree of refinement and completeness had been attained—indeed, we may say that it has never since been excelled—and that punctilious care was bestowed upon the least as well as upon the greatest factors comprehended in a decorative scheme. That this thorough and painstaking care was contributory in a great degree to the success of the Brothers Adam in their domestic work we need hardly emphasise.

In the early years of the nineteenth century, although the architectural and decorative influence of the Adelphi was still strong and far-reaching and constituted a force to be reckoned with, other influences were beginning to creep in from France as a reflection of the Empire mode, a mode altogether heavier and less inspired than the creations of the Adam Brothers. Architecturally it may be termed the style of the " Greek Revival"; in mobiliary and decorative parlance we know it as the Empire mode. In England the process of architectural change at this time was not so clearly marked as in America. Architectural traditions were, perhaps, more firmly established or, at least, more widely established; and, in the second place, there was not the widespread building activity that occurred at the very end of the eighteenth century and in the first three decades of the nineteenth in the recently established republic, where population was rapidly increasing and where a great many men, rejoicing in a fresh burst of prosperity and new-found wealth, were erecting for themselves homes commensurate with their affluence. We might, indeed, say that in England the architectural change was chiefly to be observed in a gradual falling away from those vital and blithesome qualities that had distinguished the work of earlier days and a slipping into a more sombre, stolid and inelastic form of expression. It was as though both architecture and interior decoration were suffering from an incipient hardening of the arteries. Details grew heavier and more pompous, there was less variety in the forms employed, and the numerous enlivening devices of fixed decoration, that had so glorified and characterised the hey-day of Adam influence, one by one dropped out of fashion until we come to a full realisation of the archi-

tectural and decorative bathos in the prevailing vision
of great rectangular rooms wth plain plaster walls,
whose monotony was now and then relieved by a niche;
door and window trims heavily detailed in severe and
rather monumental Greek and Roman *motifs,* among
which the key fret and the anthemion were conspicuous;
plaster cornices echoing the same inspiration, heavy
plaster ornaments to match around the edges and in
the centres of ceilings; and plain, vigorously moulded
black marble mantels without any fixed architectural
adornment above them on the chimney breast, a place
that seemed now to have become sacred either to a
family portrait or else to a large mirror set in a heavy
gilt frame. Altogether, it will be observed, the ground
had become well prepared for the final plunge and
slump into Victorian desolation, dullness and material-
istic commercialism without a ray of imagination to
lighten and redeem the benighted epoch.

In America, the Adam influence had borne ripe fruit
and continued to make itself felt in a somewhat modified, but nevertheless beautiful, form through the work
of such men as Samuel McIntire of Salem. Adam expression, however, had never attained the far-reaching
spread that it had in England and in the very late eighteenth century and the early years of the nineteenth,
when there was so much building to be done along the
whole Atlantic seaboard, building both public and domestic, in order to keep pace with the access of a newly
stimulated national expansion, and when, moreover,
there was the greatest enthusiasm everywhere throughout the country for all things French, it is not surprising that the style which we know as the "Classic" or
"Greek Revival," echoing the current phase of French
architectural sentiment should have taken deep root
and achieved a wide development, modified, it is true,

PLATE 12

From a photograph by J. E. H. Post

THE DINING ROOM AT "MT. AIRY"

From "Colonial Virginia: Its People and Customs," by Mary Newton Stanard
Eighteenth Century (late) Plain Walls as a Suitable Background for Paintings

by local conditions and necessities, but unmistakable in its parentage.

The interiors in this new evolution of domestic architecture were commonly characterised by a great deal of solid dignity and decorum, an impression materially assisted by the customarily spacious dimensions of the rooms, without much enlivening imagination or decorative resourcefulness to give to the *ensemble* that vitality that had always radiated from the background of a room conceived by the Brothers Adam or by the men who professedly followed their lead. The walls were plain, unrelieved expanses of smooth plaster (Plate 12) extending from baseboard to cornice and were either painted or tinted some pale, cool colour—grey, pearl, drab, buff, and a light green inherited from Adam usage, were in high favour—or else they were covered with wall-paper, usually of a very excellent quality and meant to last.

About the end of the eighteenth century and in the very beginning of the nineteenth, the landscape papers were extensively used alike in rooms and in halls and many of them, both polychrome and monochrome, were both beautiful and dignified and lent a peculiar charm and breadth to the rooms in which they were hung, a charm that nothing else has ever quite taken the place of. In addition to these landscape papers, papers with striking Chinese *motifs* of figures, animals, pagodas, bridges, birds and flowers, frequently in vital colouring, enjoyed some vogue. There were, also, the monochrome French papers printed with carefully cut wood blocks from cartoons by David * and other equally noted contemporary French artists. These papers pourtrayed scenes from classic mythology and were designed as panels to be hung in a sequence. Of all the

---

* These papers are now being reproduced from the original blocks.

4

early wall-papers, they were, perhaps, the finest in both conception and execution.

A little later on in the nineteenth century, when these beautiful wall coverings had either passed out of fashion or were no longer obtainable, their place was taken by papers designed to represent moulded panels, or by paper marbled, mottled and veined and laid off in vertical and horizontal lines to simulate the joints of masonry. The best of these masonry papers—and some of them were by no means bad—contained cartouches in the centre of each oblong block and within the cartouches were small monochrome scenes of classic or historical provenance. Some tone of grey was usually chosen for the execution of such papers and, it may be added, the masonry papers were as a rule hung in halls where their pattern did not conflict with the movable decorations and where their pictorial note lent a touch of interest in default of other features to arrest or amuse the eye.

Door and window trims were bold and heavy in detail and, when any attempt was made at ornamentation beyond flat, rectangular mouldings, Greek key fret and anthemion *motifs* generally appeared and also square thistle or acanthus leaf pateræ at the angles. The panels of doors and shutters were small, with the occasional exception of large panels in the lower halves of doors, and were defined by a number of small, flat mouldings which often gave them a complex appearance. The woodwork was usually painted white, although such pale colours as pearl or light grey were now and then used by way of variety. Green, or sometimes white, Venetian blinds were much in fashion at this period and added a touch of decorative interest to the windows which otherwise they would not have possessed. Floors were of plain boards without any essay at adornment. In hallways marble tiles were sometimes used, either solid white or black and white chequered.

Plaster decoration consisted of moulded cornices and of ceiling borders and central ornaments that echoed the *motifs* of the woodwork in the manner already mentioned as occurring in contemporary houses in England. Ceiling borders were not invariably used, but the central ornaments in the larger and more important rooms were rarely omitted as they formed a point of departure from the ceiling for the imposing chandelier which had by now come to be regarded as an almost indispensable adjunct.

Mantel-pieces of black or dark grey veined marble, oftentimes with two plain pillars supporting the shelf, were in common use. White marble and wood painted white, and fashioned in the same pattern, were also much used. In some of the more elegantly equipped rooms the low mantels of white marble were elaborately carved in the current French style and in some instances displayed griffin or caryatid side supports instead of the pillars just alluded to. These latter pieces of sculpture were really very beautiful and imparted an air of elegance and distinction to any room in which they were placed, quite sufficient to redeem any impression of heaviness conveyed by the other items of fixed equipment.

The architectural and decorative mode that followed the Classic Revival, which, indeed, grew from it and into which the Classic Revival gradually declined when its period of decadence set in, is discussed in Chapter IX.

Furniture and Decoration.—In the early part of the eighteenth century—the last years of the reign of William and Mary and the reign of Queen Anne—every article of furniture that we now have was in use and, besides this, there were some things that we have since allowed to fall more or less into oblivion to our own great decorative loss. While many of the mobiliary fashions of an earlier date persisted to some extent— the panelled oak pieces and the more elaborate walnut creations of late Stuart times and the walnut, marqueterie and lacquer achievements of the William and Mary era—and especially in the provincial towns and country districts, a new and powerful influence in furniture design was everywhere apparent. This new element has been called the *curvilinear* influence and was particularly manifest in the prevalence of cabriole legs for seating furniture, tables and cabinet work, shaped aprons for tables and wall furniture, shaped and curving tops or cresting for bureau bookcases, cupboards, cabinets, highboys and other pieces of wall furniture, shaped heads with cyma curves for panelling and mirror tops, and even the introduction of curved lines into structural features such as the fronts of *bombé* or "kettle-front" cabinets and chests of drawers. This influence came into England directly through Dutch channels, but was only one instance of similar concurrent influences prevailing throughout Europe which may be attributed to a complex and mixed Baroque and Oriental parentage.

Although oak continued to be used to some extent for furniture making, the favourite and fashionable, and we may also say the standard, wood was walnut, either solid or as a figured veneer laid on over a base of oak or of some other wood. The cabinet makers of the period, however, did not restrict themselves in their finer work to the expression of their talents in walnut alone. They made considerable use of other woods which increasing commercial facilities were placing within their grasp; they freely employed marqueterie in the more refined "sea weed" patterns which had superseded the larger multi-colored floral and foliated *motifs;* they continued to produce many pieces of lacquer, admirable in colour—red, green, cream, yellow, blue, brown, silver and black—and in decoration; they decorated not a few pieces with paint and parcel gilding; they strained various fabrics over carved and moulded wood bases; and last, but not least in significance, under the impetus of designs furnished by such men as Kent and his school, who required pieces of a certain scale and pomp to accord with the stately interiors then being created, they executed massive and heavily carved tables and consoles, coated with *gesso* richly gilt and topped with slabs of marble or vari-coloured *scagliola,* as well as other pieces in a similar monumental vein to match.

About 1720 mahogany began to be used and the advent of this wood as a material for furniture construction opened the way for developments in both structure and ornamentation that would not have been possible in any of the previous *media.* Before speaking more explicitly, however, of the changes induced by the popularisation of mahogany as a cabinet wood, attention should be called to what has aptly been termed "Architects' Furniture," a species of mobiliary equipment that exercised a profound effect upon the appearance of a great many interiors during the first half of the eighteenth century. Architects were designing stately rooms with lofty ceilings and broad wall spaces on a scale and in a style hitherto unknown in England. For these spacious interiors the "small calibre" furniture of the familiar "Queen Anne" pattern was totally inadequate in scale and often unsatisfactory in the minutiæ of style. The want of something more imposing was

partially filled by the heavy carved and gilded pieces *
of which mention has already been made, but there was
still an obvious need for something further in the way
of large case work. And this further need was met by
the architects who proceeded to design large bookcases, cupboards, presses and cabinets in a scale commensurate with the positions they were to occupy and
in a style that was distinctly architectural in conception, even to the details of ornamentation, free use
being made of pillars, pilasters, entablatures, pediments of various types, urns and cornices whose every
feature was transferred from architectural to mobiliary usage. This was one step farther than, and a logical development from, the built-in cupboards and
buffets previously discussed. This "architects' furniture" was constructed either in the natural cabinet
woods current at the time, chiefly walnut and mahogany, or else was made of pine or deal and painted to
accord with the fixed woodwork of the room in which
it was placed.

During the early Georgian period, and synchron-
ously with the carved and gilt Kentian pieces and the
"architects' furniture," a great deal of the other furniture underwent a process of elaboration that was more
observable in decorative details and the amount of
decoration applied than in structural forms. It began
with what is known as the "Decorated Queen Anne"
type and progressed through the heavily, and often
overly, embellished creations of chair and cabinet
makers up to the rise of Thomas Chippendale into
prominence as the arbiter of furniture fashions. About
the middle of the century there had been a recru-

---

* These imposing carved and gilt tables, consoles and the like began
to be popular in the latter part of the 17th century, thanks to the influence of Marot, whom William of Orange brought to England.

descence of the "Chinese taste" in the Oriental and
pseudo-Oriental forms inspired by the designs of Sir
William Chambers. It was left for Chippendale to tem-
per and correct the excesses of design that had prevailed prior to his *régime,* to adapt and improve upon
the precedents that he found previously established,
and to introduce new elements by which he sought to
elevate mobiliary taste of his day and, needless to say,
this he succeeded in doing.

The heritage of English precedent that Chippendale
found ready to his hand, he refined and, in many cases,
elaborated with the utmost skill, displaying his genius
and originality, not in the futile effort to create something utterly different from all preëxistent fashions, but
through a sane and reasonable adaptation to contemporary requirements as he conceived them and as the
means at his disposal prompted him. The "Chinese
taste" he interpreted in a manner perfectly consistent
with the needs and environment for which he was working; the "Gothic style" in its undiluted form, though
obviously an anachronism and a piece of affectation,
altogether out of keeping with the architectural settings then being created, he handled with tactful address and contrived to keep it from being aggressively
offensive; the Rococo inspiration, derived from current
French models, he translated successfully into an English body and, although there was nothing in any of
the phases of British architectural and decorative
backgrounds to which it in any way corresponded, managed so to express the style that it did not conflict with
its environment. But it was in what might be called his
"composite" work, in the expression of which he freely
drew from various sources and commingled elements
Chinese, Gothic and Rococo in the same piece along
with traditions of earlier English derivation, that he

achieved his most signal successes as a great master of style. Whatever diversities of origin such pieces might reveal upon close and searching scrutiny, there can be no question that their *ensemble* was in full and harmonious accord with the architectural environment of the day.

Early in the second half of the eighteenth century, under the revived classic impulse imparted by the Brothers Adam, the whole spirit of furniture design underwent a radical change and the mobiliary equipment of the period was created with the avowed and patent intent of close coincidence with the newer phase of architectural expression. Emphasis was laid upon straight structural lines and the decorative details were of obviously architectural provenance. The attenuation and restraint discernible in architectural forms were communicated to the structure of the furniture and also visibly affected not only the *forms* of the ornament employed but also the *amount* of ornament and the manner of its distribution. While Chippendale, so long as he followed the bent of his own inspiration, worked almost exclusively in mahogany and carried the manipulation of his chosen medium to the highest development of which even so facile and accommodating a material was susceptible, the access of Adam influence popularised a great diversity of materials which, while they did not displace mahogany as a cabinet wood, were freely used concurrently with it and vastly added to the resources of colour possibility and contributed to the general lightening effect of contemporary interior decoration. Satinwood especially came into high favour. At the same time painting and inlay were exploited to the full extent of their capabilities as decorative factors. Hepplewhite, Shearer, Sheraton, and also the lesser lights who wrought at the same time and followed in their wake, were all profoundly influenced by the new ideals of which the Adelphi were successful protagonists and the work of all these cabinet makers and designers exhibited a kindred regard for and observance of the reversion to purer classic principles with the attendant attenuation of proportions and dominance of straight lines as well as the use of *motifs* of more or less immediate classical provenance.

At the very end of the century we discover the classic forms merging gradually into the "Directoire" phase of expression, while early in the nineteenth century—a period synchronous with the very apparent decadence of Sheraton design—we find the more bombastic manifestations corresponding to the Empire fashion in France for, notwithstanding the abhorrence of France and of French politics, French styles were as potent and pervasive as ever. For a detailed discussion of Empire forms, as well as for the minute particulars of all the furniture variations during the period included in this chapter, the reader is referred to the "Practical Book of Period Furniture," Eberlein and McClure.

Other Decorative Accessories and Movable Decorations.—During the early part of the eighteenth century, the tapestries which had played so important a part in the decorative composition of former times, retained somewhat of their pristine popularity and remained to a certain extent in evidence, although they did not constitute one of the distinctively characteristic features of the time.

Hangings for windows consisted of either brocades, damasks or velvets in bright colours and strong patterns, much like the fabrics used for covering upholstered furniture, or else of printed linens and chintzes of agreeably bright colouring and in designs similar to those shown in the illustration. Both kinds of hangings were used either with or without valances and were often hung from box heads which were covered with the same material strained over the wood.

In large rooms chandeliers were often used; sometimes they were made of carved wood, painted and parcel gilt, sometimes of brass, sometimes of wrought iron which was occasionally embellished by colour and gilding, and sometimes of glass with large crystal pendants. Sconces, too, were conspicuous items of decorative equipment and were made in the manner just noted in the description of chandeliers as well as with various other devices of embellishment.

In addition to the mirrors employed in fixed decorative treatments, great numbers of mirrors, both large and small, were in common use. Some were tall and narrow, others were long and low, while others still were quite small. It was quite a usual thing for a mirror to be made in several divisions. The edges were often bevelled, even where the head of the mirror was elaborately shaped, and it was not an uncommon thing for the surface of the glass to be adorned with shallow cutting where such decoration would not interfere with practical utility. Then again, side panels in large tripartite mirrors were frequently adorned with polychrome paintings in reverse, in the Chinese manner, which added greatly to their decorative value. A number of the early mirrors were framed with bevelled glass of a different colour, very often a rich deep blue, although other colours were used. Most of the mirror frames, however, were of walnut and were either adorned with marqueterie or were carved and parcel gilt; or they were of pine or some other soft wood, carved and coated with *gesso* and wholly gilt; or else they were of lacquer with gilt, and also sometimes with polychrome decorations. Sconces, when not of metal or of carved wood, painted and parcel gilt, were often made in combination with small mirrors and were framed in the manner just indicated. A number of mirrors, especially those intended for overmantel decoration, were framed in combination with decorative paintings, the mirror forming the lower part of the composition and the painting the upper portion.

Pictures—portraits, landscapes and decorative paintings of fruits and flowers or of combined architectural and landscape subjects—constituted another valuable and much used decorative resource, and likewise framed prints, both plain and coloured, were extensively employed.

Sculptures, especially in marble but to some extent also in bronze, were much in vogue and were placed either on pedestals or in niches designed to receive them. These marbles and bronzes were often in the form of urns and vases as well as busts, figures and groups. Porcelains, in the shape of urns, vases, jars and other articles, both large and small, especially during the China-mad days in the early part of the century, were freely employed as decorative adjuncts.

From the middle of the century onward, when the Adam influence had become dominant, the same decorative accessories as just enumerated continued to be used, but their forms naturally underwent such modifications as rendered them in keeping with the altered conceptions of elegant design. With the ornate wall surfaces of many of the Adam rooms, there was less opportunity to use the tapestries which earlier in the century had continued to enjoy at least a certain curtailed degree of favour. The method of draping window hangings was often more involved and the cornices surmounting them frequently assumed more preten-

tious forms than had hitherto been common. Chandeliers were lighter in line and more intricate in design
and there was a preference for metal with numerous
pendent glass prisms rather than for wood painted and
gilt or for brass alone in its more robust but graceful
designs. Sconces, too, reflected the same trend toward
attenuation and were quite generally adorned with cut
glass drops and pendent prisms which greatly added
to the brilliance and lustre of the illumination when the
candles were lighted. The sconces, also, not uncom-
monly displayed, along with mirror frames, the airy
surmounting or surrounding ornaments wrought in gilt
compo supported on wires. In the heads of mirrors
were often inserted paintings with classic *motifs* or designs in gilt relief on a ground of plain colour or else
devices painted in reverse on the under side of the
glass.

Materials and Colour.—In the early part of the century the woods chiefly used were oak, walnut and, for
panelling, deal and pine and fir also. About 1720 mahogany, while not wholly displacing the others, came
into use for cabinet purposes and grew more and more
popular. *Gesso* laid over a pine foundation and gilt was
also an important source of decoration.

The fabrics were brocades, velvets, plain and with
cut pile figures, brocatelles, damasks and silks. The
simpler fabrics were printed linens, muslins and
chintzes. In both cases the colours were strong and
vigorous and the designs usually bold and often large
in detail. As the century wore on the diversity and
brilliance of colouring became less pronounced. Pale
and delicate pastel colours were freely employed and
stripes had a tremendous vogue. The patterns on the
brocades were refined in scale and often attenuated in

accord with the prevalent trend of contemporary style. Even when the colours used were fairly vigorous, they were so disposed in quantity that their emphasis was appreciably modified. Needlework in *petit point* and *gros point* also played a prominent part for the covering of furniture.

After the middle of the century and all through the period of Adam ascendency, while mahogany retained a place of honour, satinwood and other light coloured woods, such as sycamore or harewood, maple and similar light toned materials enjoyed huge popularity, for the whole tendency of the time was toward a lighter and more cheerful and blithesome colour scheme. Not only was furniture very commonly made of light coloured wood or painted some light tone, but the fixed woodwork also was painted in various pale hues, as were the walls and ceilings. The scale of the earlier work, both in architectural usage and in furniture contours and decorative *motifs* was heavier and required heavier colours; the lighter scale and refined, attenuated *motifs* of the Adam period demanded lighter colours and would have looked utterly out of place with the full-bodied tones of an earlier era.

The same thing was true of fabrics. The silks, damasks, brocades, velvets and other stuffs used for hangings and upholstery were light in colour and refined in the details of their pattern. At this time also Aubusson tapestry, by the nature of its colour, design and texture, came into vogue for furniture covering and also for rugs and carpets.

Arrangement.—During the earlier part of the century, while symmetry and formality of arrangement were duly considered in the disposition of the movable furnishings, there was still a certain amount of the casual latitude of earlier days to be seen in the placement of the principal articles that entered into the composition of a room. Under the Adam *régime,* however, the principles of formality and balanced symmetry were caried to their fullest limit. It was the period of the dominance of pairs. It might be pairs of consoles, or pairs of sconces, or pairs of sofas, or pairs of candelabra—but wherever there was an opportunity to introduce the element of balance by the use of duplicates, the opportunity was seized and made the most of.

CHAPTER III

INTERIOR DECORATION IN ITALY PRIOR TO THE EIGHTEENTH CENTURY

INTRODUCTION.—The golden age of Italian wall decoration, furniture making and furnishing began about the middle of the fifteenth century and continued through the sixteenth and seventeenth. It was veritably a golden age in point of virility, freshness and fertility of conception and the national genius was manifested in the vigorous design of the furniture, in the way in which it was disposed and in the preparation of the background as well as in other important branches of art. Added to the native well springs from which flowed a copious stream of Renaissance inspiration was the powerful impetus derived from the *diaspora* of Byzantine culture resulting from the fall of Byzantium before the Ottoman onslaught in 1453.

Prior to the period at which we begin our consideration of interior decoration in Italy, wars and rumours of wars, petty though they were compared with the magnitude of modern military operations, chiefly occupied the minds and energies of the princes and the rulers of the small republics and there was almost incessant strife between two or more of the various independent states or civil jurisdictions among which the Italian peninsula was parcelled. Under the unstable conditions consequent upon the chronically disturbed state of society there was comparatively little opportunity for either the accumulation or spending of private wealth and it is scarcely to be wondered at that a native taste for household luxury and refinement found

scant scope for gratification when the development of
the arts of domestic embellishment was so seriously
retarded. In the majority of cases men's minds were
either almost wholly centred upon political and military affairs or else their mental and physical activities
were directed into ecclesiastical channels. Cultural development in the secular world was badly handicapped.

With the advent of an era of greater political stability, however, commerce revived and flourished apace,
personal and civic wealth accumulated, the resources
of the municipalities were less constantly drained by
the heavy exactions of internecine warfare, and the
spirit of creative art, never wholly dormant even during the times of greatest strife and turmoil, came
quickly into its own again, drawing renewed inspiration from the abundant treasures of Italian antiquity
and deriving likewise a quickening impulse from the
culture of Byzantium, the remnants of whose rich heritage were brought to Italy by the numerous refugees
from the fallen capital of the Eastern Empire. The re-
birth of art, in all its phases, experienced the strong
impetus of natural reaction after a period of repres-
sion. Domestic and industrial arts blossomed and
throve in new-found security. Private wealth fostered
the efforts of artists and craftsmen while princes and
potentates vied with each other in liberal patronage of
the arts both fine and applied. The story of the Medici
in Florence affords an illuminating commentary on this
phase of Italian cultural history and the story of many
other great contemporary families might likewise be
appropriately cited to the same end.

*Architectural Background and Methods of Fixed
Decoration.*—In this golden age of restored tranquillity,
stately villas, that often rivalled the splendours of their
ancient Roman prototypes, rapidly succeeded to grim

PLATE 13

CHAMBER IN SECOND FLOOR PALAZZO DAVANZATI, FIRENZE, FIFTEENTH CENTURY
Courtesy of William Helburn, Inc.

PLATE 14

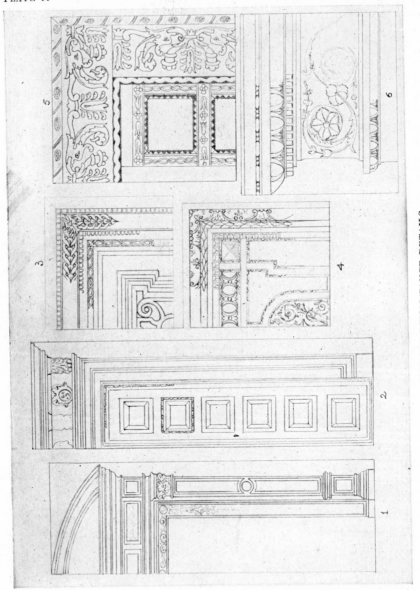

ITALIAN RENAISSANCE DETAILS

PLATE 15

A SALON ON FIRST FLOOR, PALAZZO DAVANZATI, FIRENZE, FIFTEENTH CENTURY
Courtesy of William Helburn, Inc.

B. BED CHAMBER, PALAZZO DAVANZATI, FIRENZE, FIFTEENTH CENTURY
Courtesy of William Helburn, Inc.

PLATE 16

CHAMBER IN PALAZZO VECCHIO, FIRENZE, SIXTEENTH CENTURY
Courtesy of William Helburn, Inc.

castles and fortified houses. Nobles and wealthy merchants and landowners felt free to forsake the crowded restraint of urban life for the larger liberty of residence among the groves and gardens of their estates. The abodes they built, with the aid of the best architects of the day, were broad and lofty and fully expressive of the urbane, though withal vigorous, elegance of the age. The rooms were commonly of great dimensions and their height is one of the most impressive features of their proportions. It was, indeed, the era of the great hall (Plate 13) and princely salon. Such were the habits of domestic life that the small drawing-room and intimate boudoir had little place in the household scheme and the personal requirements of the immediate members of the family were easily satisfied with the simplest of provisions. Classic conceptions of design were everywhere asserting themselves and we find a **strong** rectilinear emphasis (Plate 13) predominant in nearly all of these imposing apartments. There were, of course, plenty of round vaulted ceilings (Plate 20 A and B; Plate 18) and round arched windows or doorheads enriched by a countersunk semi-circular tympanum (Plate 15 A) above them. But, notwithstanding all this and the occasional presence of round-arched arcades, the dominant emphasis was rectilinear and this same quality was reflected in the contour of the furniture that was designed to equip these spacious interiors.

In the matter of fixed decoration and interior enrichment, Italian interiors of the period under consideration may be divided into two classes. The first class is composed of the interiors where all or a great portion of the background—walls, ceiling and floor—was highly decorated and rich in colour (Plates 15 B, 16, 18, 19 and 139). The second class is composed of interiors

5

where only a minor portion (Plates 13, 15 A, 20 A and B, and 127) or none of the background is decorated and where the physical setting presents an aspect of severe restraint and, sometimes, even of austerity. In the first class belong the rooms whose walls and ceilings are gorgeous with frescoes and gilding (Plates 16, 18 and 19), the encrustation of coloured marbles or the poly- chrome and parcel gilt enrichment of diaper work (Plate 15 B) and heraldic blasoning, while the floors accord with the rest of the scheme in their display of multi-coloured marbles (Plates 18, 19 and 139) or mo- saic. In the second class belong the rooms whose walls and vaulted ceilings are severely plain and whose floors are of plain stone, tiles (Plates 13, 15 A and B and 16) or boards. The points of architectural embellishment are the carved fireplace (Plates 15 A and 20 A and 111 C) and its hood or chimney piece, the doorways (Plate 14, 1; 15 A, 18 and 19) and, if there be a flat wooden ceiling instead of vaulting, the beams and cor- bels (Plates 13, 15 A and B and 127). Occasionally, also, a niche (Plate 127) with doors to enclose a shrine might be given architectural emphasis. In such in- teriors colour was frequently introduced on the doors themselves (Plate 14, 2), in a countersunk tympanum above the doorway, if perchance this bit of diversity were added, on the beams and boards of the ceiling (Plates 13; 14—3, 4 and 5; 15 A and B) and on the in- side shutters of the windows. It need scarcely be pointed out that such an interior provided an admirable foil for the advantageous display of hangings and fur- niture (Plates 13 and 15 A and B). No matter, how- ever, whether an interior was elaborately ornate or severely simple, the Italian furniture of the period pos- sessed such flexibility of character that it looked equally well against either background and to this peculiar

PLATE 17

THRONE ROOM—PALAZZO QUIRINALE, ROMA
Courtesy of William Helburn, Inc.

PLATE 18

Photograph from Anderson, Rome

THE HALL OF HERCULES, PALAZZO FARNESE, CAPRAROLA

Middle Sixteenth Century

By Courtesy of "Vogue"

PLATE 19

Photograph from Anderson. Rome

PALAZZO FARNESE, CAPRAROLA

The Great Maps Painted Upon the Walls Give Evidence of the Far-reaching Interests of the Farnese Family

By Courtesy of "Vogue"

quality we shall have occasion to refer more at length in a subsequent division.

Furniture and Its Decoration.—From the middle or latter part of the fifteenth century onward, the display of movable furniture in the regal rooms of Italian palaces and villas, and in the scarcely less regal rooms of the lesser country houses and town dwellings of the well-to-do citizens, was scanty when judged by modern standards. "When the walls of the galleries and saloons were covered with frescoes (Plates 16, 18 and 19), or hung with arras, tapestry, brocades (Plate 17), rich velvet from Genoa, or with stamped and gilt leather; when the ceilings were painted (Plates 16, 18 and 19) or heavily carved and gilded; when the floors were inlaid with the choicest marbles and mosaics, many objects about would detract from the magnificence of the whole and leave a confused impression on the mind. This the unerring taste of the sixteenth century decorators fully realised. The few pieces of furniture that were admitted, however, were in keeping with their surroundings, and are marvels of workmanship. Every kind of splendid material was employed in their manufacture and adornment." The chests or *cassoni,* which from the earliest times were conspicuous and highly significant pieces of furniture in Italian furnishing schemes, placed in the halls and corridors or salons, "were used to preserve tapestries, clothes, plate and most of the valuables used by wealthy Italians." Carved with scrolls, foliage and figures in high relief or richly embellished on the front and cover with paintings, "either illustrative of the lives of saints, scenes taken from classical mythology or historical incidents" and blasoned in the proper tinctures with family armorial bearings, the *cassoni* were indeed impressive pieces of furniture and well calculated to compel and centre attention. They were often lined inside with linen or even with gorgeous silks and brocades strained tightly over the wood. The *cassone* was one of the most valuable presents given to a bride, and when it fulfilled the *rôle* of a dower chest it was generally adorned by picturing some incident taken from one of the well-known love tales. To some, indeed, it may seem that these *cassoni*—and, for the matter of that, not a few of the other articles of Italian Renaissance furniture—were "almost overpoweringly decorated" without ever giving the eye a single spot on which to stop and rest. Many such profusely ornamented pieces placed in the same room, it is true, would have been unbearable. But the Italians did not so use them. The *cassone* was designed and decorated with a clear perception of the principle, so characteristic of much of the best Italian and Spanish work, whether architectural or mobiliary, of concentrating enrichment in one spot and isolating it against a background either simple, at times to the extent of austerity, or else so fully covered with elaborate repeats (Plate 15 B) that it assumed the quality of a richly coloured texture of virtually neutral action in affording the necessary contrast to whatever clearly defined object, whether simple or elaborately adorned, might be placed against it. There was wealth in the golden age of the Italian Renaissance to devote to a liberal patronage of the decorative arts and the patronage bestowed encouraged the development of furniture design and execution by the most eminent craftsmen and artists of the period. They deemed it worthy of their best efforts to design a single piece of furniture and execute it with the utmost study and care as an independent and complete work of art. Under such circumstances the making of a *cassone* was a finished and marvellous achievement in itself. Among the painters of panels for *cassoni* may be mentioned such masters as Botticelli, Andrea del Sarto, Pesellino, Pietro di Cosimo and the most capable of their pupils while, for the carvers of these same amazing chests, Jacquemart reminds us that we must seek among the foremost sculptors of the day—Donatello, Bernardino, Ferrante, Canozzo and others of equal renown. So far as furniture was concerned, they were the Adams, the Chippendales, the Hepplewhites, the Angelica Kauff-manns and the Cipriani of their era, but far greater; only, unlike the Adelphi, they did not merely draw designs for others to work from but they worked at the furniture with their own hands and thought no shame of the task. They esteemed the making of a chest or cabinet an honourable and legitimate work of art and that is why so many of the pieces from their hands are surpassingly beautiful and full of finished grace. Before passing on, it will be as well to note that there was not a little variety in the forms of the *cassoni* so that their decorative furnishing potentiality was increased thereby: some of them were merely rectangular chests, with or without feet, and being flat-topped served for seats as well as receptacles; some were shaped like a sarcophagus and had either flat or rising tops; some were low enough to sit upon comfortably; some were as high as consoles, and some were raised on stands.

While *cassoni* (Plate 13) were undoubtedly the most omnipresent, the most conspicuous and the most lavishly decorated pieces of cabinet work, there was besides a wide variety of wall furniture that went to make up the mobiliary equipment of sixteenth and seventeenth century Italian rooms. There was the *madia,* a hutch-like cupboard with doors, and perhaps several shallow drawers above them, the whole structure supported by trusses at each end. This piece of furniture was often used for the stowage of food in much the same way as the dole cupboards and kindred articles in England. There was the *credenza* (Plates 20 B and 15 A and 89 B), an imposing and much used article about four feet high and of varying length, with doors in front and with or without shallow drawers above the doors. In composition and decoration it was an object of distinctly architectonic value. It served the purpose of a sideboard or buffet or, in apartments not used for dining, it answered equally well the office of a console. Occasionally a superstructure was added at the back with one or more shelves and in this form it was really the historical precursor of the very ugly nineteenth century sideboard. In this connexion it is worth noting that the furniture designers of the nineteenth century, who perpetrated so many of the painful monstrosities of the Victorian era in black walnut, were not an *ignorant* set of men unacquainted with historical precedents. They did know somewhat of furniture history, but with their knowledge they combined an amazing degree of colossal bad taste which impelled them to choose the least-inspired models of sixteenth, seventeenth and eighteenth century Italian, French and Spanish provenance and add thereto their own fantastic aberrations of contour and embellishment. Illustrations of some of the Victorian "chefs dœuvre" parallel with other illustrations of their Continental prototypes would constitute a body of the most damning evidence.

Akin to the *credenza* in its general scheme of structure was the small console or cabinet with doors, about three or three and a half feet high by two feet or a little more in width. It served as a stand on which to place a casket or some other article of decorative significance. The exact reverse of this was a similar piece of cabinet work, with a small drawer *beneath* the doors instead of above them, and this was set upon a table or stand; in other words, it was the forerunner of the larger cabinet, with doors and drawers, upon a stand which figured so prominently in furnishing schemes of a much later date. A combination of these two pieces sometimes occurred in a two-storey structure with doors in both the lower and upper parts. This double cabinet was somewhat wider than the console first mentioned and the upper part was not quite so broad as the lower. Altogether it was a dignified and desirable article in any well-appointed room.

Not dissimilar to it in general appearance was the writing cabinet, of which examples occurred at an early date, with doors in the lower part and a falling front in the upper which, when let down, provided a place to write. A related piece of writing furniture was the cabinet with falling front which stood upon a table or stand. There were also various wider and larger cabinets and presses, either divided in two by lower and upper sections or with full length doors, in the latter case being virtually wardrobes, as we understand the term. Chests of drawers, very like in disposition to the analogous article of the eighteenth century, were by no means unknown.

Bedsteads, as was the wont of the period, were oftentimes ponderous affairs; others, again, were not of cumbrous proportions. The larger bedsteads were frequently raised a pace or two above the floor on a dais (Plate 15 B) and were both of the post and canopy (Plate 21 B) or tester type and also of the sort that had headboard and lower footboard but no canopy. Another piece of wall furniture that was not seldom elevated on a dais to give it greater state was the *cassa panca,* a kind of ceremonial bench (Plate 15 B) that was invariably given a position of prominence and seems to have been the forerunner of the drawing-room sofa of a later date as regarded certain points of etiquette in seating honoured guests. The *cassa panca* was really a long chest with high, solid, massive arms and back, the seat, which was hinged at the back, being the lid. Occasionally there was an high, throne-like back and sometimes the arms were wanting. The former type, however, was the more usual. A specimen in the Metropolitan Museum is eight feet, ten inches in length, twenty-one inches in depth, has a back and arms rising nineteen inches from the seat and stands on a dais nine and a half feet long and five inches high.

From both their structure and design it is quite obvious that not a few of the *banconi* or tables with drawers were intended to stand against the wall and many of the long tables, analogous to the English refectory tables, were likewise so placed and are, therefore, under sundry circumstances to be reckoned as wall furniture. Clothes hangers and mirror frames were objects of careful design and workmanship and are not to be overlooked in an enumeration of wall pieces. The mirror frames were small as only small mirrors were available at all and these were scarce. Great care, nevertheless, was bestowed upon the frames and they possessed considerable decorative importance.

Besides the long tables, already alluded to, and the smaller wall or writing tables with drawers in them, there was the greatest variety in shapes and sizes, as might be expected in an age of exuberant invention, and all the occasional requirements in the matter of tables were well supplied. (For a detailed discussion of the sundry varieties of sixteenth and seventeenth century Italian tables and other pieces of furniture *v.* "The Practical Book of Italian, Spanish and Portuguese Furniture," Eberlein and McClure; now in preparation.) Chairs, settees, stools and benches were of numerous types, but all were dignified and impressive and well calculated to furnishing ideals in which dignity, as well as grace, was an indispensable requirement.

Other Decorative Accessories and Movable Decorations.—The actual movable furniture in a sixteenth or seventeenth century Italian salon did not by any means comprise *all* the furnishing of the apartment. The walls and ceilings, as mentioned before, might be gloriously chromatic with frescoes or mosaic and, in addition to many-hued and rich-toned pigments, there would be the glow of gilding bestowed in appropriate places. In case the walls and ceilings were not so adorned with fixed decorations on the surface, there was the universal delight in tapestries (Plate 13) and other large hangings of needlework which were prized doubly on account of the pleasure and satisfaction to be derived from the devices thereon depicted and likewise because of their wealth of mellow colour. Besides tapestries as suitable enrichments for plain walls, there was always the resource of pictures. Then, furthermore, there were the polychrome maiolica mural ornaments and mural ornaments consisting of wood carvings (Plate 15 A) painted and gilt. This wooden mural sculpture was an highly developed art and justly prized. Another decorative resource lay in the pieces of marble sculpture, always dear to the heart of an Italian, and in various pieces of pottery of agreeable shape and colour. Nor must we forget the carved, painted and gilt wooden candlesticks (Plate 19) and candelabra, some of them of great height; nor the iron candelabra (Plate 15 A), gracefully wrought and likewise coloured and gilt in their embellishment.

Equally effective in the matter of lending interest to the composition were the fixed decorative accessories such as the paintings upon the doors themselves, paintings in the tympana above doorways, paintings upon the wooden inside shutters or paintings upon the beams of the ceilings and the corbels that supported those beams. On the doors and shutters the painting and gilding might be only partial, to enhance the tone of the wood, or it might be in a continuous diaper pattern or, again, some mythological, historical or religious subject might be fully depicted. The painting of the ceiling beams was done in a purely conventional manner and was meant merely to give the relief and warmth of colour and gilding.

Oftentimes, when not much colour appeared on doors or shutters, interest was centred there by devices executed either in studding of iron nails (Plate 13) or by wrought iron, sometimes parcel coloured and gilt, applied in a rich and delicate decorative pattern. The sixteenth and seventeenth century Italian smiths were masters in their craft and their decorative creations are among some of the most treasured relics they have left us.

Last, but by no means least, as an item in the composition of the sixteenth and seventeenth century Italian interior was the carved mantel and likewise the carved chimney piece that so often accompanied it. These were wrought in stone and in marble with the utmost finesse and displayed all the characteristic decorative *motifs* of the period, including foliage, fruits, flowers, arabesques, grotesques, masques, *amorini* and the human figure. The carving was usually in high and bold relief.

Materials and Colour.—For the fixed architectural background, the materials most commonly used were stone, inlaid and multi-coloured marbles, tiles or wood for the floors. For the walls they employed plaster, either rough or smooth, or else encrustations of marble or mosaic. When the walls were to be painted they were coated with a smooth, hard plaster; hard plaster was likewise used when moulded decorations in relief entered into the decorative scheme. These moulded decorations in plaster were often further enriched by the addition of colour. When *sgraffito* decorations were desired several successive coats of different-coloured plasters were laid on. For the ceilings either plaster or wooden beams, frequently carved and painted, were the usual materials. Cypress, oak, pine and walnut afforded the chief wood resources, although other kinds were occasionally put to use. For polychrome decorated doors it was customary to use pine, cypress or some similar soft and easily worked wood as a foundation. The surface was then carefully coated with *gesso* to give an absolutely smooth and suitable ground for the application of the pigment and gold.

For furniture, walnut was the staple wood just as oak was in England. For *cassoni* and other pieces, however, that were to be embellished with paint, polychrome decoration and parcel gilding it was customary to use pine or cypress and cover it with a preparatory coat of *gesso* before the paint and gilt were put on. If there was any carved relief, the carving was apt to be crudely done and the fine modelling was left for manipulation in the *gesso*. For furniture that was not to be adorned with gold and colour, oak, chestnut, acacia and other suitable woods from time to time made their appearance with the occasional introduction of sycamore, pear, rosewood and sundry other materials for purposes of inlay or marqueterie.

For upholstery, velvet of a full, rich red was perhaps the most favoured material. Besides this we find cut pile velvets, brocades, brocatelle and damasks of various colours as well as *gros point* and *petit point* needlework. Leather, both plain and decorated, was also used for the backs and seats of chairs. Much attention, too, was paid to fringes and gold galons which were freely employed. For the lining of *cassoni* and caskets it was not uncommon to use silks and brocades of divers colours strained upon the wood.

Nothing contributes more to the enrichment of an apartment than the use of hangings on the walls. In old Italian interiors hangings were freely used and these hangings consisted of tapestries, brocades (Plate 17) or damasks with embroidered orphreys or borders at the sides, velvets enriched with gold embroidery and needlework designs in bold *motifs* appliqué, and large pieces of multi-coloured needlework in floss or silk thread on background of silk, satin, damask or velvet. Cloth of gold and silver were also employed.

From a purely practical point of view, with reference to modern practice, it is to be noted that the old Italians fully realised—they had doubtless found out by trial and experience—that when hangings were used on the walls back of large pieces of furniture, whether those pieces were of carved or plain panelled walnut, or of a gorgeous polychrome and gilt exterior, the very nature of the furniture in design and material demanded the association of a fabric of full colour and depth, of texture, such as tapestry or heavy red or purple velvet, and that thinner or flatter textures looked jejune and unsuitable. These pieces might, with perfect propriety of effect, stand against an austere and bare wall, but if fabric was added it had to be of warm hue and full texture.

In the choice of colours for interior decoration there was universal employment of strong, full-bodied tones and vigorous contrasts. While the reds were very red

and the blues very blue, the combinations and grada-
tions were blended into a most agreeably mellow *ensemble*. An examination of old Italian interiors and
a close scrutiny of the methods the sixteenth and seventeenth century decorators used makes it quite evident
that it was the practice to concentrate enrichment
whether of objects or of colour at strategic points. It
is also to be noted, with reference to their lavish use
of gold, that they well understood that a great mass of
gold is quiet and neutral, that a little gold at carefully
selected places is quiet, refined and enriching, but that
small amounts of gold distributed here, there and
everywhere produce a flashy, cheap and noisy effect.

Arrangement.—One of the most striking things
about fine old Italian interiors is the absence of crowding and fussiness. The decorators of the sixteenth and
seventeenth centuries seem fully to have realised that
a few important pieces, well and logically placed, are
all that are needed to make a room. If there are too
many large pieces the effect of all is spoiled and the
eye is apt to ignore the individual excellences of every
object in the cluttered hodge-podge. Accordingly, a
comparatively few pieces, properly distributed, were
relied upon to produce the desired result. Unless a
room was exceptionally large, and oftentimes even then
(Plate 17), it was the custom to keep the centre of the
floor clear of all obstructions. In some instances a long
table (Plates 13, 15 A, 18 and 19) would be placed down
the middle of a very long room or, instead of this, the
length might be broken by several smaller tables placed
equidistant from the ends of the room, with their appropriate accompaniment of chairs or stools in close
proximity. The arrangements almost invariably displayed a due regard for principles of symmetry and

yet, at the same time, there was a great deal of elasticity and very little inclination to methods of stiff and oppressive formality. The inborn habit of symmetrical placement might be seen in such a grouping, for instance, as a long wall table flanked at each side by two tall-backed chairs. This was a very common arrangement but very typical and serves well enough as an example. The brummagem ideal of stuffy and cluttered "cosiness" did not appeal to them and would have been utterly abhorrent to their conceptions of dignity and elegance.

CHAPTER IV

INTERIOR DECORATION IN ITALY DURING THE EIGHTEENTH CENTURY

INTRODUCTION.—As the period before the eighteenth century had been an era of spacious dimensions, of great and lofty rooms, of dignified splendour and splendid dignity, of intense virility and vigour however rich and exuberant in the manifold manifestations of architectural setting and mobiliary equipment, of unmistakably masculine interpretation in all the phases of decorative art, so the eighteenth century was essentially a period of femininity in decorative conceptions, of intimate boudoirs and highly elaborated drawing-rooms punctiliously appointed with all the polished refinements of which fecund invention bent upon achieving an almost sybaritic degree of luxury was capable, of minute elegancy, of graceful pliability, of sunny, blithesome polychrome merriment. If the imposing amplitude and sweep of a former generation were absent, and if the foundations of decorative conception were less serious, the happy domesticity and facile playfulness of the prevalent genius, amounting at times to pure inconsequent frivolity, were very human and very fascinating and, withal, sincere, in that they faithfully mirrored the spirit of the age. The genius of the preceding age, notwithstanding all the gorgeousness of colouring and wealth of inventive ingenuity, was a trifle sombre; the genius of the eighteenth century, not less opulent in its own fashion, was fundamentally gay and debonair. Potency of colour and subtlety of form were no less keenly felt and no

79

less assiduously courted than in former years, but their application was in a lighter vein.

In a measure, the eighteenth century was a decadent period, for the quality of sturdy creative originality, which had so strongly characterised the work of the sixteenth and seventeenth centuries, was almost wholly dormant. Italy was borrowing back again the inspiration she had so lavishly poured forth in earlier centuries for the benefit of other countries and the inspiration thus borrowed back was become, in the course of transition, an indubitably second-hand commodity, bereft of fertility and *verve* so far as creative vigour and the divine spark of originality were concerned, like an outworn garment that has grown threadbare through the usage of its temporary possessor. And yet, despite this promiscuous borrowing back, the eighteenth century Italian decorators, designers and craftsmen succeeded in imparting an abundant measure of national individuality to their interpretations so that their work stands quite apart from the performances of their contemporaries in other lands and is easily recognisable by its qualities of charm which the local genius rarely failed successfully to impart. While it is undeniably true that greatness of conception, architectonic dignity of contour and strong originality of design were usually wanting, the native fertility of the Italian craftsman temperament was constantly in evidence through the wealth of decorative *motifs* and the multiplicity of decorative processes lavished on surface embellishment, a wealth that asserted itself on every hand with an indomitable persistence comparable to that of tropical vegetation. These characteristics were equally to be seen in the fixed architectural decorative background and also in the execution of the movable furnishings.

PLATE 20

A. HALL, VILLA CURONIA, FLORENCE
Showing Vaulted Ceiling, Plain Walls and Decorated Corbels
Courtesy of E. S. Dodge, Esq.

B. ROOM, VILLA CURONIA, FLORENCE
Tiled Floor, Plain Walls, Vaulted Ceiling. Note Treatment of Doors and
Arrangement of Furniture
Courtesy of E. S. Dodge, Esq.

PLATE 21

A. DETAIL OF MIRROR GALLERY, PALAZZO
DORIA, ROMA
Eighteenth Century, Baroque Transition to Rococo
Courtesy of Radillo-Pelitti Co.

B. BED CHAMBER, CASTELLO VINCIGLIATA
Courtesy of Radillo-Pelitti Co

PLATE 22

A. BEDCHAMBER, VILLA CURONIA, FLORENCE
Showing Fabric-Covered Walls
Courtesy of E. S. Dodge, Esq.

B. ANTECHAMBER, VILLA FABBRICOTTI, LATE EIGHTEENTH CENTURY
The Heavy Baroque Furniture is out of place with this Classical Background
Courtesy of Radillo-Pelitti Co.

Architectural Background and Methods of Fixed Decoration.—The diluted Baroque manifestations that had been observable in the latter part of the seventeenth century continued into the early part of the eighteenth (Plate 21A), to be succeeded, in due season, and in circles likely to be affected by new fashions, by the lighter, more playful and more involved Rococo influences patterned after the modes current in France, though slightly modified in the course of transition by the action of local traditions and local preferences of interpretation, traditions and preferences that were exceedingly subtle and difficult of definition but nevertheless very real and, in the aggregate, very perceptible. In its own time, virtually synchronous with a like prevalence in other countries, came the absorbing vogue for "the Chinese taste," and it left a strong impress of Orientalism on the work done in the immediate period of its duration, while agreeable traces of its quondam ascendency and its enduring appeal could be detected here and there long afterward.

In sharp contrast to all this stylistic medley, the middle of the century witnessed a vigorous revival of classic feeling (Plate 22 B)—the swing of the pendulum to the opposite extremity of the arc—in precisely the same way that we see the rise of the Adam influence in England and the transition to the Louis Seize mode in France. The Italian reversion to classic forms and precedents was not less vigorous in its expression than the contemporary comparable movements elsewhere, but again, as on former occasions, the local exhibition was tinged by local conception and local methods of adaptation.

The close correspondence of these successive phases of design in the several countries, and their almost exactly contemporaneous procession, reveal to us, in

6

a particularly striking manner, the internationalism
of decorative art.

In the eighteenth century the Italian salons and galleries were not less splendid and stately than they had
been during the preceding era, but there was far more
ample provision for the smaller and more intimate boudoirs and drawing-rooms as well. And whether we
are called upon to consider the great salon, the smaller
drawing-room, the boudoir or the sumptuously appointed and dainty bedroom of the eighteenth century
grandame or beauty, we encounter the same general
method of decorative treatment. The more permanent
features, such as frescoes and encrustations of mosaic
and inlay (Plate 21 A), and also the more enduring
movables of the background such as tapestries and
other gorgeous hangings of large extent, remained,
but there was an added sumptuousness and fullness of
appointments that had not hitherto existed. It is true
that the earlier classification of fixed architectural
backgrounds—richly ornate on one hand, and austere
on the other—still held good, but the severely simple
backgrounds were very apt to be much enhanced by the
addition of numerous movables. In not a few instances
walls were covered with fabrics (Plate 22 A) frequently
held in place by mouldings fastened on so as to form
panels. Then, again, there was to be seen an extensive
introduction of *boiserie,* analogous to French and English practice, with the panelling (Plate 21 B) embellished with carving and appropriately painted and
parcel gilt. In many instances, large painted panels,
sometimes on canvas, sometimes on wooden grounds
overlaid with a smooth coating of *gesso* according to
traditional Italian practice, were set into the walls and
surrounded with mouldings. The subjects were warm-
toned landscapes with prominent architectural features

in the manner of Piranesi, pastoral scenes in emulation of the French creations of Watteau, episodes or scenes from classic mythology, fruit and flower devices or gaily coloured and sometimes gilt Chinese *motifs*. Not seldom, also, were mirrors introduced into the panelling as an highly effective decorative device. In the tale of mural resources must likewise be reckoned wallpaper, printed from wood blocks, with landscape, architectural and classic subjects executed in either polychrome or monotone effects. Nor should we forget another expedient sometimes resorted to, especially for the embellishment of *loggie* or partially open-air apartments—the use of canvas hanging friezes and panels painted with classic *motifs*, fruits, flowers and landscapes. By every available means the sumptuousness and multi-colored gaiety of the background were ensured.

The tall and elaborately ornamented chimney piece, reaching from the mantel to the ceiling or nearly to the ceiling, gradually disappeared as an inseparable structurally incorporated factor of the permanent background and was succeeded by lower mantels and fireplace surrounds reflecting in their decoration the successive Baroque, Rococo and Classic modes of the period that held sway in the procession of fashions already enumerated. These mantels were made of carved stone, carved wood and carved and inlaid marble, the latter sometimes displaying an exquisite combination of colours in conjunction with the most delicate intaglio work. Above the mantels were set carved wooden panelling, paintings, hangings or elaborately framed mirrors.

Carved, panelled or inlaid doors still formed important parts of the fixed decorative background, but the methods of carving, panelling and inlaying all reflected the successively prevailing stylistic phases of the age. The doors were often divided into many panels of different sizes and each panel contained a different subject. Sometimes the doors were wholly without panels on one side and painted with a continuous polychrome landscape, while the obverse displayed numerous panels each one of which exhibited a landscape with an architectural feature or else, in the very small panels, a decorative repeat. The obverse of these interesting and characteristic doors is also a valuable study in mouldings. Again, there might be several large panels of Rococo outline enclosing polychrome and gilt decorative *motifs*. Doors of this description often bear eloquent evidence to the all-prevalent popularity of Chinoiserie during a certain epoch of Italian interior decoration. On the gold background are painted Chinese figures and sundry other Oriental *motifs,* but, curiously enough, the connecting arabesques are of unmistakably Renaissance provenance and betray the peculiarly local Italian touch of interpretation. No matter what method of ornamentation might be employed for the embellishment of doors, the Italian decorators were fully alive to the importance of the door as an effective means of enrichment and they failed not to make the most of their opportunities in this direction, a practice that we in our day are only beginning to appreciate.

Along with the decoration of the door, and closely related to it, was the use of the overdoor panel wrought with some painted *motif* or else the employment of some sculptured overdoor embellishment in wood or stone or marble. The painted overdoor panels showed much the same kind of treatment as was to be seen on the painted doors themselves or on the painted panels inserted in the walls and surrounded with mouldings.

During the eighteenth century vastly more attention was paid to carefully draped and hung door and window hangings than had formerly been the case. As a suitable capping to these hangings, carefully designed lambrequins and valances were often used and lent an additional touch of elegance.

Furniture and Decoration.—As furniture design is always more sensitive to stylistic changes than is architecture, and registers them much more promptly, we are prepared to find the eighteenth century Italian mobiliary record showing all the characteristic indications of the age (*v.* illustrations in Part III), which have already been noted in the introductory section at the beginning of the chapter. The femininity of the period manifested in a variety of forms that were obviously designed to win the approval of feminine patronage; the urbanity, subtlety and opulence of contour as contrasted with the strength of line, boldness and dignity of aspect, proceeding from vigorous conception, observable in the former centuries of heroic ability and originality; the plenitude of decoration and the diversity of decorative processes utilised—all these peculiarities figured prominently in the mobiliary *ensemble* of the era. While furniture proportions ranged all the way from studied elegance to downright dumpy stodginess reminiscent of the physique of some of the *contadini,* it must be conceded that even the frequent stoutness of dimensions was generally coupled with great suavity, grace and subtlety of line. In almost all cases, the furniture of the day possessed the admirable quality of domesticity along with the amiable, sunny urbanity of its genial makers. And just because of its pliability of character and its easy domesticity it lends itself with peculiar readiness to modern uses in manifold environments where the architectural background is not insistently rigid in its emphasis.

If we miss the well-nigh heroic qualities and vigour of so much of the earlier work, yet we are to some degree compensated by an ingenuous and companionable informality, a measure of adaptability not there before, a frequent dash of refreshing playfulness and a facile decorative value. Whether eighteenth century Italian furniture was daintily elegant or most informally domestic, it was always polite. The table manners of the sixteenth and seventeenth centuries were vigorous and effective, but not pretty nor pleasant; lacking what we nowadays consider the indispensables of table appointment, people fell back upon first principles, used their fingers freely, got greasy chins and even picked their teeth at the table. In the eighteenth century table refinements had very appreciably advanced and, though folk somewhat came short of the straightforward creative virility of an earlier day, their manners were vastly more elegant and agreeable. Furniture has always faithfully reflected the social life of the period. Eighteenth century Italian furniture was no exception to the rule and, though it may be accused of occasional artificiality and the lack of marked originality of design, it invariably exhibited that urbanity of aspect that was suited to the politer habits of the generation that used it.

At the very beginning of the eighteenth century, the last traces of old Italian vigour and individuality were observable in the lines of furniture that closely corresponded with a well-known contemporary William and Mary type in England—the type presenting straight, tapered legs, square, octagonal or round, and shaped stretchers—an heritage from the Baroque school of influence. This type was soon succeeded by forms of conspicuously curvilinear dominance (Plate 22 A) corresponding pretty closely with the Queen Anne and early Georgian manifestations in England. The mellowness of contour in much of this furniture is singularly commendable and engaging.

As to the great variety of contours to be met with throughout the century, it is well for the reader to remember that analogies in form between Italian furniture and contemporary types in England and France were sufficiently close to enable anyone with a fair knowledge of French and English mobiliary developments to classify Italian pieces chronologically and to understand their affinities and concomitant decorative phenomena. Whatever we find in English and French furniture—Queen Anne forms, evidences of "the Chinese taste," Chippendale elaborations, Adam, Hepplewhite and Sheraton refinements, Louis Quinze frivolities, Louis Seize classicism, the pedantic literalness of the Directoire or the pomp and occasional bombast of the Empire—that we are almost certain to find echoed also in the Italian furniture of the same date.

The least happy and prepossessing of all the eighteenth century Italian furniture manifestations were the adaptations of the Louis Quinze Rococo extravagances and exaggerations. The French prototypes, when once they escaped from the discreet and cunning hands of master designers, might descend—a fact we have all too often been obliged to witness—to shallow weakness, flippancy, or even positive imbecility. The Italian emulators of the less inspired Louis Quinze models might arrive at any of the faults just mentioned and, in addition, complete the *débacle* by achieving a result either grotesque or simperingly flaccid. The foregoing strictures, of course, do not apply to well-executed pieces patterned after worthy Louis Quinze models—and there were such, endowed with real beauty. Unfortunately, however, the ill-favoured kind were in the majority.

Of altogether different calibre was the type of furniture that succeeded when the revival of Classicism made itself felt about the middle of the century. Thence onward there was genuine and almost universal artistic merit in the handiwork of the Italian chair and cabinet makers. The square-backed seating furniture is worthy of special praise and either originals dating from this time or reproductions are among some of the best decorative assets to which the present generation has fallen heir. A great proportion of the contemporary cabinet work was not less lovely both in point of refined contour and in the matter of the decoration bestowed. The later Directoire and Empire manifestations likewise were dignified in contour and highly agreeable in their decoration.

It must be remembered that the eighteenth century Italians were an highly polished and cultured people, habitually accustomed to all the elegancies and refinements of life. In this respect they were second to none. It was at this period that the sons of the English gentry and nobility were customarily sent to take the "grand tour," after they had completed their course at the universities, as an indispensable crowning touch to their education. Their stay in Italy was regarded as peculiarly conducive to a humanising result and their intercourse with educated Italians was deemed a *sine qua non* to the broadening of their intellectual outlook. Under such conditions, then, it would be folly to imagine that the Italians should in any wise fall short of the most punctiliously complete sumptuary equipment. The eighteenth century, so often referred to in English history as the very heyday of fine furniture making

and refinements of domestic art, was an age indeed
when everything in the realm of furniture was highly
specialised and when every requirement was satisfied
by a piece of furniture especially designed to meet it.
This condition, with which we are all more or less familiar in its English aspect, was quite as prevalent
elsewhere and a fully itemised tale of all the furnishing accessories commonly made use of in the equipment
of a well-appointed Italian household of the period
would make a list far too long to give in this place.
Nor is there any real need to do so. (For detailed information on this subject the reader is referred to "The
Practical Book of Italian, Spanish and Portuguese
Furniture," Eberlein and McClure, now in preparation.) It will suffice if we direct attention to some of
the most characteristic pieces. Under the general
classification of wall furniture, besides the standard
complement of bedsteads, wardrobes, secretaries, bur-
eau-bookcases, bookcases, chests of drawers, dressing
stands, chests, cabinets and cupboards to be found in
use in every country, especial heed should be paid to
the numerous forms of corner cabinets, to the sundry
types of bedside tables, to the *credenze,* console cabinets and consoles, to the *prie-dieus,* to the writing
tables and to the spinet cases. Under the head of
seating furniture and tables we meet with an uncom-
monly rich diversity of chairs, sofas, window seats,
stools, benches and a great variety of tables, many of
them of exceedingly ingenious contrivance for occasional or special uses.

The quarter circle corner cabinets or cupboards,
hanging or standing upon legs; the *bombé* front corner
cabinet; the shaped front full length corner cupboards;
the highly decorated wardrobes; the Venetian *credenze;* the large and small consoles and sets of consoles;

the bedside tables and manifold other special small tables—all of these are fascinating in themselves and should be especially investigated because they impart a distinctly characteristic local note to eighteenth century Italian interior decoration and also because they will prove fruitful sources of inspiration by which we may profit in our own present-day decorative ventures.

The decorative processes commonly employed to enrich the furniture of the eighteenth century were inlay of woods in contrasting colours, inlay with mosaics and marbles, inlay of engraved bone—an heritage from Spanish precedents and also from Venetian practice based upon examples imported from the East—marqueterie, lacquer, polychrome painting, gilding both in combination with the natural wood and in conjunction with painting, inlay in conjunction with traced and painted devices, *sgraffito* painting with gilding—a practice, which, however, had become almost obsolete—the application of printed and coloured paper devices upon a painted or lacquered ground, the application of panels painted on canvas to a painted ground and, finally, carving, the latter being one of the most important decorative resources, as was universally the case in all European countries. Nearly all of these processes were conducive to the production of brilliant chromatic effects and we are quite justified in regarding Italian furniture of the eighteenth century as one of the strongest and most facile exponents of the intense national sense and love of colour. In considering the mobiliary productions of the period a convenient division may be made of those pieces in which the natural colour and grain of the wood appear; and, secondly, of those in which the whole body is covered with an applied ground of colour. (Full details of all the aforementioned processes are contained in "The Practical Book of

Italian, Spanish and Portuguese Furniture,'' already mentioned.)

The decorative devices used as *motifs* in the application of the foregoing decorative processes were numerous and widely varied but seemed to enjoy periods of special favour and follow each other in cycles of fashion. Very early in the century we find a predilection for the fine-leaved foliated scroll inlay, somewhat analogous to the seaweed marqueterie of the late William and Mary epoch in England, but derived from precedents of Venetian provenance. There were also Baroque scrolls, cockleshells and cartouches which afforded fruitful opportunities for adaptation. Early in the century, also, about the time when ''the Chinese taste'' was exerting a powerful influence upon popular fancy, we find the decorators having recourse to tea houses, bridges, pagodas, mandarins, coolies and ladies of Cathay adopted bodily without other alteration than was inevitable from an Occidental touch in the process of execution, and, still more did the Italian decorators levy upon the *motifs* taken from Chinese vases in the shape of light panels, reserved on a deeper ground of another colour, and an infinity of small polychrome flowers. These small flowers of obviously Chinese inspiration were also plentifully supplemented by small flowers and leaves of a more naturalistic European source in drawing and colour. Many of these floral decorations were minute in scale and, abundantly spread over the surface to be decorated, gave the effect of a powdered design. The Venetians, even late in the century, manifested a marked fondness for this type of embellishment.

The Italians have always evinced an attachment to stripes and chequerings, and stripes and chequerings, ingeniously and effectively disposed and often with

the greatest delicacy, recur again and again, very frequently along with herring bone borders of alternating
colours, throughout the period. Foliations of various
sorts, *guilloche* bands, rosettes and sundry forms of
acanthus had an almost uninterrupted vogue, especially
in carved work.

With the return of a strong Classic impetus about
the middle of the century there was naturally a reversion to Classic *motifs*. From this time onward we find
concurrently employed not only the devices drawn directly from the pure well-spring of Greek and Roman
antiquity but also the more mixed devices of the Renaissance—arabesques, grotesques, masques, amorini,
chimæras and the like along with acanthus and other
foliated forms. Late in the century we come to the
vogue for griffin and military attributes that marked
the Directoire and Empire phases. During the whole
period landscapes of one sort or another were in continuous use, from the pastoral subjects of the mid century, in emulation of Watteau, to the strangely diversified paper *appliqué* creations that remind one of
decalcomanias.

Decorative Accessories and Movable Decorations—
In this fully furnished century, so amply provided with
all other items of movable equipment, the sundry accessories of furnishing are correspondingly numerous
and divers. In their tale are to be reckoned carpets and
rugs, pictures, the most elaborate and varied sconces,
mirrors and girandoles, hangings not only such as tapestries, embroideries and decorative *appliqué* on fabrics
of rich colour and texture but also the hangings of silks,
brocades and velvets along with embroidered and *appliqué* valances, all of which belonged more definitely in
the realm of upholstery; sculptures in the shape of
statuary and beautifully modelled urns and vases,

Chinese porcelain jars and vases, multi-coloured maiolica plaques and bright-hued jars of large size, candelabra, standards and other objects of deftly wrought
ironwork enriched with parcel colouring and gilt, and
ornate chandeliers which in the eighteenth century had
begun to assume an importance and popularity in decorative schemes far beyond the wont of earlier periods.
Surely a goodly array of resources to aid the interior
decorator!

Materials and Colour.—The materials called into
service for furnishings included woods of many varieties and colours along with bone, mosaic and marbles
for inlay and the metal mounts employed; ironwork in
sundry forms; marble for the stately benches and other
monumental and exceedingly formal articles of furniture used in halls and also the marble used in sculpture
and for table and console tops; the costly textures for
tapestries, hangings and carpets; and an almost endless list of silks, velvets, brocades, satins, brocatelles
and other fabrics used for upholstery and hangings.

Among the woods walnut seems always to have retained its ascendency, although mahogany enjoyed a
vogue by no means inconsiderable. In addition to these
we find a frequent recourse to sycamore, rosewood,
lemon wood and a long list of other woods of more or
less rarity which were in demand for their striking
colour or beautiful grain. For the painted furniture,
cypress, pine and similar so-called "meaner woods"
were used, although it is by no means an uncommon
thing to find decorations painted over a ground of walnut or mahogany.

Among the textures in use, apart from the tapestries, probably the most striking and the most indicative of the spirit of the century were the Aubusson carpets, while the fabrics for upholstery from the looms

of Genoa, Milan and Venice ranged through every possibility of colour and pattern which one could imagine.

In the matter of the use and distribution of colour, it is to be noted that while full, rich and vivid colouring was in favour at the beginning of the century, a taste for lighter, paler, more subdued colours and less vigorous contrasts became apparent as the century progressed, although the Italian colour taste, even at its most restrained period, cannot be said to have been at all anæmic. The same phenomenon was to be witnessed in the decoration of painted furniture, much of which at an early date exhibited a body colour of vigorous tone, while the later pieces almost invariably displayed a ground of lighter hue, there being observable a marked preference for pale greens, lavender, whitish yellow, pale blue or bluish white against which the designs stood out in strong relief. It may be noted also that the Venetians showed a partiality for the lighter toned furniture, while painted furniture of Roman or Tuscan origin often showed an heavier and deeper ground colour.

Arrangement.—Considering all the wealth of resources at hand, the temptation to forsake early principles and the practice of restraint can at least be understood if not sympathised with. Though overdressing was not an invariable fault of the eighteenth century, and especially late eighteenth century, Italian rooms, it must be admitted that they often contained an unfortunate surplus of fitments and that popular taste too often seemed to revel in the satisfactions afforded by individual pieces rather than in the qualities of the composition as an whole. The foregoing criticism is not to be taken as an unqualified condemnation of all the methods of the period or even of a majority of the decorative practice. There was frequently exhibited a genuine sense of restraint, a distinct appreciation of simplicity and a due reverence for symmetrical arrangements and there were many admirable examples of good taste and judgment furnished, but it is unfortunately necessary to admit that the eighteenth century, despite all its marvellous excellence, saw the beginning of the inclination to condone tawdriness which has spoiled so many really admirable Italian things of subsequent date.

CHAPTER V

INTERIOR DECORATION IN SPAIN PRIOR TO THE EIGHTEENTH CENTURY

INTERIOR decoration in Spain prior to the eighteenth century presents a curious combination of Moorish characteristics, on the one hand, and of Renaissance and Baroque features on the other.

In considering this subject, one must bear in mind the peculiarly conservative character of the Spanish people, their almost religious attachment to time-honoured usage and precedent, and their fixed aversion from change, especially when the change has no stronger sanction than the mere compliance with a newly-set fashion.

The wherewithal to have what other nations of the period would have deemed fully furnished and even sumptuous interiors was not lacking. The inclination, however, was towards a paucity of movables. For generations, people had been wont to sit upon cushions on the floor. This was a Moorish custom, to be sure, but Moorish customs had permeated Christian Spain and Christians held to the custom with the same tenacity as the Moors themselves, among whom the usage had more or less religious obligation.

Therefore chairs and seating furniture in general were not so commonly used as in other places. Consequently, there was one factor accounted for that contributed to the comparative austerity and bareness of the Spanish interior. It was a matter of principle with the Moors not to cumber their apartments with articles they did not definitely need. And they were simple in their habits and did not need much. Here, again, was another cause for the characteristic austerity and restraint of the Spanish interior.

Let the reader not imagine, however, that a sixteenth or seventeenth century interior in Spain lacked either richness or interest. Both characteristics were present in a pronounced degree. Concentrated enrichment, and the interest attaching thereto, gathered intensity by contrast with an austere environment which acted as a foil.

In studying Spanish exterior architecture of the early Renaissance, one cannot fail to be deeply impressed by the wonderfully rich effect of the intricate, lace-like carving of a doorway set in a severely plain wall without a trace of other decoration to break its expanse. Much the same phenomenon of sharp contrast was repeated inside the houses where the marvellous cabinets, for which Spain was deservedly famous, had their sumptuous splendour accented by the complete absence of all elements that could in any way detract from their preëminence. The eye was involuntarily focussed there and compelled to take in what was presented to it.

Another factor contributory to interest and enrichment was the frequent use of expanses of gorgeously polychrome tiling (Plate 23 B), at times almost barbaric in its bewildering splendour of colour and pattern. This heritage of Moorish civilisation was incorporated with the Renaissance forms that prevailed in the sixteenth century.

Architectural Background and Fixed Decoration.— If the sixteenth and seventeenth century Spaniards had not the frescoed or marble-encrusted walls of the Italians of the same period, nor the wood-panelled walls of the French and English, and had instead plain plas-

7

ter walls (Plates 23 A and 24), or walls relieved for a portion of their height by multi-coloured tiling or by dados of painted canvas or cloth, their rooms, nevertheless, were by no means lacking in mural interest.

Love of strong colour and of vivid contrast and trenchant design is deeply implanted in the Spanish disposition and this chromatic taste was amply satisfied by the variety of hangings with which they adorned the walls of their apartments in lieu of embellishment incorporated in the actual wall structure. No nation, perhaps, was ever more addicted to the profuse display of wall hangings.

There were, to begin with, tapestries, for tapestries were the common possession of all civilised countries and were esteemed alike in all. There were "fine Italian hangings," which meant brocades, damasks and velvet, the last named of which materials, when hung as a wall embellishment, was usually enriched with embroidery in the form of *appliqué* medallions, cartouches and the like, with an appropriate accompaniment of scrolls, tendrils and arabesques of gold thread or gold galons. When the ground was a rich crimson or a full, brilliant green velvet, this form of wall decoration, often enlivened with armorial bearings as a part of the *appliqué* needlework, was both dignified and effective.

There were painted canvas hangings which presented both vivid colour and emphatic design. There were painted and scalloped canvas friezes or scalloped velvet frieze hangings rich with gold braid and fringe. There was—and this was peculiarly distinctive of Spain, although the fashion afterwards spread to other countries—the gorgeous stamped and engraved leather, polychromed and, later on, polychromed and gilt. The skins were either sewed together to make hangings or

PLATE 23

A. SPANISH RENAISSANCE INTERIOR
Plain Plaster Walls with Moulded and Panelled Door Trims. Baroque Influence Showing in
Door at Left
Courtesy of "Vogue"

B. WALLS PARTIALLY ENCRUSTED IN SPANISH MANNER WITH POLY-
CHROME GLAZED TILES MADE AT TALAVERA 1600–1700
Courtesy of Henry Chapman Mercer, Esq., Font Hill, Doylestown, Bucks, Pennsylvania

PLATE 24

SPANISH RENAISSANCE ROOM WITH PLAIN PLASTER WALLS AND PILLARED CHIMNEY PIECE
Furniture Renaissance and Baroque
Courtesy of "Vogue"

else the pieces of leather were applied directly to the wall. Add to these, "India fabrics," doubtless brought in from Portugal, "delicate summer hangings," Toledo cloths, red and yellow and Roman linens, and it becomes quite plain that the Spanish interior, although it might display certain evidences of austerity, at times, and a sparseness of movables as compared with the fashions of other countries, was by no means void of interest.

In the seventeenth century, the Italian "domino" paper, in small sections, was sometimes applied to the walls, as it was also in Italy and France, its mottled or marbleised pattern and colouring having always found favour in the Iberian peninsula.

Fireplaces showed practically the same lines of structure and ornamentation as were to be noted in Italy and France during the same period, there being, of course, some evidences of national interpretation in the matter of details. In this connexion it should be noted that the brasier was so essential an item of equipment that it may almost be regarded as a part of the fixed outfit. The brasier was generally an ornate specimen of brass craftsmanship, chased, engraved and embossed, supported either on an high stand, so that the hands might conveniently be warmed at its rim, or on a low stand where feet could be toasted. The stands were of wrought iron or of turned and carved walnut.

The beams of the ceilings and the panels of doors Plate 23 A) were especially favourite objects of decorative enrichment and were often intricately carved or inlaid. The facility for working in small panel divisions, with telling decorative effect, was an accomplishment learned from the Moors, and the practice was retained and elaborated with happy results. The carving on doors and on ceiling beams was not seldom enhanced by the application of colour and gilding as well. The floors were of tiles, stone and wood. During the seventeenth century some gorgeously coloured hard woods were brought from the Spanish colonies and incorporated in the parquetted floorings.

Wrought ironwork, in the form of grilles for windows and openings and as handrails, frequently added a decorative emphasis of strong character. The design and workmanship of these bits of ironwork were admirable. Colour and gilding were generally added to them.

Furniture and Decoration.—The two most significant and characteristic items of Spanish Renaissance furniture were the chest and the *vargueño* cabinet (*v.* illustration in Part III). There were chests of all varieties and shapes and contrived for all purposes. There were no less than seven distinct classifications into which they could be divided. Of these, the bride's chest was deemed an absolutely indispensable piece of household equipment—very much like a marriage certificate, in fact—whatever other chests might or might not be represented in an inventory of possessions.

In addition to the chests, which usually manifested conspicuous marks of national taste, there were the *vargueño* cabinets and the *papeleras,* both of which were set on stands. The *vargueño* cabinet had a drop front, hinged at the bottom, which could be used to write upon, and the inside contained tiers of small drawers. It was, in a word, the direct ancestor of the later drop front secretary. The inside of the *vargueño* was generally a splendid blaze of bone inlay, brilliant colour and gold. The *papelera* (Plate 140) was a cabinet of small drawers but had no drop front. It, likewise, was often decorated in a gorgeous and colourful manner.

Besides these, there were hanging cabinets or cupboards, massive walnut tables (Plate 24) of many varieties, settles, benches, stools and chairs. Some of the chests were covered with velvet strained tightly over the wood—bright green was a favourite colour—with gilded iron mounts and ornamental bands or studding.

The characteristic contours and *motifs* of decoration indicated the gradual transition from Renaissance, or Renaissance mingled with Moorish, forms to Baroque conceptions. The dimensions and structure of the period were bold and substantial. Walnut was the staple and favourite material, although oak and chestnut were used also in cabinetwork and occasionally pine likewise.

The mounts and studdings, both of brass and of wrought iron, gilt or plain, were especially indicative of sixteenth and seventeenth century Spanish form conception and added a very appreciable share to the rich and striking effect of the interiors of the period.

Other Decorative Accessories and Movable Decorations.—Tapestries and other hangings were discussed in the section dealing with fixed decoration because their function was permanent rather than otherwise. It is only necessary to add, with respect to hangings, that canopies of green or crimson velvet or brocade, fringed with gold, often played a conspicuous rôle when they were hung over seats or tables of state. Damask, velvet and lace for table covers, embroideries, Cuenca green cloth, Spanish carpets and Turkey carpets, as items in the inventory of fabrics afforded considerable resources of vivid colour.

Large pictures, both portraits and religious paintings, occupied a prominent place in decorative schemes. Porcelains came in through Portuguese trade with the

Orient and were highly prized; maiolica pottery of admirable colour, design and shape, was made in considerable quantity in Spain as well as the glazed tiles; glass vessels of large size and good shape, cut, engraved and sometimes gilded, were also made in Spain and had distinct decorative value; finally, the Spanish smiths were unsurpassed in their manipulation of brass and iron, from which they fashioned candlesticks, candelabra, sconces, chandeliers (Plate 24), brasiers and a host of lesser accessories for various purposes, all of which, in both metals, were wrought with a fascinating invention.

Materials and Colour.—The texture of materials, their contrast with their structural background, and the emphasis of their colour, were such essential parts of the *ensemble* in the composition of a sixteenth or seventeenth century Spanish interior that one can scarcely dissociate them from the actual architectural structure.

The velvets, plain and figured, the brocades and damasks, and the linens, imported from Italy were supplemented by Oriental fabrics brought by Portuguese traders from India and China, and by the gay-coloured cloths and carpets woven at Toledo, Cuenca or Alcaroz.

The colours were vivid and rich to the fullest degree. This applied to the leathers as well as to textiles. As to pattern, it should be noted that while the vigorous and somewhat large figures, so generally to be found in Italy, in France and in England, and which were quite consistent in scale with the colouring in which they were interpreted, were also approved in Spain, at the same time, the Moorish tradition for fine interlacing pattern and compact distribution and the Indian tendency toward attenuation with a certain openness of design, both disposed the Spaniard to an appreciation of refinement as well as vigour in pattern.

Arrangement.—The one important lesson in arrangement to be learned from Spanish interiors is that their restraint in the number of objects employed, and the consequent necessity of wide open spaces for pieces to stand alone, contributed to dignity and served also to enhance the decorative balance of each object when there was nothing to detract from its individual effect.

CHAPTER VI

INTERIOR DECORATION IN SPAIN DURING THE EIGHTEENTH CENTURY

THE eighteenth century so far as Spanish invention in architecture or decorative art was concerned was a singularly barren period. Spain had nothing to contribute beyond a few evidences of national interpretation of styles she had borrowed, mainly from France, but to some extent from England and Italy also.

It is scarcely too much to say that the well of Spanish invention, which had contributed so handsomely and so generously to the common international sum of decorative art in former centuries, was now pumped dry and that a period of creative stagnation followed. The Rococo and Neo-Classic phases of Spanish decoration were but reflections of what was going on in France, in Italy and in England.

Style development simply followed the procession and added only a few local touches in the matter of unimportant details. In the east of Spain and in the Balearic Islands, regions most in contact with active trade relations, the craftsmen added certain delicate elaborations to patterns that came from other sources, but, considered by and large, Spain had nothing new of great consequence to give.

Architectural Background and Fixed Decoration.— Spanish conservatism held on to precedents that had prevailed in former centuries and the architectural backgrounds, influenced by this tenacity of usage, presented much the same features as mentioned in the previous chapter. Tastes remained the same; the mode

PLATE 25

SPANISH INTERIOR WITH BAROQUE AND ROCOCO FURNITURE (CHAIR IN ARCHWAY, EMPIRE)

Courtesy of "*Vogue*"

of expression only was modified to meet the sway of current fashion.

Plain walls (Plate 25) with their applied fabric decorations or hangings continued. The love of vivid colour was unchanged and the facility for compounding striking contrasts, without falling into the snare of garishness, was little abated. Stamped and polychromed leather for wall embellishment passed out of use and this was a loss to be deplored.

Fireplaces and chimney-pieces suffered the same subduing process they underwent in other countries. During the Rococo period, mirrors as a factor in wall decoration came into play for panelling and for incorporation as overmantel features.

Doors were still decorated in a somewhat distinctive manner and the plastered ceilings were painted and gilt without the same success of restraint as similar decorations usually exhibited in France. In many of these exotic features, which the Spaniards had borrowed, they showed an unfortunate tendency to exaggeration. They were not dealing with things akin to their genius and they made frequent mistakes in consequence.

The flooring materials were the same as in the foregoing centuries, except that the various-coloured woods from the Spanish colonies came more and more into use and that wood was preferred to the sterner materials for flooring purposes.

Furniture and Decorations.—Practically every phase of furniture known in England, France or Italy during the eighteenth century was represented by an analogous Spanish type (Plate 25 and illustrations in Part III). The items in use and the amount of equipment employed virtually corresponded to what would be found in any well-appointed establishment in other countries.

The general design of the individual pieces of furniture was the same as elsewhere, but there was a distinct tendency to enlarge the proportions and make the structure heavier and even, at times, a bit stodgy. Bulk, therefore, did create a minor point of difference.

Also, the fashion happily persisted of covering chests and other similar receptacles with strained fabric and using thereon somewhat ample and elaborated mounts. The elaboration and diversity of mounts, however, never equalled the mark set by Spanish cabinet-makers of the sixteenth and seventeenth centuries nor the performance of contemporary French designers.

Other Decorative Accessories and Movable Decorations.—An inventory of these items would tally almost precisely with the items of a similar inventory prepared in France, England or Italy, and as most of the articles of *vertu* were now imported, or if made by native craftsmen, were copied from foreign models, there is little that was distinctive to point to, with a few trifling exceptions, such as the Bilboa mirrors with the marbleised *gesso* frames.

Materials and Colours.—Precisely similar conditions of decorative stagnation obtained with reference to materials and colours, except that Spanish colonial possessions supplied the mother country with some exceptionally fine decorative woods, which the cabinet-makers fortunately availed themselves of now and again.

As to all else, the Spanish taste of the time is to be gauged merely by what it selected; and as, in many cases, the Spaniard was working with materials and colours not germane to his peculiar national genius, he often failed to make the happiest choice or effect the most felicitous combinations.

Arrangement.—Spanish decoration of the earlier period was distinguished for its wholesome reticence in the number of articles used and by the really strategic manner in which they were disposed to compass the greatest effect.

Eighteenth century ideals of arrangement, being borrowed along with all the material properties, failed to exhibit that erstwhile happy trait and Spanish rooms unfortunately often fell into an unedifying condition of tawdry formality.

CHAPTER VII

INTERIOR DECORATION IN FRANCE PRIOR TO THE EIGHTEENTH CENTURY

*I*NTRODUCTION.—The story of interior decoration in France prior to the eighteenth century begins with a phase in which the body was Gothic and the clothes Renaissance; it ends with the full development of Baroque grandiosity and elaboration in what was known as the "Grand Manner" under the lavish patronage and control of Louis XIV, who evinced an extraordinary interest in decoration and regarded decorative pomp and magnificence as indispensable adjuncts of his court.

The military farings of Charles VIII into Italy, at the end of the fifteenth century, opened the door to a great influx of Italian Renaissance influences into France and fostered an appetite for the refinements of Classicism in decoration and architecture, a vivid recollection of which the returning expeditionaries brought back with them. The motives of the expedition were military; the chief results were cultural. Further expeditions into Italy on the part of the French kings who succeeded Charles had the same outcome. Kings, nobles, and soldiery alike had gazed upon the fruits of the Italian Renaissance only to become enamoured of them and imbued with a determination to emulate them in their own land and for their own behoof.

Besides the returning nobles and soldiery, other important factors that served to spread the Renaissance influence in France were the missions and embassies to Italian courts, Italian missions to the French

108

court, and a growing influx of Italian bankers and merchants who brought in their train sundry articles of "goldsmiths' work, medals and cameos, books, pictures, furniture and intarsias, casts and bronze work, terra-cottas and maiolica," all of which "helped to accustom French eyes to Renaissance forms." The sincere admiration of French travellers and ambassadors for what they saw in Italy is typically voiced in the words of Philippe de Comines who, in 1495, conducted a mission to Venice which he described as "the most triumphant citie that ever I sawe" and enthusiastically wrote of the Grand Canal, "Sure in my opinion, it is the goodliest streete in the world and the best built."

But even more important than the agencies just mentioned, in completing Italy's peaceful conquest of France, were the lessons French artists learnt in Italy and the things that Italian artists and artificers taught in France. During the fifteenth century there were comparatively few Italians in France; "but from its closing years onwards a continuous stream of architects and engineers, decorators and all manner of artificers poured across the Alps, beginning with Charles VIII's colonies at Amboise and Tours, and continued by that of Francis I at Paris and Fontainebleau."

Generous royal patronage and, to some extent, the patronage of great and wealthy nobles played a significant part in the Renaissance development of the decorative arts in France. The colonies of Italian artificers established and maintained by Charles VIII and Francis I were only the first instances of this royal interest and support. Throughout the sixteenth and seventeenth centuries the crown, either directly or else indirectly through its ministers, gave substantial encouragement to decorative progress. This whole

architectural and decorative development in France
during the sixteenth and seventeenth centuries may
be divided into five phases of style. The dates are to
some degree approximate as there were necessarily
overlappings and survivals.

The Style Louis XII, 1495–1515 (Charles VIII,
1483–1498; Louis XII, 1498–1515; contemporary rulers
in England, Henry VII and Henry VIII) embraced the
beginnings of Italian Renaissance influence—the deck-
ing of the Gothic body in Renaissance clothes—and
marked the incorporation of a few of the delicate characteristics of the Tuscan school, a school marked by a
"certain austerity . . . and a rather minute type of
ornament, evolved by a race of architects of goldsmith
training." The Style Louis XII was only a preliminary phase, a feeling of the way.

The second phase is known as the Style of Francis
I, 1515–1545 (Francis I, 1515–1547: Henry VIII contemporary ruler in England) marked the complete
fusion (Plate 26) of the native French elements and
the Lombard Renaissance forms, the latter representing a style of eminent "charm and delicacy" exuberant
with the devising of new features and impressive both
from its wealth of ornament and the "beauty of its
detail."

The Style Henry II, 1530–1590, the third stage of
development (Henri II, 1547–1559; Francis II, 1559–
1560; Charles IX, 1560–1574; Henri III, 1574–1589;
Henry VIII, Edward VI, Mary, and Elizabeth, contemporary rulers in England), which followed in close succession, saw the assimilation of the Roman phase of the
Renaissance, that phase which took shape in Rome during the last quarter of the fifteenth century and continued dominant during the first quarter of the sixteenth. The mature Roman phase, inspired by a more

systematic study of ancient monuments, and "pruned of earlier exuberances," "became bolder, surer, more balanced in its composition, gaining in calm monumentality and masculine strength what it lost in youthful vitality and variety of decorative motives."

The three foregoing phases belong wholly and purely to the Renaissance in all their characteristics of style except in so far as chance Gothic traits survived here and there. Of the two that follow, the former embodied the beginnings of Baroque influence and its commingling with the ripe Renaissance conceptions; the latter comprised the full fruition of the Baroque mode and its complete ascendancy over the purer and more restrained forms of Renaissance provenance.

The Style Henri IV and Louis XIII, 1590–1660 (Henri IV, 1589–1610; Louis XIII, 1610–1643: Elizabeth, James I, and Charles I, contemporary rulers in England) was a phase of fusion when curvilinear forms and bolder, heavier detail began gradually to make their progress into popular favour.

The Style Louis XIV, 1640–1710 (Louis XIII, 1610–1643; Louis XIV, 1643–1715: Charles II, James II, William and Mary, and Queen Anne, contemporary rulers in England) marked the apotheosis of ponderous curves and scrolls, singly and in combination, of pomposity, redundance, oftentimes heaviness of detail and all that conceptions of superabundant splendour could devise to create the "Grand Manner." What was naturally imposing, the exponents of Baroque essayed to make more so and did not hesitate to create structure for the sole purpose of carrying their massive decorations which were, it is true, mightily imposing but could scarcely be called logical. The exaggerations of this period belong to the earlier portion (1610–1650). Directly the influence of Louis XIV began to make itself felt there was far more restraint and the style was perceptibly tempered by an infusion of Classicism and a more studied sobriety in composition.

During all this period of five phases there was a steady and rapid development in the technical mastery of decorative processes and resources which combined to make the sixteenth and seventeenth centuries in French decorative art one of the most resplendent epochs in history.

Architectural Background and Methods of Fixed Decoration.—Throughout the sixteenth and seventeenth centuries the rooms of French *châteaux* and houses were commonly of large size. Indeed, they were often oppressively so, especially in the formal and grandiose days of Louis XIV. As was natural, and in fact necessary under the circumstances, the fixed or architectural background formed a vitally important part of the composition. The ceilings were lofty.

Style Louis XII.—In the interiors of the Style Louis XII the embrasured windows were of good size, had either square heads or very flat elliptical arches, and were usually two lights wide, divided in the centre by a substantial vertical stone mullion, intersected by one or more transverse mullions or transomes. The casements were of metal. In the less important rooms oiled linen or oiled paper were used; in the better rooms the casements were glazed with roundels or with small quarries set in lead. Inside shutters were used and, in some cases, the lower lights had also perforated outside shutters. Door heads, like window heads, were square or had flat elliptical arches.

Walls were sometimes panelled, either wholly or in part, with small panels, but were more commonly of stone or plaster, which might be painted or frescoed, but they were more frequently relieved by hangings of painted cloth or canvas or by tapestries and embroideries. *Complete* schemes of permanent decoration were rather exceptions than otherwise but gradually came more and more into vogue under spreading Italian influence. The *motifs* used in the panelling, medallions and other carved, sculptured or moulded features of door and window trim or wall decoration were a medley of Gothic and Renaissance details.

Fireplaces, with their surmounting chimney-pieces, afforded an opportunity for rich and imposing structure and a wealth of carved detail. Some of the structures left the fire largely exposed at the sides, the hood receding upwards from a bold vertical mantel whose weight was carried on half-piers or corbels; other overmantel structures consisted of an elaborate pilastered and panelled architectural composition carried up vertically part or all of the way to the ceiling and resting on a vigorous vertical mantel which, in turn, was supported on a pillared substructure that left only the front of the fireplace open.

Ceilings were either vaulted, with a more or less complicated system of ribbing, or else of wooden construction with the timbers, as a rule, exposed to view. At times the timbers were concealed by temporary cloth or tapestry testers attached by hooks. In other cases, the ceiling timbers were boarded in the manner of a barrel vault with wooden rib divisions. Panelled wood ceilings, with square, hexagon or octagon-shaped panels, affixed to the under side of joists gradually appeared as a result of Italian influence and were frequently enriched with colour and gilding.

Flooring consisted of stone slabs, of bricks, of encaustic tiles and also, as a direct outcome of Italian teaching, of maiolica tiles and of parquetted wood.

Style Francis I.—The most numerous type of win-

8

dow in the Francis I style was square-headed. An occasional variation was the rounding of the shoulders. This detail, however, chiefly appeared outside and did not affect the interior aspect. Besides these, there were also in lesser number round-arched windows and windows with flat elliptical-arched tops. The windows were generally large, two lights wide, and divided vertically by a mullion which was crossed by a transverse mullion or transome, nearer the top than the bottom, thus forming a cross, hence the name *fenêtre croisée*. There were also smaller windows without mullions, square-headed, and filled by two full-length casements. Besides the leaded quarries or roundels in the metal casements, stained-glass cartoons were occasionally introduced. Door heads corresponded in shape to window heads and above the door heads carved or sculptured decoration was often added.

As in the preceding style, walls were panelled wholly or in part (Plate 26), stone-faced, or plastered. At times the plaster surface above the panelled wainscot was embellished by reliefs in stucco-duro (Plates 26 and 27). Paint and fresco adornment, as previously, were sometimes employed, but *complete* permanent decorations were still, for the most part, to be found only in the houses of the very great and very wealthy and it remained a common practice to deck comparatively austere walls with tapestries or with painted cloth and canvas hangings that could be taken down at will and moved elsewhere. The chief features of the rooms, however—fireplaces, overdoors and the like— were accorded rich permanent treatment.

The panels for wainscotted walls and for other interior woodwork were generally small (Plate 27) and very frequently square in shape, defined by mouldings of low profile, in a manner strongly reminiscent of

PLATE 26

WOODWORK AND PLASTERWORK, GALLERY, FONTAINEBLEAU. STYLE
FRANCIS I

From "Le Palais de Fontainebleau," A. Guérinet

Courtesy of William Helburn, Inc.

PLATE 27

LONG GALLERY, FONTAINEBLEAU. STYLE FRANCIS I

From "Librairie D'Architecture and D'Art Decoratif," Armand Guérinet

Courtesy of William Helburn, Inc.

PLATE 28

FIREPLACE AND CHIMNEY PIECE, FONTAINEBLEAU. STYLE HENRI II

From "Le Palais de Fontainebleau." Guérinet

Courtesy of William Helburn, Inc.

PLATE 29

HALL OF ST. LOUIS—FONTAINEBLEAU. STYLE HENRI IV-LOUIS XIII
From "Le Palais de Fontainebleau," A. Guérinet
Courtesy of William Helburn, Inc.

North Italian Renaissance panelling of an earlier date.
The *motifs* with which the panels were often enriched,
as well as other decorated woodwork and interior stone
carving, included arabesques, pateræ, monograms
(Plate 27), initials, emblems, mottoes on ribbon scrolls,
cockleshells, ox skulls, plant forms and human and
animal forms and heads. Gothic details had quite disappeared. All of these just mentioned, and others of
similar nature, appeared more especially in chimney-
piece carvings and in door trims and overdoor enrichments, where also one might find divers classic orders,
of different scale, brought into the same composition
without reference to classic precedent; capitals combining cornucopiæ, fanciful volutes and heads; and
panelled pilasters enriched with arabesques, interlacing
scrolls or strapwork, or with circles and lozenges, the
former and latter of which were especially characteristic of Francis I decoration. The relief of all carved
(Plate 26) ornament was almost invariably low and
restrained, and the detail exceptionally refined.

Fireplaces were quite generally surmounted with
a distinctly architectural chimney-piece composition
carried up vertically to the ceiling. The chimney-piece
of sculptured stone or carven wood displayed niches,
canopies, pilasters, panelling and sculptured devices
in impressive array above a suitable corresponding
mantel carried on piers, corbels or caryatides.

Vaulted and stone slab ceilings were used in places
that readily admitted their construction, but ceilings
with exposed timbers and panelled ceilings were steadily becoming more and more the rule. The beamed and
panelled wood ceilings were often divided up into small
panels (Plate 27) and enriched with delicate carving
or with colour and gold.

Stone, marble and encaustic tile floorings continued

in use, but parquetted wood floors (Plate 27) were winning wider and wider favour as were also the floors of Italian enamelled or maiolica tiles in bright colours or with divers subjects in colour on a white ground.

Style Henri II.—The Style Henri II marks the very height and flower of the French Renaissance, the climax to which all previous development was only preparatory. It is logical and straightforward in all its characteristics and its creations carry a sense of satisfaction and conviction unequalled by the work that preceded or followed. The composition of a room in this style possessed unity of conception and did not represent merely a more or less unrelated group of fixed decorative items.

Windows to a great extent retained their mullioned and transomed divisions and their two-light width, although mullions and transomes were not invariable, and square-headed windows without them and with two full-length casements were not uncommon. Round-arched windows also occurred to some extent. Panelled inside shutters were used. Door heads were of corresponding shape to window heads and over-door decoration often took the form of a pediment, either rectilinear or arc-shaped, with appropriate accompaniments.

While movable hangings, such as those mentioned in the review of the preceding styles, continued to some extent in use, permanent *complete* decorations (Plate 28) were much more common. Walls were often panelled, either wholly or in part, and the panelling, which tended to become larger and more diversified (Plate 28) in the shapes of its divisions, was not infrequently embellished with carving and gilding and sometimes also "with marqueterie of coloured woods, and inlays of ivory, ebony, precious metals and even of marble."

Oftentimes walls that had an high-panelled dado (Plate 28) were of decorated and moulded plaster above, with colour and gilding applied to the plaster relief, or else there were frescoes (Plate 28) framed in moulded plaster cartouches with all their attendant scroll embellishments. Again, whole wall surfaces were frescoed, or were hung with tapestries or decorated leather hangings which were framed in with stucco or plaster frames wrought in high relief and embellished with scrolls, strapwork and figures in the round. Wall coverings were also made from embossed and stamped leather decorated in the Spanish manner, polychromed and gilt in repeat patterns, and affixed to the wall. A much less pretentious wall covering, but one nevertheless capable of agreeable decorative effect when wisely used, was the Italian motley marbleised paper made in small squares and applied to the walls. This paper, similar in pattern to that used for book covers, was called "domino" paper and was made in Italy from the fifteenth century on.

The *motifs* employed for the sundry wall decorations—this includes likewise the adornments of the chimney-pieces and door trims—showed, for one thing, an increased use of the orders (Plate 28) in a systematised and consistent arrangement with due recognition of their proportions and parts. The combinations of members and forms were somewhat more restricted in variety than previously by a more conscientious attention to classic rules. Capitals, for instance, adhered more nearly to traditional types (Plate 28) and the variations from precedent were chiefly in minor matters such as the incorporation of monograms, sprays of foliage and the like. *Bay, olive, myrtle, oak, acanthus* and *palm* were the usual sorts of foliage. It was very significant and characteristic that pilasters were *fluted,* or now and then *wreathed,* instead of being *panelled* and adorned with *arabesques* or with *circles* and *lozenges,* a treatment thoroughly indicative of the Francis I style. Strapwork, scrolls, interlacings, frets and running borders were among the "properties" in evidence.

While the profiles of mouldings and the cutting of all enrichments were cleanly and incisively wrought with extreme delicacy, a larger scale in general was adopted, patterns were less complex and "in the treatment of doors, shutters, panelling, and indeed all features, larger and bolder patterns were preferred, with a tendency to make of each a single, centralised design with one dominant feature, while the characteristic of the best rooms is the manner in which all the features were combined into a consistent whole." In other words, whereas the earlier styles had been largely methods of enriched decoration of spaces with small enrichments, the style of Henry II was far more architectural in its feeling and in its well-rounded scheme of composition.

The general contour and structure of the chimneypiece, which still continued the most significant single feature (Plate 28) in the room, remained substantially the same as previously. The only notable differences were that its composition was more closely governed by classic precedent and that it was not seldom executed in coloured marbles as well as in the stone or wood of former times.

Plaster ceilings had now come into high favour and were wrought with all the mastery of design and delicacy of finish of which the best Italian and Italian-taught French plasterers were capable. To the rare artistry of pattern and modelling these ceilings added the living glory of colour and gold in brilliant and glow-

ing schemes. In addition to flat and coffered plaster
ceilings, there were simple and intersecting barrel
vaults and domes. The wooden ceilings also glowed
with rich colour and gold and were beamed and panelled or coffered in hexagons, octagons and the like.
Oftentimes the beams were encased in panelling. Occasionally the wooden ceilings were inlaid instead of
being painted and gilt.

While the formerly mentioned flooring materials
were still employed, carefully laid wooden floors, enriched with parquetting, were more than ever in high
esteem. Likewise, glazed polychrome tiles, now made
in France after the inspiration of the Italian maiolica
tiles, played an important part as flooring materials.

Style Henri IV and Louis XIII.—In this style of
decoration Baroque influences, and especially Flemish
Baroque influences, began to make themselves more
and more conspicuous. The crisp delicacy and restraint
of the Style Henri II were supplanted by a more bulbous, obtuse and ponderous conception of line and
design.

Windows under Henri IV grew larger and longer
but, generally speaking, kept their stone mullions and
transomes, making the divisions previously noted.
The openings were commonly square-headed but were
occasionally varied by round-arched heads. The two-
light width remained unchanged. Later in the period,
under Louis XIII, many windows were further increased in size, so that they extended nearly all the way
from floor to ceiling. About the same time, also, stone
mullions and transomes began to fall into disuse, being
replaced by wooden substitutes or by wooden casement
frames with broad stiles and rails. Door heads, as
usual, followed the fashion of window openings.

Save in the most sumptuous rooms, the bare plaster

of the walls was exposed, thus leaving a broad expanse
to be decorated with frescoes or treated with "domino"
paper as indicated in the previous style. While, of
course, tapestries were plentifully used, they no longer
formed an inseparable adjunct to the general scheme as
indicated by the earlier plaster or stucco mouldings,
especially contrived to frame them. A low-panelled
dado or wainscot, with small divisions (Plate 31 B),
was often used and embellished with painted decorations of landscapes, flowers, foliage and the like.

The prevailing *motifs* for mural decoration—in
which may also be reckoned the carved wood, stone or
modelled plaster adornments for chimney-pieces (Plates
29 and 30 B) and overdoor enrichments (Plate 30 A),
where they were especially prominent, included the
"cartouche" form (Plate 30 A), one of the most ubiquitous and important—with its surrounding "scrol-
liage" pierced and slashed, and pulpy strapwork,
heaving convex cabochons, masques, pudgy cherubs,
which one wit has humourously dubbed "pukids,"
volutes, conucopiæ, ovoid bulging shields, massive
draperies, scrolls, rectilinear pediments, arc-shaped
pediments (Plate 30 A), and both kinds of pediments
interrupted, scrolled pediments, and several kinds of
pediments combined in a redundant medley, swags and
drops of foliage and flowers, palm branches, laurel
leaves, human figures, caryatides, quadrangular term-
shaped pedestals or pilasters tapered toward the base,
along with the various other characteristic Baroque
"properties" which found an analogue to their thick,
pulpy gobbiness in the contemporary big-scale, fat
women painted by Rubens. The same conception of
the properties of line was back of both. Mouldings, as
contrasted with their sharp crispness and incisive delicacy in the Henri II style, now appeared obtuse and

PLATE 30

A. VESTIBULE D'HONNEUR, FONTAINEBLEAU. STYLE LOUIS XIII
(EXTREME BAROQUE)
From "Le Palais de Fontainebleau," A. Guérinet
Courtesy of William Helburn, Inc.

B. SALLE DES GARDES, FONTAINEBLEAU. STYLE LOUIS XIII. (TRANSITION
FROM HENRI II)
From "Le Palais de Fontainebleau," A. Guérinet
Courtesy of William Helburn, Inc.

PLATE 31

A. SALON, MARIE DE MÉDECIS, LUXEMBOURG PALACE. STYLE LOUIS XIII
From "Le Palais du Luxembourg," A. Guérinet
Courtesy of William Helburn, Inc.

B SALON, FONTAINEBLEAU. STYLE LOUIS XIII
From "Le Palais de Fontainebleu," A. Guérinet
Courtesy of William Helburn, Inc.

PLATE 32

THRONE ROOM, LUXEMBOURG PALACE. STYLE LOUIS XIV
From "Le Palais du Luxembourg." A. Guérinet
Courtesy of William Helburn, Inc.

PLATE 33

CHARACTERISTIC BAROQUE DECORATIVE *MOTIFS* FROM PANELLING, OVERMANTELS AND ELSEWHERE

1. Section of Louis XIV Panel Head. 2 and 3. Sections of Louis XIV Panel Ornament. 4 and 5. Corner Sections of
Louis XIV Panel Heads. 6 and 7. Details of Louis XIV Overmantel Ornament

blunted (Plates 29 and 30 A) as well as rotund and massive. And yet, notwithstanding the tumid pomposity and exaggerated emphasis of the Baroque style, its often grotesque conception and lack of refinement, we must concede that it could be both imposing and distinguished and, when discreetly managed, was not without a certain agreeable quality of charm. It should be added that in France the tendency to extravagance of expression was generally kept within bounds, thanks to the national trait of moderation.

Although the fireplace openings began to be appreciably reduced in size (Plates 29, 30 B and 31 A), the chimney-piece superstructure extending to the ceiling lost none of its pristine importance and was duly embellished with all the decorative assets of the time. The scheme usually included some central feature—a decorative panel or picture—surrounded by a composition of some of the *motifs* just enumerated. The whole composition might be in stone, wood or stucco.

Ceiling beams (Plate 30 B) were often decorated with painted and gilt patterns as were also the enclosed panels (Plate 31 B). Sometimes the panels were of stucco wrought and coloured. Again, the whole ceiling was an elaborate production of the plasterer's art (Plates 29 and 31 A) with heavy stucco details and gorgeous colouring.

The formerly mentioned flooring materials continued in use in varying degrees of popularity, but marble tiling and parquetted wooden floors (Plates 29 and 30 A and B) were regarded with most favour.

Style Louis XIV.—In his admirable summarisation of characteristics that dominated the style of Louis XIV, W. H. Ward (Architecture of the Renaissance in France) says, "No government, however powerful, and no monarch, however good his taste—and within cer-

tain limits that of Louis XIV was excellent—can create
an art or a literature to order. Success was achieved
in virtue of a coincidence in aim with the artistic tendencies of the century and a skillful choice of agents.''
To put the matter a little differently, one might say
that the almost universal prevalence, at any one given
period, of a great wave of popular taste or, in other
words, the vogue of a particular style, may be likened
to the on-sweeping epidemic of a contagious disease
that few or none can wholly escape. One person, for instance, may have a light case of small-pox and be apparently little affected by the disorder; another may
be severely ill with all the attendant symptoms fully
developed. But the same influence has been at work
in both cases. So is it in the matter of falling under a
style of influence and so is it that the epidemic of a
style merges into a clearly defined and crystallised
fashion.

Thus was it also in the case of the Style Louis XIV.
There were certain antecedents back of it whose presence, in the new style development, could not be ignored
and from whose influence there could be no complete
escape, no matter what fresh elements came into play,
unless there was to be an absolute and drastic revolution in all conceptions and in all methods of style
expression. And such a sweeping revolution it would
have been exceedingly difficult to compass even had it
been desirable or desired. As a matter of fact, it was
not desired and the obvious solution, therefore, was
a compromise with the infusion of a large and vigorous
new element of ideals. The Style Louis XIV was just
such a compromise. It was a full coördination of the
elements that had gone to make up the Henri IV–Louis
XIII style with something added—a very appreciable
addition, indeed. In architecture, and to a very much

PLATE 34

BED CHAMBER OF LOUIS XIV. VERSAILLES. STYLE LOUIS XIV
From "Librarie Centrale d'Art et d'Architecture"
Courtesy of William Helburn, Inc.

PLATE 35

HALL OF HERCULES, VERSAILLES. STYLE LOUIS XIV
From "Librarie Centrale d'Art et d'Architecture"
Courtesy of William Helburn, Inc.

PLATE 36

A. DOORWAY, LUXEMBOURG PALACE
STYLE LOUIS XIV

From "Le Palais du Luxembourg, A. Guérinet
Courtesy of William Helburn, Inc.

B. THRONE ROOM, LUXEMBOURG PALACE
STYLE LOUIS XIV

greater extent in decoration, it was a compromise, and on the whole a sane and satisfying compromise, between Palladianism—the scholastic interpretation of Classicism as formulated during the late Italian Renaissance —and Baroque tendencies. The result was Baroque idealised, purged of its grossness and abnormal, swollen heaviness, presented in a tempering and restraining setting of Classicism (Plate 35), a rationalised style that incorporated what was best in the preceding episode and added positive elements of fresh provenance. Its physical affinities were Baroque, a chastened and reasoned Baroque; its spiritual affinities were Classic and Renaissance.

The foremost artists and craftsmen of the age— and it was a truly great age, despite certain defects— encouraged and assisted by the king, aided in making the Style Louis XIV one of the most sumptuous and impressive that the world has ever seen. Simon Vouet, Eugene Le Sueur, Nicholas Poussin, Charles Le Brun, Le Pautre, Marot, Francesco Romanelli, Berain, Jacques Sarrazin, Laurent Magnier, these are a few of the names of men who added lustre to the decorative work of the period, their association with the practice of their several *metiers* proving a guarantee of the excellence therein realised.

If the cartouche and all its satellite entourage of auxiliary *motifs* was the "trade-mark" of the Style Louis XIII, the rayed sun, the Gallic cock, along with the shaped panel (Plate 33, Figs. 1–5) and all its kindred variations, may be regarded as the badges of Louis XIV decorative expression. Other distinguishing traits were the impressive applied orders (Plates 34, 35 and 36 A), the general architectural composition of interiors (Plate 35), the full convex sections of mouldings (Plates 32, 34 and 35) and projecting members, often deeply undercut, the frequent use of the torus and of the *cyma reversa,* reticulated diaperwork (Plate 33, Fig. 7) in otherwise unoccupied spaces such as spandrels, and the striking use of shadow. It was, in short, an opulent, masculine and magnificent style.

Windows and doors were commonly square-headed (Plate 36 A) or round-arched (Plate 35), the former being far more numerous. The divisions of casements and panes were, as a rule, much the same as in the preceding style. Mouldings of door frames were full and often richly ornate, and above important doorways was generally an imposing architectural and decorative composition (Plate 34) in bold relief, subsidiary features of the decoration not infrequently extending to the floor on either side. The doors themselves were richly panelled (Plates 34, 35 and 36 A) and decorated in relief or colour or both.

Order and organised symmetry were two of the most characteristic traits of the style and the wall spaces, vast as many of them were, afforded opportunity for impressive architectural composition with the use of orders of pilasters and rich panelling between. The whole *ensemble* represented "symmetrical and careful scheme, distributed into large well-defined divisions, and these sometimes subdivided into smaller compartments." The tops of panels were commonly shaped (Plate 33, Figs. 1–5), or rounded, and angles were apt to be softened into quadrants.

Where orders of pilasters were not used, walls were, nevertheless, divided into compartments or broad rectangular panels (Plate 32), extending from floor or dado to cornice, with enriched borders, "the centre either plain or containing a tapestry, a picture, a relief, a carved or painted arabesque, or octagonal panel in the centre."

The *motifs* and "properties" most in evidence, besides those already mentioned, were the lion, eagle and griffin among animal forms, normal and robust human figures quite different from Rubens's specimens of unwholesome obesity; and, in the vegetable types, oak, laurel and olive in full, close-packed and be-ribboned wreaths, acanthus, heavy swags and drops of fruit and foliage. Shells and scrolls, cherubs and masques (Plate 33, Figs. 6 and 7), were used to break the centres of lintels or arches; while the cartouche, in conjunction with architectural mouldings and pediments, was reduced to "its original function of framing a shield or panel." Architraves and kindred members forming "frames to panels and openings were broad and bold, and carved with close-packed foliage or other enrichments."

When tapestries were used, it was a common practice to stretch them in a fixed frame like a painting or to empanel them. Wall adornment also often consisted of modelled stucco (Plate 32), of paintings or frescoes (Plate 32), and of inlays or coatings of various and richly coloured marbles. Mirrors also began to be employed for wall panelling and for incorporation in chimney-pieces. The colour schemes were full and vigorous and gilding was freely called into service.

Fireplaces with their accompanying overmantel decorations were focal features in the composition of the room (Plates 35 and 36 B), although the chimney breast was now often disguised in the thickness of the wall and, instead of the fireplace and chimney-piece constituting an architectural projection, it became a massively detailed and impressive piece of applied decoration. The overmantel embellishment, whether a picture empanelled in an ornate and heavily moulded surround, or some other feature, usually extended to the cornice.

Cornices were distinctly architectural (Plates 34 and 35) in their interpretation. Ceilings, which were frequently plastered with a flat surface throughout their expanse, were commonly enriched with heavily moulded plaster or stucco ornamentation of an elaborate character to which the additional touches of colour and gilding were added. The larger panels of the ceilings were often the vehicles for gorgeous frescoes. At other times the beams were visible and coloured and gilt decoration was added to coffered panels and projections. Barrel vaulted (Plate 32), domed and coved (Plate 35) ceilings were used as well as flat. The floors were of various-coloured marbles, of tiles and of wood, plain or parquetted in patterns.

Furniture and Decoration.—During the sixteenth century, Renaissance forms of furniture completely ousted any remaining traces of Gothic design. Gothic influence, however, persisted for a time in the high-backed, stall-like seigneurial chairs of state. Oak and walnut were the staple cabinet woods and yielded a ready medium for the interpretation of Renaissance ideals, especially the latter, which was much more responsive to the carver's efforts.

The chief articles of furniture (*v.* illustrations, Part III) were chests and cabinets, a few chairs of state—the use of a chair was still a mark of distinction and rank—and tables, either of the draw or refectory variety. Contours were bold and structure heavy, although the lines were graceful, for French artisans had proved apt pupils and shown themselves alert to grasp the new ideas of style and oftentimes to improve upon them. Upholstery, more as a bit of elegance than for comfort, was introduced fairly early in the century, but it was not until the latter part of the century that it figured to any appreciable extent. Carving was the chief decorative resource and the *motifs* used by the carver, as well as the structural contour of the objects, closely reflected contemporary architectural features.

From about the beginning of the seventeenth century, the progress of French mobiliary art made rapid strides. The variety of articles in use increased, structure became lighter, contours more graceful, decorative processes more diversified, and altogether the characteristics of a politer age, or at least a more luxurious age, were unmistakable. Indeed, the French cabinet-makers and carvers of the end of the sixteenth century and the beginning of the seventeenth quite equalled in skill and taste their Italian preceptors and, in addition to other excellences, they succeeded in imparting a very distinct touch of national individuality to their handiwork. By this time Baroque influence had perceptibly affected French mobiliary design and we find curvilinear structural elements, such as scrolled legs, arms and stretchers, profusion of ornament, and detail in vigorous relief, in distinction to the rectilinear, flatter and more reticent qualities that marked the earlier styles.

Under the lavish patronage of Louis XIV, the making of furniture attained a degree of finish and perfection hitherto unprecedented in any country. Furniture, likewise, branched out into various new phases. Besides employing the staple oak and walnut, rare woods of divers colours and ornamental grains were freely drawn upon for veneer, inlay and marqueterie. One of the most significant developments was the introduction of the wonderful Boule inlay of tortoise-shell and brass. To set off properly this extraordinarily rich combination, elaborate *ormolu* mounts

and metal *appliqués,* cast, chiselled and engraved, were
profusely resorted to. Painting, gilding, lacquering,
and carving also played their respective parts, but
there were so many decorative processes now available
that carving lost its paramount position. Although
Baroque scrolls and curves had long since established
themselves, structural lines, especially in cabinet work,
were mainly rectilinear. Cabinets and armoires were
among some of the most resplendent examples of this
resplendent age.

*Other Decorative Accessories and Movable Decora-
tions.*—Throughout the sixteenth century there poured
into France choice products of craftsmanship from
Italy and the East—ivories, intarsias, goldsmiths'
work, maiolicas, small mirrors from Venice curiously
set, and divers objects of like nature—which, however,
came more in the capacity of curios and cherished personal possessions than as accessories to decoration.
Apart from the wrought-iron or brass candelabra and
sconces (Plate 32), and the banners, arms and trophies
of the chase, the chief decorative accessories were such
as have already been noted in connexion with the fixed
background.

In the seventeenth century the story was quite different. Besides the tapestries, hangings and pictures
whose presence was mentioned in discussing the fixed
decorations, foreign trade had brought porcelains and
bronzes from the Orient, zeal for classic research had
stimulated the use of sculpture in marble and bronze,
and lacquer from the East was beginning to count as an
appreciable item. The brass founders and the smiths
were contributing chandeliers and sconces of admirable
design and these were employed to the full extent of
their decorative as well as utilitarian capacity.

During the reign of Louis XIV all of the aforementioned accessories were multiplied in number and the recently started manufacture, in France, of mirrors of greater size than heretofore contributed another item of effective decoration, while the metal workers excelled their past performances in the fashioning of lamps, candelabra and sconces, which performed a more conspicuous function in the decorative schemes than ever before. Glass and crystal lustres for chandeliers and sconces also helped to create brilliant results.

Materials and Colour.—The materials of furniture and the fixed decorations have been noted in preceding paragraphs. The fabrics employed during this period, besides embroideries and tapestries, numbered silks, satins, brocades, damasks, brocatelles, velvets plain and figured, and printed linens. Copious importations from Italy were later supplemented by the excellent products of the French looms. Throughout the period the colours were rich, full and varied, and the patterns were, for the most part, vigorous and large.

Arrangement.—During much of the sixteenth century the arrangement of furniture was determined more by considerations of convenience than by notions of symmetrical composition or systematic grouping. By the end of the century principles of formal balance were beginning to be heeded and by the middle of the seventeenth century, in the reign of Louis XIV, conceptions of formalism and symmetry in arrangement had reached their full fruition and pairs of objects were symmetrically disposed where they would produce the most impressive effect.

CHAPTER VIII

INTERIOR DECORATION IN FRANCE DURING THE EIGHTEENTH CENTURY AND THE FIRST DECADES OF THE NINETEENTH

*I*NTRODUCTION.—The story of interior decoration in France during the eighteenth century and the first decades of the nineteenth is not only dramatically fascinating from the merely human point of view, and intensely suggestive of innumerable precedents susceptible of modern application with the most felicitious results, but it is also thoroughly illuminating to the student of *how* and *why* things were done and of the methods of composition and design manipulation. The French were then, as they always had been, such consummate masters in the art of assimilating divers elements and of evolving therefrom, with rare selective insight, new combinations and striking forms of expression that a careful survey of their processes well repays investigation. Indeed, it is indispensable as a part of preparation for dealing successfully with modern requirements in the decorative field.

It will suit our purpose best and conduce to a truer and more coherent estimate of the character of the period if we begin our discussion with the accession of Louis XV in the year 1715. The earlier years of the century really belong to the preceding period, although the influences that blossomed forth in full force upon the demise of the *Grand Monarque,* and the letting down of the restrictions and conventions that had been rigorously upheld during his lifetime, had been at work for a number of years prior to that event. The year

130

1715, so far as any one specific date can signalise a line of demarcation between two styles, which are nearly always necessarily of gradual growth and are wont to overlap each other in their course of progress, marked the final breaking away from the old spirit of ponderosity and oppressive formalism which had been rigidly maintained, in theory at least, with a sense of almost religious obligation, so long as the "Roi Soleil" sate upon the throne. Once the restraining force was removed, reaction set in as swiftly as a bow flies back when the arrow is shot.

One phase of the revulsion materially affected the very character of the houses and influenced not only such building activities as were newly undertaken but set in motion a significant train of alterations and readjustments in the palaces, châteaux and houses that already existed. The people were determined to be rid of the palatial atmosphere of the old *régime* that had grievously weighed upon their spirits and irritated their nerves. "The chilly splendours of the vast and imposing halls, which had persisted in the last century, might be an admirable setting for state pageants, but they no longer answered the wants of society, whose chief requirement was a congenial *milieu* for intimate gatherings, combining cosiness, daintiness, and gaiety. The age of the withdrawing-room and boudoir had arrived." Outwardly, indeed, the architectural character of the newer domestic edifices exhibited little if any noticeable departure from former precedent. "Many of the chief monuments erected at this period might, except for relatively unimportant details, belong equally well to the periods which preceded or followed; the majority of its buildings betray their Louis Quinze character externally, if at all, only by the few features which were carved or otherwise enriched."

It was *inside* that the notable changes took place. People preferred smaller houses, it is true, and built smaller houses, and, in the country, the *petites maisons,* where they could quickly escape from all tedious formalities, were often more regularly occupied than the châteaux to which they belonged, but the people likewise fell to breaking up large apartments into suites of smaller ones—the precedent for this had been set at Versailles—and prepared themselves an environment in which to *live* rather than a setting in which to be *on parade.* And it is with the interiors of such houses and apartments, "devoted to pleasure and social life," that we are here concerned, with their decorations and furnishings to which, under their various guises, we apply the generic term, *"Style Louis Quinze."*

In a broad, general way, when speaking of the great decorative styles, the term *Rococo* is usually regarded as synonymous with the Style Louis Quinze. And for purposes of convenience and the sense of identity that has sprung up, we may let it go at that. In doing so, however, we must make this reservation for the sake of historical accuracy. The early years of the Regency, while the Duke of Orleans held the reins of government, saw the development of a style commonly termed *Régence,* which marked the transition between the "Style Louis Quatorze" and the later full-fledged Rococo. We must also add, and insist that the facts be kept clearly in mind, that the Rococo style, in the larger signification of the term, had really struck root in the latter years of the reign of Louis XIV and that it had run its full course long before the close of the Fifteenth Louis's reign. Furthermore, we must call attention to the fact that the neo-Classic style, with which we are wont to associate the name of Louis Seize when speak-

PLATE 37

RÉGENCE PANELLING IN CARVED OAK, PARCEL GILT
Collection Lelouz
Courtesy of Messrs. L. Alavoine & Co.

PLATE 38

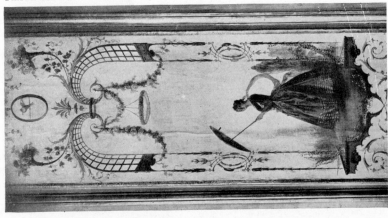

B. PAINTED PANEL BY LANCRET, ROCOCO
Ancien Hôtel de Boullougne, Paris
From "Les Vieux Hôtels de Paris"
Courtesy of William Helburn, Inc.

A. LOUIS XV (ROCOCO) OVERMANTEL MIRROR WITH
PAINTING IN HEAD
Courtesy of Mr. Karl Freund

ing of French decoration, had already been well developed and established for years in popular favour when the last-named Louis ascended the throne.

Rococo, using the term in its more comprehensive sense, was of two kinds, good and bad. It may be likened to the proverbial little girl with the curl. When it was good, it was very, very good, instinct with grace and delicacy and full of a most refreshing, blithesome *naïveté* of conception and a remarkable *finesse* of execution. Altogether, it was a decidedly agreeable and optimistic style to live with and radiated a kind of decorative sunshine. Quite on the other side of the picture, when it was bad, it was excessively horrid. Nothing, in fact, could have been worse, more offensively vulgar, more nauseatingly saccharine, more distorted, more extravagant. Adjectives, indeed, completely fail adequately to describe the thoroughly odious and inconsequently vicious character of the strumpet phase of Rococo decoration.

That Rococo should have run to irresponsible extravagance was, perhaps, not unnatural when we remember the rigid "centralised systematisation" of "life, thought," and of every kind of decorative expression that had previously confined all efforts within strait and prescribed limits. The change was not merely a rebound; it was an out and out rebellion, and that any of its fruits should have been tempered with common sense and artistic judgment is cause for wonder rather than otherwise. That it was so is a tribute and testimony to the innate mental balance and logical attitude of the French people.

There was the utmost diversity of expression in this newly dawned era which may be regarded as a period of free-thinking and anarchy in decorative art, despite the many really fine things it produced. Some one has characterised it as a "hot-house period"; whether this be quite justifiable or not, it was certainly exotic. It was an era of flux and changing ideals. The quest for novelty was the one constant element that seemed dominant. Everything was grist that came to the Rococoist's mill. The subjects that might be used with high approval as inspirations for decorative treatment were drawn indiscriminately from the "country, animal life, the customs of foreign lands," Oriental art and every other conceivable source. There was the utmost freedom in the use of all manner of naturalism. "The subject, indeed, was indifferent, provided it was novel in itself, and that its artistic presentment had *esprit* and invested it with *le bel air*. . . . All known rules of architecture might be set aside with impunity, if the result had but style, piquancy and perfect technique."

When the course of decorative license had run to its utmost limits, it was to be expected that a revulsion of feeling should ensue. And this reaction came in the form of the neo-Classic style. While the decorative forces let loose in the early part of the reign of Louis Fifteenth had "undoubtedly pushed defiance of Classical traditions further than any other period since the Renaissance," they ultimately "reached a climax beyond which no further advance in the same direction was possible," and a "fresh return to the sources" became not only necessary but inevitable. The impartial student of the work of the Rococo age "cannot but recognise that it has never been surpassed for finish, both of design and execution, for sparkling elegance and coquettish playfulness—in a word, for complete adaptation to the life of the age which, with all its faults, had many delightful qualities"; but the impartial student will likewise recognise that it had not in

it the element of permanence. While it was often most
agreeable it was, nevertheless, essentially ephemeral.
It was also essentially restless. And the time had
come when there was a common craving for something
more restful in decorative expression.

By fortunate coincidence, there had gradually
grown up a widespread disposition toward archæological research. Perhaps it may have been partly
due to the skeptical spirit of the age which was unwill-
ing to accept without question the standards and conceptions that had been handed on to it by preceding
ages. At any rate, the fact remained that antiquarian
studies and appreciation, hitherto unparalleled except
in the beginning of the Renaissance period, if indeed
then, exerted a most compelling influence upon the
popular mind. The ruins of the palace of Diocletian
at Spalato had been not only explored and sketched but
accurately measured and drawn to scale by the Brothers
Adam and the results of their labours were in due
course published in several volumes. The ruins of
Herculaneum and Pompeii had been excavated and
most thoroughly studied and the publication of the
results of this work exercised an enormous influence.
Similar undertakings, dependent upon a freshly awakened ardour for antiquarian research, were also pushed
forward elsewhere in Italy, in Greece and in other portions of what had once been the Roman Empire.

The outcome of all this activity was that there soon
followed a consciousness, growing into an overwhelming and general conviction, that the models of ancient
architecture and ancient decoration, and the principles
deduced therefrom, once acclaimed as standards by the
fathers of the Renaissance and their successors, did
not by any means represent *all* the architectural and
decorative wealth of Classic antiquity nor even, neces-

sarily, what was *best*. The full realisation of this larger horizon with its larger liberty of interpretation, along with such rationalistic attacks upon the affectations of Palladianism as that put forth by the Abbé Langier, spelled the doom of Vitruvianism, which quite collapsed. Architects and decorators disregarded the earlier norms that were thus proved to be artificial and arbitrary, and not infallible as they had once been supposed, and went back direct to fresh springs for inspiration.

This new influence was felt not only in France but also in England and all throughout the Continent. In France it assumed a concrete form that we know as the "Style Louis Seize." It was architecturally and decoratively consistent and there was no longer any tolerance shown for that earlier compromise between Palladianism and Rococo, strict architecture and free decoration, an anomalous pairing off that was very like condoning a Saturday night drunk on condition that the Sabbatarian inebriate would remain sober the rest of the time. Along with the renewed ascendancy of straight lines in architecture and decoration, characteristic of the Style Louis Seize, and along with a certain degree of Classic severity, we can see also the addition of many elements of local grace, tempering blithesomeness and restrained naturalism, the latter due in great measure to the influence of Rousseau, which taken all together gave the style its peculiar individuality.

It was the elimination of many of these added graces and amenities and the pushing of certain influences to a logical and somewhat puristic conclusion that resulted in the Directoire Style. The urbanity and mellowness of the old *régime* were now taboo and a kind of archæological mania seemed to have possessed

men's minds and impelled them to find their highest
satisfaction in discerning parallels between their own
ideals and practice and the precedents afforded by a
certain period of Roman public and domestic life. To
such an extent did they carry the infatuation that, not
content with reproducing as nearly as circumstances
would permit the architectural and decorative background of their chosen prototypal Roman period, they
even tried to emulate Roman peculiarities of costume
and domestic usage and, arrayed in tunics and togas,
would sit or recline to eat a meal from a tripod
table, doubtless with more archæological than bodily
satisfaction.

While the Directoire Style was professedly a revolt
and a departure from the Style Louis Seize, it was in
reality a development from it or, at any rate, a development from the same parent stock, pushed to extremes
and a little attenuated and formalised in the process.
In its best manifestation, the Directoire Style was pure
and graceful, but the very rigidity of archæological
interpretation to which its sponsors seem to have been
unalterably committed, would soon have proved its
undoing had it not, ere long, been completely supplanted by the Empire Style. Contemplating the two
together it seems hard to understand how two modes,
drawn as were both Directoire and Empire, from
much the same well-spring of inspiration could have
turned out so different in their final developments.

The determination to make a clean break with all
traditional backgrounds, so far as French history was
concerned, and to give the people a new system of art
and architecture as well as a brand-new political organisation resulted in Napoleonic fiat authorising
Percier and Fontaine to devise an entirely unprecedented system of decoration which they based, indeed,

upon Classic models, but upon that aspect of Classic models most calculated to appeal to aggressive militaristic ideals. Military trophies and symbols, and the emblems of imperial pomp, were freely and preponderantly introduced among the properties of their schemes of decoration along with the more graceful forms that had characterised Roman decorative art in the early imperial period. Their system, though often overloaded with ornament and excessively profuse, was, nevertheless, impressively rich and sometimes displayed considerable grace and charm despite its obvious opulence. In the earlier stages of the Empire Style there were frequently manifestations worthy of sincere commendation. That was, however, before the style became heavy, debased, vulgarised and bombastic to suit the tastes of a body of rich parvenus who had taken the place of the old *noblesse*. This phase of the style merits only condemnation.

In architecture what is known as the Greek Revival parallelled the Empire Style in decoration. Its interpretation was usually stolid, pompous and heavy, but its saving grace was that it was generally simple and fortunately took its direction mainly from an archæological bias of inspiration.

Architectural Background and Methods of Fixed Decoration.—In the preparation of the fixed architectural or interior decorative backgrounds of the Louis Quinze or Rococo style of decoration, using the latter term in the sense previously explained, we find certain general characteristics common to all the phases that come under that comprehensive heading, whether or not we choose to attach to those phases the names *Régence, Watteau, Boucher* or *Rocaille*. These characteristics, which betokened an amazing fluidity of conception and manipulation in all the aforesaid varieties, were the *studied avoidance of everything formal or ponderous;* the neglect, or rather the deliberate defiance, of all strict Classical canons or rules; the elimination of deep shadows (Plates 37 and 39 A), the disuse of straight, especially of horizontally straight, lines and of right angles, and a consuming "delight in caprices and surprises, playful forms and piquant combinations." Everywhere was studied irregularity and complication of *motifs* and the whole system of decoration may be said to have been reduced to a fluid state and, occasionally, to a frenzy of anarchistic riot. After the rigidity of the Louis Quatorze period, everything was undergoing a process of mollification.

The *architectural* foundation upon which the Louis Quinze episodes of *decoration* were grafted was essentially symmetrical in its genius and so it remained. Even during the period of utmost license in decorative practice, the French mind had too sincere a perception of fundamental values and too profound a respect for constructive sanity to make any radical departures from the *structural* principles and usages of the preceding age. Rooms, therefore, still retained their symmetry of form and were well proportioned in respect of their usually symmetrical disposition of doors, windows and other distinctly architectural features.

There was a tendency to accentuate the size of windows, and the window openings, in a great many cases extending all the way to the floor, had square- or arc-shaped heads or else terminated in either round-headed arches or arches very much flattened at the top. It was a common thing for the upper part of the windows to contain some heavy wooden tracery with curved flowing lines or else to be separated from the larger and lower part by an horizontal mullion or transome, and the small casements of the upper portion opened independently of the long casements under them. Door heads, like the tops of windows, were square, arc-shaped, round-arched, or flat-arched.

In some cases, by the manipulation of the interior trim, there was a tendency to bound even door and window openings, especially at their heads, not by lines of geometrical regularity that would indicate their limits as structural features, but by a succession of curves, retaining only the chief vertical lines. Such exaggerations of treatment, however, exaggerations that justified the accusation that the Rococo style was naught but a series of "tormented and broken lines," were to be found rather in extreme cases and were not the rule, as the limits of structural features were ordinarily clearly defined in a reasonable manner. The contours of mouldings and other members of door and window trims, in accordance with the prevailing practice, although frequently ornate and complicated in line, were almost invariably flattened (Plates 41 and 47 A) so that the openings did not assume the aspect of dominant features, as they often had done in preceding periods.

The treatment of walls in the Louis Quinze style was a matter of paramount concern. The Classic orders, which had hitherto played so conspicuous a part in the make-up of the architectural background, were now adjudged quite too formal as a dominant element in decoration and were either left out altogether or else so radically disguised by fantastic treatment that they could scarcely be recognised at all. In the wall scheme for important rooms, pilasters and rectangular architraves yielded place to elaborate framing and bordering of panels.

Panelling, indeed, was the chief resource (Plates 37, 38 B, 42, 43, 44 and 46) by which the momentous item of wall treatment was compassed. Wood was the favourite and most universally satisfactory medium for this purpose and was used both in its natural state and likewise painted or painted and parcel gilt. When the natural wood was employed (Plate 37), it was frequently oak or light-coloured walnut, and its users had the sanity to let it alone and not smear it over with any artificial darkening mixture. Other natural woods than the two just mentioned also occurred.

When paint and gilt played a part in the scheme of decorative foundation, one favourite combination was white and gold, the flat surfaces being painted white and the mouldings and other carved projections gilt. White and gold, however, were by no means preponderantly in vogue. Colours were freely used (Plates 38 B, 40, 41 and 42), either by themselves or in conjunction with gilding. As a rule the colour schemes, as judging from the social character of the times we might fancy they would be, were prevailingly light and gay—light green, citron, tender pink, green blues and blue greens, yellow or buff, light warm greys, fawns or putty tones and occasionally graining. Sometimes deeper tones were used, such as fairly dark blues or greens, sufficiently greyed, and the necessary lightening was supplied by a judicious addition of gilding.

Again, when wood was not used throughout for interior finish, the panels were often executed on canvas and then the canvasses were defined and held in place by wooden mouldings. Besides these *media* of execution, the panelling was sometimes wrought in plaster and then painted and gilt. In some cases, too, while the mouldings were of wood, the elaborate scroll, shell, leaf and other decorations were wrought in compo which, indeed, supplied a better base for gilding than wood, which had first to be gesso-coated before applying the gold leaf.

The panels were large and vertically oblong in their emphasis, extending all the way from a low dado to the cornice (Plates 40, 41, 42, and 44, Fig. 3). The width varied according to the exigencies of the room and the distribution of openings. Some of the panels were very narrow, others were fairly wide (Plates 40, 41 and 42). They were always spaced and balanced with a sense of symmetry despite the tendencies to irregularity elsewhere manifested.

These panels, notwithstanding all their "enrichment and complication," by force of sheer height acquired a value in vertical emphasis equal to that of the erstwhile conspicuous pilasters that had been suppressed. This process of flattening out or completely suppressing the major members of wall projections was consistently carried out in minor details. For one thing, the projections of all mouldings were substantially reduced (Plate 39 A and B), a marked departure from the practice of the Louis Quatorze style. Not only did the contours of all mouldings become appreciably flatter and slimmer, but all other projections likewise were radically modified; cornices (Plate 39 A and B) and pediments that had cast bold and vigorous shadows were replaced by "gentle coves (Plates 40, 41 and 42) and graceful volutes," sculpture in the round or trophies and emblems in high relief yielded precedence to paintings, while massive carven and moulded fruit and foliage swags and drops or similar features of imbricated laurel leaves were cast aside for "dainty wreaths of roses and fluttering ribbons." Everywhere the forces of flattening out and attenuation were simultaneously in operation with the dominant curvilinear force.

Attention has already been called to the general aversion from straight horizontal lines and the tendency to bound spaces "not by geometrical figures, but by a series of curves and to retain only their main vertical lines, while consoles and the pedestals were diversified by gentle swellings and taperings." In accordance with this all-prevalent impetus, the *bottoms* (Plates 40, 41, 42, 43, Figs. 7 and 8; 44, Fig. 3, and 47) as well as the tops of panels were often curved and broken, while "angles and junctions of all sorts were managed by means of scrolls, flourishes and other softening devices." It was quite the common thing for the only horizontally straight lines in a room to be the top of the dado below and the cornice at the top (Plates 40, 42 and 47), and sometimes the latter was encroached upon by flamboyant *motifs* (Plate 41) that climbed from the wall or sprawled over the ceiling. In the more exaggerated phases of the style, even the vertical bounding lines of the panels were not free from occasional curvilinear interference. Ordinarily, however, vertical boundaries of panels and of door and window openings were allowed to retain their customary emphasis modified only by curvilinear treatment at panel tops and bottoms or, perhaps, by small superposed interruptions in the forms of leafage or floral sprays or entwinements (Plate 38 A).

The curvilinear shaping at the tops and bottoms of panels, or above doors and windows, might be symmetrical (Plates 42, 43, Figs. 2, 4, 5 and 6; 44, Figs. 2 and 3, and 47), in such cases usually centring in a shell (Plate 43, Figs. 1 and 4) or some similar *motif*. Again, and this was peculiarly characteristic of the *Rocaille* episode, it might be altogether *asymmetrical,* depending upon adroitly counterposed flexures to convey to the eye a sustaining and satisfying ultimate sense of balance. Here, too, a centring was frequently made by a shell, a cartouche or a mascaron and the general treatment was apt to be somewhat flamboyant in the rapid action of its curves.

Before speaking specifically of the character of the decorative *motifs* customarily employed in Louis Quinze decoration, it seems advisable to say a word about the manner of distribution. In a period of such license and breaking away from all previous canons of restraint, it is not surprising that decorators should have given free rein to their fancy and indulged in the utmost exuberance. It often seemed as though a space left undecorated was abhorrent to them and that every space carried with it an obligation to lavish thereon some kind of ornament. If one may be permitted to paraphrase the advice of the bellicose old Irishman to his son who was about to set out for the Donnybrook Fair: "Mike, wherever you see a head, hit it!" one might say that the motto of the decorator of this epoch was, "Wherever you see a space, decorate it!" Not by any means *all* of the work of this period was thus decorated to excess. Some of the simpler things showed admirable restraint and reticence. The more elaborate creations, however, and especially during the *Rocaille* stage, often laboured under a redundancy of ornament.

One of the most characteristic *motifs* employed— we should not be far amiss in calling it the "trademark" of the *Rocaille* phase of Louis Quinze decoration, just as the scroll composed of interrupted curves had virtually been the trade-mark of Baroque decorative design—was the *shell* (Plate 38 A). It was often shaped very much indeed like a large oyster shell, more elongated than the usual Baroque cockle or escallop shell and much flared at the top with clearly defined

flutings, scallops or frillings of surface and edges.
Along with rockwork, it was one of the stock *motifs* of
the *Rocaille* system and was worked for all its might
and main, being constantly in evidence under a wide
diversity of guises but always recognisable. By cutting out all the body of the shell (Plate 43, Figs. 1
and 4) so that only the outer rim was left they derived
a cartouche form which they sometimes employed for
small mirror frames and for sconces as well as for the
centres of decorative compositions.

Sinuous leaf and vegetable *motifs* (Plate 40), which
lent themselves readily to expression in flamboyant
curves, along with sundry scrolls and flourishes were
likewise everywhere in evidence as were also ribbons,
scrolled or tied in loose bows, wreaths and bunches of
roses and other flowers, divers naturalistic details and
masques.

One important resource of decorative enrichment,
of which the Louis Quinze decorators fully availed
themselves, was the use of chequered, latticed and other
geometrically diapered groundwork (Plate 43, Figs.
4 and 8) to fill in the spaces between the rectilinear lines
of panel heads or sides and the multiplex curving forms
of other bounding lines; to fill in the distance between
curving boundaries; and, finally, as a base upon which
to superpose free groupings of decorative *motifs*. This
device was a direct reflection of Spanish influence, derived by the Spaniards, in turn, from the Moors. The
effect of this closely chequered or latticed diapering,
with its seemingly endless succession of uniform repeats, was, as it always is, to produce a rich *texture*
rather than to convey any conscious impression of
pattern. Furthermore, it served as a medium to blend
and pull together diverse forms into an united composition and helped to modify the sharpness of contrasts

10

that, without some such tempering influence, might
have seemed too incisive.

One evidence of the naturalistic tendency of the
period in decoration is to be seen in the popularity of
pastoral *motifs* (Plates 38 B and 42) of which Watteau,
Fragonard, Lancret and other artists of scarcely less
note were the chief exponents. Besides making use of
the familiar shell, scroll and foliated accessories, they
introduced into their panel paintings dainty, elegant
dames and slim courtly beaux in gay attire, or masquer-
ading as shepherds and shepherdesses, disporting
themselves in the most fanciful pastoral scenes furnished forth with hedges, trees, flowers, fountains, birds
and animals and the additional accompaniments of
grilles, lattices and trellised arbours. Panels of a different tone, but in the same vein of elaborate and refined
execution, were painted by Francois Boucher and his
school who decorated both boudoirs and salons with
voluptuous and erotic scenes from Classic mythology
(Plates 38 A and 41).

All manner of Chinese *motifs* were combined into
genial compositions for panels and other features, and
from these graceful Chinoiseries it was but a step to
the playful singeries or representations of apes and
monkeys in human costume engaged in sundry pranks.
Chinoiseries, singeries, bergeries and other pastoral
scenes were commonly incorporated with and surrounded by freely rendered arabesques, many of which
were even more open and slender in composition than
were Bérain's, and more modern and naturalistic in the
subjects depicted.

To the foregoing stock of properties of the Louis
Quinze decorator we must add the complement of
palms, cartouches, ribbons, amorini, sprigs of "slim
spidery foliage" of nondescript genus, along with a

medley for ceiling adornment consisting of gods and goddesses, blue skies, birds, scattered flowers, butterflies, and rosy clouds inhabited by chubby cherubs.

Mirrors were immensely popular as decorative factors (Plates 38 A, 39 A and B, 40, 41 and 47) and were freely used in panels and incorporated in doors, as well as occupying an important place over mantels. Indeed, they were used to such an extent that, between them and the painted panels, there was little chance for pictures most of which, as a matter of fact, were of distinctly decorative character and were customarily empanelled as overdoor decorations or set into the heads of empanelled mirrors (Plates 38 A, 39 B, 41 and 42).

In not a few rooms, coved niches were provided at appropriate places for the display of sculpture or of carved urns, porcelain vases or other similar items of adornment.

As a natural accompaniment to the many mirrors there were numerous sconces (Plates 39 A and 40) elaborately wrought in chiselled *ormulu,* affixed to small mirrors of cartouche shape, or made of glass and crystal with pendants to catch and reflect the rays of the candles. Chandeliers also (Plates 39 B, 42 and 47), either in *ormulu* or made of glass and crystal, were objects of ingenious design and finished workmanship.

Fireplaces were low in dimension (Plates 39 A and B, 40 and 47) and sometimes wide, with low mantelpieces of wood, marble or stone carved in *motifs* consistent with the rest of the curvilinear decoration. The low mantel shelf terminated the decorative construction of the fireplace; there were no structural "continued chimney-pieces." The front of the chimney jamb above the mantel shelf was graced by a mirror or by panelling and treated in a manner precisely similar to the rest of the walls.

Cornices were low in projection (Plate 39 A), but were frequently coved (Plates 39 B, 40, 41, 42 and 47) and sometimes of considerable width. It was not an uncommon practice to divide the cornice into oblong panels with groups of decoration centred in them thus, in a way, echoing the treatment of the walls. Then again, as previously noted, the cornice decoration occasionally climbed up and encroached upon the ceiling (Plates 39 B, 40 and 41). Ceilings were frescoed or else decorated with a certain amount of relief in plaster which could be coloured or gilt.

While marble-tiled floors might now and then be employed in galleries and a few large apartments, wooden floors were almost universally prevalent and were very commonly parquetted with varicoloured woods and divers patterns.

In contrast with the "Style Louis Quinze," the "Style Louis Seize" was marked architecturally by a "four-square sobriety" and decoratively by a return to classical purity of expression and more restraint in the quantity and distribution of ornament. Both architecture and decoration became perceptibly simpler and more reserved, though not severe. There was no diminution in refinement of design nor in rendering, but there was a readier disposition to acquiesce in the "guidance of antiquity." There was no longer an "architectural tendency pulling in one direction and a decorative tendency pulling in another." Architecture and decoration were again wholly consistent the one with the other and the Style Louis Seize, with reference to both architecture and decoration, was unquestionably a "more completely homogeneous style than any of those which had obtained since Henri II."

For the chief specific characteristics of the Style Louis Seize and items of contrast with the preceding

PLATE 39

A. SALON, HÔTEL DE BRETEUIL, PARIS
STYLE LOUIS XV (SIMPLE ROCOCO)
From "Les Vieux Hôtels de Paris," F. Contet
Courtesy of William Helburn, Inc.

B. SALON, HÔTEL DELISLE-MANSART, PARIS
STYLE LOUIS XV (SIMPLE ROCOCO)

PLATE 40

CHIMNEY-PIECE, HÔTEL DE MATIGNON, PARIS. STYLE LOUIS XV
(EXTREME ROCOCO)
From "Les Vieux Hôtels de Paris," F. Contet
Courtesy of William Helburn, Inc.

PLATE 41

BED CHAMBER, DECORATED BY BOFFRAND, HÔTEL DE SOUBISE, PARIS. EXTREME ROCOCO
From "Les Vieux Hôtels de Paris," F. Contet
Courtesy of William Helburn, Inc.

PLATE 42

APE ROOM, DECORATED BY HUET. HÔTEL DE ROHAN, PARIS. EXTREME ROCOCO

From "Les Vieux Hôtels de Paris," F. Contet

Courtesy of William Helburn, Inc.

style, we may point to the *reassertion of the principles
of symmetry* and of *rectilinear* and *rectangular treatment* (Plates 44, Fig. 1, and 46) ; the general *avoidance*
of *curved forms* with the occasional exception of simple
circles and ellipses which, however, were always kept
subservient to the rectangular environment; the carrying through of straight lines with the least possible in-
terruption; the inclusion of such arched forms as were
used within a rectangular panel or recess (Plates 48 B
and 49) ; the use of undisguised and unrounded angles
(Plate 46) except occasionally in the framing of panels
whose corners were modified by square re-entering
angles, the space thus formed being filled by a rosette
(Plate 46) except occasionally in the framing of panels
cornices, friezes, balustrades and lintels uninterrupted
by cartouches, ornate keyblocks or sculpture.

Rooms were scrupulously symmetrical and well proportioned in their dimensions and in the balanced disposition of windows and doors. Windows commonly
extended all the way to the floor and even those that
did not had low cills. They were almost invariably of
the casement type with wooden muntins, stiles and rails
and were frequently divided vertically by a mullion and
horizontally by a transome, the upper section, when
such divisions were made, being smaller than the lower,
and, of course, opening independently. Window and
door heads were commonly rectangular (Plates 47 A
and B and 48 A), or, when round-arched (Plate 48 B),
straight lines and rectangular elements were so disposed as to maintain the rectilinear predominance.

Trims for doors and windows were of low projection
and refined contour (Plates 47 B and 48). They were
also of far more restrained design and of rectilinear
emphasis. Wherever any curved features were retained in door heads (Plate 45, Fig. 1) or in overdoor

treatment, they were always subordinated to the rectilinear note in composition as in all similar instances
to which attention has already been called. Classic
pilasters often framed door and window openings in
the larger and more important rooms, while in smaller
rooms, where it was desirable to keep the scale
down and to flatten projections, the pilasters were
not seldom replaced by thin strips (Plate 44, Fig. 1).
All mouldings and projections were derived from
Classic precedents and maintained the aspect of purity
and severe restraint consistent with their source of
inspiration.

Walls were both panelled (Plates 46, 47 B, 48 and
49) and plain of surface. Panelled walls were executed
in wood, either in its natural finish or painted, the latter being the more usual. They were also executed in
plaster with mouldings of plaster or compo or of wood
applied to the plaster background. Small ornaments
of more or less intricate character in themselves were
sometimes moulded in *carton pierre* or in compo and
then applied.

The plain walls might be covered with wall-paper
or with fabrics strained over their surface. For this
purpose brocades, silks, reps, poplins, printed linens,
chintzes and other appropriate fabrics were employed.
Wall-paper, up to the latter part of the century, was
printed with hand-blocks upon sheets about three feet
long by a little more than a foot wide. About 1790 it
began to be made in rolls.

It was customary to divide the walls horizontally
by a dado about two and three-quarters feet to three
feet high (Plates 46, 47 B, 48 and 49). This relieved
what might otherwise sometimes have seemed too
strong an emphasis of verticality, especially in the case
of panelled walls where a number of the panels were

PLATE 43

CHARACTERISTIC ROCOCO DECORATIVE *MOTIFS* FROM PANELLING

1. Rococo Pierced Shell *Motif.* 2, 3, 5 and 6. Panel Head Details. 4 and 8. Sections of Characteristically Diapered Ground. 7. Section of *Motif* from Panel Base

PLATE 44

CHARACTERISTIC ROCOCO AND NEO-CLASSIC PANEL *MOTIFS*

1. Louis XVI (Neo-Classic) Style. 2. Restrained Louis XV. Rococo Transition to Neo-Classic. 3. Restrained Louis XV. Rococo

PLATE 45

CHARACTERISTIC NEO–CLASSIC PANELLING *MOTIFS*
1. Full Section Louis XVI Cupboard Panelling. 2. Section of Overmantel Detail. 3. Louis XVI
Panel Corner Detail

PLATE 46

BOUDOIR, HÔTEL DE LA FAYETTE, PARIS. STYLE LOUIS XVI
From "Les Vieux de Hôtels de Paris," F. Contet
Courtesy of William Helburn, Inc.

tall and narrow. It likewise added an architectural
note to the composition. Niches for sculpture, for
urns and for large porcelain vases were now and then
introduced into the walls of large rooms where such
features of decoration were becoming.

Panels were large and vertically oblong and varied
in width. One very common treatment was to alternate
broad and narrow panels (Plate 47 B), and this alternation of panel widths, corresponding with the widths
above, was often continued in the dado or immediately
below the chair rail. The panels were regular in shape
with straight sides, tops and bottoms, and all ornament was strictly confined within the limits imposed
by the frames of moulding. Furthermore, the panels
were either entirely rectangular or else relieved at the
corners by square re-entrant angles, as previously
mentioned, rosettes or some similar small device being introduced to fill out the vacancy thus created.

Colour was quite as important a factor in Louis
Seize interiors as it had been in those of the preceding
mode, although the schemes were somewhat differently
managed. The prevailing colours were cool and generally receding in character and soft in tone. White
and gold figured to some extent, but more characteristic of the spirit of the period were silver rose, pearly
grey, tender blues and pale greens and putty colour.
The colours just mentioned, of course, were chiefly
employed for backgrounds and served as foils for the
decorations subsequently painted thereon and the other
items entering into the furnishing schemes.

During the preceding epoch mirrors had proved too
valuable a decorative accessory to be dispensed with
and they continued in high favour for the spaces over
mantels and likewise for insertion in panels (Plates
46 and 48) at other appropriate positions in rooms,

although, in this latter capacity, they were not, perhaps, utilised to such an extent as they had been during the Louis Quinze period. Decorative landscapes (Plates 46 and 47 B) and other decorative subjects on large canvasses were to a certain degree employed as panel embellishments, but the favourite devices for ornamentation were arabesques, classical subjects introduced in the form of medallions or tablets, groupings of trophies or attributes, enriched or decorative bands, and floral compositions in the shape of pendants, swags, garlands, interlaced wreathings and borders (Plates 47 B, 48 and 49). The disposition of all ornament was well-ordered and logical and the compositions were always confined within geometrically regular boundaries.

Decorative paintings that filled whole panels were chiefly of two sorts, landscapes and architectural subjects in the eighteenth century Italian manner, which were also largely employed at the same time in England under the Adam influence, or else paintings apotheosising rustic life, these latter inspired by the influence of Jean Jacques Rousseau. In some cases, whole panels, usually of small dimension, were filled with classic subjects executed in monochrome.

It was more customary, however, to use the classic figure *motifs* in the smaller form of medallions, plaques and tablets, wrought in the fashion of cameos, which made integral parts of arabesque compositions, or else executed as low reliefs on plaster walls. Arabesques were commonly of the Pompeiian type or patterned after those of the Vatican Loggie. They were quite as delicate in execution and as full of imagination as were those of the preceding period, but more restrained and occasionally less vigorous, and they were decidedly lighter in scale than those of the Louis

PLATE 47

A. SALON, HÔTEL GOUFFIER DE THOIX, PARIS. STYLE LOUIS XV (ROCOCO)
From "Les Vieux Hôtels de Paris." F. Contet
Courtesy of William Helburn, Inc.

B. SALON, HÔTEL BAUDART DE ST. JAMES, PARIS. STYLE LOUIS XVI
From "Les Vieux Hôtels de Paris," F. Contet
Courtesy of William Helburn, Inc.

PLATE 48

A. SALON, HÔTEL DU CHÂTELET, PARIS. STYLE LOUIS XVI
From "Les Vieux Hôtels de Paris," F. Contet
Courtesy of William Helburn, Inc.

B. SALON, HÔTEL DU CHÂTELET, PARIS. STYLE LOUIS XVI
From "Les Vieux Hôtels de Paris," F. Contet
Courtesy of William Helburn, Inc.

PLATE 49

SALON, HÔTEL DE LA FAYETTE, PARIS. STYLE LOUIS XVI (PART OF FURNITURE LOUIS XV)
From "Les Vieux Hôtels de Paris," F. Contet
Courtesy of William Helburn, Inc.

Treize or Louis Quatorze styles. The groupings of
trophies or attributes included a diversity of subjects,
but there seems to have been a special predilection for
musical emblems, rustic *motifs,* such as wheat sheaves,
bundles and baskets of vegetables or fruits (Plate
48 A), agricultural or horticulural hand implements,
hay-makers' hats and beehives, or distinctly "sentimental emblems, such as burning torches, quivers,
pierced hearts, and billing doves." The floral and foliated treatments occurred as pendants falling nearly
the full length of a panel, as swags and garlands; as
pairs of light and long sprays of such small-leaved
plants as myrtle or ivy or jasmine, "interlaced to form
a series of vesica shapes, or else with a series of tassel-
like knots of foliage or bell-flowers issuing one from
the other"; or as loose bands of bordering. The flowers
and blossoms themselves—roses, marigolds, daisies,
anemones, forget-me-nots, bell flowers, and many more
—were almost invariably small in size and dainty in
execution.

Besides the *motifs* and classes of *motifs* just enumerated, ribbons played an important part in much of
the painted and modelled decoration of the period and
were closely associated with flowers and foliage. They
were generally closely pleated throughout their
length and, as well as appearing in bow knots and
wreaths, were used in the foliage banding of panels
or for spiral coilings or intertwinings round staves or
mouldings. Swags and drops (Plate 45, Fig. 1) of imbricated leafage of bay, olive and myrtle appeared in
carved, moulded and painted expression. Drapery festoons sometimes took the place of foliated and floral
swags. Among the purely naturalistic items must also
be mentioned birds, insects, and single knots of fruit,
foliage and flowers. Diapers or chequerings were

retained for occasional background enrichment. The honeysuckle pattern was much in evidence as were also urns and vases, successions of Vitruvian scrolls in the "wave" *motif*—"postes," as the French call them— many kinds of *guilloche* (Plate 45, Fig. 1) or meander, pateræ, rosettes and sundry other small classic architectural *motifs*, besides the usual stock complement of tripods, sphinxes and lyres. In the depiction of human figures, classic apparel rather than modern was to be seen.

Sconces, which were extensively employed, were of brass, of carved and gilt wood, of compo painted and gilt, and of crystal. In design, rectilinear feeling was dominant and in their general purity of *motif* and restraint of treatment they fully conformed to the prevailing spirit of the style. The same observations apply to chandeliers anent which it is merely necessary to add that crystal was peculiarly in favour owing to brilliance and the manifold reflections.

Fireplaces remained low (Plates 46, 48 and 49) and there were no "continued chimney-pieces," the overmantel space (Plate 45, Fig. 2) being customarily filled by a large mirror (Plates 46, 48 and 49). If the ceiling was very high, a decorative panel might be included in the space between the head of the mirror and the cornice. Mantel shelves were low and, in the design and structure of the whole mantel composition, right angles, straight lines and parallel sides took the place of the flowing curves that had previously been in vogue. The depth and breadth of the fireplace itself were somewhat decreased by placing decorative metal side and back plates within the wood or marble trim. Mantels were made of carved and painted wood, of carved stone, or of carved and sometimes inlaid marble. The frieze beneath the shelf was supported on scrolled consoles or brackets or else upon *termes* or term-like columns.

Ceilings were much less frequently coved than formerly and were quite commonly flat, an occasional exception being made for flat elliptical vaulting. Unbroken cornices with strong horizontal accent mark (Plates 46, 47 B, 48 and 49) the boundary between walls and ceiling and are distinctly architectural in the character of their members. Not a few of the ceilings were quite plain, while others were enriched with formal plaster mouldings, bands of imbricated foliage and other devices that conformed with the generally classic architectural tone of composition. The mouldings and foliated bands often divided the ceiling into symmetrically panelled spaces. These plaster decorations, standing forth in relief, were frequently coloured and parcel gilt. In the more elaborate ceilings, the flat surfaces were not seldom frescoed or else embellished with classic *motifs* in low relief which were intensified with subdued colour. The frieze of the cornice might be filled with *motifs* of purely architectural derivation or else with swags, festoons, wreaths and other items of semi-architectural or of conventionalised naturalistic origin. These latter might be in moulded relief and coloured or gilt or they might be wholly painted on a flat surface.

Floors were usually of wood and it was customary to enhance the entire decorative *ensemble* of the room by introducing geometrical patterns parquetted (Plate 49) in several woods of different contrasting colours. Marble and marble-tiled floors were also occasionally used in the larger and more formal rooms.

The Directoire mode embodied an ideal altogether different from that which had actuated the architectural and decorative practice of the Louis Seize period.

In Louis Seize manifestations, French individuality and the fecund spirit of the time, although deriving the major part of their inspiration from classic antiquity and incorporating pure classic forms into current composition, nevertheless added thereto an abundant body of graceful and often playful amenities of detail of modern and local devising. Adaptations, likewise, were freely made, but always in a spirit consistent and harmonious with the underlying classic ideals. These additions and adaptations were responsible for the piquancy and blithesome vitality of the "Style Louis Seize."

The Directoire mode was a deliberate and intentional piece (Plate 50) of decorative archæology. From the classic body it remorselessly sheared off all the accretions of blithesome grace and vivifying invention which the Louis Seize designers and craftsmen had imparted to their handiwork and confined itself to a rigidlly literal reproduction of antique practice. It was Louis Seize stripped naked and reduced to the lowest terms. Nay more, whenever opportunity permitted, not satisfied with meticulous adherence to the *spirit* of a long dead and gone past, its interpreters strove with all their might and main to *reproduce* "*particular monuments* or as large portions of them as could by any possible means be made to accord with modern requirements." "Thus the letter took precedence over the spirit with the usual unsatifactory results and, while the details and composition of antiquity were more accurately copied, they were used to less purpose." Such forms of ornament as were retained in the new system had the specific sanction of exact historic prototypes. The process of elimination and restraint produced a fashion in many respects altogether admirable.

The Directoire style at its best excels in chaste simplicity and grace and possesses a very distinct charm worthy of sincere emulation (Plate 51). The weak point about it all, and the feature open to unfavourable criticism, was the narrow conception of its originators and fautors, a conception that absolutely limited it within the straitest bounds, stifled imagination, arrested legitimate growth and forbade development, a conception, indeed, that effectually suppressed real creative instinct and deprived it of the vitality necessary to endurance and perpetuation, a conception, in short, that embalmed the style and insisted upon putting it on exhibition instead of using it.

It was well enough for the people of the time, if it pleased their fancy, to conceive that "the ancient republics enjoyed a *régime* of pure democracy and individual liberty, and that their citizens were models of all the austere and simple virtues"; it was well enough, too, for them to light their rooms with Pompeian candelabra, to place Etruscan vases on their chimney-pieces, and "to breakfast at tripods, seated on curule chairs," but to insist upon these domestic equipments *and these only,* to the exclusion of all else, was an attitude that did not conduce to wholesome growth and a logical interpretation of precedents to meet the living needs of the day. In other words, the ultra purist promoters and adherents of the Directoire style seem to have esteemed its real elegance and graceful beauty less than its symbolism of a social condition which, to them, it seemed to embody. They made it an empty simulacrum of their political aspirations. They shut their eyes to its real value and meaning as an expression of art and reduced it to the level of a fad. Under the circumstances, it is not to be wondered at that it was soon strangled and obliged to give way before the more robustly insistent Empire mode which was shortly to follow it.

It goes without saying that the rooms were entirely symmetrical in their dimensions and regular in the disposition of their openings when there was everywhere such zeal for exact archaeology. Window and door trims were much simplified and were often bereft of their former architectural features. Indeed, the openings for doors frequently had no architraves, columns nor pilasters, and when columns or pilasters were used, they had no bases. There was a mere apology for capitals, and pillars very often carried only lintels and not entablatures. Windows were divided into fewer and larger panes and the panes were set in narrower muntins. In some cases windows had semicircular, instead of square heads, and also a few window openings were semicircular or lunette shaped. The panels of doors were shallower and the surrounding mouldings flatter. In shape the panels were horizontally rectangular and of fairly small size, or else of lozenge shape and large. The taste for lozenge-shaped panels seems to have been akin to the fancy for intersecting diagonals wherever they could be introduced in balconies or lattices.

The time-honoured custom of panelling walls was in many cases represented by painting on a flat plaster ground (Plate 51), the decorating being done in the Pompeian style, long, narrow panels alternating with broader divisions. Again, panels or divisions approximating panels would be filled with strained fabric— the *toile de Jouy* linen with its classic *motifs,* elongated octagons, ovals, circles, cameo designs and lyres, all connected by a series of arabesques, or else a linen printed in some restrained and small-sized Chinese *motif*. An even more characteristic treatment was to

PLATE 50

DINING ROOM, HÔTEL CHANAC DE POMPADOUR, PARIS
DIRECTOIRE INFLUENCE MERGING INTO EMPIRE
From "Les Vieux Hôtels de Paris," F. Contet
Courtesy of William Helburn, Inc.

PLATE 51

A. SALON, HÔTEL DE GRAMMONT, PARIS. STYLE LOUIS XVI—DIRECTOIRE
FURNITURE EMPIRE
From "Les Vieux de Hôtels de Paris," F. Contet
Courtesy of William Helburn, Inc.

B. SALON, HÔTEL DE MAILLY, PARIS. STYLE EMPIRE
From "Les Vieux Hôtels de Paris," F. Contet
Courtesy of William Helburn, Inc.

apply paper in panel forms, using for this purpose the hand-blocked designs of classic subjects in large size, done in monochrome from cartoons prepared by David. These were exceedingly beautiful and dignified and within the past few years the present owners of the blocks have again begun to make impressions from them, which are not at all prohibitive in price. Then, again, plain walls were often covered with simple paper of small design or with landscape paper in monochrome or in subdued tones. When walls had a plain papered or painted surface it was not at all unusual to introduce a deep frieze below the cornice and to dispense, on the other hand, with the dado, there being nothing but a low washboard at the base of the walls.

Mantels of marble, stone or wood, were low and severe in line (Plate 50); there was a straight lintel, and the shelf was supported on simple round columns, on elongated scroll brackets or upon caryatid figures (Plate 51). There was no set overmantel decoration, but a large mirror or painting usually occupied the space.

Ceilings were flat, separated from the wall by a restrained cornice, and they usually carried some moulded geometrical or severely classical plaster decoration around the edges and, perhaps, in the centre; or else the ceilings were concaved to a flattened arc or formed into a barrel vault. These latter ceilings might be frescoed, or, when the arc was flat enough to make the treatment effective, they might be embellished with plasterwork squares, octagons, circles and hexagons enclosing classic figures, the whole scheme being wrought in very flat relief. Floors were of marble tiling or of wood, in the latter case frequently parquetted in geometrical devices.

The key to the genius of the fully developed Empire

style is found in two factors, one political, the other social. The first was the emphasis intentionally laid upon every element that savoured of militaristic pomp and imperial display; the second was the ascendancy of a ruling class composed in the main of *parvenus,* who, " after their kind, liked pretentious display, and were not restrained, as the old aristocracy had been, by hereditary culture and a mode of life which amounted to a continual training in elegance and good taste," a condition that resulted in a " coarsening in tone of the work carried out for them."

The better examples of the Empire style were of two sorts, the elaborate kind that was executed with punctilious regard for a certain type of classic precedent and was both inspired by ideals of the utmost magnificence and supplied with means to realise the ideals with thorough elegance; and, on the other hand, the simpler sort of Empire work that exhibited a decorous reticence in the use of the current *motif* and materials. The less desirable examples, which unfortunately predominated numerically, were characterised by thorough-going ostentation and bombast.

Symmetry was one of the prime requirements and all openings were regularly disposed. Window and door openings were usually square-headed or round-arched. Trims were broad and of flat profile. Doorheads had straight, flat lintels, sometimes in the form of a very much simplified cornice supported on modillion brackets. Door and shutter panels were large, rectangular and flat, with flat moulding profiles.

Walls were almost invariably plain. The more elegant walls were covered with strained fabrics or frescoed; the simpler walls were painted or papered. The dado dropped out of fashion and the frieze became general.

Fireplaces were low and without fixed chimney-piece decoration, and the space between mantel shelf and ceiling was usually occupied by a mirror of corresponding breadth. A straight lintel, often without any decoration, topped the fireplace opening and the mantel shelf was supported by plain round columns or by caryatid figures.

The high ceilings were flat, the cornices were modest, and the moulded plaster ornament around the edges and in the centre was in geometrical or heavy classic *motifs*. Floors were of wood, plain or parquetted, and, in halls and some of the more sumptuous rooms, of marble tiles.

Furniture and Decorations.—Both wall and seating furniture, at the beginning of the reign of Louis XV, was more abundant and varied than had been the case during the preceding reign. It was a period of polished manners and luxurious habits, and once the restraint of Louis XIV formality was removed and the door opened to greater freedom of social habits, mobiliary art was quick to reflect the change in the increased number of intimate, domestic and luxurious forms introduced.

Louis Quinze furniture faithfully mirrored the dominant traits of contemporary fixed decoration as noted earlier in this chapter. The curving line was supreme. Nearly all furniture dimensions were smaller and lighter in line, a change indicative of the abandonment of pompous, stately forms in favour of greater convenience and bodily comfort.

While all the usual types of bedsteads, cupboards, or armoires, tables and seating furniture were fully in use, there was an appreciable increase in the number of forms and refinements introduced in writing furniture and in console cabinets or commodes. These latter

11

were used upon every conceivable occasion and in every conceivable place. Besides these, there were contrived numerous small stands, tables and cupboards to meet specialised demands.

While walnut was the staple wood, all sorts of rare and highly coloured woods were freely employed for veneer, inlay and marqueterie. Much of the furniture, also, was painted, painted and parcel gilt, or lacquered. The colours used were generally light. When it was possible to introduce panels painted with arabesques, pastorals, singeries or Chinoiseries, it was done. To add to the mobiliary grace and elaboration, *ormulu* mounts were lavishly employed on cabinet-work.

With the neo-Classic period, returned the dominance of rectilinear emphasis in furniture. The cabriole leg made place for the straight fluted and tapered leg; the *bombé*-fronted console cabinet with its swelling, undulating contours, yielded to a successor whose right-angled restraint of line was in sharp contrast. The kinds of articles and the amount of furniture used did not appreciably change; the difference was wholly in contours and *motifs* of decoration. Light colours in painted, painted and parcel gilt, or lacquered furniture continued in favour, as did also the great variety of multicoloured woods for veneer, inlay and marqueterie. Likewise continued the fashion of numerous metal mounts for cabinet-work, the design, however, being altered to suit the revived classical spirit.

Directoire movable furniture, like Directoire fixed decoration, was virtually a reduction of the corresponding Louis Seize elements to their lowest terms. The Empire style, while retaining a good deal of rectilinear severity, nevertheless, occasionally flourished out into flamboyant and grandiose contours, especially where seating furniture, bedsteads and, to some extent, tables, were concerned. During the Empire phase of the neo-Classic style, while painting and parcel-gilding of furniture continued to a limited degree, the favourite material was mahogany, which made an admirable foil for the elaborate filigree and embossed ornamental *appliqué* which enjoyed such vogue. Empire contours were almost invariably substantial and robust, and, at times, became even gross and clumsy.

Other Decorative Accessories and Movable Decorations.—During the dominance of the Rococo style, tapestries of the old pattern continued in use to some extent where large, formal rooms or galleries left a place for them. Other accessories, however, had usurped most of their function. Hangings at doors and windows were made of silks, taffetas, brocades, damasks, velvets and printed linens, light colours and dainty patterns being most in favour. Door and window heads were very commonly adorned with shaped valances or loopings, and the hangings were frequently draped back. Pictures for the walls of many of the rooms were not at a premium (*v.* paragraph on the use of mirrors). Porcelains, both Oriental and of Western fabrication, were in great demand, and, along with pieces of bronze or marble sculpture, were introduced with great frequency. Many of the Oriental porcelains, such, for instance, as some of the finer Chinese ginger jars, were carefully set with ornate *ormolu* mounts.

Chandeliers of crystal, brass, or of *ormolu*, depended from the centres of ceilings in the more elegant and important rooms. Sconces of chiselled *ormolu,* in graceful, flowing designs, were hung in symmetrical positions on the panelled walls. Candelabra were designed to accord with them.

During the period of neo-Classic influence, while

the love for the old tapestries never quite died out, there was a perceptible turning toward the newer Aubusson tapestries of paler, lighter hue and more blithesome pattern for such wall surfaces as required a large hanging. Door and window hangings were of practically the same fabrics as noted for the Rococo period. Light colours and dainty patterns also remained in favour, with the addition of a well-defined vogue for stripes. At door and window heads there were both straight and shaped valances, and likewise looped draping or else shirred ray-like folds centring in a button, the two latter treatments being suitable for round-arched windows. Valance mouldings or boxes were likewise in use and added a distinct note to the composition. In accordance with the prevalent rectilinear emphasis, door and window hangings generally fell in straight folds.

Pictures regained the position from which they had been temporarily ousted during the most mirror-loving days of the Rococo period. The disposition of rooms was not less symmetrical or ordered nor was the extensive use of mirrors discontinued, but it became the fashion either to hang pictures within panels that accorded with their dimensions or to remove them from their frames and empanel them. Porcelains and other objects of *vertu*, whether Oriental or Occidental, found abundant appreciation and were freely employed. In addition to the taste for Oriental forms and European fashions of recent date in ceramics, there was keen interest in revived classic forms in pottery and porcelain. At the same time, with the re-awakened classic sense, bronze and marble sculpture enjoyed increased favour. What was said of lighting appliances for the foregoing period applies with equal force for the neo-

Classic, the only significant difference being the substitution of Classic for the Rococo design.

Tapestries in the Empire period were distinctly out of place. They were tolerated where they had to be retained, but their presence was not sought as a factor in decorative schemes. Hangings of silk, satin, brocade or velvet were voluminous and impressive by their ample folds and by their shaped valances and cornice mouldings or by their intricate loopings at window heads. Pictures had more leeway in decorative practice, as many of the wall surfaces were unbroken by panel boundaries. Porcelains and sculpture were popular in their imposing and heroic dimensions, and where they aided vigorous contrasts of strong colour. To chandeliers, sconces and candelabra, many of which were of exceedingly beautiful design and workmanship, in glass, marble, crystal, brass, bronze and *ormolu,* must be added the lamps for mantel garniture, usually of bronze, with etched or cut-glass globes and pendent prisms. The fire iron and hearth accessories of the period also aided the *ensemble* with their polished brass fittings.

Materials and Colour.—The fabrics and other materials in use at the successive periods have already been more or less fully noted. To what has been said it is only necessary to add that during the Rococo and neo-Classic periods a great use was made of Aubusson tapestry for furniture covers and that in the Empire period a great deal of heavy brocade, brocatelle, damask, velvet and rep was used not only for hangings but also for wall coverings, likewise that haircloth, figured and plain, began to occupy an appreciable space in upholstery calculations. Throughout both the Louis Quinze and Louis Seize styles there was a marked preference for cheerful and light colourings, whether in woodwork, furniture or fabrics. At the same time, delicacy of pattern was a *sine qua non.* These characteristics were well exemplified in the Aubusson and Savonnerie rugs and carpets so much used at this date. During the Directoire episode, while the colouring occasionally became more vigorous in emulation of Pompeian precedent, the design was so restrained and shapely that there was no oppressive impression of heaviness. With the full blossoming of the Empire style, the whole colour preference changed. Strong and heavy reds, greens, purples, yellows and other vigorous hues in raw and often combative tones came into high favour and the patterns reflected the militaristic and imperial tone observable in all other decoration.

Arrangement.—Throughout the Rococo and neo-Classic periods a balanced, orderly and symmetrical disposition of furnishings and decorations was considered indispensable to a well-appointed interior. The modes might change, but the conception of order remained unaltered.

CHAPTER IX

NINETEENTH CENTURY EPISODES AND AFTER

INTRODUCTION. — Howsoever wonderful the nineteenth century may have been as an era of phenomenal material progress and of unprecedented mechanical, engineering and scientific achievement, it was distinctly *not* a period kindly to architecture or to any of the allied arts, and the art of interior decoration fared worse, if such a thing were possible, than any of the others. After about 1830 architecture, furniture design and the practice of decorative furnishing slumped into a dismal vale of barrenness or of revolting vulgarities and simpering inanities; a deplorable state with almost no bright spots at all to relieve the artificiality, dreariness and stupidity. From the day of the so-called "carpenters' Classic" style in domestic architecture and the synchronous gobby, clumsy and tumid mahogany-veneered travesties upon the Empire style in furniture, both of which spread over the United States about the date above mentioned, there was a dreary procession of one abnormality after another until near the very end of the century—in architecture, the Gothic revival with its wooden crenellations painted and sanded to simulate stone, and jig-saw tracery and fretwork, the mansard roof episode with its attendant bastard Rococo enormities of decorative detail, the still more atrocious whimsicalities of the Centennial fashion with bird-box masses and details that were a most unhappy medley derived from Gothic tracery, Moorish fretwork and Hamburg edging, and next following this nightmare the aberrations of the "dreadful 80's"; in furniture, the rosewood fantasticalities, the black walnut perversions when designers so frequently adapted and parodied the least inspired eighteenth century Italian and Spanish precedents—an exhibition not of ignorance but of abysmal bad taste—the Eastlake trivialities, the golden oak brutalities of unhappy memory and still more unhappy survivals; and, to complete the tale of iniquities, the shocking "art nouveau" demonstrations of what an utterly unbalanced and depraved, and we might add starved, imagination could descend to. Even in the last decade of the nineteenth century and after the beginning of the twentieth, when the invitable but long delayed reaction against all the preceding abominations had set in and the trend towards reasonable taste and sane furnishing had gained appreciable impetus, occasional discouraging reversions to mobiliary imbecility were to be noted and, along with them, reversions to decorative imbecility as well. Witness the extravagances and faddish, inane gaucheries perpetrated under the inspiration of Viennese influence.

Bad as things were in America, conditions were little if any better in England or on the Continent. As a fit accompaniment to the ill-shapen furniture, the acme of decorative effort in Great Britain seems to have been reached in a very orgy of kakochromous needlework in Berlin wool and a dolorous achievement of dexterity in decalcomania plastering, to be followed slightly later by a succession of equally unedifying performances. Like absurdities made their appearance locally elsewhere. And in all this mad age, which seems to have run riot in a delirium of delight over the fancied possibility of creating art by purely mechanical processes, there was a drab, unmitigated monotony of decorative horrors relieved only by such infrequent and sporadic episodes as the Biedermeier period in Bavaria or some of the better efforts of William Morris and his contemporaries in England. One of the most deplorable and pathetic features of the period was the universal self-satisfaction and the universal striving to attain the smug and genteel—*verbum horribile!*—result. There was no lack of mental capacity among decorators and designers—would that there had been! The outcome might have been less appallingly hideous, but the mental capacity was prostituted to the pursuit of copious and banal activity wholly devoid of imagination and of worthy ideals. The minds of those who should have created worthy things were grovelling in a moil of the grossest mechanical materialism.

Architectural Background and Methods of Fixed Decoration.—During the period of "carpenters' Classic" ascendancy there is little that can be said, in a positive way, of the architectural background. Its qualities were chiefly negative. Apart from the rectangular door and window openings with their rectangularly detailed and perfunctory trims and rectangularly detailed, perfunctory and flat fireplace surrounds and mantels to match, there was little that could be dignified by the name of interior architecture. The best that can be said of these items of equipment is that they were simple. The rooms were apt to be lofty and of fairly good proportions and the door and window openings were generous; so that, despite the lack of any real spirit of inspiration, there was a certain amount of dignity because there was no great pretense. To be sure, it was the dignity of a large box, an altogether passive and negative dignity. The soul of the room was often throttled by blocking up the fireplace and substituting an hot-air register to serve in lieu of the living fire. The walls were merely expanses of white plaster above an insignificant baseboard and the cornices, while respectable, were neither impressive nor of any positive decorative value.

Succeeding this period of "carpenters' Classic" dominance, when the woodwork was customarily painted an unobtrusive white or cream and the walls were either painted or else papered in banal or even worse than banal taste, came an era of the same barren walls which offered an expansive opportunity for the display of atrociously hideous wall-paper, soulless registers set beneath vulgarly proportioned marble mantels, and pompous, tumid, ill-detailed woodwork executed either in expensive walnut or else fashioned from some humbler wood and painted white or dirty chocolate brown or grained. The finishing touch to this delectable interior would be a grotesque and pretentious chandelier dropping out of a no less grotesque and pretentious cast plaster centre-piece affixed to the middle of the ceiling. At this same time we often find doors and windows with heads either semicircular or else showing the segment of an arc, supposedly conveying a bit of distinction, and, when affluent vulgarity was minded to splurge in elaboration of woodwork, there were sometimes added borders of heavy machine-carved flowers, thick rope mouldings and heavy gadrooned edges, borrowed unintelligently from eighteenth century Italian models of not the best type. City houses of the brown-stone-front vintage supply plentiful examples of these depressing items.

The next phase of ugliness was the Centennial episode with nothing new or better to contribute to the architectural background and only a variation in the matter of fretted gingerbread woodwork more plenti-

fully diffused, besides the supplementary horror of
so-called frescoes consisting of awkward designs
printed on paper and pasted on ceilings. An Eastlake
spirit also manifested itself in the woodwork. Next
came the dreary, ponderous and stupid period of the
80's with its attendant monstrosities of wainscot, grotesque galleried and fussy mantel-pieces and overmantels with mirrors; stair rails and grilles with multi-
tudinous spool and globular turnings; panels and fireplace hoods with muscular griffins and caryatides and
a maze of foliations and grisly masques derived from
clumsy mediæval German *motifs,* all substantially
wrought in golden oak or, perhaps, in red-stained mahogany. A frequent *piéce de résistance* of fixed decoration at this time was a terrifying composition in
"stained" glass of virulent colouring or else a bewildering maelstrom of much be-leaded fragments of thick
white glass, set in unusual shaped windows on stair
landings or above sideboards. Almost synchronous
with this hectic era was the "Art Nouveau" craze with
its attenuations, its contortions and its misshapen sinu-
osities that closely resemble hanks of molasses toffy
being pulled at a candy frolic.

From all this moil of aberrations there was bound
to be a revulsion of feeling and a recrudescence of sanity; the human mind had done its worst and the pendulum was due to swing back to better things. The day
of better things had dawned, there were searchings
among the saner precedents of the past and considerable progress had been achieved when there arose a
brief reversion to anarchy in the extravagant gaucheries of the ultra-Viennese school, an isolated ebullition,
however, which endured in vigour for only a brief season and did not serve to stay or seriously hinder the

course of decorative progress to which we have since held.

Furniture and Decoration.—The furniture properly cognate to the "carpenters' Classic" phase, in the matter of architectural background, was of the swollen and clumsy late American Empire type, which was usually of solid mahogany or else veneered with crotch wood over the tumid proportions. There is so much of it still extant, and unfortunately some of it is being extensively reproduced and palmed off on the unenlightened in out of the way regions, that it is unnecessary to describe it in detail. This mobiliary type was closely followed by the rosewood furniture with much meaningless sinuosity of members and profuse carving of details. Such pieces as *étagères* or "what-nots" flourished in polite drawing-rooms as did also marble-topped tables, oftentimes surmounted with coloured wax flowers under glass domes as becoming central features of ornament. The rosewood period gave place in due season to the period of black walnut, a time in which mobiliary design made no improvement and only succeeded in debauching sundry eighteenth century Spanish and Italian *motifs* and making them infinitely worse than they were originally. Upon the heels of black walnut came the procession of golden oak with its tedious ponderosity and revival of loutish German mediæval details, there being but a brief episode of Eastlake creations in walnut before the toffy-coloured tyranny became universal. After the chief vogue of golden oak, with its monstrous sideboards and ungainly tables, a medley of styles began to crop up. Then the dry bones were stirred and towards the end of the nineteenth century there began to be a revival of sane design in furniture which has improved steadily to the present day without serious let or hindrance, save for

the "Art Nouveau" and ultra-impressionistic modern
Viennese furores which, however, soon ran their ephemeral course and subsided into deserved obscurity.
There were, undoubtedly, analogies during all this ster-
ile and misguided period between the design of furniture and the architectural characteristics, but in a time
when there was little domestic building that deserved
the name of architecture and little furniture of any
merit, it would be idle to point out correspondences of
glaring imperfection.

*Other Decorative Accessories and Movable Decor-
ations.*—During nearly the whole of this dreary period
of progressive horrors, which may be said to have
reached its culmination in the Turkish cosy corner
with all the grotesque and inappropriate accompaniments thereto appertaining, the "decorative accessories" were not decorative but quite the reverse and
their room would have been better than their presence.

There were wall-papers, which were usually bad, and
there were numerous draperies and fringes, which were
generally far worse, about as bad, indeed, as perverted
and fantastic imagination could make them. Carpets
there were, and rugs, ingrain, Brussels, Wilton, Axmin-
ster and sundry other weaves, physically admirable
but, for the most part, either poor or actively objectionable in colour and pattern. It was *de rigueur* as a
rule to have the carpets cover every inch of floor space.
Later on, towards the end of the century when there
began to be a taste for parquetted floors of hard wood
and ornamental (?) designs, rugs came into greater
vogue, especially after the impulse given towards the
collection of Oriental rugs by the Centennial.

Barring these and shocking bad lighting fixtures and
very mediocre sculpture in marble or bronze, with occasional excursions into the least inspired phases of

Sevres, Royal Worcester and other ceramic productions, the period was barren of decorative accessories
and movable decorations. The wall-papers designed
by William Morris and the Japanese bronzes and some
of the porcelains that appeared after the Centennial
ought not to be unconditionally included in this category of condemnation, but their influence went only a
little way towards mitigating the otherwise objectionable tone of the era.

Materials and Colour.—Reference has already been
made to the woods used for furniture and interior finish. It remains only to mention the materials employed
for upholstery and hangings. Haircloth, both plain
and patterned, enjoyed great popularity at the beginning of the period and deserved furniture of better design on which to be applied. Velvets, both plain and
figured, brocades, damasks, brocatelles, poplins, satins
and silks of the best quality were lavishly used for
upholstery and draperies but, as a rule, far more could
be said for their quality than for either their colour
or their design. Carpets, likewise, were of the best
possible quality but shared the same limitations regarding colour and pattern as the other fabrics.

The colours most favoured were either sombre and
dull or else vigorous and full, in the latter case being
employed without the requisite knowledge of their
properties and relations to do them justice. The Viennese episode, almost coincident with cubism and post-
impressionism in painting, launched into riotous excesses of both colour and design, if much of it can be
called design, with an utter disregard for chromatic
psychology. Perhaps the psychology involved was
Teutonic, which would account for its inscrutability.

Arrangement.—This was essentially the period of
the "what-not" and the centre table—it might be more

proper to spell it Centre Table with capitals as indicating the almost religious veneration paid it—of grim, sumptuous, uncomfortable and depressing formality and "genteel," middle-class propriety in arrangement without consideration for either practical utility or comfort. One cause, perhaps, for all the dreary, expensive banality and lack of either humanity or a modicum of taste was the fact that it was a period of preëminently material prosperity and rapid accumulation of wealth which brought to the fore a vast crowd of *nouveaux riches* who had neither the knowledge nor traditions back of them to impel them to better things. They allowed themselves to be outfitted by purely commercial purveyors who were enjoined to make the establishments of their patrons thoroughly respectable and *au fait*. And unfortunately those who, from their antecedents, should have known better, allowed themselves to be infected by the ill example of the vulgarly affluent majority.

During the last few years a new movement has arisen. As it has gained a very considerable following, particularly among those who are strongly individual in their tastes and preferences, it is desirable that a separate section be given to its consideration.

THE "NEW" DECORATION
AN EXAMINATION OF THE "MODERN" METHOD

When a new tendency or movement first reaches the attention of the public, and particularly if in some of its manifestations it be rather startling, several attitudes of mind immediately become evident. One temperament shrinks from the unusual, sometimes with repulsion and hard language, while another, with equal lack of examination, runs to embrace it as *le dernier cri;* still another regards that as everything else with a tolerant smile of amused indifference, while it is reserved for a fourth class to weigh merits and demerits before passing judgment.

As it is to this last group that the readers of this book will doubtless belong, they will probably be glad of a consideration of this comparatively new movement in household decoration which shall be at once sympathetic and impartial.

WHAT IT IS

While the newer tendency is derived from the Modernistic Movement abroad, it would be fairer to say that its American manifestation is a *reflection* of that influence rather than a continuation. The European movement, developed in its turn from the Austrian Secession, a recognised school so long ago as the closing years of the last century, is decidedly iconoclastic and will be referred to later. We do not think that there has been a great deal of this spirit shown in household decoration here, and, with the exception of the work of a few exponents of European origin, what has been done in this direction has probably been by way of interesting experiment. We need hardly look for any outbreak of erratic tendencies, and the conservative need not therefore greatly concern themselvs at the few manifestations of *outré* decoration which have appeared. There naturally will be some in every movement who go further than others, so that we may expect to find here as elsewhere all shades of opinion and practice, from decided innovation to comparative conservatism.

The movement is the product of a number of clever minds, and there is no organisation for the promulga-

PLATE 52

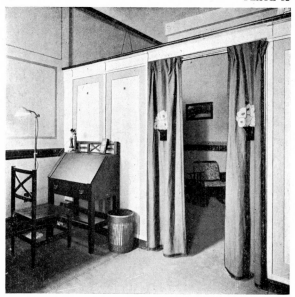

OFFICE AND RECEPTION ROOM: AN EXCELLENT EXAMPLE OF "MODERN" WORK

Walls, Blue-green Divided into Panels by a Rich Dark Rose Band and Black Line; Base, Chair-rail and Picture Moulding, Black; Partitions, same as Walls; Ceiling, Grey; Carpet, Plain, same Rose as Walls; Furniture, Black; Draperies, Rose Linen with Appliqué in Grey, Black and Rose Velvet; Draperies in Reception-room, Rose Linen with All-over Design in Green, Red-violet and Blue.

By Courtesy of the Aschermann Studio, New York

SCHEME FOR A DINING-ROOM IN "MODERN" STYLE

Walls, White Enamel; Ceiling and Walls above Woodwork Painted White; Baseboard, Black; Pilasters, Marqueterie, Black and White; Furniture, Ebony Finish; Draperies, Upholstery and Rug, Intense Blue and Black; Lighting-fixtures and Bowls, Hammered Copper.

By Courtesy of the Aschermann Studio, New York

PLATE 53

MODERN BRITISH COTTAGE INTERIOR WITH BUILT-IN FURNITURE AND
MOVABLE PIECES OF CORRESPONDING TYPE

By Courtesy of Messrs. Barry Parker and Raymond Unwin, Letchworth, Herts.

PLATE 54

PANEL INSERTS OF JAPANESE PAPER, LAMP AND
SIMPLE TABLE, ALL APPROPRIATE TO "MODERN"
DECORATION
William Chester Chase, Architect

tion of certain principles: the tendency here seems simply a reaction from "Period" furnishing and the supplying of another method of treatment which shall be more in accord with our life to-day. How well and how fully it does this is the aim of this section to enquire.

If we interpret aright the movement in this country its ideal—and what a fine one it is!—is to teach use, convenience and beauty by way of simplicity and balance on the one hand and fine, frank, cheerful colour on the other. Now there is nothing very "new" about all this—and it is none the worse for that. It is what many of us have "been after" for many days. As the thing which comes nearest to their solution of the problem is Peasant Art (including the British Cottage) this has largely been the inspiration of the new movement. The humorous side of this is that while some at least of the new movers have been scathing in their criticisms of Period Art as unable to embody the spirit of to-day, Peasant Art is as much Period Art as any other. None of us, however, is entirely logical and we need not stress this, especially as mingled with this older inspiration is the use of anything from any source which will aid in the realising of the object desired.

In itself the use of varying materials is also unobjectionable, providing they can be welded and harmonised into a complete and beautiful whole. It is in the definition of the aim to be realised that we come to our first question.

If the Modern Movement is an effort to realise, and to provide homes in correct relation to, human life to-day, it is evident that the result will depend upon the conception of what that life is.

12

WHAT IS OUR MODERN LIFE?

It is undeniable that there is in our present existence (and those whose disposition it is to ignore the
past are invited to remember that there has also been
in most ages) an element which is hectic, freakish,
anarchistic and unwholesome. In Europe before the
war this tendency was growing to an alarming extent
and many brilliant but erratic minds so stressed this
phase of our existence as either wilfully to deny its
other elements or so to dislike them as to wish them
begone. The extreme wing of this group would have
liked to cut loose from and abolish the past with its
lessons and make all new after its own devices. It is
little wonder that we have seen an outpouring of cubism, vorticism, futurism, attempts to depict emotional-
ism and movement without sufficient regard to the basis
of form, strident and discordant colour, and the more
hectic and immodest tendencies in woman's dress.

We do not say and we do not think that this spirit
has entered to any great extent into decorative art in
America and probably the war has eradicated it abroad.

Here, we may well believe, the movement in general simply recognises the variety, the virility, the
elasticity, yes and the restlessness and excitability
of modern life and attempts to meet and interpret it.
Whether it would not be better to endeavour to *neutralise* the latter phases is a question worth the asking.

With the difference in aim comes the difference in
result, and consequently we shall find examples which
continue with the fine qualities of simplicity and
strength of line the stiffness and want of home feeling
which somehow prevails in much of the Vienna Secession; other houses a bouquet, with rooms in colour-
schemes representing various and unrelated flowers;

and still others in which the unities are rightly kept
and which have the cheer and charm and freshness of
simplicity and beautiful colour beautifully used.

VERVE AND FRESHNESS

That the injection of these qualities into our homes
would be an exceedingly desirable thing was effectively
borne in upon the writers when for selective purposes
they had the task of going over some three hundred
photographs of the interiors of tasteful houses. With
few of them could particular fault be found (otherwise the photographs would not have been taken), *but
in less than a quarter of this number was any particular
individuality shown.*

Most tasteful Americans are unduly conservative
and too content to follow precedent, and a movement
which awakens and "gives them to think" is decidedly
at present a needed spur. It does not follow that we
must rush to adopt the new decoration, but it is well
to consider it carefully, for it has much to offer. In
addition to providing many hints even to those who
prefer the old it certainly affords at much less expense
than period furnishing a method of decoration well
adapted to modest houses, cottages and some apartments, which is simple and at the same time artistic,
bright and attractive.

There is no obligation to adopt its more *outré* features if unsuited to our temperaments, for it presents
alternatives from which to choose. In order that full
consideration be given this method its detailed characteristics have been treated in Part II in the chapters on
Colour, Walls, Floors, Furniture and Fabrics.

A very practical question is: How far is it adapted
to the possessions we already have? If, upon examination, we find this spirit or ideal appeals to us, can we

avail ourselves of it wholly, or to what extent, without an entire redecoration and refurnishing of our homes?

To those who own handsome Period Furniture and furnishings it may be said that such things will not be superseded by this or any other new method which may arise. The "modern" method, charming as it may be at its best, is in any event rather limited to small houses or apartments, and indeed not to all of these. It is an excellent sign that many Americans of the better and more thoughtful class are taking account of something other than *size*. Small families often wish to eliminate the care and continual bother large properties involve and are moving into apartments or smaller houses, even erecting smaller country abodes as well. The tastes of these people may be highly formed and rather luxurious, and merely simple and charming houses would reflect neither their personalities nor their lives. They may then wish these abodes to be jewel caskets enshrining gems in the way of rare furniture, textiles, vases and pictures, and there should be none to say them nay in their desire to surround themselves with beauty. In such cases the new decoration obviously does not apply.

Then, too, if the colouring in any house is rather attenuated it is plain that patches of brighter hue cannot be introduced without working havoc with all that remains; so that in such instances again one must either take or leave it—redecorate or let all remain largely as it is.

But there are many houses furnished in non-committal style, and others containing period furniture, but which are generally eclectic in character, and these may sometimes be greatly helped by hints from this newer method. As the simplicity of spaciousness is one of its finest features, there may be some elimination, and the improvement wrought by the mere removal of cumbersome and less desirable pieces is often immeasurable.

The colouring of a room generally exists in the walls, rugs and fabrics. If the walls are good and are neutral they are perfectly adapted to this new style, and if they are "fussy" they are not adapted to *any* style and should be changed. If they are in poor condition they may be renewed either in the neutral or more colourful vein.

Of rugs much the same may be said. If neutral they are perfectly correct, and so if they are colourful, provided they are not restless in pattern or contrast. If objectionable, bare floors would be better with any style of decoration. An expanse of bare, well-polished floor with a few simple rugs in good solid colouring, or two tones, or bordered, is always attractive. Good Oriental rugs will do excellently well if the new colouring to be introduced is made to accord with them.

Now with the simple change of upholstery, hangings and cushions wonders may be done in the vivifying of such a house. But before *anything* is done plan the whole. Consult the section on "Unity and Variety" and the Peasant colour-combinations given in the chapter on Colour, and scheme out what is to be done in each room. If there is a large couch its cover may be colourful, but let it be of solid colour and then use pillows of decidedly ornamental character, with one of black.

For upholstery stripes always have an intrinsic style of their own, and these may be strong and varied, or plain strong tones may be chosen, or printed linen or cretonne.

If there is great variety in the other furnishings

keep the portieres and window curtains in solid colour. If variety is lacking it may be introduced here.

Much may be done by Oriental, Batik, or other decorative hangings, screens, lamps, vases, and the like.

The probability is that in most houses many of the pictures may be discarded to advantage. Those that are retained should be good in themselves and for the decorative purpose for which they are used, and their frames should be fitting and unobtrusive.

Merely nondescript homes may be made coherent and attractive by following the plan outlined in the preceding paragraphs with the addition of an overhauling of the furniture. Badly designed, tortuously carved or machine-impressed pieces should be simplified or discarded. "Foolish" bric-à-brac, calendars, photographs and general litter should especially be weeded out. Better a few good things than much which is distracting and inharmonious.

Regarding the new decoration we may then finally say that in its saner forms it is attractive, practical and inexpensive. As to its more *outré* aspects one could not close more fittingly than to quote the words of Mr. Aymar Embury regarding strained and eccentric effects in general: "Whatever fascination this wayward cleverness may afford at first sight is not lasting, but is sure to dwindle and become a weariness when once the novelty has given place to the habit of familiar contrast day after day."

PART II

PRACTICAL DECORATION
AND FURNISHING

—you cannot separate art and recreation, and you cannot separate art and business. The list includes items which we consider as amusements, and items which we think of as business. We began with dancing and ended with upholstery. Make them all beautiful.

"THE ORGANISATION OF THOUGHT."

By A. N. Whitehead, Sc.D., F. R. S.

London: Williams & Norgate.

Philadelphia: J. B. Lippincott Company.

PART II
PRACTICAL DECORATION AND FURNISHING

CHAPTER I

THE BASIS OF SUCCESSFUL DECORATION

THE INTERIOR AS A WHOLE. PLANNING. FOUR METHODS
OF FURNISHING

IT would be a comparatively easy task for the writers
to lay down an accumulation of abstract principles,
governing the different phases of Interior Decoration. They hope, however, to do much more than this;
and, fully recognising the many varying conditions
under which the decorator—either professional or amateur—must work, to cover these conditions in such a
practical way as to afford the greatest aid in the simplest and most systematic manner. Needless to say the
salesman will similarly be able to derive much aid in
intelligently advising his customers.

Part I of this book has dealt with the various Period
styles in their purity in which anyone may gather many
hints for present-day usage of the same. The present
portion of the work treats in detail of the fitting up
of our modern houses and apartments and will afford
help to those who can make but a limited expenditure
in the improvement of their homes as well as to those
who are financially so situated as to be able to carry out
such plans as they may wish.

Notwithstanding the great improvement made in the
decoration of the interior during recent years, a fault
continually manifest is the failure in many instances to

consider the house or apartment as a *whole*. Instead
of the clean, coherent effect which should everywhere
be evident as the result of a well-mapped decorative
campaign—be the property large or small—is felt a fit-
fulness of purpose, a lack of grasp. The individual
rooms may be charming, but the fact that they have been
separately considered, strung like beautiful but incongruous beads upon a string, is often but too plain.

So far are our best architects and decorators from
erring in this respect that their first and guiding principle is unity, but—not always through their own fault
as we shall see—the want of architectonic quality is
frequently manifest in the work of clever and competent
people, not to mention that of those decorators who are
simply tradesmen, while houses which are furnished by
their owners are seldom free from this defect.

The temporary craze for some particular style is
responsible for much of this: the householder furnishes
a room or two in the manner then in special fashion, or
commissions a decorator to do it, and a year or two
thereafter, that vogue having had its little day, other
rooms are done, also in the style which is then "just the
thing," but in a style which is likely to be totally at
variance with the first. Do not householders know that
such crazes are fostered by manufacturers and dealers
for trade purposes, that art is a matter of sanity and
equilibrium, and that worthy interior decoration recognises no such thing as the fad?

There may be choice and preference, and it is the
aim of this book to lay before the householder and the
decorator facts and principles that will enable choice
and preference to be arrived at *intelligently;* so that
they shall be the honest expression of the individual
temperament, and not mere whim or a temporary

"liking," to be effaced by the next attraction that grasps the attention.

As such an intelligent choice and appreciation must be based on knowledge, and as decoration by any method or in any style is a *whole,* its parts being intimately related and inseparable, it is urged that no decision be made or work begun until that knowledge be made one's own. Special attention has here been given to making its acquirement easy through simple, systematic and logical arrangement and treatment, but the contents of one chapter should not be acted upon until the others also have been studied. If a window cannot be curtained without reference to the other furnishings of the room, to the room itself, the others in the house, and the exterior of that house—and it cannot—then it is plain that these other things should be taken into account before we curtain the window.

The basis of all good decoration is *plan*—well-selected and adhered to; and as there are four methods of furnishing these will forthwith be stated.

The instances in which an entire house (or apartment) is newly decorated and supplied with new furniture throughout are few in comparison with those in which already acquired possessions are used at least to a partial extent: these possessions will naturally therefore have their influence in the selection of a style of furnishing. But it is advisable to see that they do not have too *great* an influence, and to remember that improvement can gradually be carried out. The plan may therefore be built upon future rather than existing conditions. It is possible even with limited means to change the whole character of an interior during the course of a few years, and each of these years may be marked by constant interest and pleasure. It is questionable if such gradual development worked out by the house-holder himself does not give quite as keen and solid satisfaction as the placing of a large commission with a professional decorator may give his wealthy neigh-bour. For those of abundant means to allow the posses-sion of certain bad furnishings to hamper and mar right planning would be poor policy indeed—it is better to rid oneself of the incubus and have done with it.

FOUR METHODS OF FURNISHING

I. INTERNATIONAL—INTER PERIOD DECORATION

By far the most satisfactory method of furnishing, either for the elaborate or the simple house or apart-ment, is that combining nationalities and periods which properly accompany each other as under sufficiently close decorative influences. Of such importance is this plan that it has been fully developed and exemplified in Part III. Its title indicates the scope of this method, its infinite variety, and its freedom from all narrowness of view.

Full provision is also there made for period furnish-ing where the walls must necessarily be simple, owing to the property being rented, or for other reasons. Many new houses and apartments are finished interiorly with wood-work of simple, classical design appropriate to almost any epoch. Doors and windows are usually in good proportion, the former being simply panelled. These features are so unobtrusive and non-committal that they may be left as they are, and with a treatment of the walls either in simple, tasteful style, or adapted more closely to the period chosen, furnishing may be in accordance with almost any period style. In many con-ditions and for non-plethoric purses this is an excellent method.

PLATE 55

ONE-PERIOD DECORATION, A LOUIS XV DRAWING ROOM

PLATE 56

INTERNATIONAL-INTERPERIOD DECORATION IN A MODERN APARTMENT

Cabinet, Arm Chair and Stool to Right, Italian: Settee and Chair to Left, French, Louis XV: Tapestry, Flemish: Bust, Italian

Charles A. Platt, Architect

(See Part III, Chapter III)

PLATE 57

"MODERN" DECORATION. HOTEL TRAYMORE, ATLANTIC CITY, N. J.

II. THE ONE-PERIOD METHOD

This method with its limitations is also mentioned in Part III, which see.

III. THE "MODERN" METHOD, OR THE "NEWER DECORATION"

This is a various, adaptable, and inexpensive style of decoration enabling those occupying small houses or apartments, if possessed of taste and judgment, to secure excellent and artistic results by simple means. It is fully described in Part I, Chapter IX, and details for its carrying out are provided in the various chapters of Part II.

IV. THE NON-COMMITTAL METHOD

In many cases families possess much modern furniture, including wicker, of various kinds and of no particular style, and there is no alternative to using it. While it is not an advisable method of furnishing to be deliberately chosen, where it already exists and the owners have taste the results may be very charming and homelike.

Frequently it is possible to weed out gradually the less desirable pieces and substitute more desirable things. Many hints may be taken from the "Modern Method," or a transformation effected by easy stages to Inter-period style. If either is done the decision made should be adhered to, as a fluctuating policy hinders good results here as elsewhere.

The improvement of our home-life and surroundings throughout the country, on the farm, and in remote districts as well as in the centres of civilisation should be a purpose dear to all of us. On holidays and anniversaries no better gift to relatives and intimate friends

could be found than pieces of furniture or furnishings
which are good in themselves and appropriate to the
surroundings of those receiving them. As it is to the
rising generation that we must look for improvement,
so every boy and girl should be encouraged to take pride
in the rooms they occupy and be helped in their
development.

Great insistence has been laid upon the need of
" expressing one's own personality in one's surroundings." The counsel when so baldly stated is apt to lead
to self-consciousness, artificiality and a false striving
to be different, resulting merely in freakishness of
effect. If, with sincerity, we endeavour simply to make
our surroundings as beautiful as in us lies, as homelike,
as consistent with our needs and our social standing,
we shall in the end find that we *have* expressed ourselves—as we *are,* and not according to some vain
imagining of what our personality is.

Of the four methods of furnishing above described
it will be seen that two contemplate the use of Period
Furniture. There seems to be an impression among
many who have given no particular attention to the subject that there is something esoteric about Period Furniture, that it is beyond their comprehension—and also
that the furniture itself is beyond their pocketbooks.
Both suppositions are probably wrong for readers of
this book. Half the time spent on bridge, motors or
"movies" for a few weeks would give them much valuable information, and for those who cannot afford genuine antiques there are always faithful reproductions.

"But why should I trouble myself about the styles
of the past?" may be asked. Because there we find a
beauty unapproached by modern designers. With the
decadence of the Empire style the art of great furni-
ture-design died, and we still await its resurrection.

CHAPTER II

COLOUR AND COLOUR-SCHEMES

PRINCIPLES AND CHARACTERISTICS OF COLOUR. ACCENTS AND DOMINANTS. COLOUR IN DECORATION. COLOUR AS DICTATED BY PERIOD STYLES. VALUE. SCALE. THE PROPORTIONS OF COLOUR. UNITY AND VARIETY IN DECORATION. COLOUR IN THE "MODERN" DECORATION.

FORM and Colour are the twin foundation stones of art. Form must come first, before the application of colour, but construction is the province of the architect. Wall decoration when extensive may be done by the architect, the decorator, or by both working conjointly. Part I of this book gives a thorough consideration of the treatment of walls in all periods, so that nothing pertaining to form remains here for consideration excepting the arrangement and balance of the furniture and other objects to be introduced into the interior and the matters of design and scale. Consideration of these points will naturally come later.

On the other hand, it is impossible for us even to plan our scheme of decoration without reference to the universally interesting subject of colour.

COLOUR

In this chapter colour will be treated from a simple and practical point of view. It is a subject upon which a vast deal of theory is usually expended, all in itself excellent but usually resulting simply in the obfuscation of the general reader. There is perhaps a better way to communicate it.

191

As everyone knows, the primary colours are yellow, red and blue, and the binary colours (those composed of two) are orange (yellow and red), violet (red and blue) and green (yellow and blue).

Red, yellow and blue are called primary colours because white light in the solar spectrum separates into these three basic colours. As pure light these colours would fuse back into white. In material pigment they do not quite accomplish this but fuse into grey.

Two simple little diagrams will explain the matter of colour. Yellow, red and blue may be called the "eternal triangle" of colour—let us so arrange them.

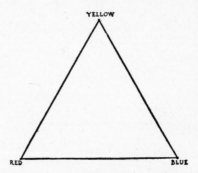

As orange is an equal mixture of normal yellow and red, let us place it midway between its two components, also placing the other two binary colours between the components of each. We then have superimposed a second triangle upon the first.

The dotted lines will show at once the opposing or complementary colours. They are opposing because each of these contains none of the other. Orange is a mixture of yellow and red and contains no blue. Blue and orange are therefore opposing. A glance at the diagram will likewise show the other opposing colours. It is simplicity itself.

There is a curious effect which while, of course,

experienced by all artists, has not, to the writers' knowledge, previously been formally pointed out. It is a most important one to be remembered by all who have to handle colour. Let us glance for a moment at our triangle of yellow, red and blue. Yellow and blue, though occupying opposing points of the triangle and thus contrasting, do yet form a harmony of difference, *i.e.,* they are pleasing in combination.

Blue and red also occupy two opposing points of the triangle and while they are less contrasting than

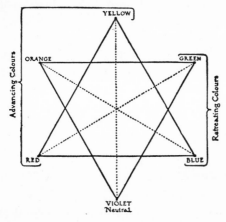

blue and yellow are at the same time less pleasing an harmony.

Yellow and red likewise occupy two opposing points of the triangle. Now these, in their pure state, form no harmony, but rather a discord. If we but remember these things, and also that the three colours in the upper left of the diagram (yellow, orange and red) are advancing or aggressive and warm colours and those in the right (green and blue) are retreating or quiet and cool colours, we have already gone far in the understanding of colour for decoration. Violet is neutral. In decorative practice gold also is neutral.

13

Our useful little diagram shows that normal orange is half way between yellow and red, *i.e.,* it is composed of an equal power of each. It is evident that if more red be added it becomes a reddish orange, and if more yellow it becomes a yellowish orange. It is also plain that if one follows the dotted line from orange across the diagram to its opponent blue and adds blue to orange he will neutralise the orange by the blue he adds until if a sufficient power of blue were added the orange would be totally destroyed and the combination become grey. It is by this adding of a portion of one colour to another, or the adding to them of white or black that tones are made.

The number of hues and tones to be produced by the mixture of colours is necessarily very large. The most prominent are those composed of any one of the six colours on the second diagram with the one next it —thus yellow and orange produce yellow orange. The others in successive order are red-orange, red-violet, blue-violet, blue-green, yellow-green.

In practice the most generally useful colours are the slightly greyed hues of these twelve colours and those known as the Tertiary and Quartenary Colours and are produced as follows:

Tertiary: The mixture of two Binary (sometimes called Secondary) colours—Slate (violet and green), citrine (green and orange), russet (orange and violet).

Quartenary: the mixture of two Tertiary colours —Sage (citrine and slate), buff (citrine and russet), plum (russet and slate).

As one thinks of such tones as buff, rose, grey, grey blue, etc., it is plain that such tones are more agreeable and subtle than the strident and hard primary yellow, red and blue.

The strong prismatic primaries and binaries are

suitable for accents, about which we shall by-and-by have much to say, but in quantity are not agreeable to cultivated tastes.

With but a few words as to the general characteristics of each colour we shall be ready to proceed to their use in decoration. It should be remembered that these characteristics are those of the pure colours and that in their tones they are modified by the amount of departure from this original.

Yellow: Although sunlight is a white light, yellow gives more of an *effect* of light than does white itself. If a piece of light yellow paper is placed out of doors on a gloomy day and glanced at through the window it will appear as if the sun were shining upon it. Yellow in its various shades is therefore useful for the lightening of dark rooms.

Red: It is perhaps safe to say that when the colour red is mentioned many understand by it the colour which is represented by vermilion; nor is this strange when even writers on interior decoration give this hue as prismatic red in their *colour charts.* Nevertheless, the real prismatic red is a quite different colour, strongly inclining toward the crimson shade and more nearly represented by rose madder or carmine.

Anyone at all familiar with the three-colour process of colour-plate making and its present remarkably faithful reproduction of tones of every description will at once realise the truth of this, as the "Red" ink used in printing these plates is of a quite carmine hue. The distinction is of high importance, a misunderstanding of the definition of a point at issue being often the main cause of dispute.

It is, for instance, usually observed that red is a very exciting colour. This is quite true of the vermilion red, which contains some yellow and is therefore really orange red, and true to a less degree of the true prismatic red. All reds have the quality of warmth.

Orange: Orange, which partakes of the nature of both yellow and red, therefore combines their qualities of light and heat.

Blue: Blue is one of the retiring colours and is quieting in its influence; it is also cool, in some shades cold. These qualities should be borne in mind.

Green: Green, which is the combination of yellow and blue, has the qualities of light, quiet and coolness.

Violet: Violet possesses richness and sumptuousness, which have associated it with royalty. It has also sombreness, which has associated it ecclesiastically with penitential seasons and death, and individually with a lesser mourning than black.

Having briefly gone over the characteristics and relations of colours, their use in decoration can be taken up, and this can perhaps best be done in an easy-going conversational way. Let us begin with an example:

As a well-dressed man might, for instance, with clothes and accessories of quiet tan, wear a tie of an orange shade, or containing it, so if the colouring of a room were of similar character a strong note might be struck by an orange bowl filled with nasturtiums, an orange screen, or other such object. This strong, introduced note would be an Accent. Without such accent a keyed and related room (or a costume), though harmonious is apt to be monotonous and dead.

But, the man with the tan costume might also, and better yet, wear a tie of blue, and so might the room have a bowl or other object of blue, and if the shade is right it will give an accent of more value and variety than the accent of kindred shade. This is because blue is the complementary or opposing colour of yellow and each therefore gives value and quality to the other.

It will thus be seen that there are two kinds of accent —the related and the opposing—and that without the one or the other a room is characterless and with use becomes exceeding tiresome.

The word accent itself shows its purpose of simply adding emphasis, so that it is at once plain that in such a tan room as we are considering we must not have too *much* orange or blue (either in mass or number of scattered objects) or instead of accent we shall then have disturbance. It is also obvious that in such a room we might have much more of orange as an emphasis than we could rightly have of blue, because the first is related and the second is not, but is opposing.

It is equally plain that our principles still hold if we reverse the combination. One of the prettiest rooms the writers remember was a simple little guest chamber in a country house. It was furnished in old mahogany and at the rather high-set double windows were curtains of blue and white, while on the floor were simple grey-blue rugs, matching in shade the blue of the curtain. Had there been introduced into this room our previously mentioned orange bowl of nasturtiums the result would have been perfection.

And the citing of this room brings us to another resource we have in furnishing. It will be noticed that in addition to the blue in the curtain there was white, and we would now also mention that the wall-paper was of a grey-white with a little scattered snowflake pattern in white talc thereon. We have, therefore, in addition to the blue and orange the introduction of a third element—white; and a fourth in the mahogany tone of the furniture.

White is not a colour, but is the combination of all the colours and therefore neutral, so that it conflicts with no other color and may safely be used with any.

In the present instance the mahogany is closely related
to the orange and contrasted pleasantly with the shade
of blue employed, so that here again we have no conflict but a safe and beautiful combination of four
colour-elements in the one room. Our resources are
growing.

Now say that we introduce, besides the above furnishings, a screen covered with cretonne of which the
same tone of blue is the dominant note, but which contains green leaves and perhaps a number of other
colours, all of which however occupy lesser space than
the blue and are pleasantly related or contrasted—so
far as colour is concerned we should still be safe.

We therefore arrive at an important point. Many
home furnishers and even some professional decorators are apt to limit themselves too closely for life,
variety and pleasantness of effect by the laying out
of colour schemes or "rhythmic notes" composed exclusively of varying shades of one colour, or adding
simply an accent. On the other hand, many women
and even women decorators indulge in a riot of colour
without a sufficiently large basis of neutral or at least
quiet and undisturbed surface. In short, we see that
the two errours to be avoided are all "harmony" without "relief" and all "relief" without "harmony."

We must, in furnishing, therefore use consideration, and a little thought will usually set us right. Take
up, as an example, the question of the introduction of
the varied cretonne screen into the blue and white room
we have been considering. It might, so far as colour
is concerned, be safe, but would it otherwise be advisable? In this room it would *not* have been, because
the room was small and the only unbroken surfaces of
blue were the two small rugs. The cretonne, therefore,
might have given the room a crowded, restless effect.

Much better, if a screen were required in this case, would be one of which the covering was a plain related blue. On the other hand, had the room been large, with correspondingly large unbroken surfaces of blue and white, the cretonne would have afforded a pleasant relief. Here, then, other questions than those of colour have entered—those of space and quantity. Its placing would also have to be taken into account, so involving the question of balance. We note, therefore, simply by way of warning, that in considering one phase of decoration, colour, we must not forget others of like importance and must not be carried off our feet and purchase goods themselves delightful in their colour effect but inadvisable in other respects for the use we wish them for.

Bearing in mind these interesting principles we can go over the various possible colour-schemes and combinations and see their suitability in many instances and their inadvisability in others, treating each colour as including all its varying shades and tones.

COLOUR IN DECORATION

WHITE AND BLACK

White, not properly a colour, is here mentioned first of all, and for that very reason. It is both a neutral and a universal harmoniser. From the decorator's point of view we should consider as "whites" not only pure white but all the varying shades, such as grey, cream, ashes of rose, etc., which are too light to be properly classed under those names.

White is also first taken up because walls and ceilings are first to be considered in any furnishing, and for this purpose light shades are most frequently advisable. Of these shades the whites, alone or in combination, are among the very best. Their own beauty and adaptability are a sufficient recommendation, but they possess the further advantage of relieving too great adherence to a given colour-scheme. There is no reason, for instance, why a blue room should be *all* blue, and proclaim the instant one enters it: "Yes, I am Blue; indubitably, unmistakably Blue." The use for walls of one of the white or light tones in such a case relieves a scheme which otherwise would be artificial and oppressive. It is quite sufficient that the dominant note of a room should be of the selected colour without that colour running riot.

Walls in "the whites" will be treated in detail under that section. The same tones are of eminent use for wood-work and curtains and will be discussed under those heads.

White in combination with black recently amounted to a fashionable craze. The combination is rather too startling for a room continually occupied but may have its uses. A reception room with black and white striped paper of not too violent a pattern, and black lacquered or painted furniture upholstered in Chinese or other gorgeous fabric would be effective and not unduly *outré*. Some of the cretonnes with black and white stripes broken by groups of roses in conventional form are very attractive, and black alone makes the best possible background for flowered cretonnes, bringing out the colours with effect and charm, and being exceedingly sensible, as it does not readily soil.

White in juxtaposition with colours heightens their effect and raises their key, while black reduces and lowers them.

YELLOW, ORANGE AND BROWN

As previously seen, yellow stands for light and in its pure shades makes for cheerfulness in rooms which have but moderate sunlight. By the same token, in strongly lighted rooms it makes for *glare*. If used in such rooms, therefore, the quieter shades of yellow, such as buff and tan, are usually chosen. Quietness need never mean dullness, but in household practice it too frequently does. We have previously inveighed against the deadness of many American homes; is it from simple inertia or from incapacity for any originality that so many rooms exist with walls of dead and dull mustard-colour oatmeal paper, which absorbs all light as a sponge does moisture; rugs and portières in perhaps a darker and still duller shade, "relieved" perchance with brown or sickly cream. Frequently added to this is Mission furniture in the dullest of oak, and leather cushions of the same hue, unrelieved by any ray of brightness, a veritable symphony of mud and mustard! If any reader is unfortunately possessed of such a room we trust he will make speed to import into it some notes of strong orange or blue as previously suggested; but in newly furnishing let us point out the better way. If one wishes to use a quiet shade of buff, etc., there is no objection to quietness if it has *life, i.e., enough* yellow or orange in its composition to avoid the deadness which, all considered, is really a note of the "ordinary" and the "neutral."

But quiet tones in even an highly lighted room are not of absolute necessity. It is to be remembered that there are always such things as awnings, shades, Venetian blinds and curtains rich and heavy enough to modify and diffuse a garish light to a happy glow. With such a light it is therefore possible, if one wishes, to employ tones of orange, buff, gold or Chinese yellow, all making for life and cheerfulness.

These tones go well with golden or dark oak, with mahogany, walnut, ivory or painted furniture, so that the yellows are among the most desirable shades for furnishing. It is well, however, not to let this colour —or any other—"run away" with one. A mingling with other harmonising and pleasantly contrasting colours is advisable in some of the draperies or in the various objects of ornament a room contains, so as to obviate the artificial air always given by an apartment too definitely of one colour. This is notably the case with a strong yellow, for it is unbecoming to some complexions and does not invariably form the best background for the dress of modern women.

The browns are derivatives from yellow mixed with red and some blue. There are many attractive shades, and brown velour for hangings is rich and handsome. The colour should, however, be sparingly used, as it makes for darkness and dullness.

RED AND ITS DERIVATIVES

In its proper shades and proper proportions red is of eminent value in interior decoration. An all red room is too suggestive of the infernal regions for sane and cultured folk. Perhaps the frieze of raw green which so often accompanies such apartments is intended as an off-set reference to the Elysian Fields.

The distinction has already been drawn between the true and vermilion reds. Both have their value, but that of the former is much wider in its application. Indeed, in this prismatic red in its slightly greyed hue of soft crimson, often seen in old silk shawls, and in its lightened tone of rose, we have one of the most useful and one of the loveliest colour resources of the decorator and the home-maker. The deep hues have vitality and warmth, and so are most suitable for city use. Rose has an enlivening and human quality without the heat of the stronger shades, and so in proper quantities may anywhere be used. As red in any shade is an advancing colour its just proportions are naturally much less than of such a retiring shade as soft green and a comparatively small quantity will make it dominant where desirable. Reference to the description of an apartment in the subsequent section on "Unity and Variety" will show a good management of such a scheme.

The soft crimsons above referred to and the soft shades of rose are excellent in solid colours with a stripe or pattern in the weave for upholstering, portières, and the like. Baby pink is weak and characterless and its use even for the young girl's room cannot be commended. Far better for this purpose would be walls in some one of "the whites" with cretonnes in a dainty French striped or flowered pattern of rose and blue, with perhaps a trifle of mauve, on a white or cream ground. This with ivory-white or mahogany or painted furniture makes a charming combination. Grey and rose is another attractive and feminine colour-scheme.

In a happy blending with other colours in cretonne and other fabrics, reds have some of their most eminent values. If we are to use colour for beauty, for cheer, for delight—and our lives might be much more enriched by it than at present—it will be found that it is by such happy combinations and blendings rather than in the laying on of colour in masses that our object will be gained.

The vermilion red is most useful for accents for out-of-doors employment. A few porch chairs of this colour, a hammock, or a small quantity of vermilion on a tent gives a festive touch, in relief to the masses of green in grass and foliage.

BLUES

There are entrancing tones of blue, the employment of which amply justifies the popularity of this colour in decorative use. There are, however, other shades of coldness or hardness of which one can only say: beware.

Furthermore, there is another difficulty in the use of blue to which attention must be called. Both men and women artistically inclined must have noticed in the matter of personal attire how hard it is to secure blue shades which "go together." With yellows there is not this difficulty; yellows which are even quite different in hue often harmonise well; various shades of red do not always dwell happily together; yet neither of these colours present the difficulty of blue, where a very slight difference in tone often is enough to result in discord. The present writers believe that they are the first to point out the extreme sensitiveness of the colour blue in this respect, and they are glad to pass on the warning to their readers.

We may go further—let us take, for instance, one of the loveliest colour schemes which the colour-loving soul of man has yet devised, old blue and old ivory— a room panelled or papered in ivory white, Louis Seize furniture painted in old ivory and upholstered in old blue, with gold picture frames and candlesticks of the period. It is of the greatest beauty; it is, as the French would say, "of an elegance," but does it not lack *humanity?* It is not the elegance which proves the obstacle, for if we painted simple cottage furniture in the same tone of ivory, upholstered it in an inexpensive material of the same old blue, and laid cotton rugs of the same hue on the floor, the result would inevitably be the same; it is the nature of the blue; for if it is cool it is also a trifle cold—*unloving.* But let one take into either of these rooms a bowl of roses (not the purplish American Beauty but the true rose shade, mingled perhaps with cream) and we have an harmony which not only sings but which makes the room a place in which to *live*.

The artistically sensitive French knew this, and continually we find them mingling with their blue either rose or its lighter shade of pink, or else old gold, which is not quite so good for the purpose.

With these reservations, blue may be heartily commended, especially in its greyed, medium and peacock shades. It is admirably adapted for country and seaside use, and as previously noted, in proper combination it possesses refinement and elegance.

If baby pink cannot be recommended neither can baby blue—both seem to indicate a "silliness."

GREEN

Green is another of the retiring colours. It is also cool in many shades, but naturally not so much so as the blue which enters into its composition and which is partially neutralised by its other component, yellow. If a greater proportion of yellow is introduced it becomes warmer and more advancing, according to the quantity added. As (we write it reverently) The Great Decorator of the World has used these two colours of blue and green in sky and sea and vegetation, we must recognise their appropriateness in larger masses than with the reds, and yellows, and brighter blues in which He paints the flowers.

As will be seen in the section on "Unity and Variety" really bright colours are not advisable for walls and ceilings. A green of considerable strength may, however, so be used and "Chelsea" green was much in vogue for panelled walls in Queen Anne's time.

Green is an eminently suitable colour in its soft tones for rugs and portières. The violent hues seen in some cheap goods have no place anywhere in decoration. Olive green is rich and handsome; but, like brown, it must be employed in moderation if heaviness is to be avoided. Blue greens are frequently used in painted furniture and when sufficiently relieved with other colours are excellent for this purpose. It may be said that green universally *needs* relief; while a thoroughly wholesome colour as a background and in combination, an *all* green room would be almost unbearable in its influence, even in the lighter shades. We feel the need of enhancing yellow, orange, or rose.

Soft green, white, and rose is an excellent colour-scheme employed by some British decorators with great success (Plate 64) and too seldom used here.

Blue may also be used with green if the shades of both are right.

Of all colours there are vivid hues which in small quantities may be effectively and beautifully blended with other vivid colours. One of these shades is Paris green. We have seen this combined with vivid rose in a pair of Chinese slippers. But the Chinese are masters of colour: *perhaps* some day we shall know colour as they do. Meanwhile, the Anglo-Saxon who looks down upon them may sit at their feet and learn.

VIOLET, MAUVE AND MULBERRY

As will later be seen Violet is a heavily worked colour in the "Newer" decoration, elsewhere it is not so greatly employed as others.

We sometimes see rather effective rooms for women in its lighter shade of mauve. There is a dullish, reddish mauve used in the new French decorations and we have seen wall-paper in this shade striped with greyish white. With textiles of the same shade of mauve much might be done, as it is a firmer and less feminine hue than the usual shade.

Mulberry is a violet so filled with red that perhaps it might better have been included under that colour. It is dark and rich, and if used with a sufficient quantity of lighter colouring is handsome for draperies. Care should be used in selection, for under artificial light some shades of mulberry look brown.

THE GREYS

Normal grey is a fusion of equal powers of the three primary colours, yellow, red and blue. But if there is an excess of any one or two of these the tone would naturally lean toward the colour or colours in excess, so that there are really numerous hues of grey. The warm greys are naturally therefore those which have a yellowish or pinkish tone, while those of bluish or greenish cast are cool.

Greys are preëminently useful as backgrounds, *i.e.*, for walls and ceilings, and of great value in the mingling of various colours in cretonnes and other fabrics; with green and blue, it prevents the hotness which would result from too much red or yellow.

Occasionally it is employed for the coverings of settees and chairs, and certain shades go well with ivory or gold furniture, the combination being of great refinement and elegance. In such cases, however, grey like blue requires the presence of rose or yellow to give relief.

The cream-grey of linen furniture-covering is cool and refreshing in the heat of summer, but not everyone realises how much the effect will be improved if a few coloured objects, such as couch pillows, etc., are left out to give relief. It would hardly seem needful to point out what a bowl of flowers will do in this respect and yet how often do we see country houses with abundant blooms without and ne'er a flower within.

While probably, if pressed for a close statement, such a theory would be disclaimed, some writers who philosophise upon the subject of colour seem to convey the impression in portions of their text that the qualities of colours are *due* to their association—that green and blue, for instance, are quiet and refreshing *because* we associate them with vegetation and the sky. Such a theory would be a' distinct errour. Doubtless these associations may have caused a quicker apprehension and heightening of those qualities in the human mind; but, as indubitably, every true colourist realises that, apart from any association whatever, the qualities we have mentioned are *inherently possessed* by the colours.

The distinction is of much importance, because we must realise that in dealing with colour we are not employing mere symbolism but are handling media whose character is fixed and known.

It is perhaps because of such cloudiness of statement as we have noted that "practical people" who know the actualities of steel, for instance, and respect the builder of the bridge or the skyscraper for its use, often feel that the man who insists upon employing colour in a way fully as appropriate for *his* purposes is but "fanciful and foolish."

The simple fact is that no branch of human endeavour is more firmly based upon principles of eternal truth than is Art.

PLATE 58

A STUDY IN VALUES

The Overmantel Painting and the Cabinet are of the Same Value: The Mantel and Vase Likewise
Agree, in a Different Value: The Walls are Between the Two in Value

Courtesy of Mrs. Lyman Kendall

COLOUR AS DICTATED BY PERIODS AND STYLES

It should be remembered that in certain periods certain colours, patterns, and textiles were most used with the interiors and furniture of those periods. These have all been duly treated under those periods in Part I of this book, and if a period furnishing is to be followed, should be thoroughly studied.

These details will not usually be found hampering, as goods in appropriate textures and colours may nearly always be had sufficiently near to the period use to be appropriate.

It should be remembered that with dark-panelled walls full-bodied colour was naturally used as relief.

VALUE

So far, the term value has not been used, and yet the thing itself has virtually been dealt with in our discussions regarding colour and will necessarily occur again and again throughout this volume. It might conversationally be defined as the *lightness* or *darkness* of objects irrespective of their colour. To illustrate, suppose we have before us two samples of goods, one a turquoise blue and the other a crimson. Now, putting aside for a moment all question of colour, we at once see that relatively the first is light and the second is dark—these are the " values " of those respective pieces of goods. A study in values is given in Plate 58.

The question of value comes into decoration in the form of contrast. We may think of introducing a certain object into the furnishing of a room; its colour may be perfectly satisfactory, but when we try the effect we may find that the object is so light or so dark that it separates itself from all others and "jumps" at us. Its "value" therefore is too high or too low for the room.

14

SCALE

Scale in colour is a proper correspondence in the intensity of the colours used. An *absolute* correspondence would be either the use of all the colours in their strongest hues or else a greying of them all in a like degree. Such correspondence as this makes for harmony—and also for monotony. A total want of correspondence makes for entire incongruity. Let us exemplify—as to the first, a whole room done in pastel shades, all equally greyed, would be uninteresting to the last degree. As to the second: bring into another room, in which the textiles are precious antiques of quite sufficient but time-softened colour, a new cushion of raw, untamed red-orange or brilliant blue—and you bring disaster. The existing beautiful tones would be "killed" by the new arrival, and of that itself we should immediately exclaim: "Take it away; it is all out of scale!"

Entire correspondence or entire dissonance should therefore be avoided and an *harmonising but not equal degree* of intensity decided upon. The reason for this is plain. *Some* accent is needed for relief and contrast, but over accent simply produces disturbance. We have, it is true, the contrast of the colours themselves, but to avail ourselves of the *whole gamut of colour* we should add a proper degree of contrast in their intensities also.

A quiet or soft colouring is one in which most of the tones are greyed, with a few of somewhat greater strength: a brilliant colouring is one in which most of the colours are high with a few of somewhat lesser intensity: and necessarily there is a succession of degrees between. The degree decided upon is the *pitch or key*.

And not only may a certain key of colour exist in

an individual fabric, but throughout a room full of them: and the same plan of accent may there also prevail. Many decorators, for instance, use *in general* fabrics of soft colouring—because they are naturally harmonious and easy to manage—and then "key up the room" with a few notes of more intense but not incongruous colour with perhaps a black satin cushion or two to add to the contrast. But if one has a proper colour-sense it is not necessary to "play safe" to this degree—the Orientals have never found it obligatory to be anæmic in order to be harmonious. We may take the cue from them and from the age of Louis Quinze, when colouring was exquisite but nevertheless in good strong tones—in *tones,* however, not in raw and undiluted rainbow hues.

THE PROPORTIONS OF COLOURS

The proportions in which the respective colours in a colour-scheme should be used have been given and we may mention those in a particular harmony:

Sage $^{14}\!/_{32}$, slate and citron $^{5}\!/_{32}$ each, green $^{3}\!/_{32}$ and blue and yellow $^{1}\!/_{32}$ each.*

Such examples are useful as indicating the large amount of neutral tone as opposed to stronger hues commonly advisable; especially for amateurs in furnishing and those who have not a strongly developed colour-sense. It would manifestly be absurd, however, to attempt to apply in practice such tables literally or in any "rule of thumb" manner, measuring off so many square feet to be in such a colour, so many in another, and so on. As there is nothing like actual demonstration let us try it and see.

The proportions in each instance are based on the *normal colours,* and the moment these are departed

---

* Color Value, by C. R. Clifford.

from the conditions are changed. In the example given the green would (from its quantity) naturally be employed in the textiles—furniture-coverings, curtains and door-hangings. We should hope that no one would use for these the unadulterated prismatic green, yet that is the hue provided for in the above proportion-table. A modified green would, of course, be chosen, and according to the extent of its modification so could a larger proportion of this colour be employed with a consequent reduction of the amount of whichever neutral the modification impinged upon.

Ceilings usually approximate white, and woodwork and sash curtains are very frequently white; in such cases, then, we have the intrusion of another neutral, still further lessening the necessity, at least, for the employment of so great a body of sage, slate and citron.

But more important still is the advisability (not reckoned with in the proportion table) of introducing other colour. There has been entirely too much of this "keying and relating" of quiet tones, resulting in the reaction of the modernists who in some phases have run riot in the contrary direction. Let us be both scientific and sane. To stick to our example the general effect of a room in this colour-scheme would be greenish, and the relieving strong colours yellow and blue also equal green. Now the complementary of green is red, and the complementary should always be introduced to give relief. There should, therefore, be some touches somewhere of a modified red, such as rose, garnet or the like. Look at the blue and yellow scheme with a touch of rose in Plate 63: now lay a piece of white paper over the rose and see how the scheme immediately "goes dead."

And with all the exemplifications of the past, why in

the name of art should we confine ourselves to the poverty-stricken colour-combinations we so often see? We might sometimes think from these that *blended colour* does not exist. Consider the frescoes and tapestries and banners, the glorious needlework, velvets and brocades from the Renaissance to the days of Louis Seize; visit the museums and observe the wonders of Oriental art: look at the indications of colour evident even through the medium of half-tone reproduction in such an interior as Plate 139 and in such textiles as are shown in Plates 130 A, 143 B, 144, 145 A, B and C, 152 B, 162 A and B. We may then realise what colour has been and may be again!

The secret of the decorative effect of blended colour is an open and very simple one. Let us take, for example, a picture or a piece of textile. The hues of either may be of much variety and even brilliant in themselves, but to a great extent they complement and thus neutralise each other, some one colour, however, being dominant. If we look at a picture or a fabric, then, we shall see two results—if good it counts as a beautiful piece of blended colour; nevertheless its *total effect* is not a confusion but is generally neutral, with red, yellow or another hue somewhat in ascendancy over the rest. This explains why we may, if we so wish, use an immense deal of colour *provided it is properly balanced.*

UNITY AND VARIETY IN HOUSEHOLD DECORATION

The improvement in household decoration is one of the most encouraging signs of American artistic development, but in many instances it is but partial: only in the case of the most widely cultured, or those employing the best decorators, can it be called complete. Most reforms begin in the same manner; the improvement at first is usually one of details, finally sweeping on to their proper end.

Household decoration in this country, then, began with the room as its unit, whereas the proper conception is the *house,* or apartment, as the unit, each room being merely an integral part of a consistent whole. The faulty point of view so largely obtaining has usually resulted in disunity—greater or less in degree according to the taste of the owner. To the average householder, and equally the average decorator, the thought of complete consistency in decoration has hardly occurred, and when it has the result has been at the expense of the equally desirable and necessary variety. It will be the purpose of the present section to point out, and for the first time, how both may be obtained.

DISUNITY

What then is the disunity against which our attention should be directed? Let us at once realise that a home, a club-house or even a hotel is not to be a congeries of rooms of various styles, characters or colourings: it is an entity, and if in the final result we do not *feel* it to be such then *there* is disunity.

Happily the day is past when we have such examples as "Harthover," amusingly described in "The Water-Babies," where the third floor was Norman, the second cinquecento, the first Elizabethan, the right wing Pure Doric and the back staircase from the Taj Mahal, but unfortunately we may still cite such examples as the following—examples that would be unthinkable at the hands of the best men but which are not beyond the perpetration of some whose establishments bear the sign "Interior Decorators." The hall wall then, say, is of a greenish-gray sand-finish, and the furniture of mahogany. In open view at the left is the library, in Tudor style, with panelled walls and bookcases of dark oak and with upholstery and hangings of a deep crimson red. On the right is the drawing-room, with walls of yellow damask, and Louis Seize furniture in ivory-white, covered in the yellow of the walls. At the rear we discover the hospitable dining-room papered in blue, with its festive board and other furniture in quartered oak of golden hue. Each one of these rooms may be consistent in itself—*but fancy the prospect to the visitor entering the hall and from his point of vantage glancing about at the disunity opened before him in these four rooms.*

Even if the construction of the house made it possible for us to view but one of these rooms at a time the result would intrinsically be nearly as bad, because one's optical memory is not so short that the character of one room is forgotten in passing into the hall and on into another room.

We may still say that there are builders who are not architects, that there are artisans who are not artists.

THE IDEAL

The most certain method of improvement in any direction is the keeping before us of an ideal; or, to phrase it in our more modern way, the scheme of "what we are after," and that scheme must be firmly based upon the facts and circumstances.

The home, to suit the requirements of modern life, must possess two sets of qualities. On the one hand our aim should be to secure a restful habitation, not a museum or a *melange*. The watchwords here may be rest, peace, sleep. On the other hand we are living, active human beings, fond of variety and filled with many interests. These may be comprised in the words cheer, action, companionship. Our homes must express both. The first means unity: the second variety. How shall we accomplish the securing of the one without sacrificing the other?

UNITY

Unity must exist in many directions but one of the most important of these is colour—and it is one of those most frequently violated. Unity in its other relations will be considered in other chapters.

As shown in the chapter on "Walls: as Decoration and as Background," neutral backgrounds are by no means a necessity; they are, however, largely employed by all good decorators and certainly much simplify the work of the person superintending his own furnishing. Indeed, when we consider the following line of thought regarding backgrounds, it will be plain that treating the walls of a *series of rooms* in other than a rather neutral manner will land the amateur among problems which while susceptible of solution he might find beyond his management.

BACKGROUND

I. If we preserve unity in the background (walls and ceilings) we shall then have a basis throughout the house which will act as a balance to the various other colours that we may and should introduce in attractively furnishing it. Naturally this unity does not need to be actual identity; it will suffice where rooms are but singly visible if a general *impression* be kept. Where rooms communicate it is certainly better that the likeness should be very close: if, for instance, one is panelled it would be better that both should be, and that the tones should be the same in each. If the walls are painted or papered the general tone of wall-surface should be kept, but identity is not necessary, especially if the purpose of the rooms be different.

II. A moment's practical thought will show us that if we keep this unity throughout and choose any strong colouring for our walls, we should have a definitely yellow, red, blue, green or purple house—a condition which would be intolerable. We are therefore guided to the selection of a more neutral colouring.

III. Neutrality means to many—drabness. To the lover of beauty it means some of the most beautiful tones in a beautiful world. Among these are the ivories, champagne, dull gold, creams, buffs and certain tans; pinkish grey or ashes of rose, bluish grey, greenish grey and mauve grey, or the combinations of these.

FLOORS

Some good decorators also extensively use rugs of the same character, or at least general colouring, throughout the house, considering the floors as a portion of the background and likewise choosing neutral shades such as grey and taupe. This is usually unnecessary and involves too great a sacrifice of decorative opportunity.

FURNISHINGS

The securing of unity by harmonious and closely related backgrounds is much, but suppose we should now proceed to fill this beautiful shell of the house, apartment or club-house with objects of many incongruous hues! Should we not at once destroy the unity we had taken such pains to secure? And yet, speaking by and large, there is usually too *little* colour in American and British homes rather than too much—and the too little is often badly used.

The truth is that the western nations have greatly lost their colour-sense, either through materialism, drabness of life, or what other defect it behooves us not to argue here.

The principles of colour harmony which have been mentioned are true of all *intensities* of colour and are therefore perfectly adapted to any of the three tendencies in decoration—as has been mentioned some decorators use in general quiet, attenuated shades of colour and then "key up" with a few more vivid spots: others use tones such as those shown in the colour-charts, of sufficient vitality and yet of a harmonising quality: the so-called "Modern" school, considered in the next section, uses strong and positive colour. The plan which will be suggested is of equal use whichever degree of intensity may be decided upon.

THE USE OF COLOUR IN DECORATION

Blue and the greens which contain but the normal proportion of yellow are *retiring* and are *cool*.

All shades of yellow and of red, except those largely neutralised by the admixture of other colours or o. black or of white, are *advancing* and are *warm* in tone.

Suppose, then, we place in a room with neutral background rugs of a soft green and hang portières of the same in the doorway. So far, we shall have a room which is quiet, cool and restful. We shall also find that it lacks life, and in continual occupancy would prove somewhat depressing in its influence over mind and body.

If the reader will refer to Plate 59 he will find a room in which the rugs and portières are of just this character, but into which have been imported a few touches of rose. The depression has gone; the quiet remains; the room is now livable and "human." These few touches of rose have done the work.

Furthermore, although these touches are few and

PLATE 59

THE QUIET ROOM
From the Painting by Edward Stratton Holloway
(Rose Dominant Over Green)

although rose is but a modified red, it will be found that the rose is more noticeable than the green.

If yellow and blue had been used instead of rose and green the result in these respects would have been much the same. In other words yellow, orange and red are *dominant* over green and blue and such quiet shades as tans, brown and greys.

Shades of yellow and of red, and their combination orange being dominant, *if we choose any one of these shades and carry it by the use of various objects and furnishings throughout the various rooms we shall have unity.*

We may use then, with the above, other and quieter colours alone or in combination in the different rooms and we shall have variety.

Let us take a concrete example.

The illustration (Plate 59) was painted directly from an actual bedroom in an apartment. How shall unity and variety be carried through the remaining rooms? Let us take up each in detail.

Reception Room.* Such a room may well be characterised by greater elegance than a bedroom and yet should preserve an inviting and companionable atmosphere rather than the formal frigidity often experienced. Rose having been selected as the dominant (though one of the others might have been chosen as well) it must also be used here, and as it possesses both the qualities of elegance and humanity it may be used in considerable quantity. We shall need ample relieving surface, so that it would be well to employ a panel-

---

* Conditions of living are changing rapidly, and in apartments and new small houses it is a little difficult to decide upon the best name for what is properly a very small drawing-room and furnished as such. That term is a trifle pretentious for a room of that size, but living-room is scarcely sufficiently elegant, and there is often a living-room in addition. As the room discussed is primarily for the reception of friends, reception-room seems as appropriate a name as any.

ling in ivory-white or else a handsome paper of the same general tone, striped or brocaded in the surfacing and not in another colour. The bedroom shown in the illustration was afterward papered in this tone and two rooms so carried out would thus harmonise as to the wall effect.

We should also have ample relieving space in plain or approximately plain colour. Indeed, in choosing for an example the apartment, or the equivalent house with small rooms, the writers have consciously chosen the most difficult subject with which to deal. The difficulty lies in the fact that one of our most beautiful decorative resources is the rug and fabric of blended colouring, but as these cut up and crowd in effect the small room we must forbid ourselves the use of these in such instances or choose them with great discretion. As we shall have much colour in this room before we have finished, it would be wise to choose one rug, largely covering the floor, of plain warm grey, or in two tones of that colour closely approaching each other and in small and simple pattern, or plain with a deeper border. The portières had also better be of rather solid color—a rose velvet, a brocade of unobtrusive pattern or the less expensive rep of irregular weave. On the chair-coverings we may let ourselves go considerably. For these we may select preferably perhaps some such material as the stripe shown in the chart or a blend of various colourings in which rose shall be dominant. This fabric might be of cream, rose and blue stripe, not too wide in pattern, or of tapestry, or *petit point,* again not so large in design as to be out of scale with the room or the surfaces covered. If there is a sofa or settee it would naturally have the same covering as the chairs, but if there is a large couch instead it

PLATE 60

Varied Colour in Cushions and Other Objects

Satin-Stripe Paper

General Tone of Warm Grey Rug

RECEPTION-ROOM ROSE DOMINANT

Ivory-white
Trim

Couch Covering
Chair Covering

PLATE 61

Tone of Rug

ROSE DOMINANT OVER BLUE

Varied Colour in Small Objects
Narrow Stripe Paper

Rose Silk Lamp-shade and Small Objects
Chair Covering of Varied Colour

SECOND BEDROOM

PLATE 62

Cretonne in Rose and Tan

SITTING OR SEWING ROOM

Paper of Linen Shade
Possible Tone for Tan Rug

ROSE DOMINANT OVER TAN

Cretonne of Cooler Tones

PLATE 63

Furniture Covering
Tone of Rug

Ivory-white Trim
Champagne Paper or Panelling

A Touch of Rose in Small Objects
Furniture Covering
Tone of Rug

COLOUR SCHEME, BASED ON YELLOWS, FOR TWO ROOMS

would be better to use a plain material such as Burgundy rose velour and again let ourselves go with an abundance of varied but harmonious cushions. A chart of this colour-scheme is given in Plate 60, but it must be remembered that in all these charts the samples of textiles are necessarily much out of proportion to the large surfaces of walls and floors.

The lamp had better be of vase shape in grey pottery, or mottled rose, or solid black with a reflecting surface, or of Chinese porcelain, and the shade in rose silk. The black bowl is exceedingly effective and the rose of the shade reflects in its upper curves.

In any room relief may be secured, where necessary, in the smaller objects, and this relief may be either in the direction of greater neutrality or more colour. Such an article as a vase of ivory-white or grey porcelain or pottery would give the former, a handsomely tooled binding in blue, a colourful brocade or Chinese textile or embroidery under the lamp would aid in supplying the latter. The gold or silver tones of candlesticks, etc., add richness and variety.

It will have been understood from the above description that there is not only no intention of confining the readers to the materials shown in the charts but that they may go far afield in choice provided the general colour-scheme and proportions be kept. And this is true of tone as well as of fabric, for it may be considerably altered so that harmony is preserved, and the shade of one fabric may well be lighter or darker than that of another. The same effect may also be carried out in very inexpensive materials.

Second Bedroom. If this room communicates with the first (a portion of which is shown in Plate 59) it should by all means be in the same colouring of green, rose and white. This does not presuppose monotony but harmony, and variety may be gained in numerous other ways: in the disposition of the furniture, in the treatment of the bed and the windows and in the smaller objects, for instance. Other small variations may be made, such as using plain or self-figured rose for the chairs, instead of cretonne. Indeed, cretonne has been so greatly employed of late years that restraint in this respect is advisable. If the two rooms do not communicate we may use blue as the secondary colour, and of this scheme a colour chart is given (Plate 61). The paper might be of the narrow stripe in cream and grey: and we might add that this colour-combination in any form is excellent for either a warm or cold exposure. The rugs should be mainly or entirely of blue. The chair-coverings may be in any material (perhaps tapestry) giving approximately the shades and proportions of the sample—the blues not too bright and greater in quantity than the rose. Or these coverings may be in rose and an additional supply of blue be introduced elsewhere *so as to carry it through.* A room is a picture painted with materials of various sorts instead of with pigment, and the principles in both arts are the same—the prominent colours should not be in one spot of each only but be judiciously distributed in smaller quantities elsewhere as well. A screen might be in blue, or better still in blue and grey, the grey harmonising with that in the walls.

So far we have four colours—the blue, the rose, the grey of the walls and the colour of the furniture—perhaps mahogany. We may extend our palette still further. In the sample given in the chart of a possible chair-covering, tans and greens appear with harmony. Into a room furnished much in this general key was recently introduced a canary in a tan Chinese bird-cage with emerald green tassels. It proved an inspiration in the direction of varied colouring.

The blue rugs above referred to should be kept simple. The border or design could be of rose or of quiet tan if there is some quantity of this elsewhere in the room. The shade for the lamp or electric lights had better perhaps be plain rose silk.

It is to be noted that while this colour-scheme has been assigned to a bedroom it is equally available for rooms of other character, and that most of the colour-schemes are interchangeable. They have been thus assigned only to give *concreteness,* such examples being much more helpful than much loose generality.

Sitting- and Sewing-room. It is with such rooms as these that we may secure charming results at little expense. Let us take as an example the sensible shades of tan or wood-brown, with rose again dominant to carry through the unity of the apartment. The room chosen for such a purpose should naturally have a good light. If it be sunny and warm in tone choose the cooler shades: if it has a north light warmer ones should be selected. The choice of goods is wide and one may readily secure decorative materials from quiet greyish wood-browns to rich and warm tans.

In the chart (Plate 62) is exemplified a rather warm combination, but with cooler paper of a linen shade. It could run into ashes of rose, cream or light buff, if not too strong, and still not essentially depart from the general key of wall surface we are employing throughout, because it will look cooler in combination with the colouring of the other surfaces in the room than it really is.

The assortment of inexpensive rugs at our command is perhaps greater in tans and browns than in other colours, so that we may easily make a choice.

Good general tones for a bordered rug are given in the chart, but it would be well to have some small pattern in the central portion, because every thread dropped in sewing shows upon a solid colour. Any pleasing and harmonious design may be chosen, but it should be quiet if one follows the writers' suggestion that here if anywhere is the place to use cretonnes. Two samples are given in the chart, one a little brighter and cooler than the other. There are many others as good as either, and they run all the way from 75 cents to $4 a yard, or more. Neither of those shown is expensive.

Dining-room. A dining-room should always be most attractive, and we have reserved for it one of the most charming of colour-schemes—pinkish rose and silver grey. As it is not possible to give additional charts, this is omitted, as the general plan has been so fully dealt with that a few observations will be all that are necessary. As usual the quantity of the neutral shade should be larger than of the dominant, pink-rose. The rug had better therefore be of grey, though it may contain rose or have a rose border. If the sideboard is of the Sheraton type with brass rail for a curtain this latter may be of one of the beautiful pink-rose and silver-grey stripes, in which the satin of the grey lights up with a silvery sheen. The screen before the serving table may be of the same, as this material possesses both quiet style and elegance. The lights may be shaded with rose, casting a warm glow over the room. It would be much better with this combination to have the side-lights and candlesticks of silver finish rather than of brass.

While we have taken rose as the dominant note throughout there are other shades of red which might be chosen; such as Burgundy or a soft crimson. These are darker and less luminous than rose and would require more discrimination to blend happily.

When we have said that either yellow or orange may be used as the dominant over blue, green, grey, or tan, and in combination therewith, we have covered the whole gamut of colour, for the shades of any of these may be infinitely varied provided that harmony is preserved. If one prefers the still more softened and greyish tones to those given they may as readily be used, but in the *proper proportions* of the colours in the actual atmosphere of a room all of the schemes will be mellow and harmonious.

Violet has not specifically been mentioned, though it may well take its place among the blending of colours in cretonnes, tapestries, etc. In its pure tones it is a difficult colour to carry through a series of rooms. When used its natural relief is gold or cream colour or both. Grey mauve is a delicate and beautiful colour for a boudoir but inappropriate for more robust rooms.

It may here again be said that as the materials used in the colour charts and mentioned in this section are variable in many directions, the same *idea* may be carried out irrespective of the employment of costly or inexpensive goods. It is naturally difficult to suit all circumstances, as one reader may be able to use antique furniture, rare fabrics, Ming vases and costly rugs, and another, who deserves equal attention, may be limited in means but mightily interested in the improvement of his home.

Though such immense variety has already been provided for, this plan extends still further in its scope. One dominant may rule *two* quieter shades of approximately equal quantity as, for instance, rose or yellow over green and tan. Nor have we as yet considered the correlative idea.

15

THE CORRELATIVE PLAN

As has been said, yellow, orange and red are dominant and advancing colours *except* when attenuated by the admixture of other colours or of black or white. Suppose, therefore, we attenuate them. Yellow and orange when so reduced become tints and tones—creams, champagnes, buffs, tans, browns and olives. Attenuated red, except in the shades we have mentioned of rose, Burgundy and mulberry, are not so useful in decoration. Pink alone is rather jejune, though in blending with other colors it is very happy and enlivening—a pink and apple-green sprigged pattern on a cream-white ground is a good example. Brickish red has its uses, as in floor tiles and fireplaces, but is vigorous, owing to its still retaining a great strength of red. The pinkish grey known as ashes of rose, is of great delicacy and refinement and so one would hardly care to carry it through more than two rooms, unless in a woman's apartment.

Let us therefore consider the derivations of yellow; for here we have great scope. *In these tones it has lost its dominant qualities and may so be carried through a series of rooms in quantity, to produce unity, other colours being used in various rooms as relief.* This, it will be seen, is the correlative or reverse of the former plan. In *that* the dominant was carried through; in *this* the neutral will be.

In order to illustrate as fully as possible within limits we give a colour chart embracing two rooms (Plate 63). To begin with the walls—where we should always begin—those in the drawing-room may be papered in a rich stripe or brocade of champagne. Better still would be panelling, enamelled in the same shade.

Either the beautiful blue and gold brocade or the yellow and grey stripe, or something approaching

either, might be used for the chair-coverings in this
room, the unused one being employed in another. The
rug could be a plain or small-figured one of the tone
shown, or of the lighter shades seen in Chinese rugs.
It had certainly better be plain or plain with a plain
border if used with the delicately patterned blue and
gold fabric. If a Chinese rug of unobtrusive pattern,
and with the usual blue designs, very quiet in tone,
could be secured this might be used with the stripe. If
the blue and gold is employed a few touches of rose
would be required in small objects to give warmth and
life. An entirely blue shade for the lamp should be
avoided—it would give too cold a light. It should be
of a deeper champagne or yellow, either plain or with
only a little blue. Any picture frames used should be
of gold (dull) and lighting fixtures of brass, also dull.
Candlesticks should be of brass, not silver.

In carrying these modified yellows through a series
of rooms the tones used may vary considerably where
the rooms do not communicate. Instead of champagne
we may go off to creams and buffs and tans with some
use in the rugs of even browns or olives. Yellow,
mauve, and grey; yellow, blue, and grey; and buff, grey,
and rose are all exquisite combinations. A very happy
colour-arrangement recently seen was this: panelled
walls painted deep cream, softly polished black Sheraton furniture, a Chinese rug of a beautiful grey-blue
with design in buff and rose, and draperies in striped
tan and grey-blue. Transitions should nowhere be sud-
den and startling but should be gradual and harmonious. And with these many varying shades we may
and should employ other varying *colours* as relief.
Nothing so gives an apartment a ''decorated,'' arranged, and artificial look as the too great prominence
of a colour carried throughout: whether it be the dom-

inant or the base which is so carried we should simply *feel* its presence; it should not jump at us at every step.

In the colour charts it must be remembered that it is possible to show only enough of the wall material to suffice for colour. In the actual work there would be a far greater proportion. Not only must there be large surfaces of these more neutral shades, but also a sufficiency of plain or nearly plain more strongly coloured area to balance the ornamental fabrics used. In general, ornament demands the relief of plain surfaces, plain surfaces demand the relief of ornament. The writers especially wish to impress these two points, regarding a not too great prominence of any one colour and a not overloading with ornament; as, if the method given were otherwise carried out, the intention would be parodied and a sincere attempt at helpfulness quite destroyed.

THE LARGER SCOPE

A consideration of unity and variety would not be complete without thought directed toward the decoration of larger premises than those so far discussed. Their treatment is at once easier and more difficult; easier because the large room gives more scope to the play of decorative facilities; more difficult only because there are more rooms.

Their very spaciousness, if not cluttered with objects of all descriptions, has the effect of minimising pattern and harmonising colour. The smallness of a floor debars us from cutting it up with design, lest it look smaller than ever: and if we did use quiet Oriental rugs we should have to exercise our wits and our energies to find two or three sufficiently akin in tone and figure. Upon a spacious floor we may, however, by the use of due discrimination distribute several pieces even of differing characters. The few chairs which may find place in a small room must usually, for the avoiding of distraction, be covered with the same material: in the large living-room we may use one covering for most of the seating facilities and then indulge in a burst of varied colour with the big easy upholstered chairs. Chests, large cabinets, consoles and large luxurious couches are mostly forbidden by smallness of space but are the very things we need where there is abundance of room.

The opportunities for variety provided by the system here outlined are almost infinite. In a house of thirty rooms half a dozen of them might be in one general scheme and yet each be individual. If in so many the combination of rose and blue were used, for example, the rooms themselves would be on different floors and for different purposes—perhaps a drawing-room, nursery, man's room and boudoir with accompanying bedrooms. The furniture and furnishings of these various classes would naturally make a decided difference in the employment of the colouring and give very different effects. Then in one room the rose would be used in one place and in another in a different place; the shades may vary considerably; the additional colours used for relief need not be all alike; plain goods would be used in one situation and blended or patterned in another and the character and designs of the textiles would naturally not be the same. In a boudoir and adjoining bedrooms the furnishings of the former would be the more luxurious—to mention one particular alone the curtains of the boudoir would be silken, perhaps with such an *appliqué* as is suggested in the chapter on Windows; those of the bedrooms might appropriately be a beautiful white net. An indication of the varying treatment of communicating bedrooms has already been given. In a man's room the colouring might well be deeper and more masculine— mulberry or Burgundy and plum-blue; in a young girl's the lighter French flowered stripes of rose and blue on cream; thus totally varying the tone and character, yet preserving the adopted hues and the unity thus gained.

THE USE OF COLOUR IN THE "MODERN" DECORATION

The employment of colour is probably the most outstanding feature of this method of decoration, described in the last chapter of Part I, and the more extreme examples of its use are apt to irritate persons neutral by temperament or training, precisely as does "noise" in modern music. The use of positive colour in the days of William and Mary in England and Louis Quatorze in France was as great as it is among the modern men and women, and yet it is safe to believe that interiors of those periods would not affect the quieter-minded as do some examples of modern work. This is but to say that in these specially mentioned cases the use of colour is not happy and that their harmonies (?) need revision or use in a different manner. Turquoise and blue-green have run a maddening course: one might sometimes think that blue-green, strong violet and red-orange, and green, golden-yellow and blue-violet were the only colour combinations known, were it not for such others as red-orange walls with bright blue woodwork and furniture, and a typically German ugly green, red and tan "relieved" by mauve. The unentrancing terra-cotta also has its innings. Now these hues may be, or were, more unusual than the beautiful rose-reds, yellow buffs and tans, grey-blues and apple-greens—and the fact that they were *not* employed in such quantities and prominence by the master colourists of the past shows us there was a *reason*.

There is also occasionally a tendency to use but two well-harmonising colours in a room: such as ivory and blue. grey and green, yellow and cream, yellow and blue—every one of which combinations needs for relief touches of rose-red or orange.

Absolute white and black has been greatly employed, to which there is no objection except that it is much more apt to stand apart from colour than would ivory and black.

With the object of seeing just why these combinations have been so greatly exploited the writers have gone over a large body of Peasant Art, which, as has been said in Part I, is one of the inspirations of the movement. They found red-orange walls and ceilings stripped with blue-green, and the primitive yellow and vermilion red with black and white, but in the overwhelming majority of cases *tones* were used and in beautiful combinations. Many of these tones were bright and cheerful and others quiet. So useful are these combinations as suggestions for colour-schemes that it will be far more valuable to mention some of them than to recite for adaptation what has already been done by modern decorators. The manner in which these schemes may actually be used is indicated in the section on "Unity and Variety" just preceding. These colour-memoranda are given just as transcribed, mostly from costumes and textiles, as these notes sometimes show the general proportions in which the tones are used. Doubtless some of these combinations have been employed by modern decorators.

Cream white, plum brown, pale rose red, with touches of buff and pale blue.

Cream, buff and indigo, relieved with touches of soft red.

Background of gun-metal grey, design in pale buff and a tone of light red.

A tone of cranberry red, tone of bluish-green, tone of indigo, all relieved with pale-buff.

Reddish buff with relief of maroon, white and dark green (nearly black).

Cream and strong orange, light indigo and black.

Burgundy rose, medium green, light yellow, black and white.

A very odd one was cream, light plum and salmon, relieved with light yellow and black.

And a very beautiful one from an Italian costume, cream white, Burgundy rose, quiet apple-green and plum, with a spot of red (which would better have been bright rose) and small touches of indigo and bright orange.

Tan, yellow, dull blue and dull green.

Fire-cracker red, dark blue, green and black.

Regarding colour and colour-combinations, it should be remembered that even among artists and experts there is a certain amount of divergence of view as to what is attractive and harmonious, due probably either to the individual eye or temperament, and so it is unwise to indulge in too much dogmatism upon the subject. This applies also to intensity of colour, strength being a delight to some and a positive disturbance to others. As a general rule it may, however, safely be said that the prismatic colours in their purity should be employed only in small portions, but that tones, and good strong tones, too, such as those shown in the colour-plates of this chapter, will blend well when properly used and in proper proportions.

Colour in the home is productive of joyousness and cheer, and in its right use is in no way hostile to restfulness and peace.

Suggestions for the practical use of colour in this newer decoration naturally appear in their respective departments—the chapters on Walls, Floors and Textiles.

CHAPTER III

WALLS, AS DECORATION AND AS BACKGROUND

PANELLING, WAINSCOTTING. COMBINATION WALLS. MASONRY, PLASTER AND SPECIAL FINISHES. THE WHITES AND TINTS. DECORATIVE WALLS. PAPERS AND THEIR CHOICE. PAPER PANELS, FRIEZES, DADOS AND CANOPIES. CEILINGS. BORDERS AND PICTURE RAILS. WOODWORK. "THE WHITES" FOR WALL USE. THE "NEWER" DECORATION.

THE treatment of walls is one of the fundamentals of decoration; and this is evident when we realise that no furnishing, however handsome in itself, will constitute a good interior unless the walls, also, have been adequately studied and carried out in accordance with the principles of good design.

Walls, with their "trim," ceilings, and floors compose the shell of the room; and to these may be added the shades and curtains of the windows and the doors or hangings. So intimately are all these connected one with another in any scheme of decoration that no one of them should be proceeded with until all have been taken into account; nor should the treatment of that shell be decided upon without a consideration of that which is to occupy it—the furniture, with its covering, especially as to colour and pattern, and the various subsidiary objects of use and ornament.

As is indicated by the title of this chapter, walls may either be decorative or simple but adequate and beautiful backgrounds. Extremely spacious rooms, such as ball-rooms and the more public rooms of palatial houses need a decorative treatment (such as the

Italian Renaissance, Adam, Louis XV and Louis XVI styles afford) and less imposing premises are often susceptible of a due amount of decoration in the wall surfaces, which will be shown as we proceed. The drawing-rooms of small houses and apartments may frequently be given a more ornamental character than the private rooms without a disturbance of the unities, and in such properties the "Modern" decoration (considered at the end of this chapter) will also be found a resource of value. On the other hand, the treatment of walls as backgrounds is often the best, as it is the most generally feasible, method; so that both styles will have equal attention here, the simply painted or papered wall being as carefully considered as the most elaborate.

A particularly careful consideration of Walls during the historic periods has been given in Part I, and the chapters on International-Interperiod Decoration (Part III) indicates those to be used under each of the great decorative influences. The subject is now expanded by the taking up here of the methods most of value to the present-day householder, including some of the less usual effects by way of suggestion to those who wish to give individuality to their homes.

Before treating of the more simple painting or papering it will be well to consider walls of a constructional nature. In the adoption of such walls the services of an architect or decorator are required, but it is advisable that the reader should here at least consider their possibility and advantages.

PANELLED WALLS

These and their appropriate ceilings are primarily of Period character and where a distinctly period style

PLATE 64

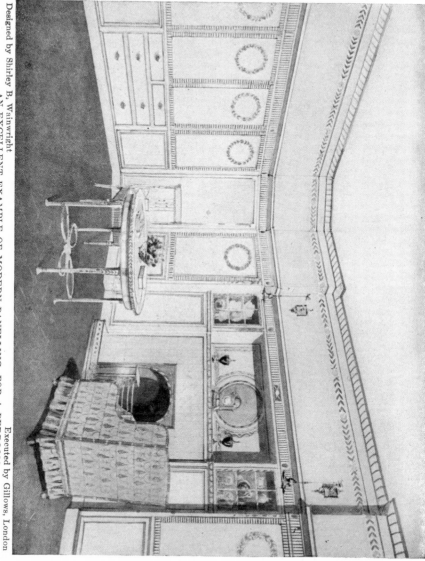

Designed by Shirley B, Wainwright   Executed by Gillows, London
AN EXCELLENT EXAMPLE OF MODERN PANELLING, FOR A BEDROOM
The Wardrobe and Drawers Built in the Left Wall Would Prove a Great Convenience
From the "Studio Year Book of Decorative Art," by Permission

of decoration is desired a correct following of that style is necessary. Modern architects have, however, designed many more non-committal derivations and these may be employed where a general method of furnishing is adopted. A charming British example of such panelling in a modern bedroom is illustrated in colour in Plate 64. It may be said here that panelling of even such an elaborate character as that in the Georgian dining-room shown in Plate 65 A, while decorative, is still of background nature, and allows, without confusion, the employment of pattern and colour in the furnishings, as does all other panelling not in itself too ornamental, colourful or of striking contrast. In eighteenth century England and America panelling was often painted not only in white but in such tones as cream, pale green, blue green, grey and chocolate, and frequently the carving was gilded or parcel gilt.

With panelled walls should be included those with painted inserts and others mentioned in the section on Modern Decoration which follows. The very simple method of panelling by canvas and applied mouldings (Plate 65 B) is deserving of special attention because of its inexpensiveness and excellent effect. In drawing-rooms, dining-rooms and boudoirs such fabrics as damask and watered silk and distinguished ornamental Japanese and other papers may be used with fine effect as panel inserts. Such treatments give excellent scope to tasteful ingenuity—a plain or figured gold Japanese paper such as comes in sheets would go excellently well with panelling of a deep cream, or a silvered paper with grey or oyster-white. Conventional, or flower, or figure decorations may also be painted in panels, doorheads, and the like.

WAINSCOTS

When, in the eighteenth century, wainscotting gradually dwindled to a panelled dado (and finally to mere baseboard and cornice) the plastered portion of the wall was either in white or in such tints as cream, grey, or light green, or else covered with fabric, or the wall-papers which by then had come in fashion. Such papers might either be in monotone or polychrome; or, as suggested above, in gold or silver.

COMBINATION WALLS

Able architects, both here and abroad, in certain instances use wood with plaster to such an extent that the result may probably be considered a combination wall. The woodwork consists of inglenooks, built-in furniture, special features and beamed ceilings, and so altogether charming and homelike are most of these effects that they are especially called to the attention of the reader. Two of these are illustrated here (Plate 66 A and B), and others will be found in Plates 53 and 78 B. In such cases the wall itself may be in white, tint, or in a strong tone, harmonising either by likeness or contrast with the woodwork and the furnishings. Woodwork will be considered at the end of this chapter.

Other combination walls are those of stone, brick or tile with plaster, and each of these may have its use in appropriate situations.

STONE, MASONRY, PLASTER AND SPECIAL FINISHES

In large houses of appropriate architectural character the walls of halls, stairways and some of the other more public portions may be of cut stone, as may also be specially designed studios, living-rooms, etc. (Plate 67 B). Palatial rooms and halls are also sometimes lined with marble, white, flecked or of colour. Some-

PLATE 65

A. A NOBLY PROPORTIONED DINING ROOM PANELLED IN GEORGIAN STYLE
By Courtesy of Sir Ernest Newton, Architect, London

B. WALLS COVERED WITH FILLED CANVAS, AND MOULDING APPLIED TO
FORM PANELS
Simple Panelling may be in Tint, Two-tone or Strong Tone. Present Instance is in Oyster
White with Ceiling of Plain Silver Japanese Paper in Sheets 19 x 47 Inches. Hangings Blue
Own Home of Edmund B. Gilchrist, Architect, Philadelphia

times these and the following but partially cover the walls with a high dado, the upper portion being tinted (such as a white marble with pale green-grey plaster) or decorated. A certain amount of roughness and texture is allowable in stone walls of entirely informal nature, but to the writers the cobblestone wall usually adjacent to a fireplace is hideous even for a "camp." It should also be mentioned that plaster imitation of stonework is a piece of architectural dishonesty and a thing to be abhorred.

Concrete blocks with mortar afford such an admirable wall of less elaborate and expensive character that an example is illustrated (Plate 67 A). No better foil for the fine Italian furniture could be imagined, and the cross-beamed ceiling with rosettes at the crossings carries out an effect of unusual and sanely architectural character. In such an instance the polychrome painting of the rosettes would give additional decorative quality.

Brick walls are useful for solaria and other informal purposes, and in their place a combination of brick with rough-cast plaster above it would be very attractive.

Tile, when appropriately chosen, is another desirable finish, either alone or with plaster.

With plaster walls we arrive at one of the most practical surfaces at our disposal and one susceptible of a variety of treatments. Sand-finished plaster, either in its natural tone or tinted, is most desirable, especially for spacious rooms such as the dining-room illustrated (Plate 68). While on first thought such a wall might seem to possess no great handsomeness it is found to make one of the most admirable finishes as background to richly carved furniture of noble proportions and hangings of tapestry or brocade. Its use

during the Renaissance period in instances where the
walls were not of decorative character, is a sufficient
credential of its merit. More smoothly finished plaster was also there, and may now, constantly, be employed. Such a wall finished with a frieze in "compo,"
as in the Adam room illustrated (Plate 69), likewise
affords an excellent background with sufficient decoration above to avoid entire plainness of effect. The
treatment of plaster walls as an architectural and decorative feature was a special *metier* with the Adam
Brothers ("The Adelphi") and anyone considering
walls of this character should consult the recently published book on their lives and work.* Tinted, painted
and decorated plaster may best be treated in subsequent sections.

WHITE AND PLAINLY TINTED WALLS

In an old Dutch Colonial house, the roof of which
descended to the hillside upon which it was built, the
interior walls bore both the tooth and tone of time. Its
purchasers, with enlightened common-sense, wished to
preserve its genuine antiquity and yet secure freshness; they whitewashed the walls (using the Light-
house Mixture† which does not rub off) and when they
had hung simple white curtains and introduced their
fine old mahogany furniture, the result was all that
could be desired.

---

* For plaster and parge treatments the reader is also referred to
Part I, Chapter I.

† The Government formula for this mixture is: Slake a half bushel
of lime with boiling water, cover during the process to keep in steam.
Strain the liquid through a fine sieve or strainer and add to it a peck of
salt, previously dissolved in warm water, three pounds of ground rice
boiled to a thin paste and stirred in while hot, half a pound of Spanish
whiting and one pound of clear glue, previously dissolved by soaking in
cold water, and then hanging over a slow fire in a small pot hung in a
larger one filled with water. Add five gallons of hot water to the mixture,
stir well and let it stand a few days, covered from dirt. To be applied hot,

PLATE 66

A. PLASTER WALLS IN COMBINATION WITH EXTENSIVE WOODWORK
By Courtesy of Sir Ernest Newton, Architect, London

B. A COMBINATION OF MANY MATERIALS IN A MODERN ENGLISH
DINING ROOM

Walls, Wood, and Plaster Painted Buff and Green; Base of Fireplace, Stone; Upper Facing,
Brick; Back, Blue Tile; Hood, Sconces and Centre Light, Copper; Bull's Eyes in Door, Dark
Green Glass; Rug, Grey-Green.

Courtesy of Percy Lancaster, Architect, Southport, England

PLATE 67

B. STONE WALLS AND FLAGGING

Courtesy of Messrs: Wilson Eyre and McIlvaine, Architects, Philadelphia

A. WALL OF CONCRETE BLOCKS: CROSS-BEAMED CEILING
WITH ROSETTES AT THE CROSSINGS

PLATE 68

SAND–FINISHED WALLS FORMING AN ADMIRABLE BACKGROUND TO
TAPESTRY AND FURNITURE
By Courtesy of Messrs. Wilson Eyre and McIlvaine, Architects, Philadelphia

PLATE 69

PLASTER WALLS WITH ADAM MANTEL, CORNICE,
CEILING AND FURNITURE

The Ceiling of this Room was Carefully Copied from a Ceiling of One
of the Rooms of "Solitude," the Seat of the Honourable John Penn,
in Philadelphia
By Courtesy of Messrs. Mellor and Meigs, Architects, Philadelphia

Walls so done, or painted in oil colours, or with some of the numerous advertised preparations, naturally possess much of the same character as those treated in the previous section—there is a simplicity and bigness about them all.

As compared with papered walls, soon to be considered, each has its own advantages. The painted wall is more sanatory than the papered wall, particularly when many layers of paper are allowed to accumulate without scraping. With paint any desired tone may readily be mixed, whereas the precise shade desired may not always be obtained in paper. Paint demands walls in perfect condition and properly prepared: paper is not so exigent and is readily applied.

That the simply painted wall possesses great charm in combination with appropriate, well-placed pictures and attractive furniture, is shown by the man's living-room illustrated (Plate 70 A).

DECORATIVE WALLS AND THEIR USES

This heading at once brings us face to face with the important query: Shall our walls be considered and treated as Background or as Decoration? and, after all, the question should not be difficult for each of us to decide. The masters of the late Italian Renaissance (Plate 139) and of some subsequent periods, revelling in ornament and colour, were quite competent to endue all their surfaces and furnishings—walls, ceilings, floors, hangings and furniture—with these qualities—and yet secure harmony and repose: it is possible for our best architects and a few decorators to-day to do likewise, but it is hardly needful to mention that the problem demands knowledge, wisdom and taste of an high order. Unless, then, the householder can avail himself of such aid he had better deny himself an universal ornateness. As a general principle ornament requires the relief of plain surfaces; strong colour the relief of neutral tones. It is evident, then, in our use of ornament that we must have relative simplicity and quietness *somewhere,* and it should not be difficult for us to decide where it shall be.

It should at once be said that *spaciousness* is a great simplifier, so that if our rooms are large and anything approaching crowding is sedulously avoided, much more ornament and colour may be employed than in smaller and necessarily well-filled apartments.

If furniture is scant and simple, walls of rather decorative character are almost demanded to avoid bareness of effect. If furniture, hangings, and the various other objects with which we surround ourselves are rich and ornamental, the relief of background is the evident prescription. If walls are decorative, and particularly if ornamental ceilings are added thereto, the floor should be restful, and the upholstery and hangings without obtrusive pattern and strong contrasts. Walls may be decorative and yet not insistent, and these naturally allow a considerable degree of these qualities of pattern and contrast elsewhere.

The principles guiding us are, therefore, plain and we may pass on to the consideration of decorative walls.

An illustration is given of a fine living-room in Plate 70 B. With the influence of Italy as inspiration this handsome and altogether happy result was secured in this manner:

The lofty walls were covered with canvas painted a dull gold, and the pattern stencilled upon it in burnt umber, not with hardness and regularity but with different quantities of colour, so that in some cases it is quite transparent. The polychrome frieze is painted,

PLATE 70

A. A SIMPLY PAINTED GREY WALL
By Courtesy of Abbot McClure, Esq.

B. WALL OF ITALIAN INSPIRATION IN OWN HOME OF WILLIAM LAWRENCE
BOTTOMLEY, ESQ., ARCHITECT, NEW YORK

PLATE 71

COMPOSITE ROOM, LANDSCAPE WALL DECORATION
Old Italian Architectural Painting as Chimney Piece Decoration
Courtesy of "Good Furniture Magazine"

PLATE 72

A HALL WITH PAPER OF TWO-TONE STRIPE

PLATE 73

B. FOLIAGE PAPER AS PANEL
INSERTS

A. WALL COVERED WITH
DAMASK

and in the cartouches are inserted a series of reprints from Piranesi.

As previously mentioned, panelled walls may be made highly or quietly decorative by inserts of all-over painted decorations, smaller, conventional designs, Watteau or Oriental figures, etc. Or the inserts may be of fabrics or of ornamental papers (Plate 54). They may also be enriched with colour and the mouldings gilded. A number of genuine Japanese papers in gold, silver, odd designs and colourings are imported by the Japan Paper Company of New York and Philadelphia. These are in small sheets and are not primarily designed for wall use, but those who are willing to go to some trouble for the sake of securing individual effects would find some of these things distinctly unusual for panel inserts or even for the papering of an entire room.

Painted walls may have panelling or a dado of lines supplemented by other painted decorations such as those mentioned in the panel section above.

A favourite device of some ingenious modern British architects is the painting or stencilling of a conventionally decorative frieze above woodwork (Plate 66 B), panelling, or with an otherwise plain wall, above a strong rail set two or three feet below the ceiling. Sometimes such a frieze is in modelled "compo" with or without colour. We recall one example of conventional trees and figures in this medium, and another in which, the rest of the wall being plain, there were strongly modelled heraldic designs above the fireplace.

Bands of conventional decoration may be used around a plain centre or run only perpendicularly down the sides of such a centre.

A very interesting treatment, in the "newer decoration," with strong colour, of wall in connexion with

16

a piano, by Mr. Aschermann, is illustrated in the last section of this chapter and a full description of the colour-scheme given beneath. (Plate 77 A.)

Walls may be entirely covered by rich fabrics or strongly ornamental papers or decorated leather.

The degree of ornament or colour in walls consistent with a considerable amount of decoration in other surfaces and objects should be carefully weighed in each instance or confusion will result. As an instance, it may be said that an ivory-white panelling with a damask insert of rose, old blue, light green or old gold would be a perfectly appropriate background for a drawing-room furnished with Sheraton painted satin-wood or painted Louis Seize furniture upholstered in the same colouring as the panel insert.

PAPERED WALLS

In *general*, walls in the whites, neutrals, and soft, light shades of colour will be found the most practical. The reasons have before been given but may be repeated here:

1. Through them we are able to key together all the various rooms in a dwelling or an apartment without that house or apartment becoming noticeably of strong yellow, or blue, pink or green.

2. They allow the employment in such rooms of a greater variety of colour.

3. They are reposeful and possess wholesomeness and cheer.

It should be noted, however, that the *general* advocacy of a good thing by no means presupposes its universal use. A truly catholic taste is as acutely conscious of the desirability of other things in their proper circumstances. In very light houses or in apartments situated on upper floors where the light pours in in undiluted glare, and where heavy curtains may not be desired, somewhat darker colours for walls are appropriate. They will give rest and richness. Even here, however, a middle tone of the chosen colour will be found sufficient, and usually it had better be of rather neutral shade. For more positive treatments the section on the Newer Decoration should be consulted.

Perhaps no other one thing has given such scope to the fiendish ingenuity of man as the designing of paper for the wall. The usual shop is a museum of horrors where out of a hundred patterns ninety are to be shunned. Yet even here one may find good and simple things, and the best shops and decorating establishments have papers of great beauty.

In viewing any possible selection four questions should mentally be asked.

I. Is it beautiful in itself?

II. Will it lie back on the wall?

III. Is it in accordance with the purposes of the room?

IV. Will it be harmonious with the room and its furnishings in colour, pattern and scale?

As a practical aid in selection, suggestions as to the best styles are given in the following paragraphs.

Stripes: Stripes have always an intrinsic style (Plate 72). They add somewhat to the apparent height of the wall, which is sometimes an advantage where the walls are low. With lofty walls they may be used if treated according to later suggestions. The narrow stripes of cream white and grey are exceedingly attractive, practical and have a modest elegance. They may advantageously be used for an entire suite of rooms except perhaps the drawing-room, where a striped paper generally agreeing in tone, but of still greater elegance, may be substituted.

There are many other good stripes in white, light shades and in all colours likely to be used, the stripes being of varying widths. The two-surface stripes are of simple but undoubted style. In these one stripe is plain and the next is of satin finish, watered, brocaded or patterned.

In addition to these two-surface papers there are those in two tones of the same colour, and also in two tints, which also often have varying surfaces as well.

While exercising care that the stripe selected should not be out of proportion to the size of the room, it should be remembered that if there is little difference in tone or surface between the alternate stripes wider ones may be used than where the contrast is strong.

Crane and Morris Designs: The papers by Walter Crane, William Morris and other designers are of strongly decorative character, possessing as they do both pattern and colour. Crane's "Macaw" design* is perhaps the most beautiful of them all.

Brocades: An all-over conventional brocade in some such pattern as the damask wall illustrated (Plate 73 A) and in pale ashes of roses or cream is very beautiful. In these papers brocaded in the surface the pattern only shows strongly on portions of the wall where the light strikes at certain angles, but adds richness to the remainder. As previously noted some papers are both brocaded and striped.

Diamond Pattern Papers: There are papers in tan, grey, and light colours in which the lines run diagonally, thus forming a diamond pattern in which there is a small figure. These are attractive, and being unob-

---

* See colour-plate in "Decorative Textiles," by George Leland Hunter.

trusive, the direction of the lines is not objectionable. As a usual principle it is not well to use lines at variance with the perpendiculars and horizontals of the room.

Solid Colourings: Where a solid-colour wall is desired in soft but definite tone, the pulp and felt papers are available, but in light shades they are characterless and the present writers advocate a plain painted wall rather than these. The following three are, however, often better than either.

Stippled Papers: These effects are in imitation of walls which are stippled with paint in various tones over a toned background and most of these are of great beauty. As the tones would not match at the joints this paper comes to such great width as fifteen feet Decorators frequently stipple papers themselves with a sponge and water colour, but it would be unwise for the inexperienced to undertake it.

Surfaced Effects: There are several styles of papers which may be grouped under this heading, all of them giving more or less the effect of solid colour. They are very slightly varied in surface or colouring so as to relieve monotony and add richness. They have a texture which is hardly that of plaster or stone, but of which these are the nearest comparisons, and they are all the better for not being a direct imitation.

There is also a sand-finished paper which gives approximately the same effect as the so-finished plaster.

Canvas Papers: The Canvas and Jasper papers are good, although they do not possess any great distinction. There is, however, a Canvas paper which is of decided richness. This is of dull gold on which the canvas lines are imprinted in brown, so that the general effect is of a golden tan.

Gold and Silver: Papers entirely covered with gold

or silver, either plain or with oriental figuring, are handsome and likewise expensive. Some of these have stamped raised patterns in different tones or with suggestions of colour.

Japanese Grass: This is one of our very desirable assets, giving a rich but unobtrusive surface. It may be found in such tones as silver grey, warmer grey, gold, green and gold, and blue and silver. There are also good imitations of grass cloth.

Two-Toned Papers: Available also are many designs of conventional character in two tones so nearly alike as to be unobtrusive. These have the advantage of richness often at moderate cost.

Sprinkled and Small Pattern Effects are simple and attractive. Snow-flakes, triangles or dots are all pleasing and especially suitable for bedrooms.

Small Effects: There is a paper with a tiny black design at frequent regular intervals on a white ground, and also on a background of Chinese yellow, and perhaps other colours. Such a wall-covering could be used in a series of rooms, though it might in time become more tiresome than stripes.

Medallions: These papers are a mistake—if one were ill he would lie and count the medallions till moved to despair. There was an instance where an occupant, though in perfect health, discarded a very beautiful medallion paper costing ninety cents per roll and substituted an eleven-cent small-specked paper to immense advantage.

Period Papers: Wall-papers are furnished by manufacturers for certain period rooms, such as Adam and Empire, and these may sometimes be appropriately used.

Attention should be called to the reproductions of French wall-papers designed by David with subjects

PLATE 74

WALLS WITH PANELS OF LATE EIGHTEENTH CENTURY ARCHITECTURAL WALL PAPER
Messrs. Peabody, Nelson & Brown, Architects
Courtesy of "Good Furniture Magazine"

PLATE 75

BLACK GROUND, FLOWERED, CRETONNE PAPER
Pictures have no Place on such a Wall

drawn from classic history and mythology. The figures are large and the subjects are in sequence and intended to be used as panels.

Late eighteenth century Architectural (Plate 74) and Landscape Papers have been reproduced and are excellent if the room be furnished as were those in which these papers were originally employed—with simplicity. If they are strong in effect the walls then become the decoration and other features should be subordinated or confusion is apt to ensue.

Cretonne Papers: Another instance is the cretonne effect of which an illustration is given in Plate 75. In this case, with black ground and conventional flowers in varied colours and with bird's-eye maple furniture in simple lines, the result is good, except for the pictures erroneously hung upon such a wall.

Foliage Effects: Foliage papers in pale tones (Plate 73 B) are less obtrusive than the landscape effects, but judgment must here also be employed.

Flowered Papers: Small all-over flowered or leaf designs in greys, creams or pale tones of colour are often charming for bedrooms or above a dado in the whites or appropriate tints.

The bower of naturalistic red roses and the garden of blooms may be relegated to the use of those who have yet to learn of what household decoration consists.

PANELS, FRIEZES, DADOS AND CANOPIES

These have all had their special vogue and, as is always the case with "crazes," have afterwards been discredited—and probably will again be revived with equal fervour. Each has its own uses and may at any time be employed. Present readers would probably properly prefer to use them when not rendered undesirable by too frequent occurrence.

Panelled Papers: When well done paper panelling is attractive, especially for drawing-rooms and boudoirs. It should always be of simple architectural character, with straight lines marking the divisions rather than flowered or other edging.

Friezes: These are usually of too heavy and obtrusive design, thus overweighing the upper wall. Their use is not recommended: however, where it may be expedient two or three bands of the same or differing colours painted around the wall below the ceiling give a more individual effect. A wide painted band down to the picture rail is also good. Fabrics with a moulding below are often applied to form friezes, but the writers advise caution in seeing that the texture does not conflict with that of the wall beneath.

Dados: These may be employed especially for halls, dining-rooms, drawing-rooms, living-rooms, and libraries if desired. The lower paper should, of course, be the darker, and if one is ornamental the other should be plain. The huge flowered effects at one time in vogue would disturb the poise of any room. On the other hand the writer once occupied as a bedroom the room formerly used in an apartment as a dining-room; the lower wall of a soft medium green in plain felt, the upper wall being of a cream shade with a stripe composed of a rose stem and conventional leaves in the same green as the base. With a four-post bed and other dignified mahogany furniture it made one of the prettiest rooms imaginable.

Canopies: Canopies may be of decided use in lofty rooms, as they lower the apparent height. The ceiling paper is carried down over the side wall, without border, to a picture-rail. This arrangement often allows the use of striped papers where otherwise they would be inappropriate. There are instances in which the division between wall and canopy was a strip of flat moulding perhaps four or five inches wide and of dark colour, matching the "trim" of the room. This moulding is set even with the top of the door trim, so becoming an extension running around the room.

CEILINGS

As the walls should be lighter than the floors, the ceilings should be lighter than the walls, but of the same colour, they being properly an extension of them. If the walls are of two tones, such as a cream and grey stripe, the ceiling should be keyed to the lighter tone— in this instance fortunately also the warmer, the cream.

In most cases there is nothing more simply elegant than a perfectly plain ceiling paper, but if the ceiling is in poor condition a dotted or small figured surface is preferable. Silver paper may sometimes be used to advantage for the ceiling surmounting a painted panelled wall. Although somewhat darker than a white wall the reflections and high lights of the metal surface remove any oppressive sense of weight. Wall-paper manufacturers have exercised their ingenuity in designing side papers, elaborate borders and decorated ceilings, "to match," but these things are usually to be avoided by the tasteful decorator.

The beamed ceiling is appropriate to certain architectural styles and if paper is used in such cases it should be only in the spaces between the beams. In the large living-room of a certain handsome country house the beams also were papered over— an indefensible practice subservient of all character.

Ceilings of plaster work, parge or "compo" are attractive when well designed, and good patterns may be secured "in stock." They should follow the period styles in which they were used or at least be based thereon, and great care should of course be exercised to have them agree in style with the architecture and furnishings and to have them in proper scale with the room.

Where the walls are white or nearly so such a ceiling may be left white, but otherwise it should be tinted a light shade of the wall tone.

BORDERS AND PICTURE RAILS

It is accepted without question by many persons that borders are a decorative necessity. So far is this from being the case that one should carefully consider whether they are needed before using them at all. If employed they should be good in design, not more than four inches wide for the ordinary room, and with straight edge. Cut-out borders destroy architectural lines to no purpose. Occasionally borders are of value in the less formal rooms for the carrying up of the dominant colour upon the wall (Plate 76), but usually there is no particular reason for the strong marking of the dividing line between walls and ceiling. If it is felt that a greater finish be required, a simple cornice-moulding is the better device. This is quite commonly simply a picture rail set just below the edge of the ceiling, leaving sufficient space for the picture hook to go over the rail. If the woodwork is dark the rail may also be stained dark and this gives a "snappy" appearance, which is sometimes desirable if there is little interest in the remainder of the wall.

This placing of the rail is a thoroughly good one when the ceiling is low, but otherwise the necessarily long picture-wires are apt to give a "stringy" appearance, and if this is the case it is better practice to

PLATE 76

NARROW, CONVENTIONAL BORDER AND SET-DOWN PICTURE-RAIL.

set down the picture rail fourteen to eighteen inches from the ceiling (Plate 76). The finish thus given is sufficient and no other is really necessary.

WOODWORK OR "TRIM"

The trim of windows and doors (and the doors themselves) with which most of us have to do are of wood, or in strictly fireproof buildings of metal. Stone or brick are, of course, also frequently used for trim, and we occasionally see tile or mosaic, but these last are such definitely architectural features that they should not be undertaken except under professional advice. (Plate 144.)

Varnished golden oak is the *bête noire* of the decorator, professional or domestic, and toffy-coloured pine is worse. If at all possible either should be got rid of by painting or staining, and this should be before moving into the premises, where one can. If one is already an occupant the change involves disturbance and dirt, but the result will be found worth while. Owners and builders should be made effectively to realise the objectionableness of this "tobacco juice" colour of woodwork so that it may quickly become a barbarity of the past.

In order to get rid of the "goldenness"—heaven save the mark!—the hard finish must be taken off with varnish remover or else rubbed down. It may then be restained an unobtrusive shade and oiled, or it may be painted.

Pleasing Finishes: Paint, enamel, mahogany and dark oak, real or stained, and many other woods less usually employed, are all good. The first two may be either in white or in tint. Great stress is laid by some upon the use of ivory or cream rather than pure white, and this is often advisable, but pure white quite usually becomes ivory and the deeper shades grow "more so."

Where walls are in tint or in colour, whether painted or papered, the painted trim may either be of white or of the same or a kindred colour, in the same or not greatly differing tone. This question will by-and-by be dealt with in detail.

If the trim is not keyed to the wall it may be keyed to the wood of the furniture. If the furniture is mahogany the woodwork had better be of mahogany tone, or in some light tint or one of the whites. Dark oak woodwork is naturally the best for furniture of the same tone. Unlimited varnish is disturbing upon any wood, not less so over that which is dark than over the lighter species.

Grey-fumed oak when well done is in itself not an unpleasing finish, but it is not a practical one except where the furniture is also grey, white enamel or harmonious in colour. The writers recently visited a new apartment-house in which this grey was the universal finish, and thought with many a head-shake of the deplorable result when the unusual mahogany or oak furniture should be placed by the tenants.

As previously mentioned, the trim may be keyed to the walls, or it may be white, or it may be dark. The first means harmony, the last contrast. If the walls be of the Whites, white trim will be harmonious; if they be in colour white will be a contrast. For strong effects the section on Modern Decoration should be consulted.

There is room for a broad and unprejudiced choice. As Mr. George Moore said of literature, "all methods are good," but all methods are not equally good in every circumstance. If our furnishings are likely to be so full of life, colour and contrast that further emphasis would be disturbing, by all means let us have harmony. If we feel that our rooms are strongly balanced in mass and colour, we may well afford ourselves some contrast.

"THE WHITES" FOR WALL USE

There is a theory abroad that white walls contrast too strongly with the furnishings of a room; and mahogany furniture used with their extreme form of white, calcimine walls, has been pronounced "impossible." Pure white curtains have for the same reason come in for their share of deprecation. In accordance with our usual policy of first-hand investigation, let us consider this question, for it has its importance not only in connexion with the so-called "Colonial" interior but in many other cases.

There is first to be noted that in any but a perfectly bare and unfurnished room there is no such thing as a dead white wall. Immediately the windows have been duly shaded and curtained and the furnishings placed, nothing remains of a true whiteness but the highest lights, the shadows and half-tones going off to grey. Just here it is well to remember Whistler's amusing search for the brown necktie. When it or its substitute had been found Mr. Eddy tells us:

"Then mark you the brown of the tie was by no means reproduced in the portrait, but the brown as modified by all the browns and notes of the entire costume, and as still further modified by all the browns and all the notes and shades and lights of the studio."*

The fact is that in any room in which there is the richness of mahogany, coupled with the hues of rugs, upholstery and hangings, there are refractions of colour upon a white wall modifying it to the tones in the

---

* Recollections and Impressions of Whistler, by Arthur Jerome Eddy.

room, refractions impalpable perhaps but nevertheless there.

We may similarly say that the moment that the
whitest of white curtains are hung at the window no
white remains of them but the highest lights. We know
how artists of the *Genre* school delight in the painting
of white curtains. Does one suppose they would do so
if the pigment pourtraying them were pure Flake
White? The artist's pleasure arises from the exquisite tones of yellow, blue, pink and violet grey, of which
these "white" curtains consist as soon as they drape
into folds.

Nor can one with an artist's eye speak of mahogany
as wholly dark. There *are* darks and decided ones, but
note also their grey half-tones and their sparkling
lights, which in their turn can only be pourtrayed in
pigment by white which is almost pure.

Let us then by all means keep to principles, but let
us develop these from fact. In such cases, then, we
shall still indubitably find contrast, and strong contrast, between white walls and mahogany, but contrast
is of the spice of life. We shall thank the purists not
to try to take away our *spice.*

The simple truth is that white is pure, wholesome
in its mental influence and noble. It is also sanatory—
for to remain white it must be kept clean.

WALL TREATMENT IN THE "NEWER" DECORATION

As has been said in Part I, Chapter IX, simplicity
and right organisation are prominent tenets of the
newer school, and it is recognised that the correct
handling of backgrounds is necessary to this result.
If they are to be prominently decorative a restful balance must elsewhere be secured and, as this involves
the sacrifice of many other decorative possibilities, it

is frequently found more feasible that they should remain backgrounds and allow the introduction of decoration in other objects. There is, therefore, with this school a recognised use of walls in greys, creams, buffs and other tints and light tones. These have now for some time past, however, been so largely employed by good decorators that it is felt by the moderns that they make somewhat for monotony and that stronger colour may often advantageously be used. This is but a return to the past, for during the period from Queen Anne to Adam walls both plain and panelled were often in virile tones. They were still tones, nevertheless, and bright blues, red orange, and the like, were certainly not used.

If we had but one or two rooms to consider, quite brightly coloured walls might easily be managed, but if a certain degree of unity be lacking in the background it will be difficult to supply it elsewhere, and if one strong colour be adopted throughout it will become exceedingly tiresome before many months of its company.

For plain-coloured walls, whether quiet or in brighter hue, any of the resources mentioned in the previous section may be drawn upon. Painted and sand-finished walls are among the very best for this method, but paper also is frequently used. That with some texture or slight mottling is better than a perfectly smooth surface. Narrow vertical stripes are also good and give an approximately plain result. Gold and silver papers are rich and handsome and grass-cloth papers are unexcelled.

As a *sense* of unity is all that is required, there may be some considerable variation in colour or surface in the different rooms. If, for example, a silver-grey grass-cloth paper is the general covering the employ-

ment of a grey blue of fairly strong shade, or of silver
paper in one or two rooms would not create undue dissimilarity; nor would strong yellow, salmon or light
tan vary too greatly from a general tone of cream.

THE AVOIDANCE OF THE USUAL

Many devices for this purpose are used by the
newer school of decoration. One of the most prominent
of them is the painting of the woodwork (the "trim")
a different shade from the walls, lighter or darker, or
a strongly contrasting colour. Another is the lining
up of the walls with a wainscot or a panel effect, or
with vertical lines, or with a frieze or canopy, or around
the ceiling, corners and doors (Plate 77 A). When
such contrasts are used by the new movers as violet
woodwork, or lines, with yellow walls, bright blue with
red-orange walls, etc., one can only ask what becomes
of restfulness: when various strong colours are used
in the different rooms of the same house, one may enquire where their theory of unity has gone: and in both
cases we may wonder how good a background these
supply for our persons and our costumes, and how good
they are to live with? Of course, if such decoration is
to be merely temporary and to afford a passing diver-
sion for variety's sake, these purposes are fulfilled.

Considerable strong colour may, however, be employed with unusual but most satisfactory results.
The office and reception room by Mr. Aschermann
(Plate 52 A) is a good example in point, and a combination used by Mrs. Grace Wood was also charming.
This was a hall-bedroom with walls of grey, panelled
with a broad band of mulberry and an inner line of
pistache green. The furniture was in the green with
mulberry lines, and the bed-cover mulberry. Such
things have a freshness and verve which it would be

PLATE 77

A. A "MODERN" TREATMENT OF WALL AND PIANO

Walls, woodwork, ceiling, piano and bench in intense canary yellow; lines on walls, blue-green; flowers on walls and furniture painted intense red, orange, green, blue and violet; furniture covered with blue-green silk velvet; carpet, plain red-violet with 18-inch block border in black, red-violet and intense emerald green like mat below bench; candlesticks painted red-violet; green candles.

By Courtesy of the Aschermann Studio, New York

B. SCHEME FOR A BILLIARD-ROOM IN "MODERN" STYLE

All woodwork, black; floor-runner around billiard table, grey and black; furniture coverings, some grey leather, others intense emerald green linen with black and yellow design; draperies, same green linen; ceiling, gold with painted design in black, emerald green and grey; fireplace, hammered brass.

By Courtesy of the Aschermann Studio, New York

PLATE 78

A. A REPOSEFUL HALL ABUNDANTLY RELIEVED BY THE DECORATION OF
UPPER WALL-SPACE

B. MODERN BRITISH PLAIN-WALL COTTAGE LIVING-ROOM WITH
APPROPRIATE FURNITURE
Letchworth, England
By Courtesy of Messrs. Barry Parker and Raymond Unwin, Architects, Letchworth

well to impart into many dull and conventional homes. Fortunately these ideas may be carried out with sanity of effect and even strong contrast be preserved. Black or indigo lines upon a Chinese yellow, which are often used, are not at all bad if not overdone, because the contrasting hue is sombre and not brilliant.

Panelling is another strong resource of this method of decoration and many effects may be gained by its use. Both the small squared and the larger panelling of later times are used, and either in one or in two colours, these being either quiet or strong. Applied mouldings (Plate 65 B) are excellent for this purpose.

One very tasteful room known by the writers has a white ceiling and canopy effect with walls of peacock-blue burlap with cornice, background and vertical strip panelling in white enamel. This, however, is a single room. In a suite the panels of one or two important rooms may be filled with a painted decoration for greater ornament or with such a beautiful polychrome heavy Japanese paper as shown in Plate 54. Effective papers may also be used above a dado (Plate 78 A).

Conventional decorations in colour are often introduced in panels, and if well done the effect is excellent. They take the place of pictures, which should not appear upon such walls as these strongly marked ones unless of appropriate decorative and colourful character.

As cottage art is looked to for inspiration in one phase of "modern" decoration an exceptionally good example is given in Plate 78 B. In this instance the tones are quiet, but such restful interiors as this and those on Plate 93 would sustain a great deal of colour without disturbance.

17

CHAPTER IV

FLOORS AND THEIR COVERINGS

THE FOUNDATION. FLOOR COVERINGS. SIMPLE RUGS. PAT-
TERNED RUGS. THE "MODERN" DECORATION. STRUC-
TURAL FLOORS. POLISHES.

FLOORS THE FOUNDATION

THE usual theory regarding floors is that they are a portion of the background of the room, the other two portions being walls and ceiling. This is quite true, but floors are more than this— they are the Foundation.

For this reason it is evident that they should be darker than the walls, so as to give the effect of stability, as otherwise we should have the effect of the floor flying up into our faces. An apparent exception to this will be noted later on.

The structural floors nowadays commonly provided are of hard wood, finished in a fairly light shade. If it is desired to refinish them in another or darker tone it is necessary to remove the existing finish, which is a rather "large order" and necessitates the absence of furniture while the work is under way. Furthermore, many new apartment houses forbid in their leases that this be done.

In the circumstances under which most of us live, therefore, there can be little variety from the usual shade except in houses built to the occupant's order. When that is the case there are many desirable materials and colourings at our service, all of which, as well as the treatment of floors in old houses, will be taken up later in this chapter. It is well for the present

258

to pass on to the subject of floor *coverings,* not only because the more unusual materials for floors are not
available for all readers, but for the special reason
that the principles regarding floors are better shown in
the discussion of their coverings.

FLOOR COVERINGS

Balance: Upon the floor being darker than the walls
the whole balance of the room depends. And by this
is immediately condemned the entire series of light
cotton rugs, which in the joyous springtime fill the
shop windows to the beguilement and sorrow of the
unwary householder, particularly when they are full
of pattern: for even though they may be slightly darker
than a particularly light wall, they are not sufficiently
so in effect to lie down in their place.

One of the advantages of light walls is that the tone
of even the usual structural floor will generally be
found sufficiently dark and quiet to balance those walls,
whereas a dark paper would immediately turn the room
upside down. We shall in any event wish some rugs
for finish and comfort, and if the floor itself is too light
for balance and cannot be changed, no resource is left
us but largely to cover it.

Colour: We shall soon see that the truer point of
view, that the floor is the Foundation, makes for
greater truth and beauty in decoration, and emanci-
pates us from some hampering and unnecessary restrictions that are laid down for our use when floors are
regarded as backgrounds only. From this way of considering them probably arises the theory that in colour
floors must be keyed to the walls. We should say that
they may be, or may not be—and often preferably not.
There is no objection whatever to theory provided that
it be based on all the conditions. The difficulty with

some particular theorists is that although they may intimate that the house or apartment should be an entity, they do not practically provide for it. In order that it be an entity the thing in general most needful is that those large surfaces, the walls, should be close in their general effect throughout. If, then, the floors are to key with the walls in colour this would necessitate a close agreement in the colour of rugs over the whole house with a monotonous result. We may rightly wish to use several varieties or colourings of rugs in our rooms and we have already found in the chapter on colour (section "Unity and Variety") how this may be done with perfect harmony.

Some of our best decorators employ an excellent method which secures both unity and variety. The floor is covered throughout with a perfectly plain rich carpet and then upon this Oriental rugs are laid where required. Among the best colours for this carpet are very deep rose, blues, taupes and tans.

THE FLOOR AS A BACKGROUND OR AS DECORATION

In the chapter on walls it was said that they might either be treated as background or as decoration. The same is often true of floors and with them we are sometimes still more free to choose which method we shall employ. The floor being darker than the walls, and being in appearance held down by the furniture upon it, has greater apparent artistic stability than the walls, and is less sensitive to disturbance. Furthermore, being under our feet and not opposite our eyes, a larger variety of tone and contrast does not so greatly obtrude as it would in a higher position. We may, therefore, regard the floors in either light, and will consider the respective advantages of each method.

PLATE 79

A. LARGE RUG FORMED OF STRIPS OF CARPET
SEWED TOGETHER

B. PLAIN–CENTRE RUG WITH BORDER OF ORIENTAL CHARACTER
The Inter-period Selection of English Furniture and the Textile chosen for the Settee
are both good

PLATE 80

B. PLAIN-CENTRE RUG WITH BORDER IN
EXCELLENT ACCORD WITH THE CHARACTER
OF INTERIOR

A. ORIENTAL RUGS AND ORNAMENTAL HANGING
AFFORDING THE RELIEF OF COLOR AND PATTERN
TO SEVERELY PLAIN WALLS

PLATE 81

A. CEMENT FLOOR WITH INSERTED DESIGN IN COLOURED TILE
By Courtesy of George Howe, Architect

TILED FLOOR AND BASE WITH PLASTER WALL
Well-arranged Chippendale Furniture and Appropriate Lights
By Courtesy of William Chester Chase, Architect

THE FLOOR AS BACKGROUND—SIMPLE COVERINGS

There is much to be said in favour of comparatively plain floor coverings. These, with equally simple walls, at once make sure of repose, even though we relieve them with strong colour—in fact, if we wish to use decided and varied colour (for which there is also much to be said) we should first insure the plain surfaces for their necessary balance.

It is evident that the simple rug or carpet presents fewer complications and is easier to manage decoratively than one of more obtrusive nature. It is equally plain that no matter how simple they may be, a number of small rugs upon a strongly contrasting floor is destructive of all repose, and if these be thrown down at *angles* the result is simply harassing. If *simplicity* of floor space is needed it will therefore be advisable to use but one or two rugs largely covering it where the room is of moderate dimensions. In a larger room the floor may similarly be largely covered; or it may be left mostly bare, with but a few small rugs; or a proportionate number may be employed if not too various in pattern or colour. If there be an occasion to lay rugs otherwise than parallel to the walls of the room, we have not discovered it. If a triangular china closet occupies the corner of a room, that practically becomes the line of wall at that particular point, and a small rug placed parallel to its front is permissible provided other rugs are not so close as to present interfering lines. The same is true of a rug before a fireplace built into the corner of a room.

Simple rugs may be of solid colour with or without a border, or they may be of two tones of the same colour, or of two or more colours, providing that the pattern, where it exists, is not large or too strongly contrasting to be simple (Plates 79 and 80 B). Borders on rugs of solid colours may likewise be of two tones or colours if not too prominent. In a painting by Oswald Birley of an interior at James Prydes', the London artist, there is a solid colour rug of rich rose with a border of soft green, and just within its outline on each side a narrow band of rose. Such a rug has considerable colour quality without being obtrusive. Another British rug, with a block border, is shown in Plate 66 B.

Needless to say, rug designs should always be conventional. We have the metaphor "Sleeping upon a bed of roses," but no one cares to walk upon roses, either literally or naturalistically displayed upon a carpet: when sufficiently conventionalised these and other natural objects become merely decorative *motifs* based upon nature and the objection no longer holds.

These simple rugs are to be found in both imported and domestic goods and in most of the colours we may desire. There are also the hand-woven rugs in both wool and cotton, and some of the makers will dye and weave these in any shade desired (Plate 59). Braided rugs, rag carpets, and rugs made therefrom are appropriate for "old-time" rooms and cottage use.

Rugs are more convenient and sanatory than carpets, because they may easily be removed; and, as they do not need tacking down, the flooring is not marred.

A rather serious objection to the perfectly plain rug, especially in first-floor rooms, is its showing every mark and stain. Where there are children running in and out, each dusty little footprint is evident; and if there is sewing done every thread left upon the floor is visible. For rooms subject to constant use it is better to choose rugs which have a considerable, though not necessarily a' strongly contrasting, pattern (Plate 92 B). It may be observed that many patterned and colourful rugs—even many Oriental ones—may be classed as simple for purposes of present consideration; the sole test being: is it quiet enough not to interfere with the other decorative materials we shall use?

Furnishings to accompany simple rugs.—As has been noted the use of simple rugs with simple walls allows the utmost freedom in the choice of fabrics: they may be marked in both colour and pattern provided that the first is harmonious and the second proper in both scale and character. Colour and pattern, rightly employed, are never splashy nor offensive; on the contrary they add to beauty, happiness and the joy of living. The remark is frequently sounded in our ears: " My taste runs to plainness! " when a glance at the costume and surroundings of the speaker tells us that it runs simply to mediocrity. If some of these drab souls were transplanted to more cheerful surroundings their outlook on life might be improved. Violence must, of course, be avoided and good taste should always obtain.

If it is insisted that plain solid colours be used for coverings and hangings as well as for rugs, at least let our upholstery have pattern in the weave, so as to give variety and avoid the bareness which would otherwise ensue. Also for variety's sake, if the fabrics and rugs are to match as to colour it is better that they be not of the same shade of that colour but either lighter or darker, the harmony being preserved.

THE FLOOR AS DECORATION—HIGHLY PATTERNED RUGS

Oriental rugs,* which first demand attention, have been subjected to alternate laudation and detraction: let us give them unprejudiced consideration.

There are some bad and cheap modern Oriental

---

* See " The Practical Book of Oriental Rugs " by G. Griffin Lewis.

rugs, as we shall find to be the case with everything else, and, as with such other things, we may dismiss them without delay. Rugs with zigzag lines (they are but few) may go with them, as they but distract. Those with diagonal stripes are also difficult to manage successfully. Very large and spreading patterns are usually to be avoided, though it would take all the strength of design and colour of a Kazak to redeem from drabness the " symphony in mud and mustard " we have previously described. A large pattern in a very large rug is naturally not so evident. They, therefore, have their use in spacious offices, corridors, halls, and the like.

We may now consider those rugs that are adaptable for general household use, and weigh the supposed demerits that have been urged against them. The foremost cause of offending in the eye of many is their strength of colour, and yet anyone familiar with the subject knows that almost every rug imported into America (and probably also the western portion of Europe) is "washed" to reduce its colour. When we remember not only this but the fact that in our western "civilisation" a rug cannot lie upon the floor two weeks without its shades being subdued by the soil of shoe leather and accumulating dust—be we as cleanly housekeepers as we may—the question comes seriously to the front whether the rugs are at fault or whether our culture is not growing too pale, too anæmic, for wholesome and robust man-and-womanhood. We use the word "seriously" in all advisability, for even straws are indicators, and this is a question affecting not merely decoration but character.

In any event sufficiently quiet rugs can be found among the Orientals. We all realise that in good examples the blending of tones in the Oriental rug is beyond western ability, and as there is an infinite variety from which to choose, if the rug is not successful upon the floor usually the fault is ours. If a rug to be purchased is for a certain position it should not be purchased *away* from that position—in other words, such rugs should be sent on approval, seen in their place, and well considered before payment is made. In the chapter on Textiles (section Hints on Purchasing) this whole subject of trying things "in loco" is discussed.

The second objection to Oriental rugs is pattern, and this objection is at least partly justified. There are worrying, "wormy," angular and badly proportioned designs in Oriental rugs even when otherwise of merit, and such rugs should be avoided for domestic use, though they may be valued by a collector. There are other patterns that are excellent for our purposes. The Mina Khani designs found in Kurdistan Rugs are admirable, and these rugs are among the best for general household use. The Herati and Pear designs are good if we avoid those that are too small and monotonous. When we add that many of Turkish and Persian designs are most pleasing, it will be seen that we have practically said that there are good styles in all Oriental Rugs—it is our part to avoid the bad ones. The fact that by far the larger number of handsome modern interiors illustrated in Part II of this book show Oriental and Chinese rugs upon the floors certainly has its weight.

The durability of Oriental Rugs for our Western use has perhaps been exaggerated and under the constant wear of leather footgear they will hardly last the traditional lifetime. When, however, the pile is of a fair length, they are among the best floor coverings we have.

Most Chinese rugs are of good pattern and colour and there are very good reproductions to be had at reasonable prices. The Chinese products are of great variety and yet, almost without exception, they possess the happy quality of harmonising with nearly every environment. A Chinese rug, excellent in both pattern and scale, will be seen in Plate 8. The Korean rug shown in Plate 111 is decidedly attractive. The colouring of this example is whitish-grey, yellow and blue.

Domestics. The East has been the inspiration for most of the best Saxony and Wilton rugs, but there are some good ones in conventional patterns. In the cheaper grades of Wiltons and Brussels the inspiration, to use a phrase of Mr. Kipling's, has "gone very far wrong, indeed," and nothing could be more hideous than some specimens with their raw greens and reds interspersed with light cream.

Occasionally one may come across specimens of the old cross-stitch rug. Some of these are ugly, but others are good in design and colour, especially those with black ground and flowered design and border.

Certain period carpets, such as the Aubussons and Savonneries, are colourful in medium shades and are appropriate when the room is of the proper period. Too large patterns—some of them are very sweeping —should be avoided if the room is small.

FLOORS IN THE "MODERN" DECORATION

The tendency here is toward simplicity of design, though violent or at least strong colouring is used here as elsewhere. Block borders and sometimes block patterns are favourites, and unless these are closely harmonised there is nothing more insistent (Plate 77 A).

Oriental rugs are apparently largely taboo, owing to their pattern, and yet Chinese rugs, in which the design is simple but often more aggressive, are frequently employed.

The woodwork of the floors is sometimes painted to accord with the walls, but rather darker in shade, and sometimes stained or painted. Often black floors are used (and there is nothing better) (Plate 125) and sometimes black rugs when relieved with plenty of colour elsewhere in the room.

STRUCTURAL FLOORS

The regarding of the floor as Foundation will be found particularly appropriate when we consider such Structural Floors as light-coloured tile (Plate 81 B), white marble, mosaic and cement, all of which are deficient in depth of colour. Fortunately, we not only possess a colour-sense but also that which appreciates *weight,* and in these instances we so feel the *solidity* of the Foundation that the balance is supplied to the weakness of "value." Even then if we use floors so light in tone we shall usually need to keep the walls light and quiet in effect, though here as elsewhere the old masters of decoration surmounted every obstacle and solved all problems of balance (see Plate 139).

Red tiles make excellent flooring of good colour value, but we shall here need to use caution as to the tones of reds we employ in rugs, draperies, etc., so as to avoid conflict.

Cement floors may be successfully executed by incorporating borders of polychrome tiles or medallion-like inlays at certain intervals. The illustration (Plate 81 A) shows part of a cement floor in an oval breakfast room with tile border and polychrome tile medallions at ends and sides.

From such examples as the above we see that we may employ resources whch come near to opposing usual principles, provided that we frankly recognise the difficulty and offset it by proper action in other directions. The wide-boarded floors are so obviously structural that they convey to the eye a satisfying sense of adequate foundation, despite their colour, but with very light-toned hardwood floors of narrow boards we do not feel the helpful sense of weight, and if they are lighter than the walls and cannot be darkened, they should be fairly well covered with rugs which are somewhat darker. But here again we must go with caution: if we laid down upon such a floor but a few small rugs as dark and heavy as the Beluchistans, for instance, we should then have such violent contrast that the result would probably be more upsetting than the original floor. Rugs, therefore, in such conditions should be of but medium strength, or else the light flooring should be almost *covered* with one or two larger rugs or a carpet.

Finish: Waxing is usually recommended as the best treatment for hardwood floors, but their slipperiness is the cause of painful and even fatal accidents. Shellac is also commonly used.

In old houses the flooring is often of wide boards (a survival of the Colonial method) sometimes coarse and badly worn. If not too hopeless, staining and shellacking will give good results; if very bad the cracks and crevices may be filled with putty and the floor painted and varnished. Sometimes nothing remains but to carpet them entirely, or to cover with a "filling" or matting, in which case rugs can be used over this preliminary surface.

CHAPTER V

WINDOWS AND THEIR TREATMENT

RETAINING PURPOSE AND ENHANCING DECORATIVE VALUE.
LENGTH AND ARRANGEMENT OF CURTAINS. VALANCES.
MATERIALS AND EMPLOYMENT. COLOURED SASH CUR-
TAINS. OVERCURTAINS. UNHACKNEYED EFFECTS. FIX-
TURES. DOOR-HANGINGS.

THE windows in many abodes suggest that the householder has forgotten that their primary purpose is the admission of light and air. To be sure there are seasons when the latter is needed but sufficiently for ventilation, and many times when we may have too much sunlight: it is for the modification of light that window hangings have been devised. It is also but right to remember that nothing gives so bare and desolate an appearance to a room as an undraped window, and that upon the quality and quantity of admitted light much of its charm depends. The two necessities of light and ventilation on the one hand and modification and decoration on the other will not be found conflicting if we proceed with proper information and judgment. Beginning with the simpler treatments we shall find before we have finished that many things may be done to give special interest.

The most generally sensible treatment for the usual double-sash window is that of simple curtains of white or ivory white on rings, suspended from a simple brass rod. Traverse rings and cord will be found a great convenience. When it is desired that the window be entirely unobstructed for light, for air, or for cleaning, the curtains may be drawn fully back at the sides and secured by simple cords to knobs or catches.

To the above may be added, if desired, one-sash curtains of the same material or of thin silk, suspended on rings from a brass rod attached in this case to the upper part of the lower sash. The long side-curtains may then be left undrawn, and, if the shade is pulled half way down, the room is in the daytime obscured from outside view.

For the sake of privacy when the lights are lighted and also for the tempering of glare by day it is necessary that further obstruction be provided; either in the form of blinds or shades, or heavy inside curtains which may be drawn across the windows.

The good old Venetian blind is unsurpassed and adds to the advantage of shades that of admitting more air. It may be painted any tint to agree with its surroundings. If shades are used they should be heavy and opaque. White or light tints are certainly best with white curtains. The *idea* of the two-colour shade —white within and dark outside—is good as the opacity is increased, but the green outside usually seen does not properly accompany exterior architecture. Perhaps other shades and colours may be secured.

If coloured curtains are added to the shade and long curtains of white, the one-sash curtains had better be omitted, as the long white curtains may then continuously be drawn across the window. Decorators sometimes employ two or three sets of sash curtains of gauze for the tempering of light to the exact tone they desire, but one curtain of silk can usually be secured of a shade which accomplishes this result. A voluminous and "befrazzling" window *"dressing"*—we might then call it—is too apt to remind one of the maze of lingerie, silk and furbelows with which women of a former time (not now!) felt compelled to bedeck their persons. Nevertheless, sometimes a shimmering effect is desirable and this can be achieved by the use of double gauze curtains of different shades, such as rose and aquamarine, blue and silver-grey, etc.

Our own feeling is that in simple and small rooms and especially in bedrooms, the simplest arrangement is the very best, while other rooms of a more ornamental character may well be more elaborately treated.

When shades or blinds are used heavy curtains are no longer a necessity (the pulling down of the shades totally excluding the view from outside) so that we are free to choose medium or light-weight fabrics, as, frequently, we may prefer.

Sash curtains, whether of white goods or casement cloth or silk, may be arranged in two tiers—one for each sash—so that the upper set may remain closed to modify light and the lower set be drawn back to admit it (Plate 82 A).

THE LENGTH AND ARRANGEMENT OF CURTAINS

The architecture of the window naturally plays an important part in the determination of curtain treatment. Where the wall beneath the window is recessed as well as is the window itself, the obvious suggestion is that the curtains should be long. It is undeniable that in handsome apartments rich curtains sweeping over the floor give an opulence of appearance, but for reasons of cleanliness it is certainly better that they should escape the floor by an inch or so.

Where the window only is recessed and the cill has a pronounced extension, curtains of cill length are naturally indicated. A slight cill extension is no obstacle to long curtains if desired, as the curtain flows gracefully over it. Even if a radiator or piece of furniture, such as a dressing-table, occupies the central portion of the window, long curtains may still be used, hanging straight at the sides and not being drawn (Plate 82 B).

Thin curtains have usually been made of cill length, but if this is done the draught takes them out of the window immediately the sash is raised, and they become soiled. Furthermore, thin curtains must be carefully placed on stretchers when laundered or they will shrink till they no longer reach the cill. Another objection is that where there is no furniture below the window cill-length curtains give a "boxed-in" appearance. A better plan, therefore, is to have these curtains extend slightly below the woodwork under the window— how much depends upon convenience and proportion. Where two pairs of curtains are used, it is customary to have the thin pair short whether the coloured pair be short or long.

The most usual plan where there are over-curtains and valance is to have them cover the window casings, but unless these are bad in style, condition or colour there is no reason why this arrangement should prevail, and there is a valid objection to it which seems to have been universally overlooked. Where curtains cover the woodwork they naturally stand out somewhat further beyond it, so that the general effect is the projection of the outline of the window into the room, while the feeling should be that a window is *recessed*. If, therefore, the exceptional circumstances mentioned above do not exist, it is preferable that over-curtains be contained within the casing. The rod is then run across slightly back of the fore edge of the woodwork and the valance placed in front of it but still within the casing (Plate 85). When the curtains are translucent or transparent there is still greater reason for this arrangement, as if they were placed over the outside woodwork this would show through and the result would probably be disagreeable.

PLATE 82

A. TWO TIERS OF SASH-CURTAINS

B. SHORT SASH-CURTAINS AND LONG TRANS-
LUCENT SIDE-CURTAINS

By Courtesy of B. Russell Herts, Decorator, New York

PLATE 83

B. THREE SETS OF CURTAINS—SASH,
DRAW AND ORNAMENTAL

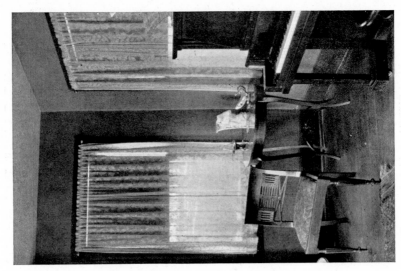

A. SIMPLE CURTAINS OF FIGURED NET
WITH SHADES

PLATE 84

A. CURTAINS OF STRIPED SILK
With this effective material the addition of a valance
would have been a great improvement

B. CASEMENT BOW-WINDOW WITH VALANCE
FOLLOWING THE WINDOWS
By Courtesy of Messrs. Story & Triggs, London

PLATE 85

SHAPED VALANCE AND CURTAINS ADMIRABLY CONTAINED
WITHIN THEIR ARCHITECTURAL SETTING
The Huge Lamp is Badly Out of Scale.   The Side Lights are Good

Another advantage of the showing of the wood-work where it is good, is the preservation of architectural lines.

If, because of ugliness, it is found better to hide the casing, opaque curtains should be used. By the same means much may be done in remedying defects of size or proportion. If the window is noticeably small for the room, the setting out of such curtains somewhat along the side wall and the raising of the top of the valance above the framework will naturally increase its apparent size. If high and narrow, the curtains may be set out at the sides and a deep valance employed (reducing the apparent height), the head of the latter then being set even with the top of the casing. If a window is low a valance had better be omitted, or confined to a narrow strip merely to carry the colour across.

For a deeply recessed bow with three or more windows there are two most attractive treatments, both of which are illustrated:

I. A valance run across the front of the alcove, and curtains to the floor at each side, these being of heavy and rich material. Light silk or casement-cloth short curtains of a different but harmonising colour at the windows themselves. (See Frontispiece.)

II. Long curtains at the two sides of the bow, valance following the tops of the windows with short curtains (Plate 84 B).

Ranges of casement windows, so frequent in Tudor houses, are treated in this same manner without the long curtains.

For double and triple windows but slightly recessed with cill straight across, it is best to run a long rod straight across the front, from which hang side and dividing curtains all of the same length, to the cill, be-

18

low the woodwork, or full length, as will give the best appearance under the existing conditions. To these a valance may be added.

VALANCES

Valances are not only a strong decorative asset but often seem required as a finish: it appears rather illogical, for instance, that coloured draperies should hang at the sides of a window without their being connected by a similar drapery running across the top. This necessity has been felt by some decorators who, in cases where a valance is not advisable, have covered a pole with the material of the curtains. Such a coloured cylinder is, however, inappropriate, and the result can be much more reasonably attained by the use of a valance so narrow that it is but a band of colour, giving the advisable connexion and finish.

With white curtains and white woodwork there is no necessity for a valance, but simply pleated valances may frequently be used with attractive results.

Valances naturally have a lowering effect, so that, as previously said, in many cases it will be advisable either to omit them or use the narrow band described. This lowering quality, on the other hand, makes them extremely useful in too lofty rooms.

Valances may be plain, shaped or pleated, and some unusual effects are mentioned in a succeeding section.

In period rooms cornices may sometimes be used advantageously and an illustration is given of an excellent selection in Neo-Classic style (Plate 86).

MATERIALS AND THEIR EMPLOYMENT

In the reaction from the elaborate and costly creations of lace which were the pride of our mothers, the frequent present prescription of absolutely plain material for thin curtains goes, perhaps, too far. Especially is this the case in drawing-rooms facing upon the street, for from that point inner curtains are not visible, and perfectly plain materials are not appropriate to the front of a handsome house, however well they may answer for simpler ones. In such instances it is advisable to have strength and simplicity in the design chosen but to add to these a certain richness. If no inner curtains are used, or if they are of solid colouring, there is much freedom of choice, but if inner curtains are patterned and varied in colouring a greater severity in the thin curtains must obtain and the two must not conflict in design or scale. Drawing-rooms, reception-rooms and boudoirs are all "of an elegance," and, unless redeemed by handsome inner curtains, plain thin materials leave something to be desired. There are many beautiful stripes, figures and patterns in net and madras (Plate 83 A).

Dining-rooms and living-rooms are sometimes elegant and sometimes simple, and the curtains chosen should be in accordance.

For cottages, many apartments and simple bedrooms nothing is prettier than flounced muslin curtains: they have a charm all their own and are most convenient, as they can be purchased ready to put up. Other execellent selections are plain materials with insertion near the edge, or with a wide hem and a narrow edge of Cluny lace sewed on the inner side and foot. Plain materials, from scrim to theatrical-net, are so numerous that it is hardly worth while to attempt to record them; all that is necessary being the selection of what is appropriate and pleasing for its particular use.

If the woodwork is ivory, cream or buff, it is better that the curtains should be similar in tone, but if it is pure white or of another colour, pure white curtains will be better: they seem to retain their freshness longer than the tones.

COLOURED SASH CURTAINS

Coloured curtains next the sash are sometimes advisable for adding richness, the modification of light, or to carry out a decorative effect. If the natural light of a room is cold or dreary, thin curtains in one of the shades of yellow will brighten it and enliven the whole atmosphere of the room. Rose will warm it without so greatly increasing the effect of light. If, on the other hand, there is too great glare, cool green, blue-lavender or soft blue will modify it. In making a choice the colour-scheme of the room must, of course, be considered.

Among the materials for such purposes are thin silk, Japanese gauze, Japanese crêpe, thin poplin, sunfast and English casement cloth.

OVER-CURTAINS

The moment that definite colour, and especially patterned colour, is introduced in window hangings they become a vital part of the decoration of the room and need special consideration. The windows are decoratively more than a continuation of the wall area, and may therefore be given a livelier interest, but it is seldom that they should become the strongest colour-note in a room—that to which the eye first travels. An exception to this rule is covered in the following section.

If the walls have been treated so as to maintain their place as background, if there is a sufficient sense of restful spaciousness in the room, and not already too much colour, then the windows may be given richness and decorative value by the use of over-curtains in solid colouring, plain, striped or patterned, or in two colours, or varied colour if not too insistent in effect. The degree of prominence the windows will stand is determined by the room and its furnishings. If the room seems already small and stuffy, over-curtains will increase both defects if they be heavy—usually they had better not be used at all. It is always to be remembered that white curtains increase the apparent size of a room while those of colour lessen it.

As has been noted, it is not necessary that over-curtains be heavy if shades or Venetian blinds are used: our facilities for securing just what is desired in colour and effect are therefore much extended. In many rooms, especially those which already are sufficiently dark, the translucent effect given by unlined striped and plain silks (Plate 84 A), poplin, printed linens and cretonnes, thin brocades, etc., is superior to the lined and heavy velvet, corduroy, damask, brocade, tapestry, heavy silk and other goods which are appropriate where opacity is desired.

A study of the room will indicate whether translucence or opacity is best

EXCEPTIONAL AND UNHACKNEYED EFFECTS

Sometimes a window is the one distinguished feature in an otherwise difficult room and it then seems advisable to "play up" this interest in order to redeem it from the commonplace. Close consideration should be given the materials used, their colour, pattern and arrangement.

Coloured curtains may here be used throughout, and two suggestive effects are mentioned. Simply for exemplification we will take rose as the dominant in both, though any other colouring may be used according to the scheme of decoration.

I. Sash curtains of thin silk in stripes of rose and champagne with a thin black line. Over-curtains and valances of thicker but still translucent rose silk of solid colour. Edge these with black and make the looping band of solid black, or use black silk cord and tassels. There would be no objection to a self figure or stripe in the weave of the over-curtains and valance.

II. Sash curtains of thin rose silk, or else the shimmering effect given by two sets of gauze—rose and grey-blue, rose and pale green, or rose and champagne. Translucent over-curtains with valance in two colours or varied colouring in rich or in striking combinations in which rose is dominant. Oriental silks, brocades, striped silks, printed linens and cretonnes are all appropriate—any material, in fact, which gives the effect desired.

There are many variations from the usual. Some of these may be mentioned, and originality will suggest others.

Valances to solid colour curtains are commonly made of the same material. Why not use, instead, a handsome brocade, stripe or other goods, in varied colourings in which the hue of the curtains is dominant? Such a combination is shown in one of the illustrations (Plate 87 A).

Plain valances and curtains may be banded with broad bands in the same way that braid is applied to a costume. The design should, however, not be elaborate or fussy but rather architectural in its lines. This is also illustrated (Plate 87 B).

In Italian decoration we frequently find valances of wood, either of plain surface or carved, painted, in either case, with a polychrome design and often gilded.

Handsomely stamped and ornamented paper, duly protected by shellac, is sometimes used for screens, and in an instance known to the writers this was also em-

PLATE 86

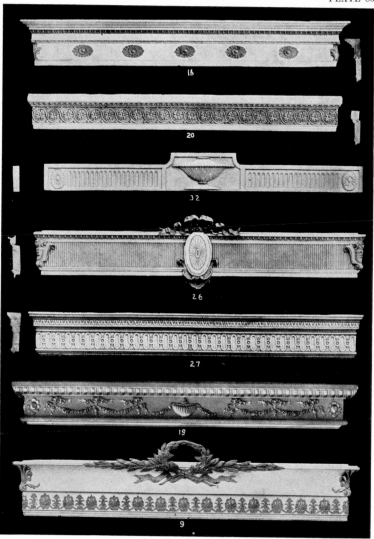

CORNICES IN THE NEO–CLASSIC MODE
By Courtesy of Newcomb-Macklin Co., Chicago and New York

PLATE 87

B. VALANCE AND CURTAINS WITH BROAD BANDS
OF STRONGLY CONTRASTING EFFECT

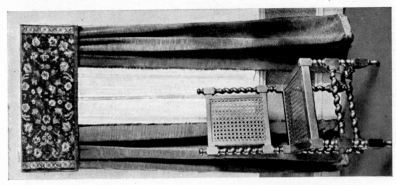

A. ORNAMENTAL VALANCE
WITH PLAIN CURTAINS

ployed for valances, so as to carry out the decorative effect. This could be mounted upon either a stiff buckram or thin board.

Fringes of silk are, of course, appropriate for the edges of valances if desired.

A heavy silk tassel depending from near each end of the valance and hanging over the curtain below, often gives a good effect. A drop ornament of unusual character might be employed in the same way.

The edging of curtains has previously been suggested, and many excellent combinations may thus be made, with thin sash curtains as well as the heavier ones.

Bands, wide or narrow, harmonising or contrasting, may be set on curtains back from the edge. On solid colours these may either be plain or of some beautiful design cut from another fabric. A band of the narrow, embroidered Chinese strips would be admirable. On ornamental goods a band of black or solid colour is sometimes advisable.

Using the same principles, a wide band, or two or three narrower ones, may be set *across* the curtains above their foot. The distance from the bottom will naturally depend upon the length and position of the curtains. Bands of insertion may also be used across plain white curtains in the same manner.

In the so-called "Modern" style of decoration strong bands of black upon curtains of Chinese yellow or blue would be most effective. So also would be bands of colour in strong contrast.

Patterns cut from other goods may be *appliqué* upon solid colours. An example of this would be the use of the charming ovals of flowers or baskets of flowers found in French goods, set upon grey-blue curtains in a boudoir.

All of these devices give distinction if well managed.

FIXTURES

Except for use with extremely large and weighty curtains the bulky wooden pole—from which it seems so difficult to divorce the general public—is unnecessary and therefore objectionable. Those interested in art continually have cause to exclaim: "When *will* people learn to employ means proportionate to the ends desired!"

A simple brass rod (with the appropriate end-fixtures) purchasable at any first-class hardware-shop or dealer in upholsterers' supplies) is sufficiently strong for almost all domestic uses. If such a rod has to extend over a wide space, such as double or triple windows or a double doorway, a screw hook at the centre will support it and prevent sagging.

Where there is a valance this naturally hides the rod and rings. If there is none a heading can be arranged in the case of opaque curtains and the rings fastened on at its lower edge at the back so that the heading projects above the rod and hides it. Thin curtains are often run *on* the rod with a heading above (Plate 83 A). But—Why worry! The sight of rod and rings seems to disturb some writers, but things of this kind are precisely on a par with the iron tie-rods frankly run across below the arched ceilings of magnificent Italian interiors (Plate 18). Our refinement may sometimes grow too fussy.

DOOR-HANGINGS

Circumstances vary so greatly that it is unwise to give hard and fast rules, but in general it may be said that if over-curtains are used at windows it is advisable that at doorways (the corresponding apertures) the same colouring should be employed, or at least that the colouring of the one should be in relation to that of the other: if, for instance, the window hangings are to be of blended tones, the portières might be either the same or solid colour of one of the principal of those tones.

If there are no coloured curtains at the windows the choice of materials for portières is then limited only by general appropriateness and the necessity of harmony with other decorations.

The popular supposition that portières must always be heavy is, of course, unjustified. They should often be opaque—as at bedroom doors—but frequently light and unlined curtains give delightful effects.

The objection that door curtains are in the way seems also unfounded for they may be pulled back to either side of the doorway, or to both sides where they are double, in the case of wide doorways. Certainly uncurtained doorways, though not nearly to so great a degree as uncurtained windows, have a bare and unfinished effect. It is, by the way, well to leave most doors on, as it is rarely the case that they are not at some time needed.

THE IMPORTANCE OF WINDOW FURNISHINGS

It will have been seen how many circumstances there are to consider in the apparently simple matter of the furnishing of windows. It is, however, precisely this advance consideration that avoids costly mistakes. The harmony of our home depends largely upon what we do in this direction: we may have rooms irritating to the nerves through their glare, their dullness or their harshness; or restful and full of happy charm, because of a pleasing and sufficient diffusion of light, rightly placed and harmonious in tone.

CHAPTER VI

THE ARRANGEMENT AND BALANCE OF FURNITURE

BALANCE. OBJECTS OF CENTRAL INTEREST. FIREPLACES. DOUBLE AND MINOR CENTRES. CORNERS. THE SETTING OF FURNITURE OUT INTO THE ROOM. SCALE AND PROPORTION EXPERIMENTATION.

THE arrangement of furniture is taken up before the subject of furniture itself, because most persons are already possessed of at least a portion of what is to be used. Furthermore, the matter of arrangement and balance is so important that it should be mastered before new furniture is purchased.

We have already, then, in our houses the constructional items of doors, windows, fireplaces and panelling, if this be used. Frequently, too, in new houses or apartments, there are such built-in features as china-cupboards, wardrobes and bookcases. All, therefore, that usually confronts us is the existing space into which we must pleasantly arrange our household effects, and possibly provide for others. When we mobilise these effects they seem of great variety, but their uses are so well defined that this in itself often aids their placing. In a bedroom of the usual size, for instance, the purpose of the room defines the appropriate furniture. Often, too, from the construction of the room, it is at once evident where the bedstead should go, and there remain but a few wall spaces into which we may fit a chest of drawers with mirror above, or a dressing-table, a highboy, wardrobe or chiffonier, a small table or two, chairs, and perhaps, if the room

PLATE 88

A. AN ENGLISH BEDROOM, WITH APPROPRIATE SEAT AT FOOT OF BED
Balance Sustained by Curtained Alcove and Double-chest of Drawers
By Courtesy of Messrs. Story and Triggs, London

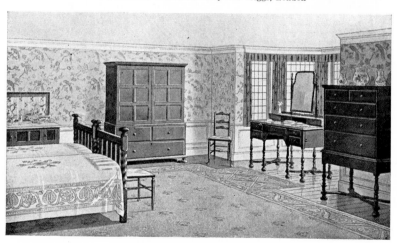

B. AN ENGLISH BEDROOM
The Light Naturally Determines the Place for the Dressing-table, while the Wardrobe and
Highboy go into Darker Spaces
By Courtesy of Messrs, Bartholomew and Fletcher, London

PLATE 89

A. AN EXCELLENT ARRANGEMENT IN
THE CORNER OF A MAN'S LIVING-ROOM

B. ITALIAN RENAISSANCE FURNITURE IN FORMAL BALANCE
By Courtesy of Mr. Alfred Villoresi, New York

PLATE 90

A. FAULTY BALANCE BETWEEN THE TWO SIDES OF AN OTHERWISE
ATTRACTIVE ROOM

B. BALANCE ACCOMPLISHED BY THE USE OF ONE LARGE PICTURE
IN PLACE OF THE TWO SMALL ONES, ABOVE

PLATE 91

AN EXAMPLE OF DISORGANISATION AND BARRENNESS IN A GENERALLY GOOD INTERIOR

be sufficiently large, a couch, and the like. The fact that we should have a good light by which to dress, will probably determine the place of the dressing-table, while a wardrobe or highboy may go into a darker space, so that by natural circumstances our progress has greatly been aided (Plate 88 A and B). In any event, we have arrived at the precept that it is well to begin with the principal pieces of furniture, afterwards disposing of the others.

BALANCE

In order, however, that the final result should show a correct balance of arrangement, we shall need to use other principles. Some of them are at once evident, as, if we were to load a boat, we should not naturally place all the bulky freight on one side and the light on the other, so we shall not arrange all the tall pieces of furniture on one side of a room and place the low pieces on the opposite side. By so doing we should not actually tip the room as we should the boat, but we should tip its appearance. Furthermore, even if we disregarded for the moment the looks of the whole room and considered either side alone, we should see how montonous is a series of pieces of more or less uniform height. We must, therefore, intersperse high and low to secure a proper balance.

Balance, in its simplest form, is that in which the objects on each side of a larger central feature are the same in character and arranged in the same manner. This is illustrated in the beautiful group of Italian Renaissance furniture in which the chairs and torchères are alike on both sides of the handsome credenza (Plate 89 B). This arrangement, being formal in its character, is particularly in place for stately rooms, but is equally appropriate in such humbler surroundings as a quiet eighteenth century room where two chairs flank a Queen Anne sofa with an old portrait above. The formality here is combined with quaintness, both of which are charming in an interior of this old-time type.

A further development of the principle of balance is that in which the objects on the two sides of the central object are not the same or even of the same character. Such an arrangement, as we shall by-and-by see, does away with formality, and imparts a more familiar and homelike atmosphere to the room where it is used.

Although balance of this nature is simple and easily accomplished, it is often neglected or but imperfectly managed. An example of such faulty balance is shown in the illustration where, on the right of a fireplace, a tea-table with two small pictures above fails to balance the antique organ on the left. The readiness with which such an imperfection can be remedied, is shown in the corresponding illustration where the two small and poorly hung pictures have given way to a larger picture properly placed (Plate 90).

An example of what amounts not only to disorganisation in furnishing, but to loss of homelike feeling, is that of a room of generally attractive character with its comfortable sofa and chair on opposing sides of a fireplace and a stand placed stiffly between (Plate 91). It is evident that the chair fails to balance the sofa in length and that the stand is disjoined from either. Now if the chair were pulled slightly forward, and the stand moved back, not directly to the side of the chair but to the side and just forward of its edge, where it would be handy to the chair's occupant, it will at once be plain that an altogether different atmosphere of invitation and restfulness had entered into the composition. If a rug were laid down before the fireplace, the windows simply curtained, some of the objects removed from the mantel and a larger clock or other object introduced to give centralisation, the whole effect would be changed. It will, therefore, be seen that the treatment of this one room is a small object-lesson in decoration, and points out what an infinite improvement a few changes in position and addition can make in an interior which is already generally good, so far as it goes.

The principle of balance being so clearly shown, it might prove interesting to try a few experiments with light pieces of furniture in one's own household, especially if there are young people in the family. The future of good household-art naturally lies with the rising generation, and if those who are now young can be interested in such matters the benefit may prove immeasurable. Parents might also find their children taking a vital interest in the attractiveness and neatness of their own rooms. The writers, therefore, indicate a few such experiments:

If, for example, we have a fireplace, or other large object, with a small space on each side of it, we may place a chair with a picture above it in each space. Such an arrangement is balanced but is formal, and we may prefer a small table in one of the spaces. If it is approximately of the size of the removed chair we shall still have balance, but, if the table is long, we shall immediately see that this balance is disturbed, and it will be better to substitute a couch for the chair on the other side, thus matching the long table in shape.

We may, however, alter the arrangement which first existed by the use of a tall object instead of a long one —we may wish to place on one side of the central fireplace a mahogany bookcase which, although not much wider than the chair, if bulky, may happen to exceed it considerably in height. It is plain that we shall have to remove the one picture in order to give place to the bookcase, and we then have the case on one side and the chair with picture above it on the other. If the picture be of strong character in a dark frame and the chair also dark, we still have a good balance to the case on the other side, but if the chair be small or light in colour and the picture be likewise, we shall *not* have balance. The question of "value" has, therefore, entered into the problem as well as that of size. Value is the lightness or darkness of an object irrespective of its colour. Balance may be described as *equal weight of effect,* and it is that which we must secure.

Another principle with which we are all familiar is the avoiding of top-heaviness—we should not place a very large picture, hanging or mirror above a small chair or table. It is really surprising sometimes to see how little is required in this direction to spoil an effect and to "get upon one's nerves" when constantly seen. In such instances, we should recall here, also, the principle of value; for, although the *sizes* of the two objects may be in proper relation, the arrangement will, nevertheless, be bad if the upper one be too strong and dark for the lower. If the lower is also frail in build, the bad result will further be intensified.

Two varieties of treatment have been considered—that in which the objects on each side of a larger central feature were alike in character and similarly arranged, and that in which they were different but were either of themselves or by the addition of other objects of equal general effect.

Occasionally in household arrangement two other contingencies arise. It may be that on the one side of the central object (such as a fireplace) we wish to use some such piece of furniture as a bookcase of mod-

erate size and on the other side a table and chair. We
so place them at equal distances from the fireplace on
its two sides, but are disappointed to find that the appearance is wrong, that the latter articles do not sufficiently balance the former. Even when we place a
lamp or other object of some height upon the table the
result is but little improved. We could build up the
effect by a picture upon the wall, but we may already
have done all we wish in this direction and may really
prefer a change from the formal balance. It may easily
be secured. It will be remembered that the writers'
definition of balance was *"equal weight of effect"*: in
order therefore to give the object or group which is the
lighter in effect the same weight which the larger
possesses we must give more *leverage to the lighter.*
In other words, as we move it *farther* from the central
object it gains in weight of effect. A few inches will
usually be sufficient, because the original discrepancy
should not be great.

The second contingency is where there is no central
object or room for one, but where the wall space is
sufficiently large for the placing of two objects or
groups. In this case the procedure is precisely the
same except that instead of working from a central
object we work from a central *point.* Measure the wall
space and find its centre; if the two objects or groups
are of equal weight of effect place them equidistant
from this central point. If one is lighter than the other
move the lighter farther away from the central point
until it is *felt* that the balance is correct. There will
likely be other circumstances in our household arrangement in which we shall have to exercise this balance of
feeling and to which this will be a guide. Mathemati-
cal calculation would be too abstruse, and a little
experiment will make is unnecessary as well.

OBJECTS OF CENTRAL INTEREST

Every large wall space should have an object of central interest about which other objects may group, and if it be not there we must either supply or create it. It may be supplied by one of the larger and taller pieces of furniture, by a large mirror, or a tapestry or other hanging; it may be created by building up a series of objects.

As these built-up effects are among the most interesting and attractive decorative facilities we possess, several of them will be suggested.

First of all, they give us the opportunity of making the most of and of bringing out the true beauty of fine pieces which yet are not of large size. One might, for instance, be the happy possessor of such a handsome inlaid console cabinet as that shown in Plate 92 A, but be so unknowing as to place it, because of its size, in some convenient but undistinguished corner where its beauty would be hidden and its effect as a decoration fatally lost. On the other hand, but little is required to make of it a centre of interest worthy the name—the placing upon it of a few choice objects and the hanging above it of the unusual but simple mirror shows its true value. This group might be flanked by handsome chairs or settees, thus furnishing the side of a room which it would be a pleasure to enter.

A different but similar result may be obtained by the use of a long but low bookcase. Above this we may hang a panel nearly as long as the bookcase and, upon the latter, place a few objects that will unite the two and give interest. These objects might be a plaque or vases, a couple of small pictures and a pair of candlesticks. Or as a centralising object we might use an attractive table or chest with a panel, mirror, or picture hanging above it, and a sconce on each side.

PLATE 92

A. A BUILT-UP EFFECT OF CONSOLE-
CABINET, MIRROR AND ACCESSORIES

B. A BUILT-UP EFFECT IN AN APARTMENT RECEPTION-ROOM
COUCH, BACKING, AND A PANEL OF FOUR JAPANESE PRINTS
(The couch has since been replaced by a Sheraton settee)

For a stately room, no better centralised group could be imagined than such an arrangement as that of the Italian Renaissance furnishings shown in Plate 89 B, and if one lack such distinguished materials much the same result might be obtained by articles of far less cost.

Probably as comfortable and homelike a composition as could be desired is that which occupies the end of a little room illustrated in Plate 92 B. Here is a roomy couch with a backing to match the covering, hung from a brass rod upon the wall. There are abundant cushions, and above it is a panel consisting of a series of four attractive and colourful Japanese prints in one mat and frame, flanked by a sconce on the one hand and an upright panel between the long one and the antique bookcase on the other. As usual, photography has emphasised the pattern of the covering. A Sheraton settee with quieter coverings has since taken the place of the couch.

Small hangings are less often used in such situations than mirrors, but if one is on the lookout for such things it would be possible sooner or later to pick up some attractive and unusual piece of drapery that would give individuality to such a setting (Plate 80 A).

Carved woodwork, polychromatic decoration, a plaster panel or a Chinese or Japanese decoration would all be appropriate for this or similar places.

Of the built-up effects that have been suggested it may be said that each of these devices has its own interest and that all might be used, each in its own situation.

FIREPLACES

We have the expression "Hearth and Home," and when there is a fireplace, it is the central object of interest and should be so treated. In many old houses, a

19

settle often stood endwise to the room at one or both sides of the fireplace, and in modern use the same device may be employed. A tea-table, sensibly set at its end, does much to relieve the stiffness of a settle and adds to the home-like atmosphere of the composition.

In more elegant rooms it is now happily quite customary to place a sofa in the same position. An excellent example of fireplace treatment is shown in Plate 56. If space is limited it is sometimes better to employ an easy-chair, with perhaps a stand or small table, for the opposing side. There should be a hearth rug and cricket, hassock or a sitting pillow or two upon the floor. Such an arrangement at once gives an air of comfort and rest. If a room is too small to admit of a full-length couch or sofa, we could use one of the double-chair settees, or simply another comfortable chair. Sofas are sometimes placed directly before the fireplace and backed by a table.

In large living-rooms or libraries, it is often pleasing to draw up a small table with books and a chair before the fireplace, placing them sufficiently far away to avoid any appearance of crowding. If, owing to the arrangement of the room, this should be found to look artificial, take them away—nothing but sincerity is tolerable.

DOUBLE AND MINOR CENTRES OF INTEREST

In a great salon, one central object (even with minor ones) on a long unbroken wall space would probably not be sufficient. In such a case two large and handsome companion cabinets could be used. They would be placed with less space between them than at their sides, so as to give good appearance and keep the companionable relations of the two without the monotony of too close a neighbourhood. With these should, of course, be pleasantly arranged other pieces of lesser size forming attractive groups. As such cases usually call for the services of an interior decorator it is hardly worth while to take up other expedients here.

In large rooms especially, all furniture should not be arranged along the wall, but some pieces should be placed out upon the floor space; on the side of a long room, it is otherwise almost impossible to escape stiffness and formality. This is taken up a little later on.

If, however, a room be long but too narrow to allow other than a wall arrangement, we should, in addition to the main centre, establish other minor centres of interest. If, however, an imposing fireplace is the main centre, we may place a cabinet or bookcase in the middle of the long wall space on one side, and one of our built-up effects on the other: these, with lower pieces of furniture interspersed, will be sure to give desirable variety and interest. In all cases where there is room for a considerable amount of furniture it should, when well arranged, fall into groups, each attractive in itself, natural in appearance, and composing well with the groups about it.

CORNERS

Corners are usually a consolation and convenience rather than a source of worry (Plate 89 A). Frequently pieces on the side wall are close enough to the corner sufficiently to occupy it, while the other corners of the room prove the natural resting places for such things as desks, tables (rectangular or round), tall clocks, small cabinets or bookcases, screens not in constant use, sewing and serving tables, and finally, in the room where it is used, the ubiquitous sewing-machine—at present usually the ugliest and often the most offensively ornamented object with which decent humanity is afflicted. To hide it with a screen is as yet the only resource.

The main precaution to take regarding corners is

that they should not look weak, and for this reason they
are not the best places in the world for chairs, unless
these be roomy.

In drawing-rooms a grand piano often finds its best
situation with its "nose" in a corner and its flat side
almost parallel with one wall, rather than swung out
into the room at a disagreeable angle. As a grand
piano is not high, a large picture or hanging on the
wall occupied by its flat side and a picture hung upon
the other wall will be advisable.

The placing of a desk or other such piece of furniture diagonally across a corner is unpleasing unless
there is a jut of the wall partially filling the space behind and so justifying the arrangement. This is frequently the case in new steel-construction apartment
houses. Kidney-shaped desks are by their form particularly suited to corners. A tea-table set in a corner
with a chair behind it and a muffin stand at the side is a
hospitable arrangement and entirely unobjectionable,
because the corner is filled. It is the empty triangular
space behind pieces of furniture that is unreasonable
and unpleasant.

THE SETTING OF FURNITURE OUT INTO THE ROOM

We have just looked over a series of interiors of
modern club-houses and handsome dwellings and the
first expression occurring thereat was decidedly unlit-
erary. It seems to be a weakness of human nature that
where an allowance is made for the sake of variety
and use it too often becomes an obsession. As many of
these interiors with furniture set "anyhow" over the
floor can only be described as a conglomeration, it is
well for us to take warning.

Let us consider then what we may properly do in
the placing of furniture out upon the floor space. We
may do *nothing* if it will result in crowding. Even the

setting of a single table in the centre of a room is bad
if we must spoil our tempers to get around it. In small
rooms we may, however, make another disposition of
a table which is pleasing and convenient. Instead of
placing it flat against a window or wall space, with a
chair before it, its back to the room, or instead of placing a chair at either end, we may set the table endwise
to the wall, or to one side of the window, and a chair at
one or both sides of the table. With a few interesting
objects upon the latter. we shall find that we have an
attractive grouping.

A small table or stand in front of an end of a sofa
or by a large chair at once commends itself because
convenient.

The arrangement of a sofa backed by a table has its
convenience—we may sit on the sofa and read by the
light placed upon the table—but we should be careful
that the two pieces chosen agree better than they sometimes do. One "set-out" arrangement which seems to
have widely spread among householders is the placing
of a couch or seat at the foot of a bedstead (Plate 88 A)
—another good device under proper conditions. But
often we have been obliged to smile at the absurdity of
an imposing couch at the foot of a negligible bedstead,
an amusing example of the "tail wagging the dog." We
often wonder why persons who use common sense in
most concerns of life fail to do so in such simple matters.
Is it that they are determined to follow a vogue of
which they have heard, at whatever cost?

Chairs in front of bookcases, wardrobes and cabinets are annoying, as each time a door is opened the
chair must be moved; and why add to human misery
by strewing chairs and stools everywhere around to
fall over or stumble against: in short, why so crowd a
room with set-out furniture that our progress through

it becomes a process or a pilgrimage? The blocking of doorways is equally bad practice.

It is also to be remembered that the littering of a room with all sorts of unrelated objects and personal effects is utterly destructive of repose and charm.

Finally, the large pieces of furniture set out upon the floor space should follow the direction of the one wall or the other. Impossible angles distract us through disturbing the harmony of line. Women, through a mistaken idea that "setting things cata-cornered" gives homelike character, are notable offenders in this respect. A chair, or resting stool or two, may be left at the convenient angle at which naturally occupied, but if we go beyond this we have disturbance.

SCALE AND PROPORTION

The importance of considering the relative sizes of various accompanying objects (the relation is techni-cally called scale) runs throughout the subject of interior decoration and must everywhere be taken into account. With it is intimately associated the matter of weight, real or apparent. Though in actual avoirdupois a wooden moulding be not heavy, we may not rightly put up a cornice so out of scale that it appears as if it might bring down the ceiling upon our heads.

This is so obvious that it seems few would transgress, yet is it more obvious than the following which we frequently see: window poles stout enough for an athlete's horizontal-bar from which depend curtains of filmy net or lace weighing but a few ounces; fragile tables groaning under the weight of huge lamps; carpets and upholstery of strong and sweeping pattern in tiny rooms, and the heterogeneous mixture of furniture formal and sprawling, heavy and light?

In every age save the present one of high enlight-

enment has there been an instinctive sense of fitness
and proportion even among "the people"—witness the
admirable congruity between furniture and interior in
the old English cottage and the houses of Continental
peasants. Hardly nowadays shall we find that sense
even among them that consider themselves the educated and elect.

"We have taken the most delightful house—Tudor,
you know: with dark oak panelling," says Mrs. A. She
has, most unfortunately, and proceeds to fill it with a
number of vanloads of accumulated mahogany furniture. Not only do oak and mahogany go badly together
as regards colour, but they are of an entirely different
provenance and spirit, having precisely as much in
common as an eighteenth century gentleman and Sir
Walter Raleigh. "Other times, other manners."

"Our apartment living-room," remarks Mr. B., the
broker, "is so homelike, with its low, heavy beamed
ceiling." By the fireplace of that truly long, low, comfortable room with its horizontal lines you would find a
big easy-chair—for Mr. B. values his comfort. But Mrs.
B. is "refined" and evidences that quality by the tall,
high-shouldered, spindle-leg furniture, upholstered in
fabrics in attenuated colour and small pattern. One
looks up from these egg-shell pieces to the massive
beams above and trusts they will not fall.

And at No. ——, —— Street (we can readily fill
the blanks) the lofty room with its fine old mantel and
woodwork in white and beautifully modelled plaster
ceiling is occupied by——dumpy mission and a mid-
Victorian black-walnut bookcase!

EXPERIMENTATION

Interior decoration is not a mystery: it is the use
of enlightened common sense. Experience leads us to

the conviction that even those who are unskilled in home arrangement have more intrinsic ability in this direction than they realise, and it is the aim of the present writers to aid them in using that which they possess. Bearing in mind the simple and gradually developed suggestions that have been made, if the reader will begin with the *practice,* we fancy that the intrinsic knowledge of which we have spoken will rally to his aid. In other words, most persons, *when they see a thing,* have a fairly good eye for balance, distance and scale; their difficulty usually has been that they have not looked and considered; even those who flatter themselves upon their artistic ability often fail to weigh sufficiently and so fall into errour.

Experimentation is the best teacher. Begin as has been suggested, with the principal and obvious pieces, afterwards grouping the others as well as possible. Then, using one's own natural eye for balance and effect, weigh the result. It will probably be seen at once that a certain piece will not do "here" but will do "there," or that it must be moved in one direction or the other. If a happy result is secured with any one group, learn to let it alone; pass on to another until each group is satisfactory, and all the groups pull satisfactorily together.

You will then have accomplished a gratifying result in interior arrangement, with correct balance, scale and line.

It has justly been said that not only must each of the four walls of a room look well, but that each must look well in relation to that next to it—that the diagonal result must also be good. To this may be added that the view from each *doorway* should be attractive and inviting.

CHAPTER VII

FURNITURE AND ITS CHOOSING

PRESENT-DAY FURNITURE AND ITS SUPPLY. WICKER. PERIOD
FURNITURE. ANTIQUES AND REPRODUCTIONS. COMMER-
CIAL FURNITURE. SUITES AND ODD PIECES. FURNITURE
FOR THE "MODERN" DECORATION.

IN the first chapter of this Part, "The Basis of Successful Decoration," we have strongly advocated
the use of Period Furniture when and where it may
be had. The facilities at hand for the purchase of this
furniture will forthwith fully be dealt with, but it may
be helpful first to consider what may be done when,
for reason of location or price it is beyond reach.

PRESENT-DAY FURNITURE

The assortment of good modern pieces is not extremely large, but we may at least be thankful for what
there is. The utter badness of all mobiliary design
after the decline of the Empire style persisted for many
years—we have but to recall the furniture of our
fathers and grandfathers, the period of black walnut
and later of varnished golden oak. "Eastlake" was a
failure, as will be every attempt to create a style not
based upon tradition and the long-established principles of beauty. "L'art Nouveau" has happily passed.

The Mission style, which as the first attempt to
escape from jig-saw and gingerbread is praiseworthy,
is strictly utilitarian, heavy, unbeautiful, ungraceful,
and with lines as antique as the ark. There is one thing
to be said in its favour—it is admirable for a happy-
go-lucky houseful of children, for it is almost impossible to destroy.

In its lighter forms particularly it is much more attractive when painted and perhaps banded or treated with a few strong, modest decorations, and upholstered in good virile style in solid colourful fabrics not too fine for its texture, in strong stripes, or in a bold printed linen or cretonne with rather striking but tasteful colour. So done it is excellent furniture for the "newer" decoration.

Then there is wicker—and is it not a comment upon the boasted artistic ability and advanced civilisation of the later nineteenth century to say that this is probably the most worthy thing in mobiliary development which it accomplished! In its way and in its *place* it is so good, however, that a separate section will be given it.

We have also the handsomer grade of department-store mahogany furniture, most of which to the tyro looks like period furniture but is not. Last summer the writers passed along a series of windows devoted to a "sale" of these goods and grew sick at heart.

There is, too, Peasant or English Cottage furniture, and for modest homes nothing better has ever been devised (Plates 78 B, 93 and 126). The reader will kindly remember, however, that this is *period* furniture as much as any other.

Some of these pieces may be found in the shops, for there are a few companies that are manufacturing it. There are also two firms, and perhaps others, that make it and sell direct to the consumer by means of representative sheets or catalogues.

Messrs. William Leavens & Co., Inc., of Boston, manufacture this cottage furniture and also pieces in the Mission vein. By use of the first a home may be charmingly fitted up—if one but has the taste; and we are trying to show the way. For the living-room a

PLATE 93

A. ENGLISH COTTAGE FURNITURE IN OWN HOME OF WALTER MELLOR, ESQ.

B. ENGLISH COTTAGE LIVING ROOM EQUIPPED WITH FURNITURE DESIGNED
BY THE ARCHITECTS
By Courtesy of Messrs. Barry Parker and Raymond Unwin, Letchworth, Herts.

PLATE 94

A. ATTRACTIVE FORMS OF REED FURNITURE
By Courtesy of the Reed Shop, New York

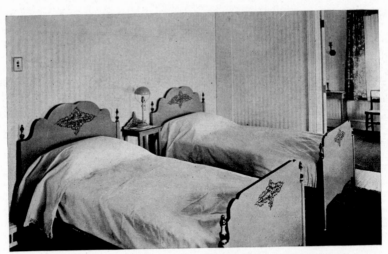

B. MODERN PAINTED FURNITURE IN A SEASIDE COTTAGE
Decorated by Abbot McClure, Esq.

large gate-legged table and one or two smaller plain
wall-tables; simple cottage chairs; some easy, comfortable wicker chairs with seat and back cushions; a large
winged upholstered chair (for this a beautiful cretonne
furniture-cover may be made which can be taken off
for cleaning) ; a box-couch with solid colour cover, perhaps of velour, and attractive pillows of various kinds;
a tapestry or brocade hanging (see Plate 128 of a remodelled farm-house) with a simple chest of drawers
below it, or else a long table in the place of the chest.
On either of the last can be placed attractive candlesticks with candles and a bowl or two. A convenient
desk is often welcome.

With these appropriately go bare, stained or
painted floors with a few simple rugs in good colouring
to accord with the colour-scheme decided upon (see section Unity and Variety) ; simple white curtains; a good
lamp; a mirror or hanging over a small table used as
a console. A few good prints in colour or monotone, or
Japanese prints, in simple, well-chosen frames, or a
really excellent water-colour or two are all the pictures
needed.

For accessories use such things as a Chinese reproduction of a Kang-Hsi or Chien-Lung vase, a bowl or
two of pottery in such solid colours as rose, blue, grey
or yellow; a cylindrical Chinese medallion-ware lidded
jar for cigarettes and a rose-bowl of transparent glass.
By referring to the various chapters under which these
matters of furnishing are discussed, many hints and
illustrations will be found. A newly married couple of
moderate means will find this method the most desirable and as inexpensive as is anything in these days
of high costs.

Some of the pieces might be painted and others
stained in the reddish-brown found on the colour-chart

(*not* imitation mahogany). As means grow larger good mahogany or walnut pieces (antique or faithful reproductions) may be substituted and some of the original furniture used elsewhere.

This same firm (Leavens & Co.) makes two excellent styles of beds—those with simple slat head and foot boards and the turned four-poster. If twin-beds are used (and they should be if two occupy one room) the slat form is the better as the others give too "postery" an appearance where two beds are employed. They also supply good plain chests of drawers. It is better to get these without the attached mirrors and secure one with old mahogany or rosewood frame, which can readily be picked up at one of the antique shops. Or such a mirror as that which hangs above the console in Plate 92 A would be excellent.

A rather more expensive and also pleasing sort of furniture is made by the Erskine-Danforth Corporation of New York. This comprises excellent pieces of the simpler forms of period furniture, some of them, fortunately for variety's sake, other than English, and good forms of Peasant furniture painted and decorated. Even in inexpensive furnishing it is well to bear in mind the facilities of International-Inter Period Decoration treated in Part III.

It is unfortunate that there is not yet upon the market a good supply of *Directoire* furniture, than which nothing can be more simply graceful and attractive. It is practically simplified Louis Seize with a little more *swing* in the arms and legs of chairs and settees (Plates 171 and 172). Decorators fully appreciate the qualities of this furniture, and it is surprising that more of it has not previously been made. It is but one additional indication of the slowness of American furniture manufacturers in realising that there is a wide field for them if they will but supply faithful reproductions of simple forms of period furniture such as this and those pieces used in the remodelled farmhouse, and at moderate prices.

It is to be hoped that in these times of reconstruction and renewed enterprise both manufacturers and dealers will awake to the fact that there are people of moderate means but cultivated tastes who are looking to them to supply their needs. If they do not, acute foreign manufacturers are likely to do so to the detriment of American interests.

There is a considerable amount of painted furniture of modern character upon the market—most of it being simplifications and variations from eighteenth century forms. These are temporarily attractive; that is, they seem fresh and modern (largely because of their colouring) until one realises their remote origin and considers how much better is the origin than the derivation. It is a pity that they do not show greater distinction of design.

WICKER FURNITURE

The making of furniture in willow, reed, rattan, cane and bamboo (the term wicker seems commonly used for all of them) is one of the most serviceable and useful of modern mobiliary developments. These materials have occasionally been tortured into forms to which they are not suited, but they have generally proved most satisfactory and durable. The reasonable price of willow furniture has been a great aid to those who have much to do upon small means. Those who have taken it up for this reason may congratulate themselves that with these and other simple forms they have done much better than those who have spent larger sums upon highly ornamented and often grotesque modern pieces.

The closely-woven reed furniture (Plate 94) is naturally more expensive, as it is also firmer and more compact. One writer designed and had made to order a small armchair in this material which after some years of use seems practically indestructible. Since then numerous beautiful forms have been brought out in all these materials and in close and open mesh, so that one may well grow enthusiastic over the possibilities of wicker furniture. Stained a mahogany shade and given attractive cushions such pieces go well in any but formal or luxurious rooms, and when painted in such tones as grey, grey blue, grey mauve, sage green, cream buff, yellow, rose or black and accompanied by upholstery in striped goods, cretonne or printed linen, they are often really handsome and perfectly suitable for city houses and apartments. For use with the "Modern" Decoration this furniture is often painted in brilliant colour. Frequently staining or painting is not necessary, for in some rooms their natural colour is entirely harmonious, and even interspersed among mahogany the lighter note proves occasionally a needed contrast.

For the country or seashore there is nothing better, and wicker is especially adapted to sun parlours, protected porches, morning and living-rooms. In the bedroom of either man or woman a comfortable arm-chair of this light, cool and serviceable material, with a back high enough to rest the head against, will prove a boon to tired minds and bodies for seizing a short rest while it can be had in the intervals of our busy lives.

The Oriental forms, with flaring backs, and the hour-glass chairs are still imported. Some are also made by American manufacturers. The "Dryad" furniture is also very attractive.

The Chinese bird-cages (Plate 126) and the old style cages of willow, largest in the middle and tapering at both top and bottom (Plate 93 A), are most pleasing. Hung in a sunny white-curtained window they give cheer and have the atmosphere of home. The flower baskets of flat basket-work may be mentioned here as equally attractive.

PERIOD FURNITURE

There remains the long and noble line of Period Furniture. In considering it a certain amount of knowledge must be taken for granted by the writers. Those not familiar with the subject are referred to "The Practical Book of Period Furniture," by Eberlein and McClure, where they will find it treated in detail.* Part I of this volume is replete with information and Part III on International-Interperiod Decoration should carefully be studied.

Not everyone can afford genuine antiques, and good examples of certain special pieces are not always to be picked up just when desired. The beautiful qualities of the old woods and the patina of time are not to be found in reproductions, but otherwise they may thoroughly be commended—when they are faithful. Just why so much "Near Period" furniture persists is rather puzzling. Doubtless, the manufacturers at first found genuine reproductions difficult to sell, for after long years biassed by the bad, the good would naturally be slow in gaining genuine appreciation. Perhaps these conditions may still exist to a certain extent, but

---

* For Italian, Spanish and Portuguese forms v. "Practical Book of Italian, Spanish and Portuguese Furniture" by Eberlein and McClure, *in preparation.*

just why adaptations nearly enough correct to cause many purchasers to think they are securing genuine styles should sell better is difficult to say, particularly as such pieces are profusely advertised as being of certain periods. Manufacturers should remember that distortions of original forms cause positive pain to those who "know," and as the number of such persons is largely increasing, the reputations of such manufacturers are bound to suffer in the end.

We think, however, that there have been indications of a return to a saner point of view, and that there will be less and less adaptation during the coming years. In the meantime, purchasers will do well to confine themselves to faithful reproductions only.

SELECTING FURNITURE ACCORDING TO QUALITIES OF MEANING

In considering Period Furniture, as indeed with the whole subject of decoration, let us appeal for a broader and more catholic spirit than is often found. Just why the sympathies and appreciation of many writers and decorators are so limited is rather puzzling. One may certainly prefer one style to all others —such preference will usually be found temperamental—without exalting that style to the depreciation of others.

There have been a few bad periods and there have been some bad pieces designed in all good periods, but these may be ignored. If we review the various periods and styles we shall find that each is excellent for its own qualities and that its qualities differ from those of others. Let us, therefore, enjoy and employ them in accordance with this and not quarrel with them because they do not possess that which belongs to others. We shall, as usual, make ourselves clear by an example.

There are some whose temperament inclines them toward the classic, the refined and the formal who are scathing in their remarks upon the furniture of Queen Anne. Queen Anne furniture is not of classic style, but we find something else which the classic does not always possess—quaintness, homeliness and comfort. May we quote here a phrase from Henry James in relation to objects of far less artistic worth than Queen Anne furniture: "The infirmity of art was the candour of affection." There we have it in a few words. We may often love an object which falls short of the supremest beauty, while that beauty incarnate in another object may fill us with undying admiration but leave our affections cold.

The classic, the romantic and the quaint each has its place in our varied lives and circumstances. We need not disparage one because of the other: broadmindedness will see that in one establishment or another there is a place for each. A study of Part I and Part III on Internationl-Interperiod Decoration, will show the qualities and what might be termed the meanings of the various styles, when we can then determine which of them are best suited to our own use and circumstances.

ANTIQUES AND REPRODUCTIONS

In all the large cities there are dealers in imported antiques. These pieces are usually choice and necessarily high in price, but those who can afford them will find these dealers reliable and fully informed.

There is also the dealer in antiques who is a cabinetmaker as well. The antiques in his stock whether of British or American style, are usually of early American make, and it may be said that in beauty of the woods employed and in workmanship they are equal to the imported pieces.

20

Indeed, we are informed by a cabinet-making dealer who has handled both that the carcase-work of the American pieces is usually the stronger. Some beautifully carved and elaborate furniture was made here and such examples may well be called "museum pieces." They now fetch nearly or quite as much as British work.

Our American cabinet-makers usually concerned themselves, however, with the production of the less elaborate but sufficiently ornamented forms, together with the simple pieces, and these are still within reach of those of moderate means. Indeed these antiques and cabinet-makers' reproductions may still sometimes be purchased at lower prices than new commercial furniture. There are especially in the East well-known furniture makers handling their own product and also large establishments (which might be termed cabinet-making factories) which sell through decorators and the highest class of dealers, both of which make fine and faithful reproductions of Period Furniture of various nationalities and styles. The pieces chosen are generally more unusual and often more elaborate than those made by the smaller cabinet-makers and the prices are necessarily higher.

The cabinet-makers' reproductions do not usually consist of the more elaborate pieces, but of those of quite sufficient ornament, often very handsome, well constructed of excellent mahogany or walnut and with the soft, desirable finish.

COMMERCIAL PERIOD FURNITURE

There are many large factories throughout the country, with superb equipment, turning out quantities of furniture of excellent workmanship, mostly by machinery. This furniture is found in good furniture- and department-shops and is thoroughly satisfactory except—that much or most of it is not faithful period furniture—perhaps in many cases it does not pretend to be. With no wish to be invidious, the fact that it is not faithful is to the present writers a very large reservation indeed. An acquaintance recently observed that they are just enough wrong to be misleading and injurious to one's sense of rightness of form.

Some of these are not in themselves bad pieces of furniture, others are "reproductions," losing the proportions and virility of their originals, and many of them are merely designed more or less *after* certain styles or mixtures of styles, some of them containing features which have no congruity whatever.

It is to this furniture we have previously referred and for which we then said we see no reason; the prices asked would certainly seem to warrant a faithful reproduction. A few enquiries will show how these figures compare with those of cabinet-makers' reproductions or even with those of the correct and elaborate forms referred to in a preceding section.

A desideratum is the manufacture of simple forms of faithful Period furniture in greater quantities and within the reach of those of quite moderate means.

That our own strictures are moderate may be seen by the following quotation from an address before the Architectural League of New York by the *President of a large furniture manufacturing company*, and printed in "Good Furniture."* Referring to these reproductions of the English furniture of the seventeenth and eighteenth centuries, he says: "Not 10 per cent. of this furniture gives the public even a faint idea as to what those styles really were, wherein lies their charm, and why those products of a vigorous, active and progressive age, in their true character, should have so

* May, 1919, pages 212–213.

much of appeal for us to-day. Our great public really
knows almost nothing of them, and therefore is not
in a position to judge the good from the bad, not only
in old work, but in the novelties of design which each
year we see develop into a fad and then fade away into
nothingness.'' Later he refers to these reproductions
as ''commercial crimes committed in that name.''

This condition of affairs is largely the fault of the
furniture-buying public, and that public can change the
condition as soon as it wishes. All that is required is to
make its will known, to insist upon straight reproductions and to buy nothing else.

In the eighteenth century the number of gentlemen
who made a real study of decorative matters is surprising, and we know from the correspondence of the period
that the interest was decidedly general. Our own
public is too ill-informed to be able to discern the ''good
from the bad,'' and too lethargic to improve itself by
means of authoritative books and a little study of
authentic examples in the museums. As it is more
greatly interested in ''movies'' than in the improvement
of its homes, it is consequently quite content with
''commercial crimes.''

The exceptions—and their number is constantly
increasing—deserve the greater honour.

SUITES AND ODD PIECES

The idea that a room must be furnished exclusively
with one suite of furniture is happily defunct; and yet,
like most such popular conceptions, it contains a certain amount of validity; the errour lying in its being
narrowed into a decorative dictum. If we substitute
may for ''must'' and delete ''exclusively'' we shall
arrive at the truth that in some instances a suite of
furniture is an excellent basis upon which to work.

In a large drawing-room, particularly of the

Georgian period or in the styles of Louis Quinze or Louis Seize, it is highly advisable that sofas, chairs, stools, couches, cabinets and tables should form a suite or be sufficiently in keeping essentially to do so. To these, however, may advantageously be added other pieces, still in keeping, but sufficiently different to give variety. In the dining-room it is well that the chairs about the table should form a set, but if the room be large we may well add wall chairs of harmonising but different build to redeem the room from bareness and too great uniformity.

Even in the informal drawing- or living-room a settee and a few matching chairs among other furniture undoubtedly give an aspect of unity which is not so evident if all the pieces differ one from another.

One of the best plans in the furnishing of informal rooms is to select a sufficient number of pieces of one period or style, though not necessarily matching, to form a basis, adding to these other furniture various but not conflicting. With these may well be used a few appropriate lacquered or painted pieces.

The whole subject of the mingling of cognate styles is fully and scientifically treated in Part III on International-Interperiod Decoration.

FURNITURE FOR THE "MODERN DECORATION"

There is no doubt that of recent years, in the revival of interest in good furnishing, great attention has been given to furniture and sometimes expense has been lavished upon it not out of proportion to its deserts but in undue relation to the total sum which the furnisher has to spend; so that other household accessories have suffered. Sometimes, where funds are sufficient for all needs this has taken the form simply of an interest in furniture too exclusive of other decorative features and for its own sake rather than for its fitness in the proposed scheme. In a general reaction against past methods, furniture, therefore, and especially handsome period furniture, has come in for its share of decrial with the new movers and is relegated to a secondary place.

Anyone who has given study to the subject of household decoration will freely admit that in many homes simpler and far less costly pieces would have given a better and more coherent result; this by no means should imply a lessened interest in furniture but rather a larger and more intelligent consideration of it whether simple or handsome. It should, in short, occupy its place adequately but not unduly in the plan of decoration as regards its form, its colour and its arrangement.

The new decoration lies largely in the direction of simplicity and therefore this school advocates simple styles and takes as its models the Peasant furniture of Continental Europe and the Cottage furniture of England. Naturally, those who follow the style of the Vienna Secession also use the furniture accompanying it. Particular attention is also rightly paid to arrangement—in theory if not always in practice—and overcrowding is sedulously avoided.

Not only are old English cottages of the greatest charm (Plate 95 A), but the British architects and decorators of to-day and some of our best American men have so wonderfully absorbed and carried on the traditions of probably the most homelike civilisation the world has known, that illustrations of their work are given (Plates 78 B and 93). Colour is not with them carried to the extent that it is with these "modern" decorators, but each of these interiors is so well balanced and so simple that all of them would be susceptible of treatment in strong tones if desired.

It should be pointed out that much of the pictur-

PLATE 95

A. AN OLD COTTAGE AT WESTON–PATRICK, HAMPSHIRE
From "Old English Country Cottages" by Courtesy of "The Studio"
The Admirable Idea of a Movable Curtain on Semi-Circular Rod and the Good Forms of
Furniture are to be Noted

B. A TYPE OF PAINTED FURNITURE WELL ADAPTED TO THE "NEWER"
DECORATION

esque charm of these rooms is *constructional* and due to the architectural proportions and features, and, in some cases, to built-in furniture, so that the illustrations serve as models in these respects as well.

Naturally great insistence is laid by the newer school upon the colour values of furniture used, and to accord with the decorative scheme adopted it may be finished in the natural colour of the wood, stained to any hue and dully finished, or painted, or decorated.

Decoration may be quaint in character to accord with old-time effects, or may be most modern and brilliant. When painted, furniture *may* be in subdued tones, but is often violent, such as bright blue or emerald green chairs with rush seats in bright yellow. Good tones are ivories, greys and tans, grey-blue and grey-mauve, yellow, rose, apple-green and black, the latter often highly polished (Plate 95 B).

Such furniture is frequently ornamented with lines in a harmonising or strongly contrasting colour. Black is excellent with any of the mentioned tones. The furniture previously mentioned as sold direct to the consumers is excellent for this style of decoration. Messrs. A. L. Diament & Co., of Philadelphia, who are the American agents for the attractive modern French Desfosse and Karth printed linens and cretonnes, are now supplying furniture painted to accord in colour and design with their fabrics.

Mission furniture, so uninviting in its usual colouring, takes on new life and decorative value when painted in attractive colour.

Wicker furniture is of special use in the new decoration. It may either be painted or left in its natural tone, and be supplied with strongly decorative cushions in solid colour, stripes or modern patterns.

Wing chairs are homelike and afford great comfort.

CHAPTER VIII

DECORATIVE TEXTILES

THE SOURCE OF COLOUR AND EFFECT. EXAMPLES OF CHOICE. FABRICS FOR THE ''MODERN'' DECORATION. WALL HANGINGS. SCALE. MOVEMENT. TEXTURE. HINTS ON PURCHASING.

THE decorative importance of textiles can scarcely be overestimated because it is largely by their use that effect and colour are gained, and if the opportunity is missed here it is often altogether missed. Excellent furniture is much, but, after all, seating furniture is but a framework and if it be improperly or unattractively covered its value in impression produced is lost; while simple furniture if good in line may be greatly enhanced in effect when accompanied by delightful fabrics. In a word, if the backgrounds are unobtrusive it is largely by textiles that the room is made or marred. If the effect has already been gained by such means as decorated walls or by painted or lacquered furniture, equal discrimination should be used properly to supplement these by fabrics which will not confuse on the one hand, or themselves sink into mediocrity on the other.

Effect consists in colour, contrast, pattern, material and texture. Appropriateness to period, circumstances and use must also be considered. A moment's thought will show that these qualities are *kindly guides,* and neither hampering nor bewildering details. Instead of having to choose from the whole range of fabrics of whatever sort, the task of the decorator or home-furnisher is greatly simplified.

A concrete example will make this clear—the pur-

312

chase of fabrics for a certain room is to be made. The colour-scheme has, of course, been settled upon. If we know, then, that we shall require goods in blue, say, or blue in combination, we evidently shall not need to trouble ourselves to look at greens, or violets, or pinks. It is a drawing-room, let us say, which we are considering, and contains mahogany furniture of the late Georgian period—Sheraton and Hepplewhite—with perhaps two or three chairs of the cognate Louis Seize style. As such furniture is of handsome type we may naturally dismiss denims, poplins and other such ordinary materials. We *might* choose printed linen or cretonne, but it would be much better to employ damask, brocade, or some such goods and do as the British do— use figured chintz covers for summer and informal occasions.

Common-sense, as well as any knowledge of the period, will tell us that for furniture of this refined type we should not use the dark, large-patterned and heavily-textured goods of the Renaissance, made to accompany weighty and imposing pieces of oak and walnut; nevertheless, the simplicity of the walls advises us that it is in the fabrics we must gain our decorative effect and that we shall need colour or pattern or both. Now what were the fabrics used at that time? Reference to Part I, eighteenth century England, shows us that the textiles used for such refined furniture were brocades, damasks and silks, and that toward the latter part of the century the colours became quieter and more subtle in tone than in the previous more vigorous age and that when they were fairly strong they were so disposed in quantity that their emphasis was appreciably modified. The patterns were as refined as the furniture, and as appropriate in scale, and stripes had great vogue.

At the decorator's shop we state our needs and find some admirable things. There are two or three charming medallion patterns and some small conventional designs of Adam and Directoire character. These are in the solid colours of beautiful old blues, the pattern being in the weave.

We remember the Louis Seize pieces and, with international tendencies in mind, look at a beautiful modern reproduction of a brocade of that period with a flower-basket design surrounded by other florals—this being in many colours.

And we do not forget the stripes which were so greatly in vogue in both England and France. There is a striped and figured damask in blue and buff and others in blue and old gold, both simple alternate stripes of plain and satin finish and wide and narrow ones of satin with watered ground. We see, too, one in the same colouring with the addition of white and rose in narrow lines. We especially appreciate the introduction of the other harmonious colours with the blue.

Being well known to the decorator he sends up to the house the large two-yard samples of the several styles we prefer, where we try their effect in the actual conditions under which the fabrics are to be used and there make our choice.

In choosing fabrics it is not obligatory to limit ourselves slavishly to the designs and materials of the particular period, provided there is no incongruity. Sometimes textiles which appeared rather later will answer admirably, and there are good modern designs appropriate for many such uses. If Period furnishing is to *live* it should be allowed elbow-room. A good test of appropriateness is to ask ourselves whether such and such a fabric would likely have been employed for

PLATE 96

A. WILLIAM AND MARY ROOM PANELLED IN OAK
Settee Covered with Brocade with Scalloped Velvet and Lace Hanging on Back.   Pillows Covered
with Petit Point Needlework.   Lacquer Cabinet
Courtesy of Mrs. Lyman Kendall

B. BAD SCALE IN THE TEXTILES USED IN AN OTHERWISE ATTRACTIVE ROOM
The Chair-covering is Totally Out of Scale with the Rug

PLATE 97

A. ARMCHAIR COVERED WITH *PETIT POINT* NEEDLEWORK, TAPESTRY CURTAIN

B. CHIPPENDALE LONG STOOL COVERED WITH *GROS POINT* NEEDLEWORK
Courtesy of Mrs. Herman Duryea

PLATE 98

THE CHARM OF CHINTZ IN AN "OLD-TIME" INTERIOR

Oriental Rugs will Accompany Ornamental Fabrics when Properly Selected

The Picture Frame is a good type for a portrait of this character and it is hung in proper relation to the mantel

Courtesy of Mrs. Abbot Thorndike and Mrs. William Thorndike

PLATE 99

A FINE USE OF WALL HANGINGS.   NOTE THE USE OF MIRROR AGAINST PLAIN CENTRE OF MIDDLE HANGING
The Furniture is mostly Italian of Various Periods
By Courtesy of George Howe, Esq.

the particular purpose had it existed in the repertoire of the period.

The choice of materials for any epoch is usually, however, a wide one, for our forebears in most ages were not given to penuriousness, and were as lavish as means allowed in variety and beauty, both of costume and furnishing. For the non-committal or the "Modern" method there is an abundance from which to select, and the result is by no means dependent upon the cost. Some fabrics, by their very nature, are less expensive to manufacture than others and each sort may be thoroughly good of its kind. Sincerity should always be apparent in household decoration, and by sincerity is meant the avoidance of cheap display and of vulgar and tawdry imitations of expensive materials.

Reference to Part I will afford information as to the various fabrics employed during each of the periods, and the Chapter on *Colour* (especially the section on *Unity and Variety*) will give many suggestions as to their use. Curtains and portières have been discussed in the chapter on *Windows and Their Treatment,* and the last section of the present chapter will afford hints for the advantageous purchase of goods. Textiles themselves, of all kinds, are for the first time fully treated in Mr. Hunter's interesting volume, which should be consulted by all concerned with household art.*

FABRICS FOR "MODERN" DECORATION

While the "new" decoration is not absolutely confined to the simpler materials, its tendencies are in that direction and the fabrics chosen are usually therefore such as linens, casement-cloth, sunfast, denims, poplins and taffetas, rather than rich damask, brocades and

---

* Decorative Textiles, by George Leland Hunter. 580 plates in colour and in halftone. J. B. Lippincott Company, 1918.

velvet. The main idea is to get the *effect* desired, whatever the material. Velour is, of course, often used for couch-covers, and special decorations such as Oriental hangings, table-pieces, couch pillows, and the like, may be striking and handsome. Batik is largely employed, and any hand embroidery in strong pattern is very appropriate.

In any style of decoration table strips are usually better than table covers. For circular or oval tables a good plan is to cut the table-cover respectively square or rectangular and ornament the overhanging corners with a heavy tassel.

For upholstery purposes solid colours, stripes and striking designs are all effectively used. If there is a sufficiency of plain surface to balance them, either of the latter two may be employed. In a large room the usual chairs may be covered with a solid colour or not too insistent stripe, and large wing or wicker chairs be done in a strong design.

In any room and with any style of decoration cutting up with too much pattern should be avoided.

WALL HANGINGS

To anyone looking through the illustrations of this volume the decorative value of wall-hangings must be apparent. Tapestries and rich brocades, needlework and embroidered silks and velvets, Oriental and Batik hangings—all are of the greatest use under appropriate conditions. Hangings were employed in all periods down to the revival of Classicism in the latter half of the eighteenth century. In England, where panelling was the accepted wall treatment, they were hung over the panels as in Plate 80 B.

Those are indeed fortunate who can afford the purchase of antique tapestries and embroideries, but many of the former have been really well reproduced. In the use of either originals or reproductions care should, of course, be taken to have them appropriate in period, colour and scale. Reproductions which are evidently "cheap" should be avoided.

Handsome brocades in modern weaves and period character are always available at a not too prohibitive price, and frequently these may be given a border of tapestry or velvet for enrichment or contrast.

A hanging over a console or table with a mirror hung upon it makes an interesting grouping, as is shown in Plate 80 A, while in Plate 99 will be seen a fine Italian mirror disposed in a similar manner.

Oriental hangings might be more largely employed than they are. Japanese draperies usually are of free and flowing design and would be appropriate with the "Modern" method. The Chinese are more conventional and controlled in pattern and so are much better for most purposes. Persian, East Indian and Javanese textiles and embroideries and Portuguese prints are often very beautiful but are not largely in the market. One of the writers owns a small but effective Egyptian *appliqué*, brought from Cairo, which invariably commands the attention of visitors.

Those who are always observant and on the watch for good and unusual things are pretty sure soon or late to be rewarded. It is probably the lack of such individuality and observation that has been responsible for the bringing home of merely conventional things —which might easily have been purchased in any large American city—on the part of those who have extensively travelled. Apart from richer examples, Peasant draperies might often have been obtained which would have given life and interest to halls and bedrooms or to living- or sitting-rooms in "Modern" or informal vein.

SCALE

Once again reference must be made to the subject of scale, for nowhere is it more important than in decorative fabrics. The design or stripe chosen must not only be of appropriate *character* but in due relation as to *size* with the furniture, other surfaces and objects, and the room itself. While, as has been said, the master designers of the Renaissance and other periods proved to us the possibility of ornamenting every surface without producing confusion, in all but very elaborate modern decoration we shall not have such problems to deal with and the ornamented surfaces will likely be few. By trying draperies in actual position, as suggested in a following section, it will not be found difficult to decide upon a satisfying result in respect of scale. It need only be observed that contrast and texture have much effect—a large pattern may be permissible or advisable when blended with the background, whereas it would be intolerable if it stood boldly apart from it.

Frequently the purchase of new upholstery may be made to solve already existing difficulties. Such an instance would be where the design of a wall-hanging were felt to overpower a small and neat-patterned rug or carpet; the introduction of an upholstery design of medium size and strength might be found to unite them into a satisfying combination.

An example of bad scale is shown in Plate 96 B.

MOVEMENT

Design may be balanced and static or it may have movement; *i.e.,* its lines of construction may be so strong in a certain direction that the vision is *pulled* along their course. If the repose of a room is so great as to be somnolent it is plain that such movement will give life and vigour: if the room is unduly low and heavy an upward spring of design will impart height and lightness; while a strongly mounting movement in the covering of a high-backed chair would as unduly accentuate its apparent height.

The same principle, of course, applies horizontally, and lateral movement is therefore often of use in disproportionately lofty interiors where it tends apparently to reduce height.

Designs consisting of well-balanced, flowing curves do not lead the vision from point to point with rapidity: they therefore create interest without unrest.

Those which pull the eye *diagonally,* and hence at variance with the perpendiculars and horizontals of the room, are distracting; while zigzag lines can only be maddening. On the floor of an old Virginia mansion the writers recall a rug with such lines which all the well-known repose of the Colonial interior was insufficient to subdue.

TEXTURE

Texture is the arrangement or disposition of the material composing a substance and results in that substance having such qualities as heaviness and lightness, smoothness or roughness, fineness or coarseness, opacity or transparence, stiffness or flexibility. The subject is one of great interest to the decorator and as regards textiles is fully gone into in Mr. Hunter's book: here a few hints of practical application will be sufficient.

Warning is usually and rightly given against the employment in close proximity of substances which war in their texture, and this must always be considered not only in respect to textiles but in the whole field of decoration—a rough-cast wall, for instance, would make a poor background for delicate satinwood furniture and airy draperies scarcely accompany pieces of Jacobean oak. It will, however, render clearer to the reader the importance of, and the reason for, this avoidance if we lay emphasis upon the handsomeness or unhandsomeness of such substances resulting either alone or combinedly from material and texture. Crash is rough and so is cut-velvet, but it is the commonness of the one which unfits it for the use of the other rather than the roughness. A considerable diversity of texture is not only allowable, and really necessary by reason of the uses of various furnishings, but advisable for the avoidance of monotony: rugs are usually of heavy wool; with them silk damask furniture coverings may be employed; while the Chinese lamp may be of the finest porcelain; and yet we do not feel a discrepancy at their use in one room, though each is different both in material and texture, providing all be similarly handsome. But—if we put down an evidently cheap cotton rug, or a wollen one so rugged as to put it in a lower degree of elegance, we immediately feel the inappropriateness. The unhandsomeness of the one is caused by inferiority of material and that of the other by great divergence of texture.

A practical effect of decided texture is the appearance it gives of weight—a smooth, unpatterned silk stretched over a large sofa might look thin and flimsy, whereas a brocade of really no greater heaviness might give a perfectly satisfactory appearance of weight and richness.

Local colour is greatly modified by texture: the colour-effect of a strongly textured piece of goods viewed at the usual distance may be quite different from what a close inspection shows the actual colour to be. This is due to refraction of light, and various angles often give different colour-effects.

HINTS ON PURCHASING

A covering being needed for a new screen and it naturally being of importance in the decoration of the room the man of the house stopped in the decorator's shop at which he dealt and out of a large stock selected ten or a dozen of the two-yard samples and had them sent home. When he arrived in the late afternoon his wife had already tried them on the screen and said: "They are all beautiful, but there is just one of them for this screen and for this room. See if you agree with me." He, too, tried them and unhesitatingly picked out the same one.

This small experience illustrates several points well worth notice.

I. Each room has its own lighting, colouring, and individuality, and to select just the right thing for that room under other conditions is well nigh impossible. Goods should practically be bought *in loco; i.e.,* the actual selection should be made on the spot where they are required.

II. Apart from any other consideration it is always well to experiment. In the case mentioned the pattern was not one which either the man or his wife would have bought at the shop: it needed the situation and the isolation for its beauty to be appreciated.

III. The goods selected were not the most expensive: Some other pieces were nearly double in price but did not look nearly so well for the particular purpose and place.

IV. If one deals at a decorator's he will usually find interest and appreciation of the effort to secure a good effect. He will also find willingness to send such samples when the purchaser is a regular customer or well recommended. One meets with intel-

21

ligence and courtesy and secures goods that are not in
all the department-stores.

V. It may have been noted that it was the *man* who
made the first general selection: does it often occur,
outside of artistic circles, that a man takes the interest
he should in the beauty of his house? Yet, if he has
taste and knowledge, why not? And if these are lacking it would be well for him to realise that these are
part of the equipment of a gentleman and should be
cultivated. The Honourable Andrew Hamilton, one of
the most celebrated jurists of the Colonial period, designed the State House in Philadelphia; Thomas Jefferson designed, built and furnished Monticello; and
George Washington twice enlarged Mount Vernon and
ordered his furniture.

The successful decorator or home-furnisher is one
who is at *all times* observing and who studies and
makes mental notes of attractive things he sees that
may appeal to him as applicable for future use. The
study of *authoritative* books is of great use and such
magazines as *House and Garden, The House Beautiful,
Good Furniture* and *Country Life* are full of good
things. Other journals, such as *Town and Country,
Vogue, The Spur* and *Vanity Fair,* frequently picture
interiors of historic houses here and abroad and modern dwellings and club-houses. The decorative articles
which appear in daily and Sunday papers and some
journals should be considered with discrimination before being followed—some are written by competent
authorities, and others by those who in this particular
direction seem to know less than their readers and who,
in their probably well-meaning attempt to introduce
the newcomer, through their own ignorance clumsily
block the gate of the bazaar.

The decorators' shops in large cities afford many a hint as to materials, furniture, schemes of colour and decorative possibilities; and one great storehouse of knowledge—the Museum—should be much more utilised than it is.

In trying effects in the home the conditions should be those which usually obtain—do not, for example, throw the shades up to the top of the windows. As night effects are quite as important as those of daytime, goods should also be tried under artificial light: quite extraordinary variations are often found, not only because of the differing qualities of the lights themselves but because they are from different directions and differently concentrated.

Such precautions may seem to entail some trouble, but they will often save one from the alternative of dwelling with nightmares or doing over what might rightly have been done at first. We should also consider the pleasure and positive mental and physical benefit of feeling each time the home is entered that, though perhaps very simple, it speaks of beauty and of rest. Neither should we forget our social relations: rooms with high, glaring lights, bad forms and faulty harmonies are impossible for companionship, while others are immediately suggestive of fellowship and cheer. A rather elderly woman in humble circumstances (I reverently lift my hat and call her lady) said to the occupant of an attractive apartment: "Some things have happened, and I felt very sad when I got up, and then I remembered that I was to come down and clean for you to-day, and it's all so beautiful, and peaceful, and quiet here that it's helped me to forget." Few would soon forget those words so simple and sincere.

CHAPTER IX

ARTIFICIAL LIGHTING

PRINCIPLES AND METHODS. CANDLESTICKS AND CANDLES. LAMPS. CANDELABRA, TORCHERES AND STANDARD LIGHTS. SHADES.

ARTIFICIAL lighting is an exceedingly important subject, and yet, in many households, it seems to be ignored in inverse ratio to its importance, of course with deplorable consequences.

The whole subject falls naturally into two divisions: (1) fixed lighting, whose arrangement constitutes a part of the fixed decorations and is architectural rather than otherwise in its affinities; and (2) portable lighting, which belongs wholly in the realm of furnishing. The former, as its nature implies, is largely determined by the architectural character of the background, first as regards pattern, material and scale of the equipment, and second, as regards the placement of lighting appliances. The latter admits of almost unlimited latitude in placement, in the selection of divers types of appliance and in the choice of illuminating medium.

Whether the lights be fixed or portable, certain general principles obtain, almost without exception, and these principles must be carefully observed. To begin with, under ordinary circumstances a blazing glare is painful to the eyes as well as ugly and disastrous to the aspect of any room, even though it be well furnished. A number of dim or subdued lights, therefore, are infinitely preferable to one or two powerful, glaring lights. The diffused glow from the more numerous and mellower lights is vastly more comfortable to the eye and more kindly to the furnishings. In the next place, it is both unreasonable and uncomfortable either to have one or two blazing illuminations in proximity to the ceiling or to have a number of less vigorous luminaries lighting the upper part of the room and leaving the lower in gloom. Likewise, the various methods of indirect lighting, although purposely devised to eliminate glare and secure diffusion, which they often do admirably, nevertheless throw most of the light on the ceiling. This does very well for public places, but is usually objectionable and ugly in a house. It is not necessary, nor in many cases would it be desirable, to have the artificial light fall from precisely the same quarter as the light by day, but it *is* highly desirable and eminently logical to have the light at night coming from approximately the *same level* as the daylight and to illuminate, not the ceiling, but the region of the room humanly inhabited.

With the foregoing dicta the illuminating experts and fautors of sundry approved modern and ultra-scientific lighting systems, aye, and various doctors to boot, will probably take serious issue and promptly adduce fifty-seven different reasons to prove that they are right and we are wrong. To their accusations we cheerfully answer that their "systems," their inverted appliances and their fiercely illuminated ceilings blazing above a substratum of milder effulgence may be all very well for offices, shops, auditoria and railway stations—doubtless they are—but we humbly submit that our homes are none of these nor can we, for the life of us, see why we should seek to introduce the atmosphere of those places into our domestic circle.

In the third place, the quality and intensity of the artificial light must also be taken into account. It

should not be harsh nor sharp in effect nor of such
intensity as to distort the relative values of illumination and shadow. Above all, the colour of the rays
must not be of a character to falsify or kill the colours
in the furnishing. *Mellowness* is the chiefest desideratum in domestic lighting, save in such exceptional
cases as ball-rooms or *salons* upon occasion of large
and somewhat formal gatherings, when *brilliancy* is not
only quite permissible but often distinctly desirable.

The illuminants to be considered upon grounds of
decorative desirability or expedience are *candles, oil,
gas* and *electricity.* Of these, the first most completely
fill all the ideals of quality just mentioned. There is
no light so restful and agreeable in quality to the eye
as candle light and no light is kindlier to the appearance of a room. The radiance is mild and diffused,
shadows are not cut sharp and exaggerated, and the
colours in furniture and decorations are not outraged.
Incidentally, it may not be amiss to note that ladies
are well aware that they appear to greater advantage in
the glow of candles than by any other light.

Candles as a means of lighting are perfectly practicable. The only possible objections that can be urged
against them with any show of validity are cost and
bother. Neither obstacle is very serious; the former
can be ingeniously circumvented, if necessary; the
small amount of the latter is not worth considering if
one values the agreeable effect of their rooms. Wax
candles, of course, are desirable, but stearic acid
candles and other substitutes for wax are thoroughly
satisfactory for general use.

It is well to have a good broad glass *bobêche* for
each candle socket. Any drippings can then be easily
removed without dirt or trouble. As a rule, the use of
shades on candles is finically effeminate, foolish, fussy,

reprehensible and anomalous. A candle is, in itself, an object of grace and beauty, but its chaste and dignified simplicity of line is marred and hidden when its shaft is surmounted with a top-heavy, frilly contrivance resembling an abbreviated ballet skirt. Upon the making of such shades entirely too much valuable energy is wasted. The flame of the candle, too, is an essential part of its beauty and ought not to be concealed. Its gleams are not distressing to the eye if the candle is of proper height and properly placed. For the dinner table use tall candles, tall enough to keep the flame above the level of the eye. For the library, living-room or drawing-room, sconces will be at a sufficient height and portable candles may be so disposed on mantels, the tops of bookshelves, tables or cabinets that the flames are comfortably above eye level. Using no shades and keeping the flame a little above eye level is one of the secrets of successful candle use.

It is well both to group candles at certain points and also to use them singly or in pairs symmetrically placed. The objections to candle lighting usually come either from those that have never really been used to them and do not know how they should be used or else from those whose ridiculous and savage obsession for a multiplicity of blazing lights prompts them to jeer at candles as antiquated or obsolete. To the latter charge one may reply that good taste, like good manners, is not a thing of the moment or of caprice. Like good manners, it has a permanent, enduring quality, unaffected at bottom by minor ephemeral variations of fashion. And good taste recognises no temporal disability. If a thing is good, as the sound decorative principles on which candle lighting is based shew it to be, it is perennially in order.

Next in place comes oil. The light is agreeable to

the eye and satisfactory in its action upon decorations
and furnishings. The degree of light and its regula-
tion depend entirely upon the kinds of lamps used and
the shades employed. It is a sufficient and convenient
illuminant and practicable if the lamps are intelligently tended. For purely practical reasons small
lamps are generally undesirable and better results are
gained by using medium-sized or large lamps.

Gas, unless shaded and tempered in varying degrees, is trying to the eye, the shafts of light are sharp
and harsh in effect and colours suffer under the rays.
When burned through chemically prepared filaments or
other intensifying devices, the greenish or intense
white quality of the light is especially disagreeable to
the eye, disastrous to colour and produces a ghastly
effect. Heat and a certain amount of smoke are also
objectionable features. If gas is used, discreet shad-
ing is absolutely necessary. Its cardinal recommenda-
tions are convenience and cheapness. Diminutive, dim
flames rising from porcelain sham-candle burners are
absolutely indefensible on the score of either utility or
decorative fitness.

Electricity is convenient and clean and its brilliance
commends it to them that like floods of artificial light.
When used for domestic lighting it must be judiciously
shaded; otherwise, it is even harder on the eyes than
gas and casts sharp, exaggerated shadows. The use
of either gas mechanically or chemically intensified, or
of electricity with high voltage unshaded bulbs may
be appropriate and convenient in public places and
commercial establishments; in domestic interiors they
have no proper place. Considered from the point of
view of either convenience or decorative propriety, it
is indefensible to mount electric bulbs atop of imitation candles. They are so patently shams that they

are foolish and they have just about as much place in decoration as the vermiform appendix or wisdom teeth have in the human anatomy. Their presence is utterly inexcusable in view of the many really admirable and satisfying fixtures that competent designers have devised. Electric bulbs, whether globular or pear-shaped, are not objects of beauty and should be screened from view by shades or by devices for diffusing the light and when they are perched on sham candles the shade should be large enough and of such shape as to hide the offensive deception.

The architectural or fixed lighting appliances may be divided into those (1) that depend from the ceiling and those (2) that are affixed to the walls. (The pimples and carbuncles of glass sometimes set in the ceiling we shall not discuss. They are barbarous and would be appropriate only in german interiors.) The first or dependent group includes *chandeliers, hanging lamps, hanging lanthorns* and *drops*. The second, or affixed *group*, includes *sconces, wall lanthorns, girandoles, wall lamps* and sundry sorts of *brackets*. Impressive and large chandeliers are appropriate in large or stately and formal rooms or in lofty halls, hanging, perhaps, in the open space of the stair well (Plate 100). In small or informal rooms they have no place at all. The smaller chandeliers with only a few lights, known as "hanging branches" until the early part of the eighteenth century, allow a greater latitude of use. As designers of gas and electric appliances for chandeliers have generally conformed to candle traditions, the principles applying to the use of one sort apply to the others also. When chandeliers are used there should also be sufficient side lights at a lower level. Otherwise, unless it be for a ball-room or some similar apartment, the centre of illumination is too high to be agreeable. It is only in exceptional cases that a chandelier can be used successfully as the sole source of illumination, even when candles are burned.

Hanging lamps for halls, entries, stair wells and rooms, especially large rooms, permit more freedom of use than chandeliers. The same may be said of lanthorns (Plate 100). It is scarcely necessary to call attention to the many admirable designs to be found in both cases. Drops, usually and preferably for electric lights properly shaded, are to be recommended for use above dressing stands (Plate 170).

Sconces, girandoles, wall lanthorns, wall lamps, brackets and all other *affixed* lighting appliances, every one of which may and ought to have a very real decorative as well as utilitarian function, should be placed (1) where they will be useful; (2) not too high so that the major part of the light goes to the ceiling; (3) and, if possible, in a balanced or symmetrical manner. Whether candles, oil, gas, or electricity be the illuminant, equally good designs may be used, wholly consistent with the character of the architectural background and the general decorative *milieu*. If electricity be used, it is suggested that the bulbs be enclosed in some of the wall lanthorn or lamp forms with ground glass to diffuse the light or with a rice-paper shield, such as they often use in Japan. In this way the unprepossessing bulb is completely screened. For many admirable historic designs of affixed light appliances the reader is referred to the numerous illustrations in the fore part of the book, while adaptations and purely modern designs of merit are to be found here and there through all parts. Finally, let the number of the affixed lights as well as their placing be sufficient to ensure an agreeably diffused illumination.

PLATE 100

A. EARLY EIGHTEENTH CENTURY BRASS CHANDELIER
LIGHTING A STAIR-WELL
Messrs. Wilson Eyre and McIlvaine, Architects

B. HANGING LANTHORN AND VENETIAN PROCESSIONAL
LAMP ON STANDARD BASE
George Howe, Architect

PLATE 101

CARVED WOOD AND GILT SIDE-LIGHT
WITH LION-MASQUE CENTRE
By Courtesy of Wilson Eyre, Esq.

PLATE 102

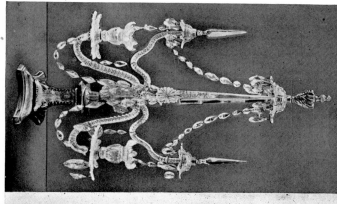

A. Unusually Fine Adam Candelabrum, Base of Blue Glass with Ornamentation enamelled in gold. Upper Part of Waterford Glass, Cut

By Courtesy of Mr. R. W. Lehne

B. Empire Candlestick (Egyptian phase) Bronze Figure, Brass Base and Sockets. Italian Early XVII Century Carved and Gilt Wood Candlestick.

Late XVIII Century Italian Carved and Gilt Wood Candlestick

By Courtesy of Wilson Eyre, Esq.

C. Empire Candlestick with Brass Gallery and Socket. Old Italian Candlestick (very tall) of Carved and Gilt Wood with Inserted Small Bits of Mirror.

Courtesy of Mr. R. W. Lehne

ANTIQUE CANDLESTICKS AND CANDELABRA OF VARIOUS PERIODS
Each is One of a Pair

Portable lighting appliances include *candlesticks, candelabra, torchères,* and *standing lanthorns* as well as all the numerous family of *lamps.*

CANDLESTICKS AND CANDLES

In addition to their obvious usefulness candlesticks are a strong decorative asset. The soft glint of metal or the beauty of colour in pottery or decorated surface which they supply would be severely missed in many decorative schemes.

As with lamp standards we may say that those of period form are best because they are the best designed (Plate 102). Those of wood, carved and gilded, are excellent, and the simple turned ones either in mahogany or painted and decorated are attractive and reasonable in price. Many beautiful candlesticks have also been made during various periods in pottery, glass and other materials, and among these should not be overlooked the unusual things of Oriental origin.

Even if but occasionally used candlesticks should not be without their candles—otherwise they are as marred as a watch without its hands. A beautiful thing primarily made for use is partially deprived of its beauty when its function is obviously removed. Besides, the cylinder of wax is of itself a beautiful thing.

Decorative candles are sometimes useful and among the best are the Japanese ones, larger at the top than at the base, with excellent conventional flower design in red and dark blue. The square white candles with black lines fit well with some decorative schemes, and those of bayberry are particularly good with odd Japanese or other candlesticks with green as part of their colouring.

Candles are also to be had specially decorated in accordance with period designs, but *handsomely* dec-

orated candles are so obviously intended not to be burnt
that their use is decidedly questionable.

Brightly hued candles, such as canary yellow, are
not open to this objection and their use often gives a
happy colour note.   They are of particular value in
"Modern" decoration and they also relieve a candlestick or torchère of iron or other dull effect.

The present writers have before now shown their
impatience of the exaltation of personal preferences
into decorative dicta and so far are they from willing
to err in this direction that they frankly and perhaps
amusingly record a considerable difference of opinion
among themselves.   One of the authors has an unalterable distaste to "things hanging down from the ceiling."   He is doubtless generally right so far as modern decoration is concerned, but another feels that as
such "things" *have* depended in all ages they are *permissible* in some cases.

The ideal lighting for the dining-room is, of course,
side-lights, with lighted candles upon the table, and if
further strength of light is required the present writers
advise the helping out of these with a pair of torchères
set conveniently near upon the floor.   This was advanced as an original suggestion, but, alas for modern
originality! since it was written we find in selecting
illustrations that precisely this arrangement was used
in the fifteenth century Davanzati palace (see Plate
15 B).

There are, however, tasteful but practical people
who in the hurry of a dark winter's breakfast, for instance, will "bother" with neither torchère nor candles
and for these the writers see no objection to an unobtrusive lighting arrangement above the table.   A
"dome," of course, is abhorrent, but there are other
devices, such as an electric drop, the bulbs and other

"machinery" being concealed at the sides by an appropriate shade and beneath by shirred gathered taffeta centred at a button or tassel.

LAMPS

Said the innocent small-householder: "I have just spent $60.00 for a new chandelier." And when we groaned: "Why a chandelier?" his injured surprise was as great as if he had been asked, "Why a breakfast?"

Yet why a chandelier in a small house or apartment? They have their appropriate places—as we have seen—but it is not here. Yet nothing seems so dear to the heart of "the people." Happily it has largely passed out of use with those of taste, except in its proper sphere, but the present affliction is scarcely less intense —the inverted dome reigns supreme! Why should the strongest light be thrown upon the ceiling? The portion of the room to be illuminated is naturally that which we ourselves occupy: the farther corners and the upper and lower areas may well go off to halftone and shadow, thus giving relief and charm.

In *general* and for the modern well-furnished home, it may be said that the only sources of illumination worth considering are side lights, lamps and candles. The first and the last may find only occasional employment, but the use of the lamp is constant.

Except for the slender standard lamp which has no receptacle for oil, the same styles are adapted for electricity, oil or gas. The electric system is the most convenient and the only objection to it is the necessary wire: this we shall have to dispose of as best we can. Perhaps some day we shall have "wireless" lamps. Here Mr. Marconi might help us out.

THE PURCHASE OF THE LAMP

Henry James, in his novel, "The Ambassadors" gives us the phrase, "a deep suspicion of the vulgar." This suspicion should constantly dwell with the decorator or homemaker in all his work but never more so than in the selection of lamps. The commercial-fixture man has laid many traps for the unwary in the way of brass and fancy metals with opalescent shades in disagreeable variations of green and yellow: there are pottery lamps—as there are jardinières—in which the tones or blending of tones have that quality of vulgarity so to be discriminated against; and even not all the Chinese and Japanese lamps of modern make are good.

Apart from its environment no decorative object should for a moment be considered, for, no matter how intrinsically beautiful it may be, if it does not fit both usefully and decoratively into the existing scheme of things, its advent will bring not beauty but discord and discontent.

There are, it will be seen, a few matters to consider before a lamp is purchased:—For what room is it to be used? Should the lamp be handsome or simple? Is a strong light needed over a large area or is a softened illumination desired? Upon what sized table is it to stand? What should be the lamp's height? Should it be slender or of more rounded form? Of what character are the furnishings with which it is to go? What is to be its background or particular situation, and of what colour or combination of colours should or might it be? Should its tone be light or dark? Do you need something striking or restrained, colourful or quiet?

The lighted lamp is likely to be the greatest centre of interest in any room, and attracts attention even when unillumined. For this reason the expenditure of perhaps fifty dollars or more for a handsome and unusual lamp would often prove a better decorative investment than the spending of the same amount on a piece of furniture. A lamp for reading or sewing should be of convenient height to give proper illumination, while the light itself should be strong and unimpeded by fringe. A fringe of beads, particularly, casts a swaying and annoying shadow. For such purposes the light should also retain its whiteness, so that, if shades of a pronounced colouring are chosen, they should be lined with white. If the light is to be diffused over a wide area, it is well that the shade should be light in tone and of sufficient transparency.

Where a room is throughout of a definite period-character the lamp—as other lighting fixtures—should of course follow the period. Where, as in many instances, it contains more or less period furniture but is pleasantly and not erratically eclectic, the choice is wide. If the room is of non-committal character, the lamp may be anything that is generally attractive and harmonious. If the room be furnished in the "newer" modern mode, the form of the lamp should be simple and the colour definite.

In a large room, even where side-lighting fixtures are supplied, a pair of matching or similar lamps will often be needed. They may be placed near the two ends of a long table as illustrated in the group of lamps in their environment, or on two smaller ones. More interesting sometimes than this uniformity is a large lamp supplemented by one or two smaller ones of differing character placed elsewhere about the room. These supplementary lamps need not always or generally be lighted, but should be placed in advantageous situations, so that if it is required to illuminate that particular portion or any interesting feature it may easily be done.

LAMPS OF MANY VARIETIES

The description and picturing of museum pieces would be of little value to the average householder. Far better will be some treatment of such lamps as are not absolutely prohibitive in price, together with simple but, in their way, artistic products. At first the variety seems bewildering, but a little consideration will consign most of them to certain classes.

Bowl or Vase and Pedestal or Standard Lamps comprise most of them, though there are attractive things which do not come under these heads and which must be treated separately. These two may be equally handsome or equally simple, and consequently a choice is apt to resolve itself into the selection of the particular example which best pleases us. It may be noted, however, that, speaking generally, the bowl shape has the more homelike appearance, while the pedestal possesses the more formal quality. If space on the table is any consideration, the pedestal lamp is naturally the one chosen; or else a tall and slender bowl.

BOWL SHAPES

These are made of almost every conceivable material, but among the best are those of porcelain and pottery with silken or parchment shades. These bases may be found in many beautiful shapes, colourings and textures, and in plain tones, mottled, blended or decorated. The shades, likewise, are of many shapes and colourings, and plain, brocaded, embroidered, or with figures, birds, plants, etc. Not only do these lamps of plain or blended colouring come from Europe and the Orient, but it is pleasing to be able to say that many kinds, and some of them among the very best, are made right here in our own land.

Two good styles of handsome lamps without dec-

PLATE 103

ATTRACTIVE LAMPS IN ATTRACTIVE ENVIRONMENTS

PLATE 104

A. LAMP OF PAULEO WARE IN
OLD ROSE

B. LAMP OF PEACOCK–FEATHER
DESIGN IN BLUE AND GREY

By Courtesy of Wolstan Herbert Dixie, Esq.

C. CHINESE PORCELAIN LAMP IN LIGHT
BLUE, WITH SHADE OF THE SAME TONE
EMBROIDERED IN BLUE, ROSE, YELLOW
AND GREEN. FINIAL OF CARVED WHITE
JADE

By Courtesy of Mr. Edward I. Farmer, New York City

PLATE 105

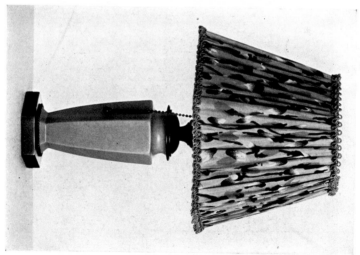

TWO VASE LAMPS OF EXCELLENT CONTOUR

PLATE 106

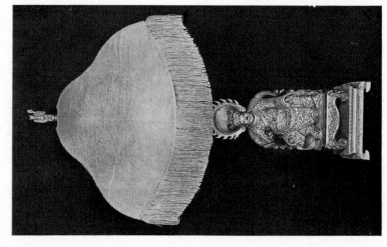

B An Old Ming Figure in Dull Gold and Red
Lacquer Mounted as a Lamp. Shade of Chinese Gold-
colour Silk Brocade

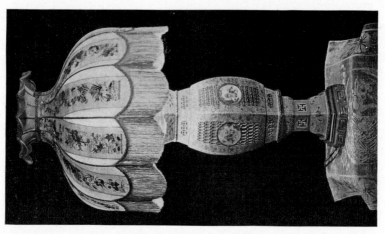

A. Chinese Egg-shell Lantern Mounted as a
Lamp. Mille Fleur Decoration in Delicate Rose,
Green, Etc. Shade of Chinese Orchid Colour Satin

By Courtesy of Mr. Edward I. Farmer, New York City

oration may be especially mentioned: vase shaped bowl
of pottery mottled in the baking, soft rose or tan, with
dark metal base, with shades in richer tones of the same
and handsome silk fringe of the same or of gold: black
porcelain, vase-shaped, with teak-wood base, the porcelain having a strongly reflective surface; dome-shaped
shade of Burgundy silk with fringe of the same and
four heavy silk cornering tassels depending but slightly
below the fringe. When illuminated, the effect of the
shade reflected in the upper surface of the bowl is of
extreme richness.

If the reader has not long ago reached the conclusion that the most beautiful vase lamps extant are
the Chinese, he will probably do so when he studies the
examples shown in the accompanying plates.

Of Chinese pottery one almost fears to let himself
go in eulogy, but nothing approaching it has ever
been accomplished in other Keramic art except in that
of their neighbours of Japan. In form the Greeks have
always been acknowledged supreme, yet it is doubtful
if even they exceeded the grace of some of the Chinese
contours, while in the realm of colour, either lavish or
restrained, the Oriental stands alone.

For the person of average means there are reproductions. Remarkably good ones were made by the
Chinese themselves, and in some of the famous European factories in early days, but these are probably
now also practically unprocurable. Modern European
reproductions are usually poor and so are some of the
modern Oriental ones, but many of the latter are of
great beauty—certainly of greater beauty for lamps
than any other porcelain at our command.

Though some writers have dwelt upon the difference in spirit between Oriental and European art,
Orientalism runs through the whole cycle of Western

22

decoration. It was even rampant among the Italians, many Renaissance *motifs* being of Asiatic influence, to say nothing of the wave of "Chinese taste" which swept eighteenth century England, France and Italy. We need, therefore, have no more hesitation in introducing Chinese lamps than Oriental rugs into any rooms where the general scale of richness and colour makes them appropriate. Those of simple design and colouring may with equal discretion be used in simple rooms and some of the tones of yellow, grey-blue and green are so exquisite that it seems as if no decoration could enhance their loveliness. A lamp of this simple contour and with a handsome but not unduly elaborate shade is shown at the left of the group of three Chinese lamps illustrated (Plate 107).

One may sometimes see in an Oriental store a vase which particularly takes his fancy and which can be bought for from $8 to $20. Base and fittings can be added by an electric-light fitter and a shade of any desired style made to accompany it.

The art of Japan is second only to that of China. The bronze lamp illustrated is an excellent example (Plate 108 C). The modern work is known to us all. Speaking in general only, the designs in the modern Keramic pieces are apt to be large and effective and usually less adapted to Western interiors than are Chinese ware and the finer patterns in the pottery and porcelain of Japan.

For rooms done in the "modern" vein, some of the plain colours previously mentioned would be admirable. The greys could have shades in rose, or yellow, and a bowl of Chinese yellow might be accompanied by a shade to match, edged and panelled in black or deep blue. A grey lamp with shade of translucent grey edged in the same way with Chinese red would be

PLATE 107

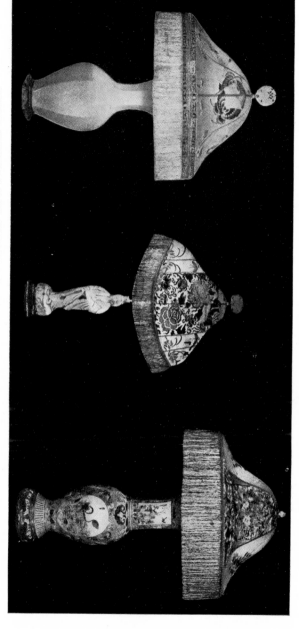

THREE CHINESE LAMPS OF VARYING TYPES, WITH SPECIALLY ADAPTED SHADES
By Courtesy of Mr. Edward I. Farmer, New York City

PLATE 108

A and *B*. ORIENTAL VASE LAMPS WITH SHADES OF FIGURED SILK AND DESIGNED
PAPER, RESPECTIVELY

By Courtesy of Messrs. Ramsey, Lyon & Humphreys, Inc., New York City

C. A BRONZE REPRODUCTION OF AN ANTIQUE
JAPANESE VASE

By Courtesy of Messrs. Ramsey, Lyon & Humphreys, Inc.,
New York City

PLATE 109

A. ITALIAN RENAISSANCE
PEDESTAL LAMP

B. PEDESTAL LAMP SUITED TO ANY
DIGNIFIED ENVIRONMENT

By Courtesy of Messrs. A. H. Notman & Co., New York City

C. PEDESTAL LAMPS OF CARVED WOOD, THE LEFT ONE GILDED, THE RIGHT
PAINTED

By Courtesy of Messrs. Ramsey, Lyon & Humphreys, Inc., New York City

PLATE 110

A and *B*. TWO ATTRACTIVE LAMPS FOR THE
BOUDOIR

C. A COLONIAL LAMP
Arranged by the Writer so that the Prisms
do not Interfere with the Direct Light

D. MAHOGANY STANDARD LAMP
Shade in Linen Color with Floral Design
in Rose, Green and Brown

equally good. The lamps of plain colour Japanese pottery with brown wicker and silk shades—also wickered—are excellent for many simple rooms, and those surrounded with basket work are equally good for porches.

The dull green pottery lamps, both American and European, have been a good deal overdone and they are neither particularly interesting nor individual.

One of the lamps illustrated has a design of peacock-feathers in blue and grey (Plate 104 B), and there are many other charming things of odd design. Wedgewood ware is dignified and appropriately accompanies eighteenth century English furniture. Those of Dresden and similar European wares are likewise attractive in appropriate situations.

In metal there are many good shapes in bowl lamps; and one should not close this section without a mention of those of this style now made in mahogany. As the wooden bowl, even in this wood, does not seem either particularly logical or elegant they are better painted or decorated. They may simply be painted and then lined about the turning with a harmonising or contrasting colour, or, as their forms are usually classical, they would be excellent with an Adam design on the bowl, or medallions, in addition to the lining. Before painting, the finish should be rubbed down with fine sandpaper, so that the colour will take well and evenly.

PEDESTAL LAMPS

The best of the pedestal lamps are naturally those of faithful period styles because they are the best designed, but there is nevertheless an almost bewildering array of attractive things of modern origin.

A word of caution has already been given as to the appropriate employment of period lamps, and one would think that flagrant and evident incongruity would naturally be avoided. Yet we recall a photograph of a particularly ornate lamp and a frivolous bust ornamenting (?) a bulbous Jacobean table in a dignified Tudor hall. Pedestals of simple classical style will accord with Georgian furniture and often with the corresponding classical periods in France and Italy.

The Empire pedestal lamps with frosted and cut glass shades and suspended prisms are excellent and too well known to need illustration.

The wooden pedestals are generally of simple contour, being based on the good old eighteenth century Classic, and are among the best reasonably priced lamps for sitting and bedrooms (Plate 110 D). Being, however, so frequently used, they need a rather unusual but appropriate shade to give them originality.

The wooden pedestals may be painted and decorated. For rooms in the "modern" style they are excellent in strong colours, striped around the turning in black, deep blue or white and with shades to match.

Pedestal lamps sometimes have an accompanying figure as has one of the charming little boudoir lamps illustrated (Plate 110 B).

Among modern things are pedestal lamps which have been more or less based on period styles but which are sufficiently non-committal for use in most situations (Plate 109 B).

VARIOUS DESIGNS

It would scarely be fair to apply the word novelty to many of these lamps, because while they are unusual they also possess dignity and value. The central example of the group of three Chinese lamps (Plate 107) where a figure is employed as a base, is of this character. So also are others in which dainty western figures, Chinese Foo dogs and other objects have been utilised in the same way.

Wrought iron standards are of excellence when well designed.

The writers recall a handsome brass affair where the base was a pan, with feet, from the centre of which arose a plain standard branched for three lights under a metal shade and with a lifting handle at the top. This would be very good for a library or living-room of strong, dignified character.

CANDELABRA, TORCHÈRES AND STANDARD LIGHTS

Candelabra and other standard lights have always played ·an important part in interior furnishing and they are of equal use to-day. They are especially appropriate with floors of marble, mosaic and tile, and decorated or sand-finished walls (Plate 100 B).

The ubiquity of the standard piano lamp has rather discredited all varieties of the floor lamp with people of individuality unless it and its shade are unusual. Certainly the candelabrum with several candles, or with electric fitting, or with the lanthorn top, possesses far greater distinction.

The suggestion of employing these for dining-rooms has already been made: they are of equal use for the illumination of desks and study tables, and for the bringing into additional relief of some special feature of decoration, such as an unusually handsome *cassone* or chest, a valuable tapestry or picture. In a rather dusky corner of a library, such a light with electric bulbs, quickly switched on, would prove of value in consulting the volumes.

Such standards, whether of metal or wood, plain, painted or decorated, may either be simple and attractive or highly wrought. Appropriateness in the use of the latter is of course necessary; *i.e.,* a magnificent lighting arrangement naturally should not be used to illuminate an inconsiderable desk or table.

SHADES

The principal requisites are that shades should be in harmony of likeness or of contrast with the lamp and appropriate to the surroundings.

Such a variety of styles, shapes and materials are illustrated that one may easily find a good model for any lamp, but a few words of caution are necessary.

The pattern, scale and spirit of lamps and shades must not be incongruous—if one is conventional in design and the other naturalistic, the spirit in each is opposed and the divergence will annoy; or if the pattern in one is larger than in the other, this will prove equally exasperating.

Shades should not come down too low on the lamp. In the group of lamps in their environment note the rather clumsy appearance given by this fault in the second example as compared with the others. Nor, on the other hand, should they stand too high, as a skimpy appearance will then result. The lines of shade and lamp together should make a graceful and pleasing contour.

CHAPTER X

MANTEL DECORATION AND GARNITURE

IMPORTANCE AS A CENTRE OF INTEREST. OVERMANTEL TREATMENT. THE MANTEL SHELF AND ITS PERILS. THE CONSIDERATION AND ARRANGEMENT OF ORNAMENT.

THE mantel began as architecture and ended, in its final development, as furniture. This is unqualifiedly true, so far as the historic styles of decoration, with which we have to do, are concerned. In modern practice the mantel is treated sometimes as one, sometimes as the other, with rather a leaning, perhaps, to the architectural interpretation. For the sake of brevity, in the present discussion we shall use the term *mantel* in its broadest acceptation, that is to say as including both the fireplace with its surrounding members and also the chimney-piece or overmantel. A mantel without a fireplace (a phenomenon one sometimes encounters) is an anomaly and has no more significance or use than a waggon without wheels or a plum pudding without plums. When such a case exists, common honesty, as well as common-sense, demands that a fireplace be made or else that the mantel be altogether eliminated. The fireplace-less mantel, therefore, requires no consideration whatever.

Whether we choose to regard the mantel as architecture or as furniture, there are two facts we cannot dodge. (1) By its very position and the space it occupies it is usually a dominating factor in the composition of a room. (2) As a focal point and important item of the fixed decoration, it naturally serves as an intermediate link between background and furniture and

343

affords a point of departure from which to attack the composition. The different methods of mantel treatment, ranging all the way from the strictly architectural conception of the Renaissance period when the overmantel structure extended either all or most of the way to the ceiling, to the mantel's treatment as little else than furniture in certain aspects of the Neo-Classic style, are duly set forth in the first part of the book and may be studied in the illustrations.

When the mantel with its attendant chimney-piece or overmantel decoration is wholly architectural in character, there is less opportunity for the injudicious to treat it with contumely and spoil its effect. It is when there is no fixed overmantel or chimney-piece that the greatest care must be exercised. It is perfectly obvious that the overmantel space demands a suitable decorative handling. That decoration may consist of a picture, preferably a portrait, or else a subject of distinctly decorative character such, for instance, as some of the eighteenth century fruit or flower pieces; a mirror, which is generally a legitimate substitute for a picture and is susceptible of considerable engaging embellishment; a bas-relief or a carving, perhaps one of the old Japanese polychrome carvings or one of the curious Chinese carved and inlaid shop signs; a decorative map or, perhaps, a decorative treatment of a plot of the grounds on the estate adjoining the house; an eighteenth century wall clock, such as one of the "sunburst" clocks of English or French design or one of the old Dutch clocks with ornate case and free hanging weights; an Oriental screen of proper size with panels laid back flat and fastened against the wall; even a well-designed and mellow but full-coloured poster— the writers have in mind a wonderful bird's-eye view of London poster got out by the tramways corporation

PLATE 111

A. A FIREPLACE IN A MODERN APARTMENT
Moulded Surround of Wood; Facing of Brass.
Korean Rug in Whitish Grey, Yellow and Blue
Courtesy of Durr Friedley, Esq.

B. CHIMNEY-PIECE BY ROBERT ADAM
20 Portman Square, London
From "Robert Adam and His Brothers"
Courtesy of B. T. Batsford, Ltd.

C. ITALIAN RENAISSANCE FIREPLACE
Carved Stone with Hooded Top
Palazzo Ruccelai, 15th Century
Courtesy of William Helburn, Inc.

The Two Classic Movements are well Contrasted in These Examples

—mounted on canvas, shellacked and set in a suitable flat frame; or any one of the various other devices that afford a suitable decorative emphasis and a point of central interest.

If the object selected as the overmantel adornment is not of sufficient size to create a proper balance, a hanging of some sort—a piece of tapestry or an old Italian, Chinese or Japanese brocade, for example—may be placed back of it or else some appropriate subsidiary decorations, such as sconces, may be used to flank the central object and complete the composition of the grouping.

Due contrast is a desirable quality to impart emphasis in the overmantel scheme. Such contrast may be attained, for example, by using a pre-Raphaelite picture in a Florentine frame against a background of dull, greenish, loose-woven old brocade, or by a Chinese painting in reverse on glass in a teak-wood frame against a rough grey plaster wall. The mantel *shelf* is one of the chief sources of decorative peril. It is almost as seductive a temptation to decorative indiscretions and overloading as the broad top of a sideboard. Only the firmest resolve and devotion to the invaluable principle of *restraint* will save it from a cluttering accumulation of things that had far better be elsewhere. Sedulously shun a number of small, trifling gimcracks and refrain from displaying photographs thereon.

When there is no mantel shelf the danger is entirely obviated. When there *is* a shelf, one must carefully study the nature of the overmantel treatment before venturing to place any movable garniture on it. Some overmantel treatments *demand* that very little be placed in front of or beneath them—such as the Stuart overmantel in Plate 3 or Plate 4, and the intrusion of conspicuous garniture would be an unpardonable impertinence; others, again, admit of more latitude in the disposition of movable garniture. In any event, six unalterable principles must be faithfully observed —*Restraint, Suitability,* from which *Dignity* follows as a corollary; *Propriety of Scale, Symmetry, Concentration* and *Contrast.*

(1) *Restraint* must be most scrupulously exercised in determining the number and nature of the objects of which the mantel garniture is to consist. Have but few things on the mantel, but let each one of them be deserving of attention. Don't choke the legitimate garniture with a weed growth of trivial things and don't be afraid of empty spaces; they are restful and dignified and act as foils to lend appropriate emphasis to objects of decorative worth.

(2) *Suitability* demands that the garniture comport with the character of the overmantel decoration and the general structural environment. Good taste, for example, will forbid elaborate Louis Quinze *ormolu* candelabra upon an early Georgian mantel with its severely architectural overmantel background; the fundamental conceptions of the use of line are utterly at variance in the two styles which mix just about as well as oil and water. There is no reason, however, why garniture of contemporary date or of obviously close stylistic affinities should be chosen. It is enough if there be some common point of contact, some harmony by either analogy or contrast of design, some basic affinity between the lines of the background and the lines of the garniture, to put garniture and background in the same or in a related decorative key.

(3) *Propriety of Scale* means that the size of the objects composing the garniture must be of a scale to accord with the whole mantel and overmantel compo-

PLATE 112

CHIMNEY PIECE IN WOOD, WHITE AND GOLD; EMPANELLED PORTRAIT

Miss Gheen, Decorator

Courtesy of "Good Furniture Magazine"

PLATE 113

ARMORIAL BEARINGS AND PLAN OF ESTATE IN COLOURS USED
AS CHIMNEY-PIECE DECORATION
A. Winter Rose, Esq., London, Architect

sition—neither too large nor too small. In other words, upon a large mantel do not put small, attenuated candlesticks, vases or the like, nor above it hang a small and insufficient mirror or picture. In extreme violations of the scale principle, whatever merit the individual pieces of garniture may have in themselves is wholly lost and the dignity of the mantel, which, under the circumstances, looks about as foolish as a very large fat man with a little pee-wee head, is destroyed. Conversely, do not overpower a small mantel with things too large for it. This principle ought not to need special insistence, and yet flagrant disregard of it offends the eye daily.

(4) *Symmetry* must be maintained in disposing the different objects both with respect to each other and with respect to the overmantel behind them which is symmetrical in its architectural or decorative expression and which also ordinarily divides the whole wall space symmetrically. If the balance is broken, a one-sided, incoherent effect follows. Symmetry does not necessarily imply stiffness, but it does imply a decorous and agreeable formality. It is plainly necessary, therefore, if there be a central object, that the arrangement of the garniture be triple—candlesticks, candelabra, vases or jars at the ends, with incense burner, porcelain bowl, bronze or other single object in the middle—or, again, in the case of a long mantel, that it be quintuple as, for instance, in using one of the old Lowestoft garnitures consisting of three jars and two vases or *vice versa*. In any event, the use of a central unit requires for the whole composition an *odd* number of reciprocally balancing units; when there is no central unit the total number of units is *even*. A quadruple arrangement, for instance, may consist of four similar, equidistant, balancing objects or of two

pairs of ornaments. The character of the overmantel decoration will largely determine the appropriate number, placing and spacing of the garniture units, but, as a rule, the triple scheme works well and, on general principle, it is safe to place the larger units—candlesticks, candelabra, jars, figures, vases, or whatever else —at the ends as flanking elements. The value of pairs in mantel garnishing is plain to be seen.

(5) *Concentration* as a principle applied to mantel treatment focuses the chief interest at one point. The interest should be centred either in the overmantel decoration or else in the mantel garniture. It is a mistake and a waste of decorative ammunition to make the overmantel decoration a feature of dominating interest and then detract from its emphasis by the character of the mantel garniture which, under the circumstances, ought really to be an auxiliary factor. The gilt sunburst wall clock, previously alluded to, is a good example of overmantel decorative interest. If, on the other hand, the overmantel treatment is in the nature of an intensified background and plays the part of a foil, then the garniture must have sufficient force of harmonious contrast (*v.* Plate 56) to make it interesting. Always beware of scattering interest too much. Settle upon the one or two points to be emphasised and make everything else play up to them. Too much diffusion perplexes the eye and muddles or even destroys the character of the decoration which, so far as ability to enjoy it is concerned, might just as well consist of a congeries of the incoherent convolutions of old Maya temple carvings.

(6) The principle of *Contrast* requires that the effect of the mantel garniture be direct and not muddled in its appeal to the eye. And remember that an effect may be *direct* and *distinct* without being *abrupt*.

There must be enough contrast in *colour, material, texture* or *contour* (*v.* Plate 120) between the background and the garniture or else the effect will be diminished and one-half of it sink into the wall. Jangling, riotous contrasts that squall aloud are neither desirable nor necessary, but one can always secure an agreeable result like one of the following: a small carved oak dole cupboard, flanked by plain silver candlesticks, against a full-coloured old brocade, embroidery or bit of verdure tapestry; or, again, bronzes against a dull, grey plaster wall.

Do not attempt to have any kind of draperies attached to the mantel shelf. The principle is bad. They are unnecessary; they are cluttering and fussy; and they are impracticable when there is a fire going in the fireplace. The utmost that is permissible in that direction is to have a narrow piece of material as a foil when its colour and texture are necessary to produce desirable definition of contour or contrast of hue. The one glimmer of intelligence displayed by the Victorian mantel designers was when they shaped their mantel shelves so that draperies became difficult, and in this they were probably blindly following the precedent of eighteenth century French practice.

With reference to the movable furniture in the room, the mantel and fireplace should serve as a centre or focus for the formation of an interesting and logical group arrangement either at the sides of or in front of it. The importance alone of the mantel with its chimney-piece decoration requires that it be the centre of a grouping, and the fascination of the fire suggests the convenient disposition of comfortable seating furniture with a suitable accompaniment of tables and lights.

CHAPTER XI

PICTURES AND THEIR FRAMING

THE NUMBER AND CHARACTER OF PICTURES. OIL PAINTINGS,
WATER-COLOURS AND PRINTS. FRAMES, GLAZING AND
MATS. THE HANGING OF PICTURES.

PICTURES

A VOLUME could not contain all the advice that
might be offered upon this subject: the present
chapter must be concise, but we shall endeavour
to make it helpful.

NUMBER AND CHARACTER

First, then, have few pictures rather than many,
and omit everything not really desirable. Avoid the
cluttering of walls—if one picture is sufficient for a
space do not use two. If the wall surface is highly
decorative (as with a Morris or Crane paper or a cretonne effect) use none. Generally speaking, we are not
attempting art-galleries: the pictures in a house are
part of the decoration, and all decoration should be
consistent and proportionate.

The writers already have a sufficient task on hand
and have no inclination to take over that of changing
human nature. Pictures are not usually purchased as
decorative units—the best possible thing for a certain
situation—but because they themselves appeal to the
buyer. The matter of fitting them in is often left for
future consideration or none at all. At least, then, let
us appeal for the buying of good pictures only: for
good art almost universally *will* fit in—somewhere.
The cultured may browse in many fields: it is difficult

PLATE 114

AN EXCELLENT FRAMING OF A PICTURE OF DECORATIVE, PERIOD CHARACTER

The panelling, however, does not allow a good placing

Louis XV Drawing Room. The Furniture is of Soft Grey with the Mouldings Painted Blue

to guide those who have paid attention to other things in life and have neglected art, but they are at least safe in buying reproductions of the work of the masters of the past and present, provided the reproductions themselves are worthy and adequate.

Avoid "Calendar art"; avoid the saccharinely sentimental of many Victorians, the harrowingly sentimental of such pictures as "The Doctor," and avoid the "soulful doggie" subject, unless perhaps for the nursery. Shun the hackneyed. Certain pictures have become so staled by over use that they only irritate anyone with individuality.

To those who wish to make their selections accord with environment it may be said: consider first the rooms in which they are to go and then their positions in these rooms. Do not put a dignified Holbein in a Rococo boudoir: do not put a distinctly modern picture in a room patently of the past; do not purchase anything that will be "out of scale" with the space in which it is to go, or out of harmony with the surroundings.

If a room is of definite period character it is naturally wise to choose pictures of that period and frame them in accordance therewith (Plate 114), always remembering the latitude allowed by the principles of International-Interperiod Decoration set forth in Part III. An Italian Renaissance picture may usually be employed in a Tudor room, and an eighteenth century French print in a Georgian room.

Where a house is not strongly period in character, there is much latitude, but due discrimination should be used.

See things as a *whole:* avoid monotony in the choice of pictures as in everything else, but do not hang right pictures in wrong rooms or put together things that are alien in character: as extremes are most quickly apprehended let us say, for illustration, a Madonna and a fox-hunt.

PAINTINGS

Really good paintings in oil or water-colour are, of course, of the first consideration. Amateurish efforts at once condemn the taste of anyone ill-advised enough to hang them.

The old conventional flower pieces with vases (Plate 58) and the landscape-and-architecture subjects of like period are of excellent decorative value. Some of these are now being reproduced by modern brushes.

Colourful and strongly decorative paintings and panels are appropriate for rooms in the "Modern" vein.

COLOUR PRINTS AND MONOTINTS

Colour prints are among the most delightful things at one's command. The original eighteenth century French and English prints are now almost priceless, but there are excellent reproductions at fair figures, as well as travesties which should be shunned at any price. This is also true of the old sporting print, so admirable in its proper environment.

"The Connoisseur" and some extra numbers of "The Studio" contain excellent reproductions of colour prints that may be used where small pictures are required.

Good old Japanese prints (not the modern garish things) are highly decorative and the work of the masters is great art. Some are naturally exceedingly rare and costly, but it is surprising how many good examples can still be bought at moderate figures.

The German lithographs are colourful but full of the deadly heaviness which seems to oppress all German art.

With the "Modern" style of decoration Bakst and other such strong and striking things are best. Some of the effective covers of such periodicals as *Vogue, Harper's Bazaar, House Beautiful,* etc., may be used to great advantage when mounted as *passe-partouts.*

Reproductions of miniatures are frequently very attractive and dainty bits of colour decoration.

Monotint reproductions, lithographs, etchings and drawings are admirable for libraries, men's rooms, professional offices and living- and other rooms if of a scholarly or rather plain character. With the exception of etchings of figure subjects in the brighter vein, monotints are not so appropriate for use in rich and handsome drawing-rooms and boudoirs. The reason for this is given in the section on framing. Furthermore, in a room where paintings in gold frames occur it is inadvisable to use monotints or other pictures in wooden mouldings.

FRAMING

Generally speaking, there are two differing classes of frames—the wide and heavy ones naturally appropriate to the solid medium of oil-colour and the lighter and slenderer mouldings used for water-colours, prints, and the like.

The good manufacturers of mouldings have eschewed the debased styles so prevalent a few years ago and excellent frames are now procurable. Very probably Whistler, who designed for his own pictures admirable frames, simple in line but sufficiently ornamental, was the leader in this reform, and the return to period styles has also had great influence (Plates 115 and 116). Bright and flashy gilt frames are now a thing of the past and duller gold is almost universally used. In this respect the pendulum occasionally swings

23

too far and a little more life would be permissible. We should remember that the walls of our rooms are seldom so strongly lighted as the framers' shops and due allowance should be made. Some mouldings are so greatly dulled that when placed in their intended positions we find that too much decorative value has been lost.

This brings us to the question of what the decorative value of the picture in its frame should be. It is a decorative unit, and in size, apparent weight, character, colour, etc., it should neither jump into undue prominence nor be so unobtrusive as to sink into oblivion. If a decorator errs it is likely to be in the direction of suppressing the picture-unit in favour of his general decorative scheme; if the artist errs it is usually in exalting it at the expense of the *ensemble;* there is a ditch on each side of the road, but it is not necessary to fall into either. In trying mouldings against a picture the attempt should therefore be made to *visualise* the combined picture and frame in the actual position they are to occupy.

FRAMES FOR OIL PAINTINGS

The landscape or sea-piece should usually have a simpler frame than the ornamental figure subject; oftentimes the simpler it is the better. Yet it is difficult to formulate rules where each picture has requirements of its own. Frequently a painting of full and mellow harmony will look well in quite an ornamental setting if that be desired (Plate 101) and again a virile piece of work may be of sufficient strength to stand almost any frame. It is the picture that is full of detail or which is none too strong in *ensemble* which should not have further and distracting detail added in its

PLATE 115

GOLD FRAMES OF STANFORD WHITE AND WHISTLER DESIGN
By Courtesy of Newcomb–Macklin Co., Chicago and New York

PLATE 116

FRENCH, PERIOD FRAMES WITH FINELY MODELLED DETAILS
By Courtesy of Newcomb–Macklin Co., Chicago and New York

PLATE 117

AN UNUSUALLY BEAUTIFUL SETTING FOR AN ARCHITECTURAL PAINTING
By Courtesy of Messrs. Wilson Eyre and McIlvaine, Architects, Philadelphia

PLATE 118

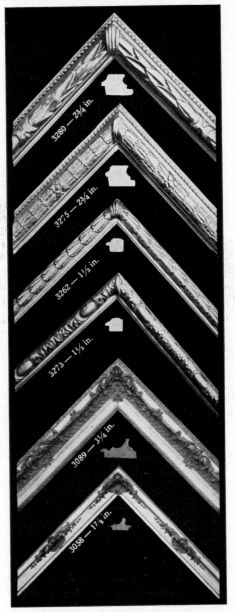

ORNAMENTAL MOULDINGS FOR WATER-
COLOURS, COLOUR–REPRODUCTIONS, ETC.
By Courtesy of Newcomb-Macklin Co.

frame. For old portraits nothing is so appropriate as the frames of their own time (Plate 98).

Unless newer portraits of women are emphatically modern in spirit we may use for them the very beautiful Adam, Louis Quinze, or Louis Seize designs. Men's portraits will be more appropriately framed in rather heavier and simpler mouldings, of which the Whistler styles are among the best examples.

There are many good non-commital designs for modern paintings of various classes.

The paintings of strongly decorative character—such as the figure-pieces of the great Frenchmen, primarily used for panels, architectural scenes and formal flower-pieces with sculptured vases—partake largely of the nature of architectural decorations and should be treated accordingly. An unusually beautiful setting is shown in Plate 117 and others occur in Plates 65 A, 58 and 112.

Glass is not usually employed over oil paintings except when they are of moderate dimensions, of much value, or of great smoothness and delicacy of treatment, as, for instance, the work of the Dutch *genre* painters, fine portraits, flowers, and the like. The protection from dust and gas fumes afforded by glass is however so great that it might more often be used than it is. A strip is set in by the frame-maker so that it does not touch the picture.

THE FRAMING OF WATER-COLOURS, DRAWINGS AND PRINTS

Glass must necessarily be used for the protection of all pictures painted or printed upon paper.

In general their frames, whether of gold or of wood, should be slender, or of but moderate width, unobtrusive and yet beautiful in form and line. They may be rather ornamental, as in Plate 118, or extremely simple and plain. Pictures with strong contrasts or masses of dark colour naturally need greater sustaining weight of effect in the frames than do those of lighter and slighter nature.

The logical frame for a colour-reproduction of a picture painted in a certain period is a reproduction, to the scale of the print, of its original frame, or at least of a frame that might appropriately have been used.

One of the beautiful Italian heads or figure-pieces with its appropriate frame would be in keeping with most homes of restrained and semi-Classic character as well as in those of the period; but if the frame were found to be too elaborate or too expensive in appearance for the particular place the picture is to occupy a simpler frame of more non-committal but generally Classical or dignified nature could be substituted.

The handsome old photograph frames of thirty to fifty years ago make admirable settings for portrait reproductions in colour. During the course of years the gold leaf has taken on dim and beautiful tones impossible to secure except through age. Such a frame, containing a reproduction of one of Sir Joshua's portraits, appears above the bookcase in Plate 119 A.

For a monotone reproduction of a period picture a wooden frame appropriate to the period should be used, or else a non-committal but not incongruous moulding. The tone of the frame should accord with that of the picture and be slightly lighter than its darkest masses. In the framing of period pictures only a man who knows this particular phase of the business should be employed.

With some of the eighteenth century monotone prints the black frames with high polish and with a narrow gold inside line may most appropriately be

PLATE 119

A. A FINE OLD PHOTOGRAPH FRAME AS A SETTING FOR A COLOUR-
REPRODUCTION OF A SIR JOSHUA REYNOLDS PORTRAIT

B. AN ARRANGEMENT OF SMALL PICTURES WELL ILLUSTRATING THE
PRINCIPLES OF BALANCE

Notwithstanding the number of small objects, this room preserves an admirable repose

used. Some of those of lighter character may have mats and narrow gold mouldings.

Writers on decoration, of course, recognise that pictures must be in proper relation to the room and that frames must be in relation both to pictures and the room. Yet nowhere have we seen a practical word of caution upon the following point. In the section on pictures we deprecated the employment of monotone pictures in handsome and colourful rooms. This was not only because of the pictures themselves but because their inappropriateness is further emphasised by the wooden frames that usually and properly accompany them, the combination being unsuited for use in handsome drawing-rooms and boudoirs, with satin-wood, mahogany or decorated furniture and rich textiles of silk or velvet.

We will go further. The almost universal prescription for Japanese prints, sanguines and drawings or reproductions in but slight colour is the wooden frame, the argument being that nothing should be used that will take away from the picture. But if such pictures are placed in handsome rooms brown, black or even grey wooden frames do precisely this: they are felt to be out of accord with the room and so both attract notice and detract from the picture. Gold was considered as a neutral by the decorative masters of the past, and dull gold mouldings of the same simplicity as the wooden frames are equally unobtrusive and still are handsome, and so appropriate for such environment. Down the long hall of an apartment known to the writers is a collection of Japanese prints on Japanese paper mounts and in frames of this narrow gold moulding: they are infinitely more attractive than they would have been in wood. But the Japanese use wooden frames for their prints! Certainly; and they are quite appropriate for the Japanese interior. They also are for some of ours, but they do not accord with the richness of others. A grouping of four Japanese prints in one mat and frame is shown in Plate 92 B.

Mahogany and rosewood are more refined than oak, and if the furniture is mahogany and these woods agree with the pictures they may be used in a room of a lesser degree of richness than those we have been considering. A narrow gold inside line may often be used with these frames.

To sum up, our general contention is that the use of a brown or black wooden frame for a picture in colour is a derogation from the picture and had better be avoided.

A suggestion well worth bearing in mind is the *painted* frame—which although occasionally seen has largely escaped the attention of writers on decoration. Yet with painted or lacquered furniture, or woodwork in a deeper tone than the walls, what could be more suitable? In some instances the frames might be related to the fabrics employed in the room. An appropriate wooden frame may be bought and painted in oil in any desired tone or colour. If there is a mat between it and the picture the frame might be in the dominant note of the picture or it might harmonise with the woodwork of the room. A few of the possibilities opened up here may be considered.

The dull green, red or blue lacquer, and imitation lacquer, tones would be very likely to suit water-colours, pastels or colour-prints used in the same room as such pieces. If there were several pictures and one did not harmonise therewith it might be used elsewhere. So also it would not be difficult to select one of the colours of body or ornament of English, French, or Venetian eighteenth century or modern decorated furniture that would admirably frame the pictures used therewith, thus doing something out of the ordinary which yet would be in impeccable taste. Among such colourings would be found entrancing shades of old rose and mulberry, old blues and greens, soft yellows, tans and buffs. Many textiles, too, would give similar inspiration, and the less positive tints used for woodwork (if darker than the walls) such as the deep ivories and creams or French greys, would be exquisite with such paintings or prints. A gold line might be introduced with advantage in many instances, especially where gold enters into the furniture decoration or where there are notable candlesticks, side-lights or lamps of brass.

In an apartment the writers once knew there hung a Beardsley figure printed in vermilion on a white ground: it was in a vermilion frame. Since then the "Modern" style of decoration has come to the fore and the wall trim is frequently pronounced in colour. If this colour is found by experiment not to "kill" the strongly decorative pictures likely to be used therewith the keying of the two together would be excellent. A bit of strong colour in simpler rooms is also often advisable and by keeping such individual things apart from other pictures conflict is avoided.

In the carrying out of any of the preceding suggestions overdoing should naturally be shunned, as a touch too much invalidates an unusual effect.

Since the writing of the above we have seen in a Fifth Avenue shop an excellent treatment of a small reproduction of one of Velasquez's infantas, the tones of which are primarily red and grey. Its frame was a narrow band with a raised ridge on either side. The band was of fawn grey, the inner ridge of red, and the outer of dull gold, the gold extending over the whole outside edge of the frame. Near it was a modern picture in which the dominant was blue-violet. The frame was the same as that just described, except that the band was of the violet.

PHOTOGRAPHS

Framed photographs are in general much better stood upon tables, low bookcases, and such places, than hung upon the wall, and many attractive standing frames are now procurable. One or two portraits of artistic merit may be hung and in such cases the simpler the frame usually the better it is. They may either be framed *passe-partout,* close or with a mat or mount. If the frame is of wood it should key with the picture. A sepia oval photograph may well be enclosed in an oval frame of dull gold with bow-knot or other simple heading. If a mount is here used it should be of Japanese vellum or something similar in tone and not white. A grey photograph in a greyish mat might have a frame of dull silver if that will accord with the surroundings.

MATS AND MOUNTS

The use of these seems greatly to have disturbed some minds. The simple truth is that many pictures of all types other than oils look well either with mats (of not too great contrast) or without them, and those that do not are usually so clear in their indication of what should be done that there is no difficulty in deciding.

Engravings and etchings are usually printed with a margin of paper and this obviously should be preserved. Apart from the artistic point of view it is to be remembered that the trimming off of such margins destroys the money-value of rare prints. Reproductions of portraits with dark backgrounds, whether rectangular or oval, frequently look better framed "close up." Perhaps, with caution, one may say that dark pictures are less likely to need mats than lighter and slighter ones, but most do so well either way that it is useless to legislate. The proper course is to consider the picture itself in connexion with the situation where it is to go. The objection that some—may we call them "hard-and-fasters?"—urge against mats and mounts is that it cuts up the decorative unit. Sometimes it does not; sometimes it does; and sometimes that is the very best thing that could happen. Suppose we consider each in order: a rather spotty water-colour will be *simplified* by a mat; a dark picture in a dark frame will be cut up by the introduction of a light mat between; and we recall a hall of such extreme repose that this very thing was absolutely needed to give relief.

Mats and mounts should not be of dead white, but of ivory, cream or grey, and sometimes of darker tones. A gold mat inside a narrow gold edging gives practically the same effect as a wide, flat gold frame.

Margin naturally enlarges a picture and this may often be the determining factor as to its use or omission.

THE HANGING OF PICTURES

The principles of placing pictures on the wall are, of course, those of balance generally. The natural height is usually that of the eye or but little above; but, as there is nearly always some piece of furniture below, the picture should be in due relation to, and form one group with, that object and those others that may rest upon it. The accessories of vases, candlesticks and kindred objects that may stand upon a console, cabinet or highboy are of great usefulness in tying together the picture and the furniture.

An evil genius seems to prompt some people to hang pictures too high; the setting down of the picture-rail, when the ceiling is disproportionally high, advocated by the writers in the chapter on Walls will not only aid in overcoming this tendency but renders unnecessary the great length of wire required when the rail is at the cornice. It also makes picture-hanging much more convenient and less laborious.

The proper relation of picture to the furniture or mantel below it and the best arrangement of groups are easiest learned by the study of good examples.

As will be seen by some of these illustrations it is quite permissible to hang one or a very few pictures upon panelling, but they must be absolutely appropriate in character, colour, scale, framing and placing (Plate 8 is a good example). It is also permissible to hang appropriate pictures upon a wall of such restrained decorative character as that in Plate 70 B, but they should never appear upon so ornamental a surface as the cretonne paper shown in Plate 75.

As the reason for avoiding diagonal lines has several times been referred to, it should now hardly be necessary to point out that the triangular wire frequently seen (and seen sometimes in our own illustrations here) should not be used and that the tops of pictures should not hang out from the wall. An exception to the rule regarding triangular wires is in the hanging of oval frames, where the converging lines of the frame make it the obvious arrangement.

Silken cords are sometimes used to decorative advantage in the hanging of eighteenth century colourprints in drawing-rooms and boudoirs. The heavy cord used with the old portrait in Plate 79 A adds to its quaintness and is in place in the attractive atmosphere of this room. When the frame is obviously heavy it is often a good device to make the hanging apparatus a deliberately decorative feature, employing silken cords and tassels as a means to suspend the frames.

The hanging of pictures with two perpendicular wires is of the simplest: the wire is passed through both screw-eyes on the back of the frame; one end of the wire is twisted into a loop over one picture hook, which is then hung upon the rail. By then placing the other hook on the rail and looping the wire over it (twisting but slightly for the moment) a picture of moderate weight can be tried at greater or less height until precisely the right altitude for appearance is determined. The second loop can then properly be made and the surplus wire cut off. The screw-eyes should be placed very near the top of the frame so that it will hang flat against the wall.

CHAPTER XII

DECORATIVE ACCESSORIES

THEIR IMPORTANCE. COLOUR-VALUE. PURCHASE. REDUN-
DANCY. SUGGESTIVE AND COMPARATIVE LIST

IT has been observed that in dress a man or woman
may be known by shoes, hats and gloves. In the
same degree in which this is true, the taste, and to
some extent the character, of the occupants of a home
are made evident by the decorative accessories to be
found therein.

A rare collection of atrocities we find them in some
instances to be: in others most of them are satisfactory
but unhappily mingled with trifling things that but
clutter and destroy repose. The worst of it is that
these annoying little things are often objects of association—small remembrances showered upon the owner
by dear and well-meaning friends—souvenirs, calendars, fancy pictures, and the host of objects from the
Women's Exchanges—that fill a man with amaze that,
when there is so much of true use and beauty which
might be done, such a waste is made of time and money!
For the sake of the givers and our love for them such
objects should be treated with respect, but—put out of
sight.

And then, finally, we see other houses in which the
accessories at once indicate strong individuality and
exquisite taste. In the British bedroom illustrated
(Plate 120), for instance, what flowers would so well
accompany the mellow tones of the panelling as the
chrysanthemums upon the table? These, with the glint

PLATE 120

STUART RENAISSANCE BED CHAMBER WITH SMALL-PANELLED OAK WAINSCOT

Note fine use of accessories

Courtesy of Sir Ernest Newton, London, Architect

PLATE 121

PORCELAINS AS ACCESSORIES IN A FINE ENGLISH HALL

PLATE 122

A. A SCREEN BOTH USEFUL AND DECORATIVE

B. HANGING, SCREEN AND PANELS USED WITH GOOD DECORATIVE EFFECT
J. Lovell Little, Esq. Architect

of metal in the three-branched candlesticks the books, the few choice porcelains on the narrow mantel-ledge, the interesting fireback and irons, the patterned curtains in relief to the plain wall-surfaces, show the greatest discrimination.

Decorative accessories are of the highest value in adding interest—the beautifully simple hall shown in Plate 121 would not be what it is without the fine porcelains used as accessories. Numerous other instances will be observed among our illustrations, and many of these will be referred to in the subsequent list.

COLOUR-VALUE

In the direction of colour these accessories may be used in three ways: as supplying strong colour *accents* where they are required for emphasis and enlivenment; as affording a *variety* of colour where the furnishing is too much in one hue; or for the carrying of colour *through* a room, as mentioned in the section on "Unity and Variety." In many instances a beautiful and colourful vase, panel or piece of tapestry has been made the keynote of a decorative scheme.

PURCHASE

As it is by such objects that we are known let us avoid hackneyed things to be found in every shop. Decorators' establishments, antique and second-hand shops, Oriental shops and Chinatown are all good places to keep in view—once in a blue moon something unusual will find its way even into a pawnbroker's window.

Expense is not always the measure of merit, and tasteful, observant people will have no difficulty in finding many attractive objects at reasonable figures.

Of course, it is futile to expect to pick up rare and valuable things for little money—artistic treasures de-mand a long pocket-book and if we have it not we shall scarcely possess museum-pieces, but may have things of beauty nevertheless.

REDUNDANCY

In the examples mentioned early in this chapter it will be seen that just *enough* has been done. Overcrowd-ing vitiates effect, and a superfluity of even the beauti-ful is unwise. We all know how tiresome the museum becomes to the casual visitor; half its beauties are lost, except to one busily studying and comparing. The motto for the decorator therefore is: Select—and again Select. Have but few accessories and choose those most advantageous for their purpose, most appropri-ate for their environment, and which will best *tell* in decorative effect.

As a practical aid a list of accessories is given for suggestion and *comparison of advantages.* To exem-plify: we may have thought of purchasing a small, ornamental mirror for a certain space on the wall: looking over the list we find such other things appro-priate to that use as wood-carvings, plaques of mai-olica and porcelains, painted panels, panels of della Robbia design or those of wood, carven, coloured and gilded or of plaster. Choice may be made from these, or an odd embroidery or other textile may be employed, or perhaps a banjo or sunburst clock. In short, we may look very considerably before we leap, and it is well to do so.

This list is merely for suggestion and reminder and makes no pretense to completeness. A few observa-tions and plate references are added.

BASKETS, DECORATIVE, for flowers. The odd shapes are very engaging.

BASKETS, WASTE. Avoid beribboned and other millinery and confectionery effects. Real baskets (such as the Chinese) stained or painted are among the best. Metal ones decorated in the same way as painted furniture are attractive.

BIRD-CAGES. The best forms are shown in plates 126 and 93 A.

BOXES AND CASKETS. Carved wood, ivory, metal, Chinese, bon-bon, jewel, etc.

BUSTS AND STATUETTES. Appropriate in formal and period rooms.

CANDLESTICKS. Of great usefulness and in endless variety. Good examples shown in plates 9, 25, 77 A, 102, 119, 120, 129, 144, 161.

CANDELABRA AND STANDARD LIGHTS. Plates 15, 19, 34, 39, 70 B, 89 B, 93 A, 100 B, 135, 150.

CHINESE DOGS, LIONS, COCKATOOS and the like.

CLOCKS. Plates 65 A, 96, 161.

CRYSTAL BALLS. Decorative and occultly interesting (those of glass are good and not so expensive).

ECCLESIASTICAL VESTMENTS. Unless these can be used in a religious connexion with a shrine or crucifix it is better not to use at all. It is surely poor taste if not irreverent to employ them as table covers, piano "throws," and the like.

FIRE SCREENS. Plate 137.

FLOWERS AND PLANTS. Plates 59, 65 B, 114, 120.

GLOBES, MAPS AND PLANS. Apparently of unlikely decorative use, but see plates 100 B, 19 and 113, respectively.

HANGINGS, small, of needlework, tapestry or Oriental work.

HEADS OF ANIMALS. Appropriate in plate 135 or a camp, but in the usual modern home are best conspicuous by their absence.

LIGHTS, HANGING, AND LANTHORNS. Plates 89 B, 93 A, 100 B, 119 A, 135.

MIRRORS. Of great decorative usefulness. Plates 25, 73, 92 A, 99, 100 B, 133, 156, 158 C.

PANELS of many sorts. Plate 122 B.

PILLOWS for couches, settees and chairs. Plate 114.

PLANT BOXES.

PLAQUES, PLASTER, etc. Plate 70 B.

POTTERY, PORCELAIN, METAL AND GLASS. Vases, jars, jardinières, mantel and table ornaments, etc., etc. Plates 19, 23, 39, 50, 55, 97 A, 100 B, 120, 121, 136 B, 160.

SAMPLERS. Old needlework pictures and the like.

SCONCES.

SCREENS. Very decorative and of much use in preventing drafts and as backgrounds. Plates 55, 114, 122 A, 122 B.

SMOKING ACCESSORIES. Beware commercial atrocities, horribly designed humidors and the like. With so many unusual carved and other boxes, Oriental jars and such receptacles which could be employed for cigars and cigarettes, such a wealth of beautiful ash trays in Benares brass, Oriental porcelain and metals of various sorts, such necessaries may be made a decorative asset instead of the too usual abomination.

TABLE COVERS AND RUNNERS.

TILES. Single Persian and other highly decorative tiles are excellent as small ornaments.

UMBRELLA HOLDERS. Use great discretion in their choice. A really *good* Chinese jar makes one of the best holders.

WALL ORNAMENTS. Carved wood, often painted and gilded. Plaques and panels of maiolica, della Robbia porcelains, plaster in the white or tinted. Plates 23, 127, 129.

WALL POCKETS, Chinese, for small growing plants.

WINDOW TRANSPARENCIES of leaded glass.

PART III

INTERNATIONAL-INTER PERIOD
DECORATION

Beautiful things have dignity. Enjoy the rhythm of your dancing and admire the beauty of your bookbinding. In whatever you do, have an ideal of excellence. Any separation between art and work is not only an error, but it is very bad business. Our brave allies, the French, have made Paris the art centre of the world. They have built up and maintain their large and lucrative trade in the decorative products of France, mainly by reason of three qualities which they possess. In the first place, they enjoy art themselves, and reverence it. In the second place, they have a tremendous power of hard work. And in the third place, every Frenchman, and still more every Frenchwoman, have within them an immense fund of common sense. The threefold secret is, Love of Art, Industry, and Common Sense.

"THE ORGANISATION OF THOUGHT."

By A. N. Whitehead, Sc.D., F. R. S.

London: Williams & Norgate

Philadelphia: J. B. Lippincott Company.

PART III

INTERNATIONAL-INTER PERIOD DECORATION

A NEW SYSTEM

INTRODUCTION

THE ASSEMBLING OF STYLES OF VARIOUS NATIONS AND PERIODS

A BROADENING OF SCOPE. INTERNATIONAL-INTER PERIOD DECORATION. THE BASIC PRINCIPLES.

A BROADENING OF SCOPE

IN these days of greater public enlightenment and appreciation of beauty it is scarcely worth while to argue the question of period furnishing. It is, rather, the purpose of these chapters to show how its scope may be broadened, rendered more flexible and adaptable to modern life, and how the disadvantages urged against what is commonly considered period furnishing may be eliminated. If such a system is to continue in use, if it is to become more than a matter of accurate copying of the past, it must prove itself alive, capable of growth and adaptable to changing conditions.

Period furnishing is commonly considered to be the reproduction in our modern dwellings and apartments of the interior decoration and furnishing of some one past period in a particular country, and it has been objected that such a method does not properly represent us to-day. The present writers are not greatly concerned in confuting this point for the simple reason

371

that a much better method is to be presented; but it might be observed that wherever the one-period style is adopted because the person is filled with such admiration and love for the work of the great designers of that period that he wishes to surround himself with its beauty and charm, there is small chance of its not being suited to his personality; for in a sense it *is* he and so is representative.

There is, however, a flaw in the one-period manner of furnishing which is less, if at all, noted—that with a wide knowledge and appreciation comes the wareness that there are other, and many other, objects of beauty that do not come within the narrow province of his particular choice.

It was doubtless some dim appreciation of this that led decorators, as the next step, to attempt an enlargement of scope or to suit varying tastes by the employment of different period styles in the various rooms of the same establishment—a dumping down, so to speak, of separate epochs under one roof—a method that utterly violated the unities and the result of which presented the appearance of a series of show-rooms in a decorator's shop.

And now, during the last few years, we have been hearing much of a reasonable eclecticism. Just what would constitute it such must have been a puzzle to the many who have given but scant attention to matters of household decoration. Doubtless even decorators who have practised this method with a fair measure of success have secured their results through their general taste and information rather than by any very careful consideration or formulation of the principles involved: so that it is by no means surprising that the decorator who is scarcely more than a tradesman and the householder unlearned in such affairs should often "come

PLATE 123

SMALL RECEPTION-ROOM OF AN APARTMENT: WITH CHIPPENDALE, HEPPLEWHITE AND AMERICAN EMPIRE FURNITURE

PLATE 124

A LOUIS SEIZE DRAWING-ROOM IN A NEW YORK APARTMENT
Messrs. McKim, Mead & White, Architects
Courtesy of "Good Furniture Magazine"

PLATE 125

DINING-ROOM IN "MODERN" STYLE IN A NEW YORK
APARTMENT

Walls Fawn; Woodwork, White; Floor, Black; Vermilion Line Around Foot
of Baseboard. Chairs, Light Green-blue; Table, Birch, Natural Colour,
Polished

Note excellent use of accessories

By Courtesy of Durr Friedley, Esq.

PLATE 126

A MAN'S ROOM WITH THE SIMPLER FORMS OF PERIOD FURNITURE AND WICKER

Excellent use of Chinese Ornaments on Mantel and Chinese Birdcage

a cropper" in a field that requires knowledge and the nicest discrimination.

The word eclecticism itself is scarcely the best that could be used in this connexion, as it implies "a selection from different systems or sources," a taking here and there that would be faulty practice; but it at least makes some approach to what is the only really satisfying and scientific method of decoration, whether for palatial establishments or for small homes or apartments where the occupant wishes to secure results in accord with cultured taste, breadth of appreciation and wideness of life.

INTERNATIONAL-INTER PERIOD DECORATION

The difficulty with period decoration in the past has lain in that, except in the hands of a few architects of distinction, it has *not been true to its name;* that it has taken account of but a selected period in but *one country* and in but *one phase of the existing movement,* and not that movement viewed as *an whole* and as *manifested throughout neighbouring nations all under the same influence or decorative impulse.* It is the old fault of narrowness, of insularity, of want of catholicity in outlook.

In our modern egotism we have been wont to consider the present the only cosmopolitan age: those who have not pursued the subject might be astonished at the amount of communication between nations at all periods, at the *wareness* that always existed among artists and craftsmen as to what their brothers of far away were about, at the *universality* with which decorative impulses spread from land to land.

It is those impulses that we shall now take into account, the four waves of influence spreading horizontally, so to speak, across the civilised world; and it will

be done so simply and so practically that all may understand. They will be considered broadly and even baldly
here, so as quickly to arrive at their helpful and practical application to-day. Not only will the more elaborate phases, suited to palatial homes, be considered,
but also the simpler and more neglected aspects of each
period, those adapted to the modest house and to property that is not owned by the occupant. The several
influences will be treated in sequence, down to the
débâcle of all decorative art in the early nineteenth
century; and the characteristics of each will be so
shown that the reader may readily see which makes
its strongest appeal to his own personality, is therefore most individual to him and most representative
of himself, his general circumstances and his life. It
will thus be no less a guide to the decorator in his endeavour to endue his client with appropriate surroundings and to the retail dealer in any of the allied
branches of furnishing in his advice to possible
purchasers.

THE BASIC PRINCIPLES

Let us begin at the beginnings of modern art. During the Dark Ages the Church saved culture and civilisation, and the Church was Gothic. (The East and
Venice were Byzantine and the West had been Romanesque, which style developed into Gothic.) This Gothic
style was naturally modified in each country by national
influences, as, for instance, by the Moorish element in
Spain. With exceptions, Italy remained Romanesque,
because there the overmastering influence of the great
Classic remains and the national characteristics and
tastes largely prevented the Gothic from "taking hold."

In that country, at about the year 1400, began the
"Revival of Learning," a Renaissance of the Classic
spirit—an awakened interest in the literature and art

of "the glory that was Greece and the grandeur that was Rome"—a revival that almost revolutionised thought and art and which swept with mighty impetus over the face of all but most northern and eastern Europe.

One civilisation or art seldom wholly routs and displaces another; but, even though absolutely different in principle, the new, somehow, grafts itself upon the old. In France this blending became the styles François Premier and Henri II: in England it became what we know as Elizabethan or Tudor.

Does our plan now begin to emerge? If one possesses an Elizabethan house not only may there be used in it Elizabethan furniture, but also furniture of Renaissance France, Flanders, Italy, Spain or Portugal— for all were of the same spirit! The Renaissance also found its way to Germany, but Germany has no consideration here.

Naturally, this is not to say that in every epoch every individual furnishing or piece of furniture made under one influence will properly accompany every other single piece, for there are qualifications which, later, will be entered into, but the recognition of the international extent of this and subsequent movements gives a wide basis upon which to work; so that with a proper regard to the unities, we may add, for example, to the English furnishings of any epoch treasures from these other countries, or reproductions thereof.

The international extent of this method of furnishing now having been established, we may go further.

Such a momentous impulse as that of the Renaissance does not soon exhaust itself; indeed, that impulse has never died, and, though temporarily obscured, revived and is exceedingly alive to-day. Before its partial obscuration it ran through several reigns in England—and England is used as a key because of its greater familiarity to most readers. The architecture (exterior and interior) of that country never thereafter lost its Classic feeling, but in furniture the Classic was, in the Jacobean period, blended with, and finally in the reign of Queen Anne almost driven out, by the succeeding Baroque influence. In other countries the Renaissance also persisted until succeeded by the Baroque.

So, to the international extent of this plan—its horizontal aspect, so to speak—we may add the chronological or vertical element, the two giving a wide field of choice, and adapting the Renaissance influence (as others which are to follow) to an extensive range of circumstances in our modern life. A chart is given at the end of this volume, showing both the international and the chronological extent of each influence.

CHAPTER I

THE RENAISSANCE

WHAT THE RENAISSANCE WAS. MODERN CONDITIONS. THREE
METHODS OF TREATMENT. ELABORATE WALLS. EXTERIOR
AND INTERIOR. TREATMENTS OF MODERATE SCOPE. PLAIN-
WALL TREATMENTS. FURNISHINGS AND FURNITURE. THE
ASSOCIATION OF FURNITURE OF VARIOUS NATIONALITIES.
THE PRACTICABILITY OF INTERNATIONAL FURNISHING.
CHARACTERISTICS OF THE RENAISSANCE. THE INTER
PERIOD ELEMENT

WHAT THE RENAISSANCE WAS

IN taking up this first influence we may, very practically, ask: How did it manifest itself in the arts
—in short, what was it?

The popular superstition is that when the great
awakening took place in Italy the masters of the Renaissance period simply brought to life the art of the
Greeks and Romans which was their heritage—a very
convenient formula for those who do not think. The
truth, briefly, is that during all the centuries which lay
between the fall of Rome and the year 1400 the wide
internationalism to which we have referred was quietly
doing its work; treasures of Oriental art were continually finding their way thither both direct and through
the Copts and Spanish Moors. Renaissance architecture
(and decoration) was never therefore the pure Classicism of Greece and Rome. It was the fusion of all three
of the great artistic influences, the Gothic, the Oriental
and the Classic, with the Classic for the time being as
the inspiration and informing influence.

MODERN CONDITIONS

So practical is the aim of these chapters that no further will they go until they take into account a very prevalent circumstance of modern life.

The very term interior decoration is indicative of the fact that through all periods the interior architecture has had its share of attention and decoration. But a large proportion of tasteful people to-day live in rented apartments or houses, and few care to panel or decorate walls for the benefit of a landlord only too likely to seize the advantage given and increase the rental so soon as the lease expires. Even those of some considerable means and occupying their own houses may not, in these days of many uncertainties, care to go to the large expense involved in elaborate wall-decoration. What, then, shall be done if such persons wish to adopt the Renaissance style of furnishing—or that of any succeeding age?

The answer must be that if period decoration is to continue in use, then it must show itself adapted to the changing conditions of modern life and circumstance; and that it *is* so adaptable is the very purpose of these chapters to demonstrate. Common sense teaches us that if we wish to surround ourselves with the beautiful objects produced by the genius of the past, or their reproductions, and yet that our walls must remain plain, the obvious course is frankly to combine the two conditions. And if any justification for such a procedure beyond the enlightened common sense, which must be the basis of all art and of all beauty, must be established, if a precedent must be found to back up all our proceedings, it is found right here—for, during the Italian Renaissance, one of the greatest art periods of the world's history, where walls were not decorated, they were *entirely plain* (Plate 127).

PLATE 127

ROOM IN PALAZZO DAVANZATI, FIRENZE, FIFTEENTH CENTURY
Note Plain Walls, Tiled Floor, Niche, Panelled Doors and Painted Timber Ceiling
Courtesy of William Helburn, Inc.

PLATE 128

AN INTERNATIONAL RENAISSANCE INTERIOR IN A REMODELLED FARM-HOUSE
English Renaissance Table and Chairs to Left: Spanish Renaissance Chairs to Right: Oriental Rugs and Lamp:
Beamed Ceiling and Verdure Tapestry
By Courtesy of Messrs Mellor & Meigs

THREE METHODS OF TREATMENT

It is at once evident, therefore, that we may adopt, according to circumstances, any one of three methods of treatment; and these apply to the subsequent epochs as well as to that we are now considering.

I. If the premises are of elaborate character and the means of the owner in accordance, the more elaborate phases of the epoch may be chosen and followed.

II. With both large and small premises the simpler but still decorative phases of any period may be adopted. Or, as in some periods these simpler forms have not been largely preserved and pictured for our guidance, simplifications may intelligently be made.

III. As first mentioned, we may use period furnishings with walls entirely plain but appropriate in colour and treatment to the period chosen.

We may also combine any two of these three—employing the more elaborate decoration for public rooms and the simpler for bedrooms, morning rooms and the less public parts of the house.

ELABORATE WALLS

In order that the statement of this method of International-Inter Period Decoration may be complete in itself and readily comprehended, it has been written independently of Part I. That Part, however, gives a complete digest of all particulars regarding the decoration of the various periods during the four great movements, and for full details regarding any epoch it should be carefully considered. Illustrations are there also given of the architectural backgrounds of all the countries.

It is only necessary, therefore, to epitomise the matter of Renaissance backgrounds by saying here that the small square or the rectangular panelling of oak was the typical style of Renaissance England; that, while such panelling was used to some extent in the northern section during early Renaissance times, it was *not typical* of Renaissance Italy, where the walls were plain, diapered, or highly decorated in colour and gilding; Spain, always influenced by Italy, largely followed the Italian ideals, but these were naturally modified by the powerful Moorish element prevailing in Spanish art; they were plain or plain on their upper portion, the lower being a dado of many coloured tiles or of painted canvas; in France, walls were sometimes at first in the small panelling, but they were more generally of stone or plaster, which might be painted or frescoed, somewhat in the Italian style. Hangings were largely employed with these walls. Later, these isolated hangings were less used and walls were panelled in larger panelling and often moulded and gilded. Or they might be frescoed or covered with tapestry or other hangings.

In the various countries under Renaissance influence there were also, of course, constructional and stylistic differences in ceilings, windows, doors and mantels—all duly treated in Part I.

EXTERIOR AND INTERIOR

In considering the use of the more ornamental backgrounds a question at once arises. As will now have been seen, great differences existed in the treatment of the interiors of the various nationalities under Renaissance influence, and in exterior architecture the dissimilarity was still more fundamental. It is obvious that, in general, exterior and interior architecture should agree, so that with our system of the use of international furnishings and furniture the enquiry at once springs to the fore: Is it permissible and is it feasible to employ the fixed architectural backgrounds of the various nationalities under Renaissance influence under one roof?

To this question the writers are not going to give as answer a categorical, but a qualified yes. This procedure has been followed by Stanford White and a few other architects of great ability—and it requires genius of this order satisfactorily to combine such elements. We know that Italian architects and craftsmen working in England and France grafted Renaissance characteristics upon the national developments of architecture both exterior and interior, and did it successfully, too. How far such national characteristics may to-day successfully be mingled will depend largely upon the ability of the architect or decorator employed. Suffice it to say that if he be a genius his versatility will be tempered by discretion and the result of his efforts will in no wise resemble a museum or a *mélange*. If architecture is to be more than correct archæology it is well to ask ourselves if it is not in this very direction of the blending of elements that are largely congruous, because informed with the same spirit, that architectural life and development lies. Absolute originality—a start *de novo,* a breaking with the traditions of the past —means foredoomed failure; intelligent combination may put new vigour into the architecture of to-day. Especially might this be true of American architecture —America being itself a combination, and, by its associations in the past war likely to become still more cosmopolitan.

In deciding upon *any* period decoration it is not only interesting but necessary to learn how far our choice is free and unhampered and how much it is determined for us by existing exterior architectural conditions. Where this exterior is *definite* it must naturally exert a largely determining influence. But this

general rule is, like every other, subject to qualifications. It does not follow that because a New York
apartment house is in style French Château or Flemish,
each one of the fifty or hundred apartments it contains must preserve that style of decoration—in apartments we may choose any style desirable in other respects. Nor, if we are reasonable and liberally inclined,
should the narrow front of a city house not pronouncedly
definite be allowed to impede our catholicity. The old
brown-stone front of New York is of a debased period
that we may well ignore, and the brick houses of Philadelphia and Boston, though derived from the earlier
Georgian, need not cause us many qualms. What there
is good in them is mainly classical and so sufficiently
adapted to most styles of decoration. A country house,
with all sides exposed and of definite exterior architecture, is another story. If one does not care to live in an
interior in accordance with the epoch of its outward
appearance he had better secure another house. The
mere mention of an Elizabethan house with Rococo
panelling will be sufficient to point the lesson.

TREATMENTS OF MODERATE SCOPE

As has been said, we may choose the less elaborate
phases of Renaissance, or any other wall decoration.
In such cases also, unless one has knowledge and facility, the services of a decorator will be required. If the
architectural lines and details are not already quite
approximately correct they should be made so before
panelling or decoration is applied. Either may be
comparatively simple but should be according to the
period. Elaborate carving of mantels, cornices and
door-jambs may be omitted, but architecturally they
should be right. In rented apartments or houses, in-
consistencies, if not pronounced, may be excused. If

the Italian Renaissance style is chosen, the diapered wall is an excellent resource. What may be done in the way of intelligent adaptation is admirably shown in the living-room illustrated by Plate 70 B in the chapter on Wall Treatment, where also is described the manner in which this attractive effect was gained.

PLAIN WALL TREATMENTS

Italian walls, when plain, were in sand-finished or smooth-finished plaster and in natural tones or of creams, ochres, light chocolate or grey. It is, therefore, evident that any such existing wall will admirably answer for a Renaissance interior. If the walls have been papered, a sand-finished paper may be applied. If the property is rented and the existing paper is in too good condition to be replaced, it would answer, providing that it has the general appearance of a perfectly plain surface in the right colouring—such as a cream felt or granite paper would afford.

An illustration is shown (Plate 128) of a remodelled farmhouse with plain walls, in which the Renaissance effect is excellently given by the tapestry and well-chosen furniture of England and Spain, with an Oriental touch in the lamp and rug.

FURNISHINGS AND FURNITURE

At this point the decorator, retailer or householder arrives at much easier going than hitherto; for it is a fact that all movable decorative objects are in all ages much more likely to be affected by the decorative influence then prevailing than is the more massive and fixed architectural structure; and so the furnishings and furniture under that influence approach each other much more nearly, though always somewhat differentiated by national characteristics. It is this very difference that adds variety and charm in our system of international decoration and gives it its value. By this plan also, as has been intimated, we are enabled to bring within our scope many beautiful objects from other lands, or their reproductions, which would be forbidden us by a closer adherence to the one-period, one-country method of furnishing. How far this immense advantage will still further be enlarged we shall realise when we come to the consideration and addition of the inter-period element of this method.

It has been felt advisable, in these chapters, to give as many illustrations of the furniture of Continental Europe as limits permit rather than to exhaust space with cuts of the well-known English furniture. Those who wish to make comparisons can readily do so by referring to "The Practical Book of Period Furniture" by Eberlein and McClure, where British and American forms are described and illustrated in detail.

There is little of the movable furnishing of strictly Renaissance provenance originating in one country that may not be employed in the interiors of another. The word "strictly" is here used because not a great while after the full flowering of this influence another movement arose—the Baroque—which blended with it. For the avoidance of all confusion, however, this will later and separately be treated, so that for the present we may confine ourselves to the furnishings of the Renaissance.

As has been mentioned, wall hangings were largely employed and may be considered one of the *notes* of Renaissance furnishing. These were of tapestry, brocade, velvet or embroidery. Any such Renaissance pieces, or reproductions thereof, may be used.

Floors were largely uncovered. In England, however, rushes were spread over them, and when these were, to phrase it gently, soiled, *more* rushes were spread over these again, till sanatory conditions became what would be as horrifying to us as we trust the present state of our streets would be to those living a few years hence. Oriental rugs have always been employed to some extent and may be used in Renaissance interiors to-day. Plain or bordered rugs might also well be employed provided the borders are plain, or of lines, or of a dignified design appropriate to a Renaissance setting (Plate 80).

The fact that the furniture of other nations in a particular period may be introduced in the interiors of any one, is fortunate for the owners of Elizabethan or Tudor houses. Probably the most creditable action of Henry VIII of tainted memory was the introduction of the Renaissance into England. There it had its influence, but England was then a less polished nation than Italy in the domestic arts, and till early Stuart times the furnishings of British houses were few. Wall furniture (chests, buffets, cupboards and cabinets) composed its bulk. Tables were but few, their place being mostly supplied by boards on trestles. Benches and joint-stools usually comprised the seating furniture. Chairs were most infrequent and were at first of the character known as wainscot chairs, and there was little upholstered furniture till the Restoration or near it. The bedsteads always occupied a position of state, and these were immensely large and heavily carved. The furniture of Renaissance England must, therefore, be supplemented from that of the succeeding epoch or from other countries under Renaissance influence if we are to have what is now considered an habitable home (Plates 136 and 3).

With such barrenness and to some extent rudeness as has been described we may contrast the dignified and

25

elegant furnishings of Continental Europe during the same period. There, too, the rooms were of enormous proportions, and anything approaching the crowding of furniture was sedulously avoided. The pieces were large and generally of the same materials—oak and walnut. Wall furniture there also occupied a position of much importance, but tables and seating furniture existed in great variety and beauty, the latter being upholstered in rich velvets, brocades, damasks and needlework. In addition to wall-hangings there were mural ornaments, pictures and carved ornaments of wood, often painted and gilt. Sculpture and pottery were abundant. Candlesticks and candelabra were of carved and gilded wood and of iron with ornament of colour and gilt.

The chests, or *cassoni,* were frequently carved by the great sculptors of Italy, the panels often embellished by the painters whose names are household words with us. These and other wall-pieces were often treated with *gesso* and then with colour and gilding.

No one knowing the indebtedness of English literature to Italian sources, realising the spread of Renaissance influence, and appreciating that only time and the march of progress were necessary to bring this added refinement to England, will hesitate to select from such furnishings and add them to those belonging to a British interior of Tudor times.

Common sense will give us the general precept that the correct course is to use principally and as a foundation the furniture appertaining to the nationality of the architectural background, *supplementing* it by that of other nations under the same influence. Where there is no distinctive background we may choose as a basis what we will, and give variety by the addition of these other pieces. National characteristics will always

PLATE 129

Photograph by Alinari
A. Carved and Inlaid Armoire, 15th Century

B. Carved Walnut Credenza and Cabinet (c. 1550)

ITALIAN RENAISSANCE WALL FURNITURE
By Courtesy of Radillo-Pelitti Co.

PLATE 130

A. Renaissance Walnut Chair   *B.* Renaissance Umbrian Chair

C. 17th Century Chair   *D.* 17th Century Circular Table   *E.* 16th Century Chair

Late Renaissance with Incipient Baroque Influence
All the above from the Volpi Collection by Courtesy of American Art Galleries

F. Renaissance Table   *G.* Late Renaissance Table
By Courtesy of Radillo-Pelitti Co.

ITALIAN RENAISSANCE CHAIRS AND TABLES

PLATE 131

A. FRENCH SIXTEENTH CENTURY CABINET ON STAND,
FLEMISH INFLUENCE
Collection Emile Gavet

By Courtesy of Messrs. L. Alavoine & Co.

B. FRENCH CARVED WALNUT CABINET À
DEUX CORPS WITH INLAID MARBLE PLAQUES
Collection Ed. Aynard

PLATE 132

A. FRENCH RENAISSANCE WALNUT CHAIRS
Lyons School, 16th Century
By Courtesy of Messrs. L. Alavoine & Co., New York

B. AN ELIZABETHAN COFFER—ENGLISH RENAISSANCE
By Courtesy of Messrs. Edwards & Sons, Ltd., London

assert themselves through a general resemblance, and they give us a happy many-sidedness and versatility of decoration impossible of being realised when we confine ourselves to an absolute reproduction of an English, French, Italian, Flemish or Spanish style. A study of the pieces of furniture illustrated herewith will demonstrate both this unity and variety. In viewing them we shall at once see their generally rectilinear character. Curves there are, to be sure, but we shall only have to become familiar with those of the succeeding Baroque and Rococo influences to realise the Classic features everywhere informing Renaissance design. It is by this comparison of varying forms that stylistic differences are quickly apprehended, rather than through reams of detailed description.

THE ASSOCIATION OF FURNITURE OF VARIOUS NATIONALITIES

In Plate 89 is a grouping of an excellent Italian cabinet flanked by two Italian chairs of the most rigidly formal type, with runner beneath the feet, and properly upholstered in velvet with gold galons. The upper finials of such chairs are almost always gilded. The candelabra are of iron.

The adaptability to association of nearly all the pieces selected for illustration will be evident. Instead of the *cabinet*, just mentioned, might be used with good result such a piece as the Italian armoire or the longer credenza in Plate 129, the double cabinet in the same plate, the French cabinet (Plate 131 B), the Elizabethan coffer (Plate 132 B) or one of the Spanish Varguenos (Plate 133 B or Plate 134 A). Even the Italian pillar-base table (Plate 130 F) placed between these chairs and aided by a pair of tall Renaissance candlesticks would do well. Associated with such furniture in imposing rooms might be the large Italian armoire

(Plate 129 A), the French armoire (Plate 131 A) or the Spanish armoire showing Moorish influence (Plate 133 C).

It is equally evident that if one of the pieces foreign to Italy were chosen, the result would be more interesting than if the cabinet remained, for of recent years the strictly Italian Renaissance period has been extensively treated and has lost its novelty. Furthermore, if one is the possessor of such a foreign piece of furniture he is by this method enabled to employ it to the greatest advantage, whereas he could not use it if he were adhering to an exclusively Italian Renaissance style of decoration.

On the other hand, should we allow the *cabinet to remain,* we might, by the present system, appropriately use with it the Italian scroll-arm chairs in the Davanzati room with plain walls (Plate 13) the curule chair in the interiors shown in Plate 15, the English wainscot in the remodelled farm-house (Plate 128), the French Renaissance (Plate 132 A), the chair in wonderful needlework (Plate 130 A), that adjoining it, or those in Plate 134 B, C and D. The Spanish chair, with brass mounts (Plate 134 F), would be of special interest in such surroundings.

Much other interesting Renaissance furniture will be seen in the rooms of the various nationalities under that influence in Part I and in Plates 127 and 135 in this chapter. They excellently illustrate the points of resemblance and difference which make for unity and variety in the furniture of different nations. A comparison of these pieces will be illuminating and will familiarise the reader with national characteristics.

Even during the Renaissance there were smaller or more homelike pieces of furniture than those so far mentioned, and some of these also are illustrated. The

PLATE 133

A. Chest with Painting Inside Lid (c. 1500). Carved Walnut Spindleback Chairs (c. 1550)
By Courtesy of C. M. Traver Co.

B. Vargueño Cabinet on Cupboard (c. 1550)
Carved Walnut, Parcel Gilt and Polychrome
By Courtesy of C. M. Traver Co.

C. Armoire of Carved Walnut (c. 1500). Small
Panels Reflecting Moorish Influence
By Courtesy of Mr. Nicholas Martin

SPANISH RENAISSANCE WALL FURNITURE

PLATE 134

A. Spanish Renaissance Vargueño
Courtesy C. M. Traver Co.

B. Renaissance, Span-
ish Colonial
(So. America)
John Wanamaker

C. Portuguese Renais-
sance, Incipient
Baroque
Mr. Nicholas Martin

D. Spanish Renais-
sance Carved Walnut

C. M. Traver Co.

E. Spanish Renaissance Table
with Wrought-iron Brace
Courtesy C. M. Traver Co.

F. Spanish Renaissance Chair
in Red Velvet, Brass Mounts
Courtesy Robinson & Farr

SPANISH AND PORTUGUESE RENAISSANCE FURNITURE

PLATE 135

A SPACIOUS MODERN HALL IN ITALIAN RENAISSANCE STYLE

Charles A. Platt, Esq., Architect

Courtesy of "Good Furniture Magazine"

English gate table used in the remodelled farmhouse (Plate 128) has proved so universally useful that we may well wonder why there are no reproductions of such pieces as the non-folding but certainly most desirable Italian circular table shown in Plate 130 D. The chair to its right is attractive, and that on the left would make an admirable hall chair. The Spanish chest and small chairs. with tapestry, in Plate 133 are good pieces, and the Spanish table (Plate 134 E), of which there are many variations, would impart decided interest into a Renaissance home.

Bedsteads are not so interchangeable as other furniture. Some of the French and Italian beds resemble each other, but the introduction of one of the well-known bulbous-posted Elizabethan bedsteads in an interior so definitely Italian and restrained as that of the Davanzati bedchamber (Plate 15 A) would be a mistake. It has already been mentioned that not every piece of furniture of Renaissance inspiration will go with every other piece, and it may be added that such discrimination as the above is necessary as regards their use in the interior to be furnished.

It is to be noted as a general principle that the introduction of but *one* piece of foreign furniture *may* be a disturbing influence: it is better to "back it up" with one or more additional pieces of the same or a different nationality, for by this procedure the *intention* of a varied furnishing is made evident and the room with all its different elements becomes immediately interesting.

The arrangement characteristic of Renaissance rooms, with the absence of any superfluity and crowding of decorative elements, is well shown in all the original Renaissance interiors illustrated and in the modern interior shown in Plate 135.

While, naturally, original pieces of furniture of the highest type or even of lesser elegance are beyond the reach of all but the wealthy, it is encouraging that good reproductions are being made. "Adaptations" are still more frequent than faithful reproductions, but the latter *can* be secured of good English and Italian forms, some French and Spanish may be obtained, and more will doubtless be placed upon the market as manufacturers perceive the demand. It is also to be hoped and expected that the practice of adapting will die out with the advance of knowledge on the part of buyers, their insistence upon authentic styles, and their refusal to accept the vagaries of commercial present-day designers in lieu of the forms and proportions provided by the masters of the past. It may here be mentioned that international furnishing in the eighteenth century periods is less expensive than Renaissance furnishing or that of other early epochs.

CHARACTERISTICS OF THE RENAISSANCE

The adaptability of Renaissance furnishing to our uses to-day may be gathered from its main characteristics. Perhaps its most outstanding qualities are spaciousness, dignity, formality and richness. Its earlier manifestations were marked by more simplicity and its later by increasing magnificence—which should be noted by those who are considering its use. That its qualities are not inconsistent with home feeling to-day is shown in all three of the modern examples referred to in this chapter.

That this style is *not* adapted to modest houses with small rooms, or to larger ones where the occupants lead a happy-go-lucky or merely frivolous existence is self-evident. It implies a certain amenity of life, a certain degree of self-respect, culture and appreciation. It is well suited to spacious apartments, particularly of the duplex variety, and to studios. If the rooms are fairly large, even though few, it would be admirably suited to the apartment of a family of scholarly or artistic attainments, because it would fit into their natural mode of life.

THE INTER PERIOD ELEMENT

The international (horizontal) phase of this system has now been considered, and we have seen how fully the furnishings of all the nations under Renaissance influence may be used together. We must now take up the inter period (perpendicular) element and learn to what degree the interiors and furnishings of the succeeding movement may be combined with those of the Renaissance.

This next influence is the Baroque. As the Renaissance did not utterly rout the Gothic, so the Baroque in its turn did not put to flight the Renaissance, but grafted itself upon it. Most curious and interesting is the manner in which a new artistic impulse, totally different in spirit from the old though it be, yet amalgamates itself with it to the production of a result not chaotic but still beautiful. The Baroque movement has been unduly condemned. Though erratic and disproportioned in its most extravagant phases, many of its developments are interesting and of permanent artistic value.

CHAPTER II

THE BAROQUE SEVENTEENTH CENTURY

THE ROMANTIC SPIRIT. ARCHITECTURAL BACKGROUND. THE
ASSOCIATION OF FURNITURE OF VARIOUS PERIODS. THE
FURNITURE OF THE BAROQUE EPOCH AND ITS EMPLOY-
MENT. PRESENT-DAY USE OF THE BAROQUE

THE ROMANTIC SPIRIT

NOT yet does it seem to be understood by many
that the spirit which is contrary to the Classic
in interior decoration is the same which
opposes it in the other arts: consequently we hear much
of Baroque, Rococo, Art Nouveau and the '' Newer
Decoration'' while feeling sure it is not generally realised they are all recrudescences of the Romantic spirit.
The failure to recognise this has been responsible for
much narrowness of view.

These two great informing influences—the Classic
and the Romantic—which affect literature and the
other arts—likewise move through the course of interior decoration and act as alternate inspirations.
These often blend, and indeed since the beginnings of
modern art (as distinguished from mediæval) have seldom been entirely separate; but one or the other is
nearly always dominant.

The Classic ideal is that of ''order,'' of restraint,
and is usually accompanied by dignified colour: the
Romantic is emotional, free, frets and champs at restraint, resents the rule of precedent and naturally re-
joices in exuberant colour.

We shall continually see the manifestations of both,
and have not long to wait; for here, almost at the be-

392

ginnings of modern decoration, the Renaissance movement, dominantly Classic though infiltrated with many
romantic features, was interrupted, we might almost
say *set upon,* by the contrary influence. Like the preceding movement, the Baroque arose in Southern Europe, and with greater or less force swept over the Continent and England.

A natural question to any enquiring mind is why
such changes occur and why new movements arise. We
shall always find the answer in natural causes, and
learn that they are in the direction of development or
reaction—sometimes partaking of both, as does the
one we are now to consider.

The Renaissance began with the classic inspiration
of order and dignity. To this was added state and magnificence. Interior architecture and furnishing became,
through political and social changes, increasingly ornate, till the original inspiration was forgotten or ignored; till the desire for display could no longer be
satisfied by the capabilities of the classic, aided, though
it was, by features unknown to Greece and Rome, and
so naturally burst its bonds and overflowed into the
romantic, curvilinear, redundant and often ill-bal-
anced Baroque. Impatience of the restrictions of the
Renaissance doubtless also aided in developing a reaction from its principles.

Although much of the rectilinear persisted in the
Baroque, its characteristic is the curve. But when,
later, we arrive at the succeeding period—the Rococo—
we shall find that its characteristic also is the curvilinear, and to a still greater degree—what, therefore,
are the outstanding features by which we shall recognise the Baroque?

They will become still more evident when we compare it with the Rococo, but as "seeing is believing," let

us look for a moment at its extreme manifestation in the cut of the diminutive Spanish chair illustrated in Plate 136 A.

In the first place, it rather increased the weight and retained the impressiveness of the Renaissance, though different in its forms, and the constructional material remained largely oak and walnut. In the second, while all sorts of curves were in use in the Baroque period an analysis seems to show the "broken curve," often called the Flemish scroll, the C curve and the cartouche to be its most prominent decorative *motifs*. In furniture, where symptoms are always the most marked, all its curves were marked by roundness of the edges, as is appropriate to their weight, and they were what we might denominate *stopped curves*, being usually closed at the ends by a whorled termination. They were not free and flowing—there is a ponderous *tightness* about them all. The shell was much used as an ornament.

Its interior architecture was marked in its use of pilasters, pillars, broken entablatures and ornament without due regard to construction and an often clumsy heaviness in mouldings and details.

In order to arrive at the practical use and application of the Baroque interior and furnishing to-day these will now be taken up in both their international and inter period relations.

ARCHITECTURAL BACKGROUND

Typical illustrations are given of interiors of the various nations under Baroque influence. So vastly do the characteristics of the fixed background of England differ from the others, and such an interesting condition then prevailed, that this may be given first consideration.

PLATE 136

A. DIMINUTIVE SPANISH
CHAIR, 19 INCHES HIGH
Showing what the Baroque could
do when it ran wild

Charles of London, Decorators, New York

B. THE ENGLISH RENAISSANCE INTERIOR ARCHITECTURE WHICH
PERSISTED TO SOME EXTENT INTO BAROQUE TIMES
Renaissance Buffet and Baroque Seating-furniture
Courtesy of Mrs. Lyman Kendall

PLATE 137

EARLY GEORGIAN ROOM WITH PAINTED AND PANELLED WALLS AND DECORATED PLASTER CEILING

Removed from Norfolk, England

By Courtesy of Messrs. Litchfield & Co., London

PLATE 138

SALON OF DIANA, VERSAILLES, STYLE LOUIS XIV
From "Librairie Centrale d'Art et d'Architecture"
Courtesy of William Helburn, Inc.

PLATE 139

Photograph from Anderson, Rome   SALA DEI ANGELI, PALAZZO FARNESE, CAPRAROLA

Note beginnings of Baroque influence in mouldings of fireplace surround and in chimney-piece sculpture. Note also tesselated floor, frescoed walls and vaulted frescoed ceiling. The chaise longue is later and not appropriate

By Courtesy of "Vogue"

England: Though there had been some earlier manifestations of Baroque tendencies, the restoration of Charles II, the ensuing gaiety, love of display and commercial enterprise let loose this and all other foreign fashions. But at the same time the Classic leanings of the great architects, Wren and Inigo Jones, and the example of their work, held in check these tendencies so far as architecture—exterior and interior—was concerned. Contemporaneously with this, the previous Renaissance style still persisted (Plate 136 B). Notwithstanding these architectural influences the Baroque movement was not restrained in the direction of movable furniture, and we therefore have the unusual combination of a Classical or nearly Classical background in Baroque times accompanied by furniture often very Baroque indeed.

This furniture will be treated in a following section and all the details of the changes in interior architecture will be found in Part I, Chapter I.

France: Across the channel the Baroque influence came in with the reign of Henri IV (1589) and persisted till the death of Louis XIV in 1715.

Beyond the ability and taste always instinctive in the French, even during the vagaries of certain periods, no restraint was there laid upon Baroque tendencies during the earlier reigns of this epoch (Plate 30 A), but, as we shall see, during the times of Louis XIV a marked change of direction became manifest (Plates 34 and 138).

Because of the faults already mentioned the backgrounds of this epoch are not particularly desirable for our houses to-day, and, notwithstanding the restraint of the latter period, the heavy magnificence of the style of Louis XIV unfits it for anything else than buildings of palatial proportions and hotels, for which it has fre-

quently been used. Even for these we may prefer less
grandiose styles, but justice must be done the remarkable work accomplished during the reign of the most
famous king of France.

After the regency of his mother, Anne of Austria,
he assumed the reins of government in 1661. By 1684
he had so humbled the power of the nobles and assem-
blies that his power was practically absolute. At court
the utmost splendour was maintained, and a ceremonial
pompous and burdensome to a degree. In literature
it was the Augustan Age in France, the age of Corneille
and Racine, Molière, Boileau, Fénelon, Bossuet and
Bourdillon. Under his talented minister, Colbert, all
the arts received the most liberal encouragement, work-
men being regularly employed by the Crown.

A pruning hand was laid upon the excrescences of
the Baroque, and what remained was combined with a
structure largely Renaissance, the result being an amal-
gamation rightly designated as "the grand manner."
To sum it in a phrase: the style of Louis Quatorze was
the effect of the spirit of Classicism working with material Renaissance and Baroque (Plates 34–36 and 138).

But the latter part of the reign of "Le Grand
Monarque" was marked by disastrous wars, consequent exorbitant taxation, the resentment of his subjects; and, leaving an almost ruined country, detested
and unmourned, in 1715 he sank into his grave.

Italy: Here the Baroque impulse found its way to
some extent into the *details* of interior architecture—
cornices, cartouches and carving, mouldings and mantels; but the Classic construction generally remained.
Its most evident effect was increasing magnificence
(Plate 139). With tesselated floors, carved mantels
and doors, every inch of the walls and ceilings often

decorated in full colour and gold, or walls encrusted in marbles; with furniture gloriously carved and some pieces painted and gilded; textiles of full bodied colour, often enhanced with *appliqué* or needlework; sculpture and Oriental porcelains; accessories of every description—with all these it is marvellous that dignity and repose were at all preserved. Yet this decoration was successful! Two requisites remained—spaciousness and artistic knowledge.

Spain: In conservative Spain the walls remained much as they were under the Renaissance, though the tiling or painting may have grown even more colourful. But the writers would particularly direct the attention of wealthy connoisseurs and their decorators to Spain as a source of interesting elements varied from those of countries decoratively better known. If the upper walls were plain, that plainness was redeemed to the last degree by the textiles which hung thereon. These were of the utmost profusion and of all known materials, light and heavy. Such colourings as crimson and brilliant green were relieved by gold. Armorial bearings were frequent *motifs*, with all their opportunity for richness of colour and interest of detail.

The leather work of Spain—stamped, engraved and coloured, and with silver or with gold—was particularly characteristic and famous. Porcelains, tiles, pottery, glass and smithwork will afford the discriminating collector of to-day unending delight. The wonderfully decorative chests and cabinets of Spain appeal to all lovers of the unusual and beautiful.

The Italian "domino" paper in small sections was sometimes applied to walls through most of southern Europe.

THE ASSOCIATION OF FURNITURE OF VARIOUS PERIODS

A varied selection of the furniture evolved in the various countries under Baroque influence is given in these pages and will be discussed in relation to their practical use in our present-day interiors with each other and in connexion with furniture of the preceding Renaissance movement. We shall also naturally wish to know whether under this system of International-Interperiod Decoration the combination may be extended still further and successive periods also be embraced with the two so far discussed.

It is the aim of these chapters not to lay down decorative dicta but to *work out* with the reader the problems that arise, all deductions being made from the existing facts. Clearheadedness is also such a desideratum that when we speak of the use of various pieces together we should stop and ask ourselves in each instance what we mean by "together"—directly adjoining, in the same room, or in the same house or apartment?

It is quickly evident that pieces of furniture placed side by side among the few furnishings of a small room might disagree, whereas they would only add a desirable variety in a very spacious room; also, that furniture of more decided differences might without incompatibility be employed in the various rooms of one residence.

We should also ask: What are the qualities that would *prevent* our using various pieces together?—in any of the above degrees.

It is again plain that the mere fact, *per se,* of one piece belonging to one era and another to a different one, forms no obstacle to their being combined in use; it is the *characteristics* belonging to the particular periods, and of which those pieces are examples, that render them reconcilable or irreconcilable.

If one were to ask in what directions great differences should be avoided, the quick reply would almost invariably be: in form, size and colour. These are, of course, fundamental, but, as we shall see, quite as noticeable are discrepancies in texture, finish, degrees of impressiveness or elegance and the upholstery employed.

Let us then take up these characteristics or qualities at once, for they will show us *what to look for* in considering furniture, not only in these two epochs but in others as well. We shall also find that differences in one or two respects, where not vital, may be sufficiently balanced by likeness in others to permit an association of the pieces.

Form: Decided difference in form is indication of a difference in spirit. Yet we have seen that the Baroque grew out of the Renaissance and amalgamated itself with it to a workable extent. There was not a *total* variance of spirit and manifestation between the late Renaissance and the Baroque—both were massive and handsome—and the difference between them, though great, was therefore not irreconcilable and fatal. So far, therefore, as *contour* goes, we may ask what furniture designed over all cultured Europe during the more than two hundred years preceding 1715 may be used together?

If our ideal is the *formal* one, then we had better confine ourselves to the Renaissance together with those forms of the Baroque that are dignified and, though more ornamental, preserve the weight and impressiveness of the Renaissance. Such a combination is shown in the dining-room illustrated in Plate 136 and in the other view of the same room shown in Plate 3.

If our ideal is more flexible, then we may be more liberal in our choice, especially in different rooms. In a hall we may lean to the formal. We may also do so in the drawing- or dining-room, but we should make them much more delightful by the use of greater variety. The private rooms may contain the smaller, lighter and more informal pieces of the times.

On considering whether the contours of the *succeeding* epochs are so radically different as to prevent their being used with the furniture of these two influences we shall find, when in turn we take them up, that in *general* they are. *Some* such combinations are, however, permissible, because, if judgment be used as regards form, differences may be reconciled by carefulness in other respects.

Size and Weight: These are two qualities, but usually go together. A large piece of furniture may, of course, be slender in its members but is usually only comparatively so. As we have seen, agreement in these respects is a strongly uniting influence and will often partially balance other discrepancies.

On the other hand, great variations in size and weight between the furniture of two periods render these pieces generally irreconcilable. Both Renaissance and late eighteenth century furniture were based upon Classic ideals, yet size and weight, with other qualities, usually differentiate them too radically to accompany each other to good effect.

Colour: Old oak and walnut go sufficiently well together in tone. Mahogany was not generally used till about 1720. The reddish tone now so frequently seen does not at all well accompany oak: the brownish shade is much better. The *tone* of satinwood would be agreeable with oak, but the lightness of the contours in which it was used are totally at variance with those of oak furniture. The matter of colour is, however, bound up with the qualities still to be considered.

Texture, Finish and Elegance: An English oaken Renaissance chair is foreign to a Hepplewhite mahogany chair in form, size and colour, but, in addition, we strongly feel the great difference between the open, coarse grain, dull finish and ponderous handsomeness of the one and the fine and close texture, the reflective surface and the light elegance of the other.

In the days when oak and walnut were the woods commonly employed for furniture they were in a dull finish. Mahogany, left in its natural state (unreddened by permanganate of potash) or in the brownish tone, and dully finished with wax, would not greatly conflict with oak, but the age of mahogany was different in spirit from that of oak and there is seldom occasion for this close use.

Marqueterie and lacquered furniture, where appropriate in spirit, may always be used.

Upholstery: In seating furniture the textile covering it is often the most noticeable feature. It is plain, therefore, what a unifying or diversifying part it may play. In the Renaissance period furniture was covered with heavy velvet or brocade in full-bodied colourings —crimsons, blues and greens being favourites—and often relieved with weighty gold galons. In the reign of Louis Seize coverings were of light-weight silks in exquisite pastel and greyed colours. These extremes are mentioned merely to show how the use together of furniture covered in styles so diverse would render such pieces incongruous irrespective of the furniture itself. On the other hand, the same upholstery employed on chairs and settees of rather varying character will pull them together in effect; and handsome covering will do much to enhance the impressiveness of pieces not

26

otherwise particularly notable. The chair shown in
Plate 145 C, for instance, is rather simple, but is rendered elegant by its elaborate embroidery and fringe.

THE FURNITURE OF THE BAROQUE EPOCH AND ITS EMPLOYMENT

A volume would be required to describe and picture
all the types of furniture of the Baroque age, bound
up as it is with the political and religious history of
the times and the action and reaction of country upon
country. Because of this intercourse—often frictional
enough—we constantly find the general forms of one
country echoed in one or more of the others, but always with those national differences that have been
mentioned.

In all practical furnishing there are four points to
be remembered as a basis:

I. Unity and variety should both be secured—the
first to avoid confusion, and the second to preclude
monotony by the providing of interest.

II. The unit to be considered is the house or apartment—*not* the single room.

III. That there are degrees in all things; and that
a closer degree of unity is necessary in the single room
than in the house as a whole, especially if the room
be not spacious.

IV. That a sliding scale may be used in the various
rooms, providing that a satisfying effect of unity is
secured throughout.

In what shall that sliding scale consist? So far as
the two epochs discussed go, the writers cannot think
of a better word than *impressiveness*. The word formality does not always hit the mark here, for a piece
of furniture may be very formal in its lines and yet be
quite simple; nor does handsome cover it, for a bed-

PLATE 140

AN EIGHTEENTH CENTURY BEDROOM, CASA DE ALTA-VILA, AGUEDA, PORTUGAL

Mainly Baroque with Incipient Rococo Tendencies in the Bedstead

By Courtesy of Carvalho Brothers

room chair may be handsome and yet not particularly impressive.

An example will make the idea clear: The two Renaissance chairs accompanying the credenza and candelabra illustrated in Plate 89 B are comparatively simple but impressive. The typical Queen Anne chair, with which we are all familiar, is Dutch and comfortable; and, notwithstanding other admirable qualities, is *unimpressive*. If we use one in a room we should not use the other.

We now arrive at the main point—we shall find ourselves able to employ in a single room both comparatively simple and comparatively ornate pieces (whether Renaissance or Baroque, or both together) provided the same degree of *impressiveness* exists in each, and provided we do not *jumble* them. We find this constantly illustrated in original interiors of the Renaissance and elsewhere. The wall furniture may be simple, but a table *set out on the floor* may have a handsomely scrolled and carved base (Plate 139), or a chest may be elaborate and its flanking chairs simple, each having its share of general impressiveness. In less formal and more intimate rooms that general degree may be less, and so the scale in the various rooms may be a sliding one.

The furniture illustrated is decidedly various in character and will enable us to consider combinations suggestive to the decorator, dealer or householder. In considering these illustrations we shall see that this furniture falls, naturally, into groups.

Having now arrived at the point where the inter period element of this plan of decoration may be exemplified, it will be most interesting first to take up Baroque pieces which will properly accompany furniture of the preceding Renaissance age.

Plate 141 B shows a fine Italian carved armoire in developed Baroque style and with a pediment fully illustrating its tendencies. Yet this handsome piece of furniture is of great dignity and would not only well accompany the more massive mobiliary forms of Renaissance provenance but would lend distinct variety and interest.

One so fortunate as to secure a piece of furniture resembling the wonderfully decorative French cabinet (Plate 142 A) with panels and diagonal marqueterie, certainly does not need to hesitate to use it in the same room with one of the equally decorative Italian painted and gilded *cassoni,* though, because of their differences, he would not place them in close proximity. Each might well form a "centre of interest."

The two cabinets, on either side of the dais, in the Portuguese interior (Plate 140) are quite of a character to go with Renaissance furniture. The one on the right is pronouncedly Baroque in its support and scrollwork, but is rectangular and impressive, while at the same time presenting decorative qualities of a different order from that of other nationalities. The table in the same room is also excellent.

Two Italian tables are shown in Plate 147 A and B; one of these early Baroque and still rectangular in its constructional lines and the other of developed style. Both would, however, look well in a Renaissance room even in close proximity.

In Plate 144 a group is shown of an Italian cabinet with a pair of candlesticks, backed by a tapestry, and two chairs. Instead of the formal Renaissance chair usually found in such company, the owner has here placed two of Baroque type with scroll arm, waved stretcher and goat feet, and, notwithstanding the variation in type, the result is pleasing. A pair of the Louis

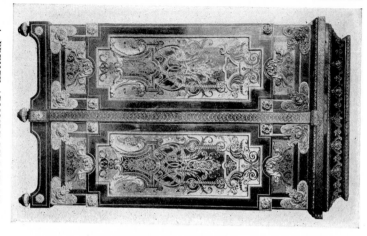

PLATE 141

A. FRENCH ARMOIRE BY BOULLE
SEVENTEENTH CENTURY
Ebony with Brass Mounts. Inlaid with Brass, Pewter
and Tortoise Shell. Collection Kraemer
By Courtesy of L. Alavoine & Co.

Photograph by Alinari
B. ITALIAN CARVED WALNUT ARMOIRE
SEVENTEENTH CENTURY
Museo d'Antichità, Parma
By Courtesy of Radillo-Pelitti Co.

PLATE 142

B. ITALIAN BAROQUE RED LACQUER AND
POLYCHROME ARMOIRE
Louis XIV and Queen Anne Affinities
By Courtesy of Pa. Museum and School of Industrial Art

A. FRENCH BAROQUE MARQUETERIE CABINET
Boxwood and Rosewood Inlaid with Holly and Ebony
By Courtesy of Anderson Art Galleries

PLATE 143

A. French Baroque Arm
Chair
Radillo-Pelitti Co.

B. Louis XIV Arm Chair
in Genoese Velvet
Metropolitan Museum

C. Louis XIV Ornamental Table with Eight Legs and Stretcher
Exhibited at the Brooklyn Museum

D. William and Mary Seaweed Marqueterie High Cabinet
By Courtesy of the Metropolitan Museum of Art

FRENCH AND ENGLISH FURNITURE, BAROQUE EPOCH

PLATE 144

AN ITALIAN RENAISSANCE CREDENZA ACCOMPANIED BY
BAROQUE CHAIRS
The Wall is Sand Finished, the Window Trim of Blue Tile and the Floor of
Biscuit-Coloured Tile
By Courtesy of George Howe, Esq.

Quatorze chairs in Genoese velvet (Plate 143 B) would go equally well here, because of general impressiveness and formal character. The cabinet is Renaissance and this chair the latest phase of Baroque, when under the Grand Monarch the Classic spirit regained a certain degree of ascendancy.

A remarkably good chair in such a situation would be the Portuguese Baroque chair with spiral members (Plate 149 B). Its generally rectangular lines, brocade upholstery and quiet dignity fit it for the neighbour-hood of most Renaissance pieces and other Baroque furniture of like character, while its back is at once noticeable because of its difference from the usual forms of other countries.

Plate 145 is occupied by a group of six different chairs, Italian and English, of ornate Baroque char-acter. Yet these chairs are dignified and impressive in character and of these, too, we may say they would by no means be out of place in a room with Renaissance forms of generally ornamental type.

We have only to consider these English chairs and the Classicism of the contemporary English back-grounds illustrated to see how far apart architecture and furniture in this age could be in that country.*

We may now take up types of Baroque furniture which do not properly accompany Renaissance forms. The Armoire (Plate 141 A) is illustrated to show the work of Boulle, the most famous *ébéniste* of all time. Pieces such as this do not find their counterpart in those of other nations and so are best accompanied by con-temporary (Louis XIV) furniture such as the chair and table on Plate 143 B and C. They are, however, practically unprocurable and any wealthy connoisseur

---

* For British furniture of all epochs, see "The Practical Book of Period Furniture," by Eberlein and McClure.

possessed of such examples would probably own museum pieces of other nationalities with which they might (notwithstanding differences) be placed in such a residence. Reproductions are made of the fine furniture of this and the succeeding reigns, but their cost is necessarily great.

While the chair and table just referred to are distinctly ornamental, it will be seen that they go excellently well with the handsome contemporary marqueterie cabinet of William and Mary on the same plate (Plate 143 D). The three are all dignified, and the resemblance of the French and English pieces is illuminating to the student of international furnishing: yet differences exist throughout and it will be observed that the three pieces of furniture exhibit as many types of stretcher. These pieces are all of the latter part of the Baroque epoch when classic feeling had regained its ascendancy. Earlier French furniture of formal character will be seen in Plate 30 A and B.

The Baroque age provides many more intimate and homelike forms than the preceding era and these are exemplified by the William and Mary and Queen Anne furniture of England and analogous pieces in other lands.

The Italian red lacquer armoire (Plate 142 B) and the French and Venetian escritoires on Plate 146 are fine specimens of Continental work, while two beautiful chests of drawers are exhibited in Plate 147 C and D. The seating-furniture is also of great interest. The form of chair usually designated as William and Mary really originated in Portugal and a Spanish example is shown to the left in Plate 148 B. The chair below it shows the Chinese influence acquired through foreign commerce. Those at the top of the plate show affinity with the earlier Yorkshire English chairs. The Portu-

PLATE 145

A. Arm Chair in
Cutpile Velvet
   B. Chair in
   Cutpile Velvet
  Radillo–Pelitti Co.
     C. Venetian Walnut Chair
   in Petit Point Embroidery
    with silk-tasselled Fringe
    American Art Galleries

DIGNIFIED ITALIAN BAROQUE CHAIRS

D. ORNATE BUT DIGNIFIED ENGLISH BAROQUE
CHAIRS
By Courtesy of Radillo-Pelitti Co.

PLATE 146

B. EIGHTEENTH CENTURY VENETIAN
LACQUERED ESCRITOIRE

A. EIGHTEENTH CENTURY FRENCH LACQUERED
ESCRITOIRE

From the Volpi Collection by Courtesy of American Art Galleries

PLATE 147

A. Early Baroque Tuscan Walnut Table
By Courtesy American Art Galleries

B. Developed Baroque Table
By Courtesy Radillo-Pelitti Co.

C. Walnut Veneer and Inlaid Chest of Drawers
(c. 1725–30)
Queen Anne and Chippendale Affinities
By Courtesy of Radillo-Pelitti Co.

D. Carved Walnut and Inlaid Chest of Drawers
(c. 1740)
Chippendale Affinity

ITALIAN BAROQUE TABLES AND CHESTS OF DRAWERS

PLATE 148

A. Crested-back Chairs of Affinity with English Yorkshire
Chairs
By Courtesy of C. M. Traver Co.

B Spanish Walnut Chairs of Following Affinities
William and Mary   Queen Anne   Early Queen Anne
By Courtesy of C. M. Traver Co.

C Painted Chair   *D*. Walnut Chair
Chinese Influence   Queen Anne Affinity
Woodville & Co.   C. M. Traver Co.

SPANISH BAROQUE CHAIRS

guese chair (Plate 149 A) and settee (Plate 149 C) are
fine and desirable pieces. Spanish Baroque and Rococo pieces will be seen in Plate 25.

Special attention is called to the two chairs Plate
148 B centre and D because they parallel a group of
furniture not so far considered—the plain forms of
Queen Anne-early Georgian with the phase of Chippendale derived from them, with which these chairs are
analogous. This furniture is Baroque and yet it
requires some special consideration apart from the
rest, for it is a group having no parallel in France and,
indeed, no close affiliation with the furniture of England either preceding or following it.

The period is contemporary with the last years of
Louis XIV and the most of those of the Rococo, but
how wonderfully different its furniture is from the mobiliary forms of the same years in France! The reason
is evident—during the reigns of William and Mary and
of Queen Anne these Dutch forms came in and persisted during the two following Hanoverian reigns.
The Dutch influence had, of course, arrived with the
accession of William and Mary, but the earlier contours of that period were different from those of Anne
and were more in accord with other Baroque mobiliary
forms.

The architectural furniture and those pieces of
cabinet-work which extended to the floor (without legs)
retained a fair degree of dignity and impressiveness,
though simple, and the ornately carved consoles and
chairs were sufficiently ornamental and Baroque; but
the plain highboys, chairs, settees, and the like, with
the typical plain cabriole leg and club foot, form a
genus apart.

Now, what shall we do with this admirable, homelike furniture? It seems to the writers that in houses

not stately, classic or formal, where the more intimate forms of the Baroque epoch are employed, that these might well be used in such apartments as men's rooms, bedrooms and living-rooms without undue incongruity.

Or, a house might be very delightfully furnished with this furniture, fine Dutch chests, and the like, some pieces of the William and Mary reign, and relieved with Italian and Spanish furniture following the same general lines. Some lacquered furniture should be used, it being a specialty of her reign. The southern pieces were often painted and decorated. The Oriental touch would also be quite in order, and blue and white porcelain especially appropriate. With such resources as these a charming result could be obtained. The latter part of the period introduced the use of mahogany, but that would sufficiently well accompany the usual walnut if the finish were the same.

PRESENT-DAY USE OF THE BAROQUE

To sum up our investigations, then, we have seen that the English fixed background of this epoch is home-like, whether handsome or more simple; that the very Baroque manifestations of the French interior are interesting and curious rather than particularly desirable for use to-day; that while certain Classic tendencies asserted themselves in the reign of Louis XIV the word best describing its general result is *pompous;* that the Italian architectural background is very ornate but generally good, and is therefore suitable for those who desire such houses; that the Spanish interior is attractive and so available for parts of America where Spanish influences prevailed but rather alien to the East and Middle West. In *general,* therefore, it would seem best to employ the English background or one of the simpler Renaissance forms.

PLATE 149

A. Carved Walnut
Arm Chair
Queen Anne Affinity
Mr. Nicholas Martin

B. Side Chair with Back
of shaped cresting and
Bottom
Spiral Members
C. M. Traver Co.

C. Walnut Triple-back Settee with Embossed Leather
Seat.   Queen Anne Affinity
By Courtesy of Mr. Nicholas Martin

PORTUGUESE BAROQUE SEATING
FURNITURE

PLATE 150

Elsie de Wolfe, Decorator
DINING–ROOM WITH COVED CEILING: LANDSCAPE WALLS
Eighteenth Century Italían and Spanish Furniture, Baroque and Neo Classic
Courtesy of "Good Furniture Magazine"

As to the furniture, it was observed in a former chapter that unless we wish a museum effect the more satisfying result will be obtained if the furniture of the country chosen for the background prevails, being relieved by the use of appropriate and interesting pieces of other nationalities.

We should not show taste and discrimination by placing together the rigidly severe furniture of the earliest Renaissance with that redolent of Baroque ornament; but there is a sliding scale between the two where we may find many companionable pieces.

If these periods have been fixed upon for a scheme of decoration we should decide upon the *general* degree of handsomeness to be observed. There should not be a *confusion* of impressive and non-impressive forms, though, of course, there may be a *pièce de résistance* or two with usually simple furnishings and this will level up the general effect.

Doubtless many more informal and homelike pieces existed in the homes of the *bourgeoisie* of the early days we have been considering than we now know of; they have likely perished, and it is to be remembered that it is usually only the more elaborate forms that are preserved in the stately buildings of the past and in museums, books and pictures.

CHAPTER III

THE ROCOCO

THE BAROQUE AND THE ROCOCO. THE AGE AND THE STYLE
OF LOUIS XV. THE ARCHITECTURAL BACKGROUND. SIMPLI-
FIED BACKGROUNDS. THE FURNITURE OF THE PERIOD.
THE PRACTICAL EMPLOYMENT OF ROCOCO FURNITURE.
THE ROCOCO STYLE AND PRESENT-DAY USE

THE BAROQUE AND THE ROCOCO

SOME usually careful writers refer to Baroque
and Rococo almost as if the terms were interchangeable. Both are the fruit of the great Romantic impulse, and the latter is directly successive to
the former, one drifting into the other. The present
writers wish, however, to make clear that the difference between them is more radical than has yet been
pointed out. It is a bit startling—is it not?—to say
that there is a larger divergence between these two
Romantic developments than there is between the
Classic Renaissance and the Romantic Baroque; and
yet is it not so? "By their fruits ye shall know them"
—do not pieces of Renaissance and Baroque furniture
accompany each other better than pieces of Baroque
and Rococo? Try the experiment and see: for we are
seeking practical results.

We have already found that notwithstanding the
difference in spirit and contour, likeness in size and
weight, material and its colour, finish and upholstery,
may all unite properly chosen pieces of Renaissance
and Baroque furniture. On the other hand, the Rococo
in its full development is slender, smaller, lighter,
graceful, spirited and gay; walnut was generally used

410

and sometimes oak, but, frequently, these pieces were painted or enamelled and sometimes gilt: to its upholstery may for the first time be applied the word exquisite. Furthermore, and for much the same reason, Rococo mobiliary forms do not well accompany those of the preceding reign, though during it there was so great a departure from usual Baroque forms—they also are widely different in spirit and effect. In the story of the period we see why this was so.

THE AGE AND THE STYLE OF LOUIS XV

The Grand Monarch had at last departed this life. His rule had been long and it was his great grandson, Louis XV, the "Well Beloved," who succeeded him. The Duke of Orleans acted as Regent during the minority of the King (1715–1723) and an immediate reaction against the pompous splendour of the previous *régime* ensued, resulting in an entire change in feeling and in mode of life. Freed from the burdensome control of that supreme egoist Louis Quatorze, the luxurious and pleasure-loving court found no restraint in the dissolute Regent nor in the young King, who only eight years later succeeded him. Tiresome functions in the great halls of Versailles gave way to the intimate meetings of the *petit cabinet*. It was an age of extreme politeness and of "manners," but also of familiar intercourse; smaller rooms came into vogue and, appropriately to them, smaller pieces of furniture and new forms suited to the new social life. Luxury, comfort, new sensations and beauty were the things sought for, and in the seeking was felt an absolute freedom from all restrictions in choice of form, material and colour and the sources from which they came. Is it too undignified to say that when freed from its heavy-handed ruler France arose and kicked its heels?

The young King (only thirteen years old when he took the throne in 1723) put the wise Cardinal Fleury at the head of affairs and this minister did his utmost for the welfare of France. Louis was amiable, but weak and inefficient. As he grew older he fell under the influence of his dissolute noblemen and the people who had rejoiced at his accession found as little consideration at his hands as they had experienced under his predecessor. Not many years ago contempt for the "public" was expressed in terse and vigorous language by the late Commodore Vanderbilt, and the ancestry of that attitude is a long one. It was never more manifest than in the reigns of the three successive Louis and it was not wonderful that it finally found its aftermath in the Revolution.

But meanwhile the exorbitant taxes were yielded by a suffering people and spent in luxury. The supreme selfishness and profligacy of the era are sufficiently well known: less popularly appreciated are its refinement, sincere appreciation of beauty, freedom from vulgarity and its intellectuality. If it was the age of the boudoir it was also that of the salon. If the Pompadour ruled King and State for the nineteen years from 1745 to her death in 1764, and if her draughts on the treasury amounted to hundreds of millions of *livres,* her taste at least was impeccable and much of the money was spent on an architecture and decoration rendering France famous for all time.

Because of her rule and that of her successor, Madame du Barry, and because of the great influence of the feminine sex in general upon the social life of the times, we constantly hear (and have grown somewhat wearied in the hearing) the half truth that the style of Louis Quinze was the result of the Reign of Woman. The present writers would prefer to say that it was the effect of the Reign of Freedom and Irresponsibility. The gaiety, brilliance of life, the expression of its revolt from control, its desire for elegance, its undisguised and irregulated search for beauty from whatever source, found relief in many frivolous phases, but the style as a whole was not only a perfect rendering of the Gallic spirit but an amazing exhibition of fertility and quality in design and consummate workmanship. The *ébénistes,* weavers of tapestries and carpets, and art-workers of all descriptions, still under the patronage of the crown, naturally breathed the pervading and exciting atmosphere and responded to the spirit and demands of the time. Nevertheless, it is to be remembered that these men had received their training under the old *régime* and did not abandon their traditions of craftsmanship, but gradually adapted them to the changed conditions and new requirements. The *Régence* style of decoration is an admirable one, retaining much of the dignity of the previous age but modified by the easier feeling characteristic of the newer time. Indications of the Rococo had appeared even during the reign of Louis Quatorze, but it was not until his successor sat upon the throne that its full flowering came.

Le Style Louis Quinze was the complete triumph of the Romantic. It was revolutionary, it was something the world had never previously seen. As the outstanding *motif* of the Baroque was the broken curve, those of the new movement were the flowing double curve, or line of beauty, and the C scroll; and in these there was nothing cumbersome nor tight; they were instinct with spring and swing and ease.

Neither of these were new, but their *employment* was very new indeed. Never before had decoration known a style in which curves so completely became construction, in which the rectilinear was to such an extent banished. Furthermore, even the usual symmetry of the opposing sides of a design was finally abolished, and balance was sustained by asymmetrical arrangement.

The name of this decoration is composed of the first syllables of *Rocaille* and *Coquille* and hence signifies rock and shell. The shell remained over from Baroque times, but it was now more than ever simply a *motif* which might be treated in any artistic direction regardless of a close adherence to its original form. The rock form was similarly handled and Chippendale made of it extraordinary use in the French mirrors appearing in his book.

It is France alone which has so far been considered, and to France belongs the premiership in this style, though Italy is generally credited with its origin and Mr. Thomson has discovered some of its characteristics in Spain much earlier than they appeared in France. We do not yet know everything and some such points still remain to be traced. Through political misfortune Italy had lost its driving power, and from the time of Louis XIV the influence of France was supreme. Not realising perhaps that the outward glory of France was secured by the ruin of its people, Italy remained under its glamour, followed as nearly as circumstances permitted its social life in an attempted but poverty-oppressed gaiety and, in a measure to be taken up later, adopted its decorative styles. This now long distracted country was disposed of by foreign powers and divided as suited their policy, and, though after 1748 peace ruled for a season, the largest part of her territory was under the despotism of the Bourbons. Tuscany was well governed by Peter Leopold, and Venice remained a Republic till 1797—but her glory was rapidly departing.

Under such conditions Italian craftsmanship had lost its virility and verve; national traditions were partially neglected and work was less thorough; cheap materials were used, and the cheapness disguised by imitative or decorated surfaces; yet, notwithstanding all this, the contribution of Italy to eighteenth century furniture was a distinct gain.

Both in Italy and on the Peninsula, where also the Rococo influence naturally had its day, there was, however, an occasional tendency to excess. How degenerate the Rococo could sometimes become outside of France is shown by the Portuguese furniture in Plate 151 B and the Venetian chair in Plate 155 B. Is not the "inspiration" for the furniture of the Victoria-General Grant period now perfectly evident? It is to the eternal credit of France that its keen intellectuality and logical level-headedness sustained it through a style that might easily have run into utter lawlessness. At its height the contrary Classic spirit was already growing, and this tendency appealed to the discriminating taste and judgment of Madame de Pompadour and met her encouragement. Of this woman Voltaire said: "She was an artist in everything."

During the last years of the reign, when the King, now sunk in the deepest profligacy, was as well hated by his subjects as once he had been well beloved; and when the unconscionable du Barry occupied the position once held by Madame de Pompadour, decorative art was kept free from license and degradation by this counter-movement, to be described in the next chapter. Even this last mistress of the King, though lacking the refinement and taste of her predecessor, had a vital interest in art and continued its encouragement.

In England there was no Rococo movement properly to be so called. Its social life might be sufficiently worldly, but the Anglo-Saxon race has never been so *light-heartedly* frivolous as the Latin, and certainly was not so under its Hanoverian sovereigns.

Interior architecture there remained unaffected by the foreign influence and indeed grew still more classical, for the Adam Brothers began their work about the middle of the century and will be considered in the next chapter. Much Louis Quinze furniture crossed the Channel into English mansions, for French fashion was always powerful, but otherwise the Rococo found there but an echo—the "French" furniture of Thomas Chippendale and the occasional divagations of other designers. Yet Chippendale's chairs, commodes and mirrors in this manner are of the greatest importance. That remarkable man, with his love of the flowing line and carved ornament, took the Rococo and made it his own. In this phase his work was French and yet it remained triumphantly Thomas Chippendale.

THE ARCHITECTURAL BACKGROUND

France: As has already been intimated, the style of Louis XIV merged into that known by the name of his successor—for in the arts such transitions are gradual. Neither do styles wait upon the death of kings, and in the later days of *le Grand Monarque* there had been decided indications of the coming of the Rococo.

The excellent qualities of the *Régence* style are seen in the wall-treatment illustrated in Plate 37. The dignity and decorum of Louis XIV are retained in the main panelling, while it is accompanied by the readily recognised surmounting ornament of the Rococo, which also makes itself manifest in the cornice.

Illustrations of the architectural background of the

Rococo itself are given in Plates 38–44. Some of these
are redolent of ornament and others examples of the
beautiful restraint that could be shown by France even
in one of the most ornate of periods. As the details of
these backgrounds are there given in the accompanying
text it is unnecessary to repeat them here.

The *motifs* were endless, natural forms being
largely employed and often with fantasy as we may
realise when apes were among the decorations used
(Plate 42). Chinoiserie was particularly welcomed
and piquantly used.

Many of the pictorial decorations were not of high
artistic quality, but to these elaborate interiors such
artists as Watteau, Fragonard, Lancret and Boucher
often added panel inserts of the greatest charm (Plate
38 B), and it is to be said for this pictorial decoration
of the period that while it might sometimes be indis-
creet it was never vulgar. In an age of such freedom
other ornamental walls were naturally employed, particularly those covered with fabrics.

Italy: In circles where the example of France was
likely to be followed there was some considerable adoption of the Rococo background with only national differences (Plate 21). Elsewhere there were no great
changes. Fabric-covered walls were here also used.

Spain: Interior architecture remained largely as before, the Rococo influence mainly making itself felt in
movable furniture.

SIMPLIFIED BACKGROUNDS

Notwithstandinng the disparities of style in the
period of Louis XIV, exterior architecture had reached
under J. H. Mansart, the king's architect, a Classic
dignity which in *exterior* work was well preserved
under the following *régime*. We therefore have in the

27

reign of Louis Quinze the felt incongruity of a Classic
exterior with often a madly Romantic interior and furniture, and a wealth of beautiful but artistically frivolous accessories. The more deeply we look into the
past the more thoroughly we realise that it was not
so logical as enthusiasm sometimes leads innocence
to think.

It may not be good practice to argue from a bad
example, but where necessity knows no law it is human
to take such comfort as we may. If, therefore, the
modern conditions to which the writers have previously
referred preclude the elaborate panelling of walls,
surely a classically plain interior is not more incongruous with Louis XV furnishings than a Romantic interior in a Classic building. We are not left wholly to
this reasoning, however, for there were some plain-
wall backgrounds in this period. It was not the prevailing style, but they were sufficient in number to
justify us in using this method.

But if an entire house or apartment may not be
panelled in a fairly ornate phase of the period, it may
in some cases at least be possible to treat the drawing-
room or boudoir in a simplified manner. Preserving
the rectangular base and tall panels, decorators, by the
use of a very few characteristic curves at their tops,
frequently supply an entirely simple but perfectly correct rendering of the style, such as was doubtless seen
in the modest houses of this period.

Where panelling is entirely precluded, a perfectly
plain painted or papered wall could be used, its tone
being one of the soft, warm French greys, fawn, or an
ivory-white. Especially in a boudoir, a grey-blue or
soft rose or a greyed blue-green or pale sage green
might be employed.

A paper-panelled wall would be permissible, provided the divisions were strictly architectural and not irregular and floral. Two shades of soft grey, or pale grey and blue, or pale grey and rose would be excellent.

French colour-prints (or their reproductions, if good) in the correct frames of the period, afford admirable wall decorations.

Tapestries appropriate in spirit are a great addition to the plain-wall treatment.

In such interiors plain or simply bordered rugs in soft greys, fawns, or such tones as the above could be used, or finely patterned Orientals in similar shades to the Aubusson or Savonnerie carpets. These were colourful but refined—no strident hues nor harsh contrasts have place in this decoration.

THE FURNITURE OF THE ROCOCO PERIOD

In such a brief and necessarily inadequate review of epochs (each of which is a field for study) as can be given in the compass of a few chapters, it is plainly impossible to cover all phases or to illustrate more than a guiding selection of furniture: but in any case it has been felt that a broad view, sufficient to evolve principles and indicate the way, is better for the purpose in view than to obscure the subject with details, however interesting in themselves.

In illustration of the merging of the Baroque into the Rococo we have an excellent example in the two outside chairs of the three shown in one cut (Plate 152 B), the remaining, central chair being a more complete assimiliation of the later style but still heavier and stiffer in its lines than subsequent manifestations. The Baroque broken-curve persists in the legs of the pair of chairs, but lengthened and straightened on its way to the formation of the flowing double-curve or line of beauty evident in the Louis XV chairs appearing in Plate 160. A survival of the Baroque will also be seen in the sumptuous Venetian arm-chair (Plate 155 C).

The Portuguese chair (Plate 151 A) is at once noticeable by the broad swelling of the leg, its individual ornament, and the claw-and-ball feet—a distinct variety indeed in the Rococo chair! Not even so apparent in the cut as in the piece itself is the severe rake of the back and the lines of the uprights of the arms which parallel it.

The Italian early Rococo chairs in Plate 157 C are also of great interest and the Spanish chairs (Plate 158 B) show an excellent restraint which we could wish might always have been employed in the furniture of the country. Such variations, in form and detail, from the usual French types as these foreign chairs afford are indeed to be appreciated in the assembling of furniture. Forcibly brought home to us is the curvilinear basis of the Rococo style when we realise that in all these chairs there is hardly a straight line.

A typical example of the French sofa appears in the modern interior illustrated in Plate 114, and with this we may compare the unusual Venetian specimen shown in Plate 155 A. The boldly swelling front of the latter, the peculiar feet and the ornament of the legs at once proclaim its interesting differences. It will be noted that this and the sumptuous chair adjoining it below are covered with the same fabric.

The textiles of the period were of great beauty (see "Decorative Textiles" by George Leland Hunter). Tapestry and the heavy brocades were appropriately employed upon seating furniture of the natural woods, while enamelled and gilt pieces were covered with the materials of lighter weight. The tones of the painting or enamelling of the framework were usually soft greys, fawns or deep ivory, often in two shades.

PLATE 151

A. Rococo Carved Walnut
Arm Chair with Claw-and-
ball Feet. Louis XV and
Chippendale Affinities

B. Portuguese Extreme Rococo Showing to what
Excess the Style Could Run Outside of France

PORTUGUESE ROCOCO FURNITURE
By Courtesy of Mr. Nicholas Martin

PLATE 152

A. SPANISH TRANSITION BAROQUE-
ROCOCO CHEST OF DRAWERS
Red Lacquer and Gilt. Mid Eighteenth
Century. Chippendale Affinity
By Courtesy of C. M. Traver Co.

B. FRENCH REGENCE CHAIRS
Collection Lelouz
By Courtesy of L. Alavoine & Co.

C. FRENCH ROCOCO CONSOLE IN WROUGHT IRON
WITH BRASS MOUNTS
Collection Kraemer
By Courtesy L. Alavoine & Co.

PLATE 153

A. LOUIS XV CABINET IN CHINESE TASTE, BLACK AND GOLD
LACQUER WITH BRASS MOUNTS
Collection Kraemer
By Courtesy of L. Alavoine & Co.

Photograph by Alinari
B. LOUIS XV MARQUETERIE COMMODE WITH BRONZE
ORNAMENTS
Musée du Louvre
By Courtesy of Radillo-Pelitti Co.

PLATE 154

A. CHIPPENDALE FRENCH MIRROR
GILT

B. CHIPPENDALE FRENCH CONSOLE CABINET WITH
ROCOCO *MOTIFS*

Both from the Collection of the Late Richard A. Canfield, Esq.

The Rococo style could not be better illustrated than by the console in wrought iron with brass mounts (Plate 152 C) and the cabinet and commode (Plate 153 A and B). In view of the now renewed commerce between France and China it was but natural that the always fascinating Chinese influence should be marked in this age, and it is exemplified in the cabinet in black and gold lacquer. The chased metal mounts of such furniture formed one of the most beautiful mobiliary developments in France.

Let us place with these the Venetian console table (Plate 155 D) and the English console cabinet veritably by Thomas Chippendale, owned by the late Mr. Canfield (Plate 154 B). In the latter the constructive material is the mahogany so beloved of that master and so adapted to the marvellous carving that was his decorative *metier*. We may consider the interest of the variety shown by such pieces as this and the above, all so illustrative of *le style Rocaille* yet so different in the means and material chosen for its embodiment. It is also to be noted that in this work of Chippendale, same as England, for the first time, has something to show comparable to the fine furniture of France.

In actual practice it will be found that this strictly Rococo furniture is not the only furniture of Chippendale's which will accompany Louis XV pieces. His lighter, more elegant and ornamental chairs and tables with their cabriole legs and handsome carving are well adapted to such association, and some of his upholstered chairs were quite in the vein of the French bergères.

In the Venetian console table the manner in which the semi-naturalistic leaves and stems are disposed to form the Rococo lower edge of the table is particularly arresting. This console is painted in golden yellow, banded in green with multicolour, and with touches of rose in the flowers, thus making an altogether engaging piece. Even the rather halting curves of the legs and their proportions add a "difference" and quaintness far from unpleasing. A carved and gilt Spanish console table is also shown (Plate 158 B). Consoles were usually gilded in order that they might properly accompany the frames of the mirrors above them. One of the madly Rococo but marvellously designed mirrors of Chippendale is seen in Plate 154 A.

There are touches of both the pathetic and courageous in the Italian furniture of this period. If penury often forbade the use of expensive woods, the cheaper ones employed were rendered cheerfully gay by painting and decoration. This treatment, though not of great moment in the naturalistic design commonly used, was nevertheless of much charm and elegant though homelike feeling. Economy in labour may also have been responsible for hasty workmanship; for certain it is that carving did not usually display the impeccable quality of the furniture of France, and the painting grounds were often ill-prepared, so that some pieces have not withstood the test of time. Examples of this Italian decorated furniture appear in the set of three pieces (Plate 156) and the Venetian console table already referred to (Plate 155 D).

In international furnishing the Italian pieces shown on Plate 157 and the Spanish furniture on Plate 158 have particular interest. They have affinities both with the usual Rococo forms and with the English vein of Chippendale and even of Queen Anne. It will be seen that they might harmoniously be employed with furniture of either style.

The little cupboard (Plate 158 C) is an engaging and almost amusing mixture of *metier*—decidedly Classic upon its front, but as decidedly buttressed at the sides by the Rococo.

PLATE 155

A. Venetian Upholstered Sofa of Unusual Form
Louis XV Affinities
By Courtesy of the Misses Hewitt

B. Carved and Gilded Walnut
Chair. Degenerate Rococo
Courtesy American Art
Galleries

C. Carved and Painted Walnut
Chair. Transition Baroque
to Rococo
Courtesy The Misses Hewitt

D. Golden Yellow Console with Green and Polychrome
By Courtesy of Mrs. M. Orme Wilson

VENETIAN ROCOCO FURNITURE

PLATE 156

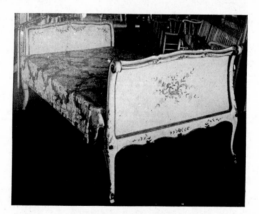

AN ITALIAN ROCOCO PAINTED SET
Cream Ground, Blue Lines and Multicolour Floral Decoration.   Louis XV Affinities
By Courtesy Cooper Institute

PLATE 157

A. Walnut Chair-back Settee, Baroque and Incipient Rococo Influences
Louis XV and Queen Anne Affinities

B. Rococo Walnut-veneer Console Cabinet with Embossed Brass
Mounts. Louis XV Affinities
By Courtesy Cooper Institute

C. Early Rococo Walnut Arm Chairs
Régence and Chippendale Affinities
Cooper Institute

D. Walnut Chair,
Louis XV, Queen
Anne and Chippen-
dale Affinities
George Howe, Esq.

ITALIAN ROCOCO FURNITURE

PLATE 158

A. Walnut Bureau Bookcase
By Courtesy of Mr. Karl Freund

B. Painted and Parcel Gilt Arm Chairs and Gilt Console. Louis XV Affinities
By Courtesy of C. M. Traver Co.

C. Painted and Parcel Gilt Cupboard
By Courtesy of C. M. Traver Co.

SPANISH ROCOCO FURNITURE

The carpets employed in this period were the Aubussons and Savonneries. These and the delightful tapestries then made are described and pictured in Mr. Hunter's ''Decorative Textiles.''

The tapestries were usually employed in the stately rooms, either hung upon the panelling or forming the panel inserts. Where plaster walls occurred they were either hung upon the wall or inset in a plaster decoration. In the Murat Mansion a tapestry is suspended in an *arched* panel, a rectangular frame below the arch enclosing the tapestry. Beneath it is a long console table.

The accessories of the period were numerous and elaborate—side lights, candlesticks, clocks, vases and mantel-ornaments, caskets, attractive boxes and objects of art of all descriptions.

THE PRACTICAL EMPLOYMENT OF ROCOCO FURNITURE

If furniture of this period is to be used, an excellent degree of variety will be secured by supplementing French pieces by those of other nations under the same influence. In a preceding section it was noted that in *general* the very distinct spirit and characteristics of Rococo furniture unfit it for association with that of other periods. In a distinctly French interior there is some reason for such a combination, and this and a method of procedure which secures sufficient unity will be discussed in the next chapter. For other interiors a superior alternative will there also be given.

By the eclectic system of furnishing—a choosing from here, there and everywhere—Louis Quinze furniture is constantly used with all sorts of other mobiliary forms, and sometimes with very unfortunate results. The writers have seen an illustration of an otherwise admirable and very dignified room in the style of the

Italian Renaissance where in the immediate foreground is *one Louis XV chair,* its framework light in hue (so that it is probably either painted or gilded) and covered with a light figured fabric, probably damask. It falls out woefully with the rest of the interior, and the want of discrimination shown in its introduction is decidedly to be deprecated.

Other instances are less disastrous, but the employment of a mixture of styles that have no real homogeneity gives such an interior the aspect of a museum. This may be unobjectionable in a studio or in the private palace, but elsewhere we may do better.

That good judgment, however, may surmount general difficulties is shown in the room so excellently arranged by Mr. Platt (Plate 56). The effect is stamped as Italian by the tapestry and bust which at once meet the eye. The cabinet and the chair in the right foreground are also Italian and of an earlier period than that of the furniture on the left, which is Louis Quinze. It is, however, a restrained and chastened form of the period. It is slender, but so is the Italian chair, and though the latter is generally rectangular the long sweeping scroll of the arm closely echoes the general lines of the French pieces. Both are also alike in hue. Here, then, we have a sufficient degree of unity with a pleasant variety, and examples such as this may be of the greatest value to salesmen advising their customers as to purchases as well as to professional decorators and buyers of their own furniture.

THE ROCOCO STYLE AND PRESENT-DAY USE

Admiration or dislike of this style is perhaps more than with any other a matter of temperament and personal character. In reaching a decision we should not fail to discriminate—one may grow very impatient of such wall decoration as that at Hôtel de Matignon and appreciate to as great a degree the beautiful reserve of that of Hôtel Delisle: one may not greatly care for apes, or too florid mantels with clocks and ornaments more florid still, and may yet very much like such pieces of furniture as the Chinese commode or the beautiful settees and chairs.

It is undoubtedly in many phases a feminine and frivolous style and yet it contains elements that, with due selection, present an interior of beauty, sufficient dignity and permanent value.

Whether or no the decoration and furniture of this age entirely meet one's own personal preference—and the writers make no bones in saying that they do not meet theirs as do those of the succeeding period—a catholic spirit appreciative of beauty cannot fail to be filled with admiration for the invention, versatility, grace, lightness and cleverness of this amazing movement and the quality of its craftsmanship.

For the house largely devoted to the life of fashion it is therefore particularly well adapted, and for a woman's apartment its chaster forms will create a home of comfort, charm and great refinement (a modern interior in this style is illustrated in Plates 55 and 114). But what would be thought of a bachelor who decorated and furnished his rooms *a la Rocaille!*

The capabilities of the period were among the first to be appreciated by decorators and the allied trades, and, as *usually treated,* it naturally therefore no longer possesses the element of novelty desired by some clients. A broader rendering of this style, combining Italian, Spanish and French-Chippendale elements with the French, opens out a new and delightful field for their endeavours.

CHAPTER IV

THE NEO-CLASSIC

THE CLASSIC REVIVAL. THE FRENCH SPIRIT. THE ARCHI-
TECTURAL BACKGROUND. THE FURNITURE OF THE PERIOD.
THE ASSEMBLING OF NEO-CLASSIC FURNITURE. BACK-
GROUNDS AND FURNITURE. THE DIRECTORY, CONSULATE
AND EMPIRE.

THE CLASSIC REVIVAL

THE cause of the Classic Revival has been much discussed but after all is extremely simple. The Romantic spirit, as expressed in the Baroque and Rococo movements, had done its utmost and could no further go without lapsing into degeneracy. As we have seen, some phases of it had already done so. After practically two centuries of this spirit all Europe was quite ready for something new, and as Classicism was now everywhere "in the air" it was seized upon as a restful and welcome relief from past irregularities, however beautiful in themselves.

There were several causes for the existing renewed interest in the Classic not necessary for our purpose to go into here; but one of them may briefly be mentioned because of its special bearing upon the decoration and furnishing we are to consider. Architects and others interested in the arts (and proportionately there were probably a greater number of titled and private gentlemen concerned in such matters then than now) had discovered that the phase of Classicism that entered into Renaissance culture—commonly called Palladianism—was *only* a phase and by no means embraced the whole art of Greece and Rome. Renewed

426

investigation at first-hand had thereupon taken place, stimulated by the discoveries at Herculaneum and Pompeii.

The movement was practically simultaneous in England and France and both were equally absorbed. Doubtless also each reacted upon the other, for certain forms of Adam and Louis Seize furniture are very close. The influence of French fashion had long been great in England, and rather strangely, considering the wars between them, there seems to have been in France a very considerable leaning toward English ways and thought which, later, still developed. Mr. Salaman says in his "French Colour Prints": "In those years just before the Revolution Paris fell head and ears in love with London, and English fashions and English customs were all the rage."

The adoption of the style in Italy was synchronous with the development in France and England. Spain, also, for the good of her artistic soul, received the same influence.

In England the outstanding figure was Robert Adam, the greatest of the Adelphi, and his work was closely followed by others. This can best be treated under the section on Architectural Backgrounds.

THE FRENCH SPIRIT

As no decoration or furniture can be understood without a right understanding of the circumstances that gave them rise, it is necessary to say a few words regarding the supposed influence of Marie Antoinette upon the ideals of France and upon its art.

Owing to the sadness of her death, her character has been idealised, and the "renovation" of the decoration of the country ascribed by popular opinion largely to her and the cleanliness of the lives of both herself and the king. Their influence was upon the side of Classicism, and it is ungracious to have to say that she was both a supremely foolish and very obstinate woman. Her extravagances, her indiscretions, her intrigues, and the affair of the Diamond Necklace are, however, in history for everyone to read. As to her influence upon French social life the words of her leading lady-in-waiting, Madame Campan, loyal to her through all her troubles, may be given: "The queen chose as her favourite the amiable, naïve duchesse de Polignac, who lived quite openly with M. de Vandreuil; the comtesse Diane, her sister, was known to have several lovers—so little did people care for morality! The public noticed that, although the king's and queen's married life was absolutely blameless, they were not overburdened with scruples, and so advantage was taken of that fact."

As to her influence upon art the same authority tells us that Marie Antoinette "cared nothing for literature or pictures." We have already seen that some years before her day the Classic feeling was espoused by Madame de Pompadour; it is a matter of history that when Madame du Barry fitted up her palatial retreat at Louveciennes, considered by some to be one of the most perfect expressions of the Style Louis Seize, the work was practically complete before Marie Antoinette ever saw France. We might as well ascribe the "cleaning up" of decoration to these two as to the queen. To be honest with ourselves we have to admit that it was the Pompadour whose taste was certain, and that Marie Antoinette's interest in decoration was marked by caprice and indecision. The acknowledgment of these truths is in no way inconsistent with our paying her all honour for the *continuance* of the interest of the crown in the arts and for her personal firmness and dignity during her last days.

The whole point, and a very necessary one to understand, is that the social life and the spirit of the age in France was *not* changed; that the Classic movement was *not* brought about by a queen who found it in full force upon her arrival, but that it was primarily an artistic movement *initiated by architects and, decorators,* and then *accepted* by fashion as a relief from a previous mode of which it had grown weary. We shall see the practical bearing of this.

Notwithstanding the change from the style of Louis XV to that of his successor, both decoration and furniture remained as characteristically "French" as before—it would be impossible to ascribe them to another nation. The difference was one of contour and form of ornament—that was indeed much but that was all! Let us apply the remaining tests mentioned in the second chapter of this part and see. In size and weight they were practically the same: the colours employed were rather more subtle and quiet, but there is no incongruity: the use of mohagony instead of marqueterie for cabinet work increased and it was given a brighter finish, but such a difference is small in its whole effect where elegance had always, and still, prevailed. The character of the fabrics employed remained the same. Both styles are slender, elegant, light-hearted and charming.

How is it *possible* that with a change from a madly Romantic to a Classic style there should be no other difference than this of form; that the *spirit* remained the same! ·

Precisely because of the points that have been discussed. The social life and trend of the age remained unchanged, and this inward and essential unity was sure to make itself felt through any variation in the mode of expression. We observe in all ages the adaptability of artists to alteration of manner, and the versatile Frenchmen seem to have found little difficulty in accommodating themselves to the new *metier*. Furthermore, we must always remember that this was an *art* movement primarily brought about by the architects and decorators themselves, and so involving no hardship in its following. Some showed themselves more eager, or more adaptable, than others; as would naturally be the case. The mode once being taken up by fashion, however, it was necessary for all to pursue it to a large extent or lose prestige.

The practical result of all this is that we feel no such vital difference between these two styles as we do between that of Louis XV and his predecessor, and in French interiors the two styles of decoration are continually employed in the same house and the two styles of furniture in the same room. The most advisable combination will be considered later.

THE ARCHITECTURAL BACKGROUND

England: It seems to the writers, at least, that the interior architecture of Robert and James Adam was decidedly more fecund and able than that of the architects of Louis Seize. The French backgrounds were dignified or charming, according to their use, generally restful, and always beautiful; yet were withal rather conventional. The Adam Brothers' work was perfectly individual and of great variety of expression. The difference seems to be that while the Adelphi *used* antiquity, the French largely *copied* it! During the Empire that copying grew to a positive obsession.

Our best architects, who *know* the interior work of the Brothers Adam are keenly appreciative of its

PLATE 159

ADAM DRAWING ROOM WITH INSET WEDGWOOD PLAQUES IN WALLS
Phyfe, Sheraton, Adam and Chippendale Furniture
By Courtesy of Wilson Eyre, Esq.

PLATE 160

SALON, HÔTEL D'ORSAY, PARIS. STYLE LOUIS XVI
Furniture to the Left, Louis XV; Chair to Extreme Right, Louis XVI
From "Les Vieux Hôtels de Paris," F. Contet
Courtesy of William Helburn, Inc.

qualities, but some writers on decoration do not realise its bigness. A closer study of the body of their achievement may bring enlightenment.

Saturated with the Classic spirit as they were, their originality was not dwarfed but stimulated. Mr. Wilson Eyre says that "the man who is most original is the man who best knows what other people have done," and if this is not invariably true it is the defect of originality rather than the fault of knowledge. Certain it is that Robert and James Adam are shining examples of the proper use of acquired information.

Robert Adam and Sir William Chambers were the king's architects. Robert was a member of Parliament, occupied an high social position, and at his burial a duke and five other gentlemen of title were his pall-bearers. His commissions were therefore important ones, comprising London mansions, large country-houses and his own enterprise at Adelphi Terrace. Such interior architecture, particularly when of classic character, is naturally imposing and of the greatest dignity, and, as is usual in this faulty world, has been faulted because it is not something else than he appropriately intended it to be.

That the style is, however, susceptible of a homelike feeling in beautiful but less palatial employment is shown by the excellent rendition of it in the modern room illustrated (Plate 159).

Adam's work (his brothers were excellent men but the originality was Robert's) was of too great variety to illustrate in all its phases. Perhaps his most individual mode and the one most closely connected with his name is the one generally exemplified in Plate 10.

Contrast with this the sumptuous back drawing-room at Lansdowne House, also his. Against the walls of old gold silk damask rise ornate pilasters of light yellow tone upon which arabesques are painted in colour. The capitals are gilded. The ceiling is modelled and painted and of arabesques containing paintings in colour. The painted furniture is of green upon which amorini appear in light tones.*

The writers admit as a fault in the work of the Adam Brothers the smallness of scale sometimes shown in details. The eighteenth century was not an age of downright assertiveness, but one of detailed refinement, and no man may rise altogether superior to his environment.

It was the ambition of Robert Adam, for completeness' sake, to design not only the room but all that it contained—an impossible task for so busy a man. It seems to the writers that Providence allowed him to proceed far enough to give the world many beautiful examples of furniture and then stepped in to prevent his going too far. Ideal as such a plan seems upon the surface to be, it is likely that the harmony of such interiors would have savoured of sameness. Certainly the mingling of other forms in these rooms as they now exist is in some instances very pleasing.

France: Though one may personally prefer a greater restraint than was evident in many of the interiors of Louis XV there is no blinking the fact that the succeeding reign shows a decline of spontaneity, verve and originality. It will not do to ascribe this to the curbing influence of Classicism, for the Adams found it a well of inspiration, as did the great architects of the Renaissance before them. It was probably due partly to the inclination for copying, previously referred to, and the copying of only certain phases at that, and to some decline in the originality of the architects them-

---

* "Robert Adam and His Brothers," by John Swarbrick.

selves. A reference to Plate 160 shows that they sometimes even did not go back to antiquity direct, but
travelled the footprints of their predecessors; for this
interior seems simply a return to the style of Louis
XIV done in the mode of Louis Seize. A number of
other interiors are shown in Plates 46–49. That of the
boudoir at Hôtel de La Fayette (Plate 46) shows no
particular individuality but is very charming. It will
be interesting to compare it with the similar room of
the style of Louis XV shown in Plate 39 B.

Italy: In the earlier part of the eighteenth century
the backgrounds had remained of the earlier Renaissance character with Baroque developments, or else in
some cases had followed the Rococo style with national
differences. The latter movement in France had also
been influential in introducing smaller, more intimate
rooms, such as drawing-rooms and boudoirs, in addition to the large salons of former times.

But, as Mr. George Moore says, "Italy never forgot
her antiquity, nor could she forget it," and as soon as
the revival of Classicism began she hastened to resume
any portion of her heritage which had been foregone
(Plate 22 B). Italy was poor, but she refused to neglect
decoration, and ornate walls were still sumptuous with
frescoes, mosaic or inlay. Fabric-covered walls also
remained in vogue, and one of these, at Villa Curonia,
is illustrated. Painted and parcel gilt panelling was
used, and mirrors were common. Plain walls were
enriched by tapestries, plaques, wood-carvings and
other movable decorations. Landscape and classical
wall-papers now also came into fashion.

Spain: The flame of inspiration in Spain had died
low and that country had little new to show at this
period beyond its own national modifications of the

28

furniture of other countries. Its walls remained largely as in previous epochs except that the use of ornamental leather was unfortunately discontinued.

THE FURNITURE OF THE PERIOD

Searching the language for the one descriptive word best applying to the furniture of the eighteenth century it would probably be found in *delightful*. We all know how rhythmic in line and homelike in feeling was the furniture of Queen Anne, we have seen how graceful and how elegant was that of Louis Quinze, and how colourful and decorative that of Italy: we shall now have the pleasure of considering what for adaptability to most present-day uses, for sheer beauty and charm, for both comfort and elegance, for richer or for poorer, is at least in the opinion of the writers, the loveliest furniture the world has ever seen. It was not the biggest in design, nor the noblest, but these qualities are not what most of us are seeking for our *homes* to-day: if it was not these it was the most *delightful*.

More than that of any other epoch, perhaps as much as all the others together, has it been employed in modern homes—and with a narrowness amounting to sameness and to tameness. More's the pity! for its capabilities in combination are almost infinite! Think of the materials alone—not only the ubiquitous dark mahogany, but satinwood, plain, decorated or brass-mounted, inlay, lacquer, light mahogany, gilding, the beautiful tones of Louis Seize painted pieces, and the decorative possibilities of those of Italy and Spain.

England will again be taken as the key for comparison because of the greater familiarity of its furniture to most readers. For the same reason it has been thought advisable to give as many illustrations of the furniture of Continental Europe as limits permitted, rather than occupy space with pieces better known. Those who wish to make close comparisons can do so by referring to Eberlein and McClure's "Practical Book of Period Furniture" for the British and American forms.

It is first necessary to give place to Thomas Chippendale, both because of his ability and position and because though he lived and worked during the Neo-Classic movement he was not for the most part of it. It seems to be the fashion to disparage Chippendale, and individual critics each take their fling at one or another phase of his work. It is amusing to note that each has his own dislike to a particular phase while giving a more or less grudging admiration to the rest —and that each of his characteristic modes is successively pitched upon and praised. Whereby we learn two things—that such criticisms are merely the expression of personal preferences owing to temperament, and that Chippendale was a more myriad-minded man than his critics. Suffice it to say that if he was not usually Classical, as was Adam, or exquisite, as was Sheraton, he was the most masculine and various of all eighteenth century English designers. His large library bookcases *were* severely classical, and most of his case pieces—bureau bookcases, wardrobes and desks—were, even when ornamented, sufficiently so to accompany contemporary furniture, for their constructional lines were straight. This may also be said of his more regular Chinese pieces; for exotic though their inspiration was, the Oriental has always played a large part in Western furnishing. The most bizarre renderings are best gathered in a room carried out in this manner, thus affording an interesting variation from others of more orthodox character. His Rococo pieces have already been provided for as accompanying cor-

responding Continental forms. His "Gothick" vein
was not largely worked and few reproductions are
made. The furniture most widely recognised as "Chippendale"—the chairs with splats containing C and
other curves and with cabriole legs and claw-and-ball
feet and other pieces with these members go excellently
well with Queen Anne forms and also accompany many
of the pieces of his contemporaries much better than
might be expected from their differences (Plate 167).
The common heritage of English feeling probably ac-
counts for this.

As the head and front of the Classic movement in
England we must give to Robert Adam first place in
furniture as in architecture. He was never a con-
structor of furniture, but, with an artistic conscience
worthy of all praise, designed, as has been mentioned,
many pieces in order that his interiors might be congruous throughout. In this he was preceded by
Chambers and also by Kent, who did some good things
but whose work was usually marred by clumsiness. Not
only was Adam's furniture of great beauty (see "The
Practical Book of Period Furniture" by Eberlein and
McClure), but his influence was strong with both Hepplewhite and Sheraton. Chippendale was intimately
associated with Adam and carried out his most important designs, notably at Harewood House, Nostel
Priory and for David Garrick. Under ordinary circumstances we might therefore have expected him to
become the most Classic of the three, but he maintained
his own individuality and followed his personal tastes,
so that we never find him supplying Neo-Classic furniture direct to his own patrons. Hepplewhite also was
original in retaining many curvilinear forms, particularly in his chair backs, though most of his constructive
lines were rectilinear. We know none too much of
Sheraton, but that strange soul—Baptist preacher,

PLATE 161

Photograph by Alinari

LOUIS XVI COMMODE WITH BRONZE ORNAMENTS
BY MARTIN CARLIN
Also note Clock and Candlesticks of the period
Musée National du Louvre
By Courtesy of Radillo-Pelitti Co.

PLATE 162

A. LOUIS SEIZE SETTEE AND CHAIRS, IN OLD NEEDLE WORK

In the possession of Messrs. Speelman Bros., London

B. CHAIRS DESIGNED BY ROBERT ADAM FOR HAREWOOD HOUSE

Tapestry of Light Field Surrounded by a Rich Rose du Barry Ground

From "Robert Adam and His Brothers"

By Courtesy of B. T. Batsford, Ltd., London

PLATE 163

A. Venetian Shield-back
Chair
American Art Galleries

B. Late Eighteenth Century, painted. Sheraton
Affinity
Cooper Institute

C. Late Eighteenth
Century, painted.
Louis XVI Affinity

D. Painted Venetian Chair
Louis XVI Affinity
By Courtesy The Misses
Hewitt

E. Walnut Square-back Chairs
Louis XVI Affinity
By Courtesy The Misses Owen

F. Walnut and Parcel Gilt
Chair
Louis XVI Affinity
By Courtesy George Howe, Esq.

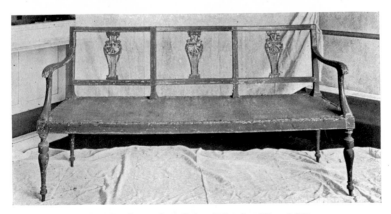

G. Italian Square-back Settee, Painted and Parcel Gilt
By Courtesy of Cooper Institute

ITALIAN NEO CLASSIC CHAIRS AND SETTEE

PLATE 164

ITALIAN NEO CLASSIC WALL FURNITURE

A. Early Neo Classic Venetian Painted Armoire (Baroque
Feet) Eighteenth Century, Polychrome and Parcel Gilt
By Courtesy of John Wanamaker

B. Console and Console Table of Veneered and Inlaid Woods
Late Eighteenth Century, Both of Louis XVI Affinity
By Courtesy of Cooper Institute

C. Falling-front Secretary of Mahogany and Rosewood
Multicolour Inlay, Sheraton Affinity
By Courtesy of George Howe, Esq.

tractarian, drawing master, designer and publisher, offensively carping in his comments on contemporaries —must have been filled with a love of beauty for its own sake, for nowhere among them all do we find work quite so *exquisite* as his. Other, lesser, English designers should find mention here, but space is limited.

Upon seeing the Venetian shield back chair (Plate 163 A) among the illustrations to this chapter upon the Neo-Classic movement some readers will probably be surprised, for it is at once recognisable as of the style of Louis XV.* This is quite true, but these curves were so subtle, so free from ornament, that they were "carried over" as being appropriate, and thus find their place among the rectilinear forms of the Classic Revival. We must not forget that the curule chairs of ancient Rome were almost entirely curvilinear. It is also to be remembered that designers do not necessarily pass away upon the death of movements: some of the French *ébénistes*, therefore, while abandoning certain characteristics of the Rococo retained other curvilinear features in their work during the succeeding reign. Especially do we see these characteristics in some of the fine cabinet pieces.

Just why so great a slenderness was adopted as the expression of the Neo-Classic in furniture has not to the writers' knowledge been touched upon. Probably it was because the heavier phase of Classicism had already been exploited by the Palladian movement and because (as opposed to the "spaciousness" of the times of Elizabeth) elegance rather than size was the characteristic note of the eighteenth century and its life: however this may be, this slenderness was universal to England and France. The instinct shown in adopting

---

* This beautiful chair is painted yellow heightened with gold, and with flower sprays in colour. Its covering is yellow silk damask.

it for these forms was doubtless a right one, for we feel a certain "stodginess" in the sometimes heavier pieces of Italy and Spain.

Within the limits of slenderness we nevertheless find a considerable variation. Some of the side chairs and tables seem extremely fragile (even Chippendale designed spider-leg tables); some of Hepplewhite's chair backs are light while their legs are substantial; but the Louis Seize arm-chairs strike precisely the right degree—for beauty and for comfort they are among the finest seating-furniture ever designed (Plate 162 A and to the right in Plate 160).

Owing probably to the faulty practice of American decorators twenty-five or thirty years ago the impression is abroad that the furniture of Louis Quinze and Seize is "gilt and gaudy"; whereas, on the contrary, it and its covering were of the highest refinement. Gilding was sometimes employed upon the framework, but the natural woods or exquisite tones of ivory or grey mostly prevailed, and the needlework or fabrics were of the greatest beauty.

It is beyond question that for high quality of design and ornament, decorative value and consummate craftsmanship the best furniture of France stands above that of any other nation. No one knew this better than the designers of those other nations themselves, and upon occasion they did not hesitate to avail themselves of its inspiration. They did not by any means always do so, however, and British craftsmen particularly succeeded in enduing their work with a homelike quality which will not cease to be prized. Each of the great furniture-producing nations contributed its national characteristics and it remains for us to appreciate this and where possible add such engaging pieces to our treasures and aid others in so doing.

PLATE 165

A VENETIAN NEO CLASSIC WALNUT TABLE
By Courtesy of American Art Galleries

B. SPANISH NEO CLASSIC PAINTED SLANT–TOP DESK
Late Eighteenth Century
By Courtesy of Montillor Brothers

PLATE 166

A. Spanish Six-legged Bedstead of Mahogany with Polychrome
Headboard and Parcel Gilding. Sheraton Affinity

B. Sheraton Affinity   C. Louis XVI Affinity   D. Hepplewhite Affinity

SPANISH NEO CLASSIC BEDSTEAD AND CHAIRS
By Courtesy of C. M. Traver Co.

PLATE 167

A COMBINATION OF NEO CLASSIC AND CHIPPENDALE FURNITURE
Courtesy of William Lawrence Bottomley, Architect

PLATE 168

THE CLASSIC REVIVAL SALON OF THOMAS JEFFERSON AT MONTICELLO, VIRGINIA
DESIGNED BY HIMSELF, WITH LOUIS SEIZE FURNITURE
By Courtesy of the Hon. Jefferson M. Levy

The furniture of Southern Europe, as in the preceding two epochs, followed to a large degree the more Northern forms but with the usual variations so interesting in International furnishing.

THE ASSEMBLING OF NEO-CLASSIC FURNITURE

As the principles of selection have been dealt with in previous chapters few remarks are necessary regarding the assembling of furniture of this epoch. With ordinary care in choice and placing most of the pieces would accompany each other, and the different treatments, plain and decorative, would add a charming variety if too many phases were not employed in the one room. Here as elsewhere confusion should be avoided.

In Plate 161 is illustrated a particularly fine console cabinet with mounts, by Carlin, in the Louvre. In the formal elegance of such furniture France stood alone and the only pieces of other nationality that would properly accompany it would be the finest furniture designed by Adam, such as the chairs shown in Plate 162 B. Such museum pieces are practically unprocurable and their value so great that few of us need be greatly concerned as to what to place with them. Specimens approaching this in merit should be used as centres of interest. The very beautiful decorated satinwood pieces of Hepplewhite and Sheraton are, with all their elegance, more intimate and homelike, and therefore more adaptable to association. Of the same general degree of elegance as this type are the Spanish and Italian cabinet pieces illustrated in Plates 164 and 165 and what a degree of variety and relief would be given the usual British or American interior by the employment of a few such different mobiliary forms. The Venetian table (Plate 165 A) is likewise very interesting. It should be noted, too, that we have in these specimens solid walnut, painted, and inlaid examples.

Seating furniture is so characteristic of style that a variety is shown. The settee in Plate 162 A, that in the New York apartment (Plate 124) and that in the La Fayette boudoir (Plate 46) afford three distinct French styles of this period. In Plate 163 is given an Italian example which with handsome covering would be a very attractive piece of furniture. A number of Italian and Spanish chairs appear in Plates 163 and 166. These are of varying degrees of elegance and (as will be seen by the legends) of different affinities.

The Spanish six-legged bedstead (Plate 166) is both interesting and charming.

As is the case with all the furniture illustrated in these chapters (except those in modern rooms) these are original pieces. More good reproductions are made of the forms of this period than of the earlier ones, and the dealer, decorator and householder will, with care in selection, be able to secure many excellent things. The woman's room shown in Plate 170 shows a successful combination of Neo-Classic furniture with a simplified panelled background.

BACKGROUNDS AND FURNITURE

In addition to the Adam room containing a variety of furniture, two particularly interesting interiors are given to show the close correspondence in spirit existing between the various nationalities. One of these is an American salon, that of Thomas Jefferson at Monticello, Virginia, designed by himself in the style of the Classic Revival. The furniture is that of Louis Seize, and what an admirable interior it is! (Plate 168.) The other is modern, by American architects, and in this the background is Louis Seize while the furniture

PLATE 169

LOUIS SEIZE FRENCH PANELLING WITH BRITISH AND AMERICAN FURNITURE

Hoppin and Koen, Architects

Hepplewhite Bedstead. Phyfe Table, Chippendale Ladder-back Chair at Window, Queen Anne Chest of Drawers
Courtesy of "Good Furniture Magazine"

PLATE 170

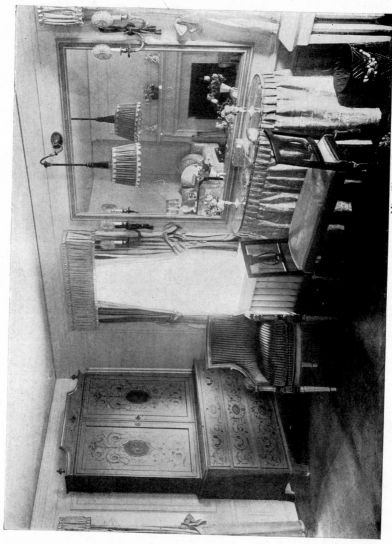

EIGHTEENTH CENTURY ITALIAN AND FRENCH FURNITURE

Miss Gheen, Decorator, Chicago and New York

The Painted Cupboard is a Modern Reproduction, Vari-coloured Decorations on a Cream Ground; the Dressing-table Seat, of Walnut, is an Italian Antique; the Chair Directoire is of various British and American styles (Plate 169).

In a preceding section it was mentioned that historic houses would naturally contain furniture of several successive periods. We continually see this in British homes, and have grown so used to the real incongruity sometimes resulting therefrom that it is less noticeable, or more forgivable, to us than would be such differences in the residences of foreign countries. It is undeniable that the national spirit pervading the furniture of any country does make for a certain unity. Notwithstanding differences of influence we *may* use William and Mary, Queen Anne, Chippendale and Neo-Classic furniture in one house, but we *must* be careful how we assemble these in the different rooms. Most certainly we should not put Queen Anne and Sheraton or Adam in close environment. Judgment should be used even in combining William and Mary and Queen Anne pieces. These two with some phases of Chippendale form one group, and other phases of Chippendale with Adam, Hepplewhite and Sheraton form another. That straight-line pieces of William and Mary will accompany even Sheraton is shown in Plate 79 B. As has been pointed out there are foreign pieces corresponding with each group that may be used therewith for the securing of interest.

A like procedure should be followed with French interiors. In the houses of that country we occasionally find the background of one period accompanied by furniture of another period or of two or more mingled together. It would be preferable that each interior be accompanied by its appropriate furniture, though, as has been said, the *restrained* forms of Louis XV go better with the succeeding style than might be expected. If mingling must be done in the same house the way to do it is shown by three rooms of the Murat Mansion as follows:

Drawing-room: Louis Seize panelled walls, Louis Quinze furniture.

Reception-room: Louis Seize fabric-covered walls, Directoire furniture.

Bedroom: Louis Seize panelled walls, Louis Seize furniture.

This is certainly better than the inconsiderate jumbling of anything and everything from all over Europe and from the fifteenth century to the nineteenth, seemingly the vogue in many new palatial American houses. Notwithstanding occasional divagations, Laurence Sterne was right—"They order this matter better in France."

THE DIRECTORY, CONSULATE AND EMPIRE

The period covered by these governments of France is a portion of the Neo-Classic epoch, but the manifestations of the Empire style were so different from those of the reign of Louis XVI that for the avoidance of confusion they have been separated here. The Directory and the Consulate of Napoleon produced styles that were uncertain and transitional.

Anarchy in France really began in 1789. In January, 1793, King Louis XVI was beheaded and the Terror followed. In October of the same year Marie Antoinette was sentenced to death. The Directory was established in 1795 and fell in 1799, Napoleon being made First Consul. In May, 1804, he made himself Emperor of France.

When such matters as decoration and furnishing were again thought of, tradition had been broken and authority lost. A style perfectly adapted to the real or imagined needs of the hour cannot be created overnight, and the designs of the period naturally followed the pseudo-Classic vein that had been the heritage of

France since the days of the Grand Monarch. Furthermore, a return to antiquity in aspiration, surroundings, dress and conversation was the mode of the hour, and the style of Louis XVI had been based upon antiquity. It was to be expected, therefore, that that manner should form at least the base for the style commonly known as Directoire; but because of republican principles and hatred of the royalty it had represented it was as natural that it should be simplified and stripped of its ornament.

As we have seen, the copying of antiquity had been a characteristic of the reign of Louis Seize, particularly during his last years, but nevertheless it had always remained an *intelligent* use of Classic material, a proper adaptation to the widely changed conditions of modern times: *now* the prevailing belief was that the Republic of France was a *duplication* of the Republic of ancient Rome, and antiquity was therefore slavishly followed.

The Directory existed for but four years and its style was a merging of that of Louis Seize into that of the Consulate and Empire. It is in general a charming style, being the result of the simplification of a mode of the greatest beauty with an added *swing* in chairs and settees, probably because of the remembrance of the curule chair of the ancients. The legs, at least the fore ones, often remained straight, either fluted or turned, but were frequently curved outward toward their lower ends. The backs of chairs were now rolled at their tops and the arms of settees flared gracefully at the sides. This furniture was generally painted, and it is to be regretted that more of it is not upon the market to-day; for no style is better adapted to our modern uses. Illustrations are given of three original pieces and a modern reproduction (Plates 171 and 172).

If the Directorate had been a republic, with its "citizens" every man a king, the advent of Napoleon to power quickly changed all this. Though nominally "Consul," his rule was practically supreme, France became once more imperialistic, and the step to the proclamation of the Empire with that military genius upon the throne was but a logical one. No longer, in the conception of France, was it Republican but Imperial Rome now reincarnate upon earth, and Cæsar again was to rule the world. Napoleon the First became King of Italy in 1805 and deposed the Bourbons in Spain in 1808.

In the ever sensitive arts of decoration and furnishing we naturally expect this spirit to find quick expression. They soon embodied the triumph of imperial antiquity, of militarism and—of vulgarity. With all stops out the organ blared and taste became ostentation. As Napoleon conscripted his soldiers so the ancient world of Egypt, Greece and Rome was commandeered for its symbols and attributes to ornament walls and furniture: the Bourbon L gave place to the N and the fleur-de-lys of France vanished in favour of the bee. The grace of the Rococo and the refinement of Louis Seize were supplanted in decoration by what we see upon the walls of the salon at Hôtel de Mailly, in furniture by massive pieces with broad surfaces in which, notwithstanding ornament, we feel not simplicity but *blankness*. With its magnificent mahogany and metal mounts this furniture was often undeniably handsome in its brutal way and we may yield it the sort of admiration we give a likewise handsome, bold and florid woman—with scant liking in our regard. Of some of it we may say it is "rather attractive" or "not so bad," but this reaches the height of our commendation.

PLATE 171

A. Side Chair with Lyre Back and Curved Legs
By Courtesy Radillo-Pelitti Co.

B. Directoire Settee-Reproduction
Dull Black with Tan Edging and Maroon Rosettes. Matching Upholstery
By Courtesy of Chapman Decorative Co.

C. Side Chair with Fluted Fore Legs
By Courtesy of L. Alavoine & Co.

DIRECTOIRE SEATING FURNITURE

PLATE 172

DIRECTOIRE SETTEE WITH FLUTED LEGS
The Architectural Background is also Original
By Courtesy of Messrs. L. Alavoine & Co.

PLATE 173

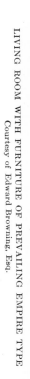

LIVING ROOM WITH FURNITURE OF PREVAILING EMPIRE TYPE
Courtesy of Edward Browning, Esq.

Without further description the illustrations show its characteristics (Plates 51 A and 173).

Despite Britain's natural fear and inveterate enmity to Napoleonic rule, French fashion strangely retained its power, influencing mobiliary styles across the channel and corrupting the beautiful *metier* of Sheraton.

America, with its adoration of France, consequent upon French aid in our troubles with our Mother Country, followed its lead with irregular results. This furniture is that commonly but, of course, quite erroneously referred to as "Colonial," Napoleon not even having become First Consul till twenty-three years after the Declaration of Independence.

Some American Empire pieces are heavier, clumsier and more debased in line than the French. On the other hand, the furniture of Duncan Phyfe deserves great praise for its appropriate lightness and grace of line. It is really more akin to the Directoire style. The acanthus-carved four-post bedsteads and the pedestal tables were American developments of heavy but unmistakably handsome character. All these are well known.

To France is due the honour of producing the most beautiful furniture ever devised for the use of man, but red republicanism and autocratic ambition had "done" for France. We should be appreciative of beauty wherever it may be found and inclined to be patient when it is not quite reached, but in contrast to the loveliness of but a few years before the brutal bombast of Napoleon's bed-chamber and the clumsy inelegance of chairs such as those from Versailles is enough to make angels weep. With the Empire all mobiliary art died, and now, in all the world for a hundred years there has been no great designer of furniture.

THE FOUR GREAT DECORATIVE INFLUENCES
RENAISSANCE, BAROQUE, ROCOCO, NEO-CLASSIC

Dates given are approximate, and are those of the first clear manifestations. Symptoms always showed themselves earlier. Influences persisted till the advent of the succeeding movement, often blending therewith.

	ENGLAND	FRANCE	ITALY	SPAIN-PORTUGAL
RENAISSANCE	Henry VIII (1509–47) introduced the new style, mainly Renaissance ornament grafted on Gothic forms. Elizabethan period 1558–1603. Inigo Jones, Palladian influence, 1619.	Introduced by Francois I (1515–47). Strongly Gothic till reign of Henri II (1547–59), when Classic influences prevailed.	Renaissance began in decoration first half fifteenth century. Its influence spread throughout civilised Europe.	Began toward end of fifteenth century. Strongly impregnated with Moorish elements.
BAROQUE	Interior architecture remained Classic with some Baroque features. Furniture Baroque from Restoration (1660). (The strongly Dutch furniture of Queen Anne-Early Georgian, and Chippendale derivations from it, form a rather separate group.)	Henri IV (1589–1610). Baroque exhibited its boldest forms in that reign and that of Louis XIII (1610–43). Under Louis XIV (1643–1715), Classic influences re-asserted themselves. France then became the dominating decorative influence in Europe and so remained.	Vigorous symptoms about the middle of sixteenth century. Culmination under Bernini.	Fully established about beginning of the seventeenth century and attained some of its most exaggerated forms in these countries. Many furniture forms usually designated as William and Mary and Queen Anne really had their inception in Portugal, due primarily to Oriental agencies arising from trade with the East.
ROCOCO (Principally on the Continent)	In England only Chippendale's "French" pieces and a few of other designers. Interior architecture, Classic.	The Regency (transitional) 1715–23. Louis XV (1715–74). Exterior architecture, Classic. Interiors and furniture, Rococo.	Simultaneous with France. Architecture occasionally disturbed and distorted into Rococo forms. Italy lost initiative in furniture design and chiefly copied forms of French provenance.	Furniture mainly derived from French forms and often carried to excess.
NEO-CLASSIC	Brothers Adam, principal exponents, established December, 1761. Hepplewhite (17— –'86). Sheraton (1750–1806). Chippendale's more Classic pieces. Shearer. "English Empire" reflection of Napoleonic influence. Decadence of Sheraton. In the United States "American Empire" marked by some individual characteristics. Best exponent, Duncan Phyfe.	Louis XVI (1774–1793). Architecture, exterior and interior, and furniture all consistently Classic. National Convention (1792–95). Directory (1795–99). Empire style— Napoleon 1st Consul, 1799. Napoleon Emperor, 1804.	Italy responded readily to Neo-Classic influences and developed forms analogous to those of England and France, but giving distinctly original interpretation and often originating peculiarly local forms. Directory and Empire furniture of France closely reflected.	Resumed Classic furniture forms, deriving inspiration chiefly from French types. Directory and Empire furniture of France closely reflected.

INDEX